JOHANNINE VOCABULARY

JOHANNINE VOCABULARY

A COMPARISON
OF THE WORDS OF THE FOURTH GOSPEL
WITH THOSE OF THE THREE

BY

EDWIN A. ABBOTT

"*Oratio imago animi*, Language
most shews a man."

BEN JONSON, *Sylva*.

PUBLISHERS
Eugene, Oregon

Wipf and Stock Publishers
199 W 8th Ave, Suite 3
Eugene, OR 97401

Johannine Vocabulary
A Comparison of the Words of the Fourth Gospel with Those of the Three
By Abbott, Edwin A.
ISBN: 1-59752-160-4
Publication date 4/25/2005
Previously published by Adam and Charles Black, 1905

TO

MY DAUGHTER

BY WHOM THE MAIN MATERIALS FOR THE WORK

WERE COLLECTED AND CLASSIFIED

AND THE RESULTS CORRECTED AND REVISED

THIS BOOK IS DEDICATED

PREFACE

ABOUT eight or nine years ago, when writing or revising for the press a commentary on the Fourth Gospel, I attempted—among other preparations for so manysided a task—to construct a key to certain verbal difficulties somewhat on the lines of a work that I wrote nearly forty years ago, called *A Shakespearian Grammar*. My "Johannine Grammar" never went beyond a rough draft: but, rough though it was, it decided me against publishing my commentary, by helping me to understand a great deal that I had never understood before, and by forcing me to perceive that a great deal more remained to be understood.

Studied with the aid of this rudimentary Johannine Grammar, the author of the Johannine Gospel revealed himself in a new light—as a prophet and yet a player on words; one of the most simple of writers yet one of the most ambiguous; with a style, in parts, apparently careless, parenthetic, irregular, abrupt, inartistic—an utterer of after-thoughts and by-thoughts putting down words just as they came into his mind, according to Mark Antony's profession, "I only speak right on"—but, in general effect, an inspired artist endowed with an art of the most varied kind, not metrical, not

PREFACE

rhetorical, never ornate, yet conforming to rules of order, repetition, and variation, that suggested, at one time the refrains of a poem, at another the arrangements of a drama, at another the ambiguous utterances of an oracle, and the symbolism of an initiation into religious mysteries.

At the same time the problem presented by the divergence of the Johannine from the Synoptic vocabulary began to seem more difficult to explain in accordance with old hypotheses but more capable of new solutions. Biographers, though differing in the style and vocabulary of their comments, cannot lawfully differ in their reports of conversations. Yet the fourth or latest of these biographers appeared to differ in this unlawful manner from the three, and this to an extent that seemed amazing unless deliberate, and, if deliberate, only justifiable on the ground that he knew his divergences to be substantially in accordance with what he conceived to be the essential truth. Perhaps (I reflected) the Fourth Evangelist might be in the right: but, if so, what about the Three? Did, or did not, Jesus of Nazareth use, and use repeatedly, such words as "faith," "repentance," "forgiveness"? Did He condemn "hypocrisy"? Did He bid men "watch" and "pray"? Did He hold up to His disciples the example of "little children" in order to answer their questions about "the greatest"? If He did, as assuredly He did, how was it possible that a Fourth Gospel—even a supplementary Gospel—could give a fair and truthful account of Jesus and set down at great length His discourses, both to the disciples and to others, without so much as mentioning (**1676** *b*) one of these fundamental words?

In order to answer these questions I began to construct a list of Synoptic words rarely or never used by John, and a list of Johannine words rarely or never used by the Synoptists: and I found that these—when compared and illustrated by quotations—shewed that in many cases John was in reality neither so silent nor so divergent as I had supposed. Where he had appeared to be taking up entirely new ground, he was sometimes saying the same thing as one or more of the Synoptists, only in a different way.

These conclusions were brought home to me more forcibly than ever when I recently began to prepare for the press a treatise on what might be called *The Fourfold Gospel*, that is to say, the passages where the Fourth Gospel intervenes in the Tradition of the Three. For the purposes of that treatise it seemed desirable to refer to a "Johannine Grammar" and a "Johannine Vocabulary" in print, instead of embodying large extracts from a manuscript. I therefore decided on printing those two volumes at once.

The "Johannine Grammar," which will form the Second Part of this work, could hardly be made intelligible to a reader unacquainted with Greek. But the "Johannine Vocabulary" stands on a different footing. There is nothing to prevent an "unlearned" reader from understanding, for example, that a difference is intended (as Origen says there is) when the Fourth Gospel describes some as "believing *in*" our Lord, and others as "believing *in His name*"; and that a play on words describes the people in Jerusalem as "trusting in His name" whereas Jesus "did not trust Himself to them"; and that a contrast is drawn between "the beloved disciple" and Thomas, both of whom "saw and believed"—but in what different circumstances! These, and a score or so of other distinctions, relate to a single word (**1463** *foll.*) "believe," and can all be understood without any knowledge of Greek. For this reason I decided to publish the Johannine Vocabulary as a separate volume[1], less costly, and more intelligible to the general reader than the Johannine Grammar which, I trust, will speedily follow.

I am indebted to several friends—in particular to Mr W. S. Aldis and Mr H. Candler—for corrections of proof and useful suggestions of a general character, and to Dr Joseph B. Mayor for valuable criticism on points of Greek. Nor must I omit thanks, due to all connected with the Cambridge University Press, for their admirable printing of the work and their arrangement of the Vocabularies.

EDWIN A. ABBOTT.

Wellside
Hampstead
24 *May*, 1905

---

[1] It must be understood, however, that Part I, though obtainable separately, frequently refers, on points of grammatical detail, to Part II, which will contain the Index to the whole work.

CONTENTS

	PAGE
REFERENCES AND ABBREVIATIONS	xvi—xviii

INTRODUCTION . . . .

§ 1 The problem (**1436—43**)
§ 2 How to deal with the problem (**1444—9**)
§ 3 A specimen of allusiveness, "hating one's own life" (**1450**)
§ 4 Another specimen, "reclining the head" (**1451—8**)
§ 5 Inferences (**1459—62**)

BOOK I

JOHANNINE "KEY-WORDS"

CHAPTER I

"BELIEVING"

§ 1 "Believing," or, "trusting," a key-word in the Fourth Gospel (**1463—6**)

§ 2 Why John prefers "believe" to "belief" (**1467—8**)

§ 3 "Believing," in the Old Testament (**1469—71**)

§ 4 "Believing," in Philo (**1472—3**)

§ 5 "Believing," in the New Testament, excluding the Fourth Gospel (**1474—7**)

§ 6 Antecedent probability of a restatement of the doctrine of "believing" (**1478—9**)

CONTENTS

- § 7 "Believing," in the Fourth Gospel (**1480**—**1**)
- § 8 "Through whom," or "what," do all "believe"? (**1482**)
- § 9 "Believing in the name" (**1483**—**7**)
- § 10 Our Lord's first mention of "believing" or "trusting" (**1488**)
- § 11 Christ's disciples "believed in him" (**1489**—**90**)
- § 12 "Believing the Scripture" (**1491**—**2**)
- § 13 "Believing," in the Dialogue with Nicodemus (**1493**—**1500**)
- § 14 After the Baptist's last words (**1501**—**2**)
- § 15 In Samaria (**1503**—**7**)
- § 16 The nobleman's "believing" (**1508**—**9**)
- § 17 "Believing" the testimony of the Father (**1510**—**1**)
- § 18 After the Feeding of the Five Thousand (**1512**—**9**)
- § 19 "Not believing" (**1520**—**1**)
- § 20 "Believing witnesses" (**1522**—**3**)
- § 21 After the Healing of the Blind Man (**1524**—**7**)
- § 22 The Raising of Lazarus (**1528**—**36**)
- § 23 "Believing in the light" (**1537**—**44**)
- § 24 The Last Discourse (**1545**—**9**)
- § 25 The Last Prayer (**1550**)
- § 26 After the Death and Resurrection (**1551**—**61**)

CHAPTER II

"AUTHORITY"

- § 1 "Authority," in the Triple Tradition of the Synoptists (**1562**)
- § 2 "Authority," in the Apocalypse (**1563**—**4**)
- § 3 Luke's view of "authority" (**1565**—**71**)
- § 4 Christ's "authority," how defined by the Synoptists (**1572**—**5**)
- § 5 "Authority," in the Fourth Gospel (**1576**—**8**)
- § 6 "Authority" to become "children" of God (**1579**—**80**)
- § 7 The "authority" of the Son to "do judgment" (**1581**—**5**)
- § 8 "Authority" in connexion with "life" (**1586**—**94**)

CONTENTS

CHAPTER III

JOHANNINE SYNONYMS

§ 1 The use of synonyms in this Gospel (**1595—6**)
§ 2 "Seeing" (**1597—1611**)
§ 3 "Hearing" (**1612—20**)
§ 4 "Knowing" (**1621—9**)
§ 5 "Coming" (**1630—9**)
§ 6 "Worshipping" (**1640—51**)
§ 7 "Going away (or, back)," and "going on a journey" (**1652—64**)

BOOK II

JOHANNINE AND SYNOPTIC DISAGREEMENTS

CHAPTER I

JOHANNINE DEVIATIONS FROM SYNOPTIC VOCABULARY

§ 1 Introductory remarks (**1665—71**)
  SYNOPTIC WORDS COMPARATIVELY SELDOM OR NEVER USED BY JOHN (**1672—96**)

CHAPTER II

SYNOPTIC DEVIATIONS FROM JOHANNINE VOCABULARY

§ 1 Introductory remarks (**1697—1706**)
  JOHANNINE WORDS COMPARATIVELY SELDOM OR NEVER USED BY THE SYNOPTISTS (**1707—28**)
  Additional Note (**1728** *m—p*)

xiii

CONTENTS

BOOK III
JOHANNINE AND SYNOPTIC AGREEMENTS

CHAPTER I
WORDS PECULIAR TO JOHN AND MARK

§ 1 Antecedent probability (1729—30)
§ 2 The fact (1731—2)
§ 3 Parallels and Quasi-parallels (1733)
  JOHN-MARK AGREEMENTS (1734—8)
§ 4 Jn xii. 9 "the common people," lit. "the great multitude" (1739—40)
§ 5 Inferences (1741—4); Additional Note (1744 (i)—(xi))

CHAPTER II
WORDS PECULIAR TO JOHN AND MATTHEW

§ 1 Parallelisms very few (1745—7)
§ 2 "Light of the world," "my brethren" (1748—9)
  JOHN-MATTHEW AGREEMENTS (1750—5)
§ 3 Inferences (1756—7)

CHAPTER III
WORDS PECULIAR TO JOHN AND LUKE

§ 1 Antecedent probability (1758—9)
§ 2 The fact (1760—1)
§ 3 Quasi-parallels (1762—3)
  JOHN-LUKE AGREEMENTS (1764—75)
§ 4 "Son of Joseph" (1776—8)
§ 5 "The Lord" meaning "Jesus" (1779—81)
§ 6 "Sons of light" (1782—3)
§ 7 "My friends" (1784—92)
§ 8 "Standing in the midst" applied to Jesus (1793—7)
§ 9 "Stooping (?) and looking in" (1798)
§ 10 What does παρακύπτω mean? (1799—1804)

CONTENTS

CHAPTER IV
WORDS PECULIAR TO JOHN, MARK, AND MATTHEW
§ 1 Introductory remarks (**1805—9**)
   JOHN-MARK-MATTHEW AGREEMENTS (**1810—16**)
§ 2 Absence of Quasi-parallels (**1817**)

CHAPTER V
WORDS PECULIAR TO JOHN, MARK, AND LUKE
§ 1 Introductory remarks (**1818—9**)
§ 2 "Latchet," "spices," "rouse up" (**1820—2**)
§ 3 Mark, Luke, and John, on "rejection" (**1823—31**)
   JOHN-MARK-LUKE AGREEMENTS (**1832—4**)
§ 4 "The Holy One of God" (**1835**)

CHAPTER VI
WORDS MOSTLY PECULIAR TO JOHN, MATTHEW, AND LUKE
§ 1 Verbal Agreements numerous, but parallelisms non-existent (**1836—8**)
§ 2 "Lay the head to rest" (**1839—46**)
§ 3 John-Matthew-Luke Agreements (in English) (**1847—50**)
   WORDS MOSTLY PECULIAR TO JOHN, MATTHEW, AND LUKE (**1851—66**); Additional Note (**1866** (i)—(iv))

CONCLUSION
§ 1 Review of the evidence (**1867—74**)
§ 2 What remains to be done (**1875—7**)
§ 3 Johannine Grammar (**1878—80**)

APPENDIX ON PREPOSITIONS
§ 1 Introductory remarks (**1881—3**); statistics (**1884—5**)

ADDENDA
Supplement to the Vocabularies **1885** (i)—(ii)

INDICES
See end of Part II, *Johannine Grammar*

REFERENCES AND ABBREVIATIONS

REFERENCES

(i) *Black Arabic numbers*, e.g. (**275**), refer to subsections indicated in this volume or in the preceding volumes of Diatessarica :—

    1— 272 = *Clue.*
    273— 552 = *Corrections.*
    553—1149 = *From Letter to Spirit.*
    1150—1435 = *Paradosis.*

(ii) The Books of Scripture are referred to by the ordinary abbreviations, except where specified below. But when it is said that Samuel, Isaiah, Matthew, or any other writer, wrote this or that, it is to be understood as meaning *the writer, whoever he may be, of the words in question*, and not as meaning that the actual writer was Samuel, Isaiah, or Matthew.

(iii) The MSS. called severally Alexandrian, Sinaitic, Vatican, and Codex Bezae, are denoted by A, א, B, and D; the Latin versions by *a*, *b*, etc., as usual. The Syriac version of the Gospels discovered by Mrs Lewis and Mrs Gibson on Mount Sinai called the "Syro-Sinaitic" or "Sinaitic Syrian," is referred to as SS. It is always quoted from Mr Burkitt's translation.

(iv) The text of the Greek Old Testament adopted is that of B, edited by Professor Swete[1]; of the New, that of Westcott and Hort.

(v) Modern works are referred to by the name of the work, or author, the vol., and the page, e.g. Levy iii. 343 *a*, i.e. column 1, page 343, vol. iii.

ABBREVIATIONS

A, B, D, and א, see (iii) above.
Apol. = Justin Martyr's First Apology.
Buhl = Buhl's edition of Gesenius, Leipzig, 1899.
Burk. = Mr F. C. Burkitt's *Evangelion Da-mepharreshe*, Cambridge University Press, 1904.
C. before numbers = circa, "about" (*e.g.* c. 10).
Chr. = *Chronicles.*
Chri. = *the words of Christ*, as distinct from narrative, see **1672***.
Clem. Alex. 42 = Clement of Alexandria in Potter's pages.

---

[1] Codex B, though more ancient than Codex A, is often less close to the Hebrew than the latter (*Clue* **33**).

REFERENCES AND ABBREVIATIONS

Dalman, *Words* = *Words of Jesus*, Eng. Transl. 1902; *Aram. G.* = *Grammatik Aramäisch*, 1894.

Diatess. = the Arabic Diatessaron, sometimes called Tatian's, translated by Rev. H. W. Hogg, B.D., in the Ante-Nicene Christian Library.

Ency. = *Encyclopaedia Biblica*.

Ephrem = Ephraemus Syrus, ed. Moesinger.

Epistle, the = the First Epistle of St John.

Esdras, the First Book of, is frequently called, in the text, Esdras.

Euseb. = the Ecclesiastical History of Eusebius.

Field = Origenis Hexaplorum quae supersunt, Oxford, 1875.

Gesen. = the edition of Gesenius now being published by the Oxford University Press.

Heb. LXX = that part of the LXX of which there is an extant Hebrew Original.

Hor. Heb. = *Horae Hebraicae*, by John Lightfoot, 1658—74, ed. Gandell, Oxf. 1859.

Iren. = the treatise of Irenaeus against Heresies.

Jer. Targ. (or Jer.) I and II = severally the Targum of "Jonathan Ben Uzziel" and the fragments of the Jerusalem Targum on the Pentateuch. Where Jer. II is missing, Jer. I is often indicated by Jer.

K. = *Kings*.

L.S. = Liddell and Scott's Greek Lexicon.

Narr. = *in narrative*, as distinct from (*a*) speech of Christ, (*b*) speech generally (**1672***).

Onk. = the Targum of Onkelos on the Pentateuch.

Origen is generally referred to in Huet's edition, 1668.

Oxf. Conc. = *The Oxford Concordance to the Septuagint*.

Pec., affixed to Mt., Lk., etc., means peculiar to Matthew, Luke, etc.

Philo is referred to by Mangey's volume and page, *e.g.* Philo ii. 234, or, as to the Latin treatises, by Aucher's pages (P. A.) (see **1608**).

Resch = Resch's *Paralleltexte* (4 vols.).

S. = *Samuel*; s. = "see."

Schöttg. = Schöttgen's *Horae Hebraicae*, Dresden and Leipzig, 1733.

Sir. = the work of Ben Sira, *i.e.* the son of Sira. It is commonly called Ecclesiasticus (see **20***a*). The original Hebrew has been edited, in part, by Cowley and Neubauer, Oxf. 1897; in part, by Schechter and Taylor, Camb. 1899.

SS, see (iii) above.

Steph. or Steph. Thes. = Stephani Thesaurus (Didot).

Sym. = Symmachus's Version of the Old Testament.

Tromm. = Trommius' *Concordance to the Septuagint*.

Tryph. = the Dialogue between Justin Martyr and Trypho the Jew.

Wetst. = Wetstein's *Comm. on the New Testament*, Amsterdam, 1751

W.H. = Westcott and Hort's New Testament.

REFERENCES AND ABBREVIATIONS

(*a*) A bracketed Arabic number, following Mk, Mt., etc., indicates the number of instances in which a word occurs in Mark, Matthew, etc., *e.g.* ἀγάπη Mk (0), Mt. (1), Lk. (1), Jn (7).

(*b*) Where verses in Hebrew, Greek, and Revised Version, are numbered differently, the number of R. V. is given alone.

INTRODUCTION

§ 1. *The problem*

[1436[1]] THE first step towards helping readers of the Fourth Gospel to solve the problem presented by its vocabulary and style is to make them see that a problem exists. The A.V. very frequently, and the R.V. not infrequently, conceal its existence. Take, for example, the Dialogue between our Lord and Peter after the Resurrection, in which the former tenderly implies a reproach for past professions of "love (ἀγαπᾶν)," while the latter, penitent and humiliated, does not venture to say any longer that he "*loves*" Jesus, but only that he "*likes* (φιλεῖν)" Him. The English "like" is too inaccurate to be admitted (even with an apology) into the rendering of such a passage; and there is no one word in our language that can exactly give the meaning; but, since it implies a humble protest on the part of the Apostle that he still retains a lower kind of love for his Master, we may, for want of anything better, paraphrase it as " I still love (**1716** *f*, **1728** *m—p*)." Then the dialogue would run as follows:

[1437] *Jesus.* Simon, son of John, *lovest* thou me more than these?

Peter. Yea, Lord, thou knowest that I *still love* thee.

Jesus. Feed my lambs.

---

[1] [**1436** *a*] See References on pp. xvi. *foll.* This is the fifth part of the series entitled *Diatessarica*. The fourth part ("*Paradosis*") terminated with subsection **1435**.

[1438] INTRODUCTION

The Master now repeats His question on a lower level, dropping the clause "more than these":

Jesus. Simon, son of John, *lovest* thou me?
Peter. Yea, Lord, thou knowest that I *still love* thee.
Jesus. Tend my young sheep[1].

On the third occasion, Jesus comes down to a yet lower level, to the standard that the humiliated disciple has himself adopted:

Jesus. Simon, son of John, *lovest* thou me *still*?
Peter. Lord, thou knowest all things, thou *feelest* (**1624** *b*) that I *love* thee *still*.
Jesus. Feed my young sheep[2].

[1438] The words "lovest thou me *more than these*" are apparently intended to mean "*more than these thy companions* whom thou hadst in mind when thou didst say, in effect, *Though all should desert thee*, yet will I never[3]." The Fourth Gospel nowhere puts into Peter's mouth this contrast between what *he* would not do, and what "*all*" might do, yet the Evangelist appears to imply the contrast here[4]. That is to say, the author writes *allusively*, alluding to tradition that he has not himself recorded.

[1439] Observe, also, the thrice repeated "Simon, son of John." It appears to call attention to the very first words uttered by Jesus to Peter, when "Jesus looked steadfastly at him and said, Thou art [at present] Simon, son of John; thou

---

[1] [1437 *a*] The Syro-Sinaitic version (which will be denoted henceforth by SS) has here "my ewes," and in xxi. 17 "my sheep." W.H. marg. and R.V. txt. have "my sheep," both here and in xxi. 17.

[2] [1437 *b*] Jn xxi. 15—17. A.V. makes no attempt to distinguish the two Greek words; R.V. translates both by "love" in its text, but adds in margin that the Greek words are different.

[3] [1438 *a*] Mk xiv. 29 "Even though *all* shall stumble yet not I." Simil. Mt. xxvi. 33. Lk. xxii. 33 words Peter's protest quite differently.

[4] [1438 *b*] Similarly he says (Jn iii. 24) "For John [the Baptist] was not yet cast into prison," alluding to the imprisonment as a well-known fact though he himself nowhere mentions it.

shalt be called Cephas," *i.e.* a stone[1]. From the level of that high and hopeful prophecy the Lord seems here deliberately to descend as though He had asked too much from His follower: he was not Cephas, after all—not yet at least—only the original Simon after the flesh, "Simon, son of John." Here again the Evangelist is writing allusively, but with allusion to a tradition recorded by himself.

[**1440**] Lastly, although the text is somewhat doubtful, the three classes indicated by SS, the "lambs" and the "sheep" that need "feeding," and the "ewes" that need "tending," appear to correspond symbolically to the distinctions indicated in the First Epistle of St John: "I write unto you little children...I write unto you fathers...I write unto you young men." The Lord might simply have said, as St Paul says to the Ephesian elders, "Feed the flock," but He adopts a three-fold iteration with slight variations, the impressiveness of which can be more readily felt than analysed and explained.

[**1441**] Thus, the dialogue resolves itself into a short dramatic poem with a triple refrain, apparently alluding to traditions mentioned in other Gospels but not in this one. Most simple yet most beautiful, artless yet in harmony with the deepest laws of art, it combines a passionate affection with subtle play on words and a most gentle yet powerful suggestion of loving reproach and helpful precept. The conclusion is at once pathetic and practical—that professions of love for the Saviour must be tested by labour for those whom the Saviour loves.

[**1442**] This passage illustrates the Johannine use of synonymous words and the iterations and variations characteristic of the Fourth Gospel; but it does not illustrate the Johannine use of different forms of the same word, as, for example, of the word "understand (γινώσκω)," which the Evangelist employs, in one and the same sentence (**1627**), first

---

[1] Jn i. 42.

as Aorist, then as Present, to mean "understand spiritually and grow in understanding spiritually," but elsewhere as Perfect, to mean "understand spiritually and perfectly." It does not illustrate the subtle shades of meaning denoted by slight variations of a clause, *e.g.* "believe" with a Dative, meaning "believe a person," and "believe" with "into," meaning "fix one's belief on a person," and again, "believe into the name of a person"—which will be discussed in the first chapter of this work. Lastly, it does not illustrate one of the author's most striking characteristics, his frequent obscurity or ambiguity.

[1443] A mere glance at the R.V. marginal notes on the Gospels will shew the reader that, in the Synoptists, the notes mostly suggest alternative *readings*, but in the Fourth Gospel they suggest alternative *renderings*. The former imply corruption in editors or scribes; the latter imply obscurity in the author, of which the following is an instance:

John i. 1—5 (R.V.)

Text	Margin
"All things were made *by* him; and *without him was not anything made that hath been made. In him was life*.... And the light shineth in the darkness; and the darkness *apprehended* it not."	"All things were made *through* him; and *without him was not anything made. That which hath been made was life in him*.... And the light shineth in the darkness; and the darkness *overcame* it not."

"*Oratio imago animi*": the specimens given above should suffice to shew that, in this case, the "oratio" is of a very extraordinary character; that, if we can get back from the "imago" to the "animus," we shall discover a very extraordinary mind; and that the attempt to get back involves a laborious as well as fascinating problem.

INTRODUCTION   [1445]

§ 2. *How to deal with the problem*

[**1444**] Many details of Johannine style may be explained by merely collecting parallel instances, as, for example, the author's use of ambiguous verbal forms (**2236**) capable of being rendered indicatively, imperatively, or interrogatively ("Believe in God," "Ye believe in God," "Believe ye in God?"), of "and" to mean "and [yet]" (**2136**) etc. This statement applies to most things in his Gospel that proceed from the author *himself*, that is to say, from the author uninfluenced by other authors. So far, a Johannine Grammar and a Johannine Vocabulary would help us to solve most of our difficulties: and it is hoped that the reader may find such help further on in the Chapter of Synonyms, the Grammar, and the various passages indicated in the Textual Index. But the case is altered when we come to ambiguities, symbolisms, and even literal statements that have the appearance of being allusive. Take, for example, the phrase quoted above from the R.V. text as "The darkness *apprehended* it not," but from the margin as "The darkness *overcame* it not." How will our Johannine Vocabulary or our Johannine Grammar help us here?

[**1445**] In the following way. In the first place, help may be derived from the Alphabetical Index referring to "Ambiguities (verbal)" at the end of the second part of this work. This will refer the reader to other instances where ambiguity arises from the twofold meaning of a word, *e.g.* where Jesus Himself is described as using language that was ambiguous or obscure to His disciples at the time, as when He spoke about "this temple," and about Lazarus as having "fallen asleep," and said to them, "A little time and ye behold me not." In the next place, the Textual Index (on Jn i. 5), or the alphabetical Verbal Index, will refer the reader to a footnote on καταλαμβάνω (**1735** *e*—*h*) which occurs in the Vocabulary under the heading of words common to Mark and

John. There it is shewn that the word generally means "catch," "take possession of," "take as a prize," and that it is used by St Paul in a play on words, by Philo in the sense of "apprehending" God, and by John himself in connexion with "a darkness" that "catches" people by surprise. The conclusion suggested is that *the primary meaning is " apprehended,"* but that there is also *a secondary meaning,* " *take captive.*"

[**1446**] If John is an allusive writer there is an antecedent probability that he would allude to the narratives of the Evangelists that preceded him. Indeed it would not have been surprising if he had quoted from them. There are, in fact, a few passages, more particularly those bearing on the Baptism, the Feeding of the Five Thousand, the Riding into Jerusalem, and the Passion, where John, whether quoting or not, does at all events exhibit a slight verbal agreement with the Synoptists, more especially with Mark. Manifestly, the first step to be taken by anyone wishing to study the relation of the Fourth Gospel to the Three, would be to set down all these passages of fourfold tradition, and their contexts, in parallel columns, and to annotate the Johannine disagreements and agreements with each of the earlier writers. A work of this kind, however, would be a work by itself, far too bulky to form a chapter in the present volume[1]: but some of the results of this work will be found in the foot-notes appended to the Vocabularies given below.

[**1447**] At this point the reader must be careful to distinguish the Triple Tradition (**318**) in which Mark, Matthew, and Luke agree, from other Traditions—Single or Double—embodied in one or more of the Synoptic Gospels. There is, for example, Matthew's story of Christ's birth and infancy; and there is Luke's story of the birth of John the

---

[1] Under the title of *The Fourfold Gospel*, I hope soon to publish such a treatise. It was completed some time ago, but its publication was deferred so that it might be revised with the aid of the present work.

Baptist, followed by an account of the birth, childhood, and early youth of Jesus. These two may be called Single Traditions, of an introductory character, in which Matthew and Luke contain hardly any points of agreement. Other Single Traditions occur at intervals in Matthew and Luke, as, for example, Matthew's story of Peter walking on the waters and the parables peculiar to Matthew, and Luke's story of "the woman that was a sinner," and the parables peculiar to Luke[1].

[**1448**] As to Double Traditions, there is one, comparatively short, peculiar to Mark and Matthew, describing the feeding of the four thousand, the walking of Christ on the waters, related also by John, and the healing of the Syrophœnician's child. There is another, far ampler[2], peculiar to Matthew and Luke, containing the Lord's Prayer, many passages from the Sermon on the Mount, and other doctrinal matters, besides the Temptation, the healing of the centurion's son, and the message of the Baptist to Christ, "Art thou he that should come?" with its sequel.

[**1449**] The bearing of these remarks will be better appreciated when the reader examines particular words in the Vocabularies given later on. He will find for example that Matthew, Luke, and John agree in using two words, "murmur" and "hallow" (or "sanctify"), never used by Mark. But the former does not occur in *any important parallel passage* of the Double Tradition, whereas the latter occurs there, as part of the parallel versions of the Lord's Prayer, in the words "*Hallowed* be thy name." The latter ("hallow") is likely to be far more important than the former ("murmur") for the purpose of ascertaining whether the Fourth Gospel is written allusively to the Three. For there is far more reason

---

[1] The Single Traditions peculiar to Mark are few and comparatively unimportant.

[2] This, owing to its relative importance (**318** (ii)), is regularly called "The Double Tradition" for brevity.

to suppose that John would write with a desire to illustrate this *doubly supported tradition* about "sanctifying" or "hallowing" than that he would be influenced by the *non-parallel* uses of the word "murmur" in Matthew and Luke[1]. For this reason, in the Vocabulary common to Matthew, Luke, and John, all words found in *parallel passages* of the Double Tradition are indicated by a special mark.

§ 3. *A specimen of allusiveness, "hating one's own life"*

[1450] Sometimes special circumstances may indicate a probability of Johannine allusiveness, even where a word or phrase is mentioned by only one of the Synoptists. This is certainly true (*Paradosis*, p. ix. preface) in many instances of similarity between Mark and John: but an instance will here be given bearing on Luke and John. Luke records a saying of our Lord that no one can become His disciple unless he *hates his own life*. This is in the Double Tradition of Matthew and Luke: but the former omits the clause. Matthew also has in the context "whosoever *loveth* father *more than me*," where the parallel Luke says that a man must "*hate*" his father[2]. These facts suggest that, as we might have anticipated, the tradition about "hating" one's "life" caused difficulty, and that Luke, though later than Matthew, has here retained the earlier text, which Matthew has paraphrased. John has "*hateth his own life*," but with a qualification that makes the meaning clearer:—"Whosoever hateth his own life *in this world*[3]." It must not, of course, be assumed, on the strength of this single passage, that John

---

[1] [1449 a] The word γογγύζω "murmur," used four times in Jn, occurs once in Mt., viz. xx. 11, of labourers, in a parable, and once in Lk., viz. v. 30, of "the Pharisees and their scribes." It happens that Mk never uses it. Consequently it appears in the "Words common to John, Matthew, and Luke." But there is not the slightest reason to suppose that Jn alludes to either of the passages in Mt.-Lk.

[2] Mt. x. 37, Lk. xiv. 26.   [3] Jn xii. 25.

is alluding to *Luke's Gospel*[1]; for he may have known the saying from other sources. But it is almost certain that John is alluding to *the saying contained in Luke's Gospel*, with an intention of explaining it, not by altering the Lord's hard word "hate" (as Matthew appears to have done) but by adding something in the context to justify the "hating."

§ 4. *Another specimen, "reclining the head"*

[1451] In the Greek Vocabulary of words common to Matthew, Luke, and John will be found (1858) κλίνω with a footnote calling attention to the phrase κλίνω κεφαλήν "recline the head." This might escape the notice of a reader unacquainted with Greek[2]: but it is of great interest as pointing to the conclusion that John knew the Double Tradition of Matthew and Luke, and occasionally alluded to it. This was made fairly probable by the apparent allusion ("hating one's own life") mentioned in the last section. If a second instance can be produced, the two will be mutually strengthened.

[1452] The only instance of "recline the head" in Matthew is in the well-known saying of our Lord (Mt. viii. 20) "Foxes have holes and birds of the air have nests: but the Son of man hath not where to *recline* his head," where no one denies that the meaning is "recline the head in sleep." The only instance in Luke (ix. 58) is in a parallel tradition agreeing with this passage of Matthew not only in meaning but in word, *verbatim*, and the meaning is equally indisputable there, "*recline* his head."

---

[1] Probably he is alluding to it; but the probability cannot be demonstrated without a comparison of a great number of passages in the Gospels.

[2] Such a reader would, however, find references to the explanation of the phrase if he turned to the Textual Index, and also in the Verbal Index, under "head": the latter would refer him to the footnote on κλίνω κεφαλήν as well as to this section.

[1453] The only instance of "recline the head" in John is in the description of our Lord's death as follows (xix. 30) "When, therefore Jesus had received the vinegar he said, It is finished, and (lit.) *having reclined his head he delivered up his spirit."* The parallel Mark and Luke have simply "he expired (ἐξέπνευσεν)," Matthew has "He let go (or, sent away) (ἀφῆκεν) his spirit." Taking the conservative and orthodox view that these three accounts of the Synoptists were accepted as authoritative by Christians several years before the end of the first century, we assume that the Fourth Evangelist knew these expressions, and preferred to describe the act otherwise. As regards the last part of his version ("he delivered up his spirit") an obvious reason for his preference suggests itself. The Johannine phrase brings out, more clearly than those of the Synoptists, the notion of martyrdom or self-sacrifice. But what as to the "reclining" of "the head"? Some may at first assume (as perhaps R. V. "bowed his head") that the physical act of bending the head ("*in*clining," not "*re*clining") is mentioned as typical of resignation or worship (**1462** *a*). Their second thought may be that resignation and worship are not so prominent in the Johannine conception of Christ as the higher feeling of absolute and unalterable filial devotion.

[1454] In fact, however, neither that first assumption about "inclining" nor that second thought about antecedent probability ought to have come so soon into our minds. The first thought should have been, What does κλίνω κεφαλήν mean elsewhere in Greek literature and more particularly in any Greek literature likely to be studied by John? Here a surprise awaits us. For Stephen's *Thesaurus* gives no instance of the phrase, under either of the two Greek words. The phrase is also absent from the Concordance to the LXX, though each of the two words, singly, is extremely common. There is indeed abundant mention of "bowing" in the Bible, but the LXX and other translators *never use this phrase for it.*

One reason appears for its non-use when we find Luke describing certain women as "bending (κλίνω) their *faces*" to the ground; for this suggests that "face" would be used in mentioning the "bending *forward*" or "bowing," whereas "head" would be used in "bending *backward*" or "reclining." "Recline," indeed, is the most natural meaning, because the verb is used so frequently in Greek for "reclining on a couch, or bed," the active, κλίνω, being sometimes used to mean "cause to lie down[1]," and the noun, κλίνη, being frequently used in N.T., as well as elsewhere, for "couch."

[1455] From the grammatical and literary point of view, then—which is also the scientific point of view—the phrase should mean "*recline the head*" in sleep, and there is not a particle of literary evidence for any other conclusion. But it may be urged that "from a common sense point of view" this meaning is out of the question, because "reclining the head in sleep" cannot possibly be intended by John, and "bowing the head in meek submission" is absolutely required.

[1456] This may be "common sense," but it is certainly not in accordance with the Johannine "sense" of what is fit and seemly for the Messiah. For where, in the whole of the Fourth Gospel, shall we find Him doing anything in "meek submission"? He is *not* "meek[2]," not at least in the usual sense of the term. Nor does He ever "submit" to the Father's will. It is His "food[3]" to do it. The first words of the Evangelist's Prologue tell us that the Logos was "with God," and its last words identify the Logos with "the Only-begotten," who is "*in the bosom of the Father.*" Almost every

---

[1] Eurip. *Alc.* 268 μέθετε μέθετέ μ' ἤδη, κλίνατε μ', "*let me lie down,*" *Orest.* 227 κλῖνόν μ' ἐς εὐνήν, "*lay me down* on the bed."

[2] [1456 a] Where Mt. xxi. 5 quotes Zech. ix. 9 "*meek* and riding upon an ass," Jn xii. 15, quoting the same prophecy, omits "*meek.*"

[3] Jn iv. 34.

INTRODUCTION

subsequent page contains some doctrine suggesting that the home of the Son is the home, or immediate presence, of the Father; that He came from this home to do the Father's will; that He is "going to the Father" because the work is on the point of completion; and that He was from the beginning, and is, "one with the Father." What more natural, then, not indeed for a common-place writer, but for such a one as we are considering, that he should connect the cry "It is finished" with the statement that the Son, in finishing the Father's work, *found at last that perfect rest which He could never find on earth*? Other martyrs, such as Stephen, might be described as "falling asleep," but this would have been inappropriate for the Johannine character of the Son of God, the Strength of Israel, who can "neither slumber nor sleep," but who might well be described as laying His head to rest on the bosom of the Father.

[1457] Chrysostom's interpretation, though it does not expressly say that the phrase means "rest," does clearly distinguish it from bowing the head in token of submission; for he mentions it as an indication that our Lord acted "*with authority*." Moreover he contrasts the action with that of ordinary men who, as he says, "recline the head" *after* breathing their last, whereas Christ did it *before*[1]: and surely

---

[1] [1457 a] Chrysost. ad loc. Λαβὼν οὖν φησι, Τετέλεσται. Εἶδες ἀταράχως καὶ μετ' ἐξουσίας πάντα πράττοντα; Καὶ τὸ ἑξῆς δὲ τοῦτο δηλοῖ. Ἐπειδὴ γὰρ πάντα ἀπηρτίσθη, κλίνας τὴν κεφαλὴν (οὐδὲ γὰρ αὕτη προσήλωτο), τὸ πνεῦμα ἀφῆκε, τουτέστιν, ἀπέψυξε. Καίτοι οὐ μετὰ τὸ κλῖναι τὴν κεφαλὴν τὸ ἐκπνεῦσαι· ἐνταῦθα δὲ τοὐναντίον. Οὐδὲ γὰρ ἐπειδὴ ἐξέπνευσεν, ἔκλινε τὴν κεφαλήν, ὅπερ ἐφ' ἡμῶν γίνεται· ἀλλ' ἐπειδὴ ἔκλινε τὴν κεφαλήν, τότε ἐξέπνευσε. Δι' ὧν πάντων ἐδήλωσεν ὁ εὐαγγελιστὴς ὅτι τοῦ παντὸς Κύριος αὐτὸς ἦν.

[1457 b] It may, however, be urged against Chrysostom that the position of a man lying, or sitting up, in bed, is quite different from that of one crucified, and that, in the latter case, the head must be *inclined forward* in death. I have seen one modern French realistic picture of the Crucifixion representing the head so bent down that the face is hardly visible. But (1) that attitude, as far as I know, is quite exceptional

it must be admitted that the usual course with a dying man (**1462** *a—c*) would be that his head would bend *backward or sideward, not forward in the act of* " *bowing.*"

[**1458**] Possibly it may be objected that the universally admitted usage of Matthew, and of Luke, and the apparent interpretation of Chrysostom, do not constitute sufficient evidence of the use of κλίνω κεφαλήν in the sense "lay one's head to rest" to establish the conclusion that John used it thus. But the reply is that the evidence, so far as it goes, tends indisputably to that conclusion, and that *there is no evidence at all derivable from Greek literature to justify* the supposition *that he used it in any other sense*[1]. The verdict "insufficient evidence" on the one side is, therefore, met by the verdict "no evidence at all" on the other. The right course would seem to be, either to mark the passage as corrupt and leave it untranslated, or to translate it in accordance with such evidence as at present exists.

§ 5. *Inferences*

[**1459**] From the facts above stated it follows that, whereas the grammar of the Fourth Gospel may be in large measure studied by itself, the vocabulary of that Gospel— though often capable of being illustrated and elucidated from

---

in the pictures of the Crucifixion; (2) it seems possible that the head— being, as Chrysostom says, "not nailed to [the cross]"—would have freedom to droop backwards, or at all events sidewards, under the relaxing touch of death, in *an attitude of rest as distinct from an attitude of submission*: and that is all that is needed to satisfy the linguistic requirements, namely that κλίνω means "bend in rest," not "bend in resignation."

[1] [**1458** *a*] The only basis for the hypothesis that John may have used κλίνω κεφαλήν to mean "bow the head (in resignation)" is that which may be obtained from translations of the Greek. It is very natural that translators should take the phrase to mean "bow." Such a view would harmonize with the spirit of Roman imperialism. It might also seem to some to suit the Synoptic character of Christ. But it certainly does not harmonize with the Johannine character.

13

Johannine sources alone—will sometimes not be fully understood without reference to the vocabulary of the Synoptists. Hence we shall proceed to study John's use of words from two points of view, first the Johannine, then the Synoptic.

[1460] We shall begin with one clue-word, so to speak, "believe"—which pervades the whole of the Fourth Gospel in such a way that to follow the Evangelist's use of it is to trace, in brief, the development of his doctrine as well as the methods of his style. From a summary of passages about "believing" we shall try to gain a general view of the writer's use of words—his repetitions of the same word in the same phrase, his repetitions of the same word in a slightly different form of the phrase, his repetitions of the same (or nearly the same) phrase with a slightly different form of the word. From "believe" we shall pass to other words, and especially to those that are synonymous, treating them in the same way and always keeping in view the author's general intention in the use of the word as well as the meaning of the particular passage under discussion.

[1461] In the next place we shall compare the vocabulary of the Fourth Gospel with those of the Triple, Double, and Single, Traditions of the Synoptists. As regards the Triple Tradition, this will be done negatively, as well as positively. That is to say, we shall shew what words John does *not* use though they are frequent in the Synoptists, as well as what he *does* use although the Synoptists rarely or never use them. The statistics of these uses must of course be expressed by bare numbers: but the footnotes to many of these numbers will quote passages of importance containing the words, and will adduce facts bearing upon their interpretation. Some of these footnotes will be intended to suggest research rather than demonstrate conclusion.

[1462] For example, under the head of "Remission of sins," connected by Mark and Luke with John the Baptist, it will be shewn (**1690** *a*—*h*) that Matthew omits it there;

that he also substitutes "debts" for "sins" (the same Hebrew word having either meaning) in his version of the Lord's Prayer; and that the Greek word *Aphesis*, or Remission, was the word regularly applied to the Remission of Debts in the Sabbatical Year—contended for by Jeremiah and Nehemiah, but recently abrogated (so it is said) by Hillel the venerated head of the Pharisees. In its bearing on the Fourth Gospel this detail is not of great importance (except as explaining why the author may have avoided the term, deeming it to be obscure or misunderstood). But it might have important bearings on the history of the origin of the Church, and possibly—for us now—upon its prospective development[1].

---

[1] [1462 a] As regards Jn xix. 30 (R.V.) "bowed his head," it should be noted that "bow" and "head" together, in the English O.T. Concordance, occur six times, and always in connexion with worship expressed or implied: "bow down" and "head" occur four times similarly, and once apparently in a bad sense (Is. lviii. 5) "to *bow down his head* as a bulrush."

[1462 b] I have not found κλίνω κεφαλήν in the very copious Indices to Aristotle and Lucian. The suggestion that the phrase simply meant "the head drooped in death" appears to me to ignore two considerations. (1) If a Greek author meant this, he would have used—as *Iliad* xiii. 543 ἐκλίνθη δ' ἑτέρωσε κάρη—the passive, and all the more certainly because the passive may mean (*Iliad* vii. 254 ἐκλίνθη) "bent his body," so that the active is only used in very few instances to mean "lay on a couch," "lay to rest," "lean anything" etc. (2) Even if κλίνω κεφαλήν could mean "I droop my head," such a phrase—appropriate enough in Homer or Virgil, Hippocrates or Galen, to describe the death of a warrior or a patient—could not have been used by the author of the Fourth Gospel to describe the outward sign of the spiritual departure of the Son of God to the bosom of the Father.

[1462 c] In 1457 a, the extract from Chrys., after ἐκπνεῦσαι, prob. om. by error (Cramer) γίνεται, ἀλλὰ μετὰ τὸ ἐκπνεῦσαι τὸ κλῖναι. We may fairly presume that Chrys.—when saying (in effect) "*the act* occurred with Him, before death; with us, it occurs after death"—repeats κλῖναι for brevity, to denote the "*act*," though, strictly speaking, the act of Christ was κλῖναι, the act with us is κλιθῆναι (not indeed being an "act" at all, but a passive relaxing of the muscles).

BOOK I
JOHANNINE "KEY-WORDS"

CHAPTER I

"BELIEVING"

§ 1. *"Believing," or, "trusting," a key-word in the Fourth Gospel*

[**1463**] The Johannine use of the word "believe" deserves a separate consideration for two reasons. In the first place, in a work dealing with Johannine grammar and vocabulary, the word is of special importance because the Evangelist uses it in various phrases and with various constructions in such a way as to throw light upon his general style and method of composition. In the next place, he exhibits "believing" in so many different phases, attributes it (in different phases) to so many persons and classes, assigns so many sayings about it to our Lord Himself, and makes so many evangelistic comments about it in his own person, that a summary of the Johannine *dicta* about "believing," amounting almost to a summary of the Gospel itself, may give a clue to its scheme and motive.

[**1464**] Look at the Gospel as a drama, and you will find that few of the leading characters are not placed at some time in such circumstances as to shew us—or make us ask—what, or whom, and how, and why, they "believed," or why, and what, and whom, they were exhorted to believe. The Baptist himself, though he soon disappears from the scene, is connected with the very first mention of the word because his rudimentary work was to produce "belief[1]." After that, Nathanael is gently reproved—apparently for believing too easily[2]. Then came the "glory" of Christ at Cana, and "his disciples believed in him[3]." Many at Jerusalem "believe," or "*trust*," because of His signs; but—a strange play upon the word—Christ "did not *trust* himself to them[4]." Nicodemus and the Samaritan woman are instructed in believing or exhorted to believe[5]. The nobleman, pleading for his sick child, is told that people in his condition "will not believe" without "signs and wonders." But he does believe—"himself and his whole house[6]." Then Peter makes his confession, "We completely believe and know." He says "we," and speaks in the name of "the Twelve." Yet Christ has said to the disciples "there are some of you that believe not[6]"; and now He declares that one of the Twelve "is a devil[7]." After this, "many" of the multitude, "many" of "the Jews," the man born blind, Martha, "many even of the rulers" (after a fashion)—all, in turn, believe or avow belief[8]. In the Last Discourse, Philip and the disciples are stimulated to believe; and they confidently protest their belief just before their Master warns them that they will abandon Him[9]. It is also said that the world is to be judged because men "do not believe[10]." Finally, in His Last Prayer, the Lord declares that the disciples "have believed" and prays that the world "may believe[11]."

[1465] Speaking in his own person, and describing the Passion, the Evangelist breaks off from his narrative to protest that he "sayeth true" "that ye also may believe[12]." After the Resurrection there is a curious repetition of traditions about "seeing" and "believing." It is said that "the

---

[1] i. 7.
[2] i. 50. [3] ii. 11. [4] ii. 23—4. [5] iii. 12, iv. 21.
[6] iv. 48, 53. [7] vi. 64—70. [8] vii. 31, viii. 30, ix. 38, xi. 27, xii. 42.
[9] xiv. 1—12, xvi. 30—1. [10] xvi. 9. [11] xvii. 8, 20—1.
[12] xix. 35.

other disciple" (but not Peter his companion) "*saw* and *believed.*" Thomas says "If I *see* not......I will not *believe*"; and Christ's last use of the word is in a solemn combination of blessing and warning, "Blessed are they that have *not seen and believed*[1]." Then immediately follows the Evangelist's statement, "These things have been written that ye may believe...and that, believing, ye may have life in his name[2]": and this is the Evangelist's last *dictum* about "believing."

[1466] Almost the only leading characters not connected with the word "believe" are Mary the sister of Lazarus and Mary Magdalene. These are not said to believe in anyone or in anything nor do they ever use the word. But both "weep[3]" in the Lord's presence. And the weeping of one precedes the weeping of Jesus and the Raising of Lazarus; the weeping of the other precedes the first manifestation of the Risen Saviour Himself. Do not all these widely differing facts converge to the conclusion that the Evangelist recognises many kinds and shades of believing and desires to subordinate it, even at its highest, to some still higher process of receiving spiritual truth?

§ 2. *Why John prefers "believe" to "belief"*

[1467] The Synoptic Vocabulary shews that John never uses the noun "faith," "belief," or "trust," but that he compensates for this by an abundant use of the verb "have faith," "believe," or "trust." His reason for doing this may be illustrated by two passages in Mark. One of these gives, as part of Christ's first public utterance, the words "*Believe in the Gospel,*" not repeated in any shape by the parallel Matthew or Luke and unique in N.T.[4] Another is (lit.) "Have [*the*] *faith of God,*" where the context refers to the uprooting of

---

[1] xx. 8, 25, 29.   [2] xx. 31.   [3] xi. 33, xx. 11.
[4] Mk i. 15, SS "*his* (*i.e.* God's) Gospel"; *b* and *f* om. "in," and so does Origen (Huet ii. 150).

trees or mountains and teaches that everything—but possibly the meaning is every spiritual thing—will be granted to faith[1]. Here again the other Synoptists deviate from Mark. Matthew omits the words "of God," and says "If ye have faith": Luke, in a different context, has "If ye have faith as a grain of mustard seed[2]."

[1468] These textual divergences are very natural. The influx of wonder-working faith into the Christian Church must have been felt much more definitely than it could be expressed. Men were conscious that "faith" had led them from death into life. Yet some found it difficult to explain to others precisely why they had "faith." The First Epistle of St Peter bids converts be ready to "give a reason" for the "hope" that was in them: so, the Fourth Evangelist might naturally desire to help Christians to "give a reason" when they were asked to explain or describe the faith that was in them: "Why, and what, or whom, or in whom, or to whom, or to what, do you trust?" This he does by substituting the verb for the Synoptic noun and by adding various objects or modifying phrases answering these questions.

§ 3. *"Believing," in the Old Testament*

[1469] The Hebrew verb, "trust," or "believe," is radically connected with the words "support," "nourish," "foster-father," "foster-mother," "nurse," "pillar (of a house)[3]." In the Passive, it means "supported," "confirmed," "steadfast." In the Causal, it means "stand firm," "trust," "believe"— but "believe" in a moral sense, not a mere act of the intellect. The best (or least inadequate) rendering is often "trust,"

---

[1] Mk xi. 22 ἔχετε πίστιν θεοῦ: a and k om. θεοῦ, D has εἰ ἔχετε πίστιν τοῦ θεοῦ, ℵ a b etc. ins. εἰ—conforming the text to Mt. or Lk.

[2] Mt. xxi. 21 ἐὰν ἔχητε, Lk. xvii. 6 εἰ ἔχετε.

[3] For these and the following facts relating to the Hebrew forms see Gesen. 52 *foll.*

because our English "trust" is connected etymologically with "true," and with words suggestive of firmness and confidence. The Hebrew *aman*, "support," is connected with our *amen* (an utterance of "confirmation") and with the Hebrew *emeth*, "truth," and *âmoun* "master-workman," the word applied in Proverbs to the Wisdom that cooperated with God in the Creation[1]. This Hebrew "trust" differs widely from that kind of belief (upon more or less of evidence) which we mean in English when we say "I *believe* it is about half past two."

[1470] In Hebrew, one may trust (1) absolutely, (2) "to" a person or thing, (3) "in" a person or thing, or (4) "that" a statement is true. The third of these constructions is usually employed in describing trust in God[2], *e.g.* "And he [Abraham] *trusted in* the Lord and he counted it to him for righteousness." But the LXX—rendering Abraham's "trusting" by πιστεύω, *which is never followed by a preposition in classical Greek*[3]—has "he trusted the Lord" (dat.). This often-quoted passage reveals the general inability of classical Greek to represent Semitic traditions about "*trust*" *in God*. Now and then, especially with a negative, the translators of O.T. use "in" to denote that Israel did *not* "stand fast, or trust, *in* God[4]"; but, as a rule, they are content with the dative to represent *both* of the Hebrew prepositions. As for the Greek "to," "trust *to*," πιστεύειν εἰς, it is never thus used by the LXX.

---

[1] Prov. viii. 30.
[2] Gesen. 53 *a* "the usual construction with God Gn. xv. 6."
[3] Steph.
[4] [1470 *a*] With negative in Ps. lxxviii. 22 "because they trusted not *in* (ב) (ἐν) God and hoped not in (ב) (ἐπί) his salvation,'" Jer. xii. 6 "trust not *in* (ב) them" (comp. Sir. xxxii. 21 "Trust not *in* (ב) the way," μὴ πιστεύσῃς ἐν ὁδῷ); without negative in Ps. cvi. 12 (R.V.) "then *believed* they his words," Dan. vi. 23 (Theod.) R.V. "because he had trusted in his God" (A om. ἐν).

[1470 *b*] Ἐπί never occurs with π. in LXX except in Wisd. xii. 2 π. ἐπὶ σέ (i.e. God).

"BELIEVING"

[1471] Besides this inadequacy in Greek construction there is inadequacy in the Greek verb itself to represent the moral meanings of the Hebrew verb in its different forms and its associations with firmness and stability. When Isaiah, playing on these shades of meaning, says " If ye be not *firm* [*in faith*] ye shall surely not be *made firm* [*in fact*] " (*i.e.* " if ye will not *believe* ye shall not be *established*") the LXX has, for the latter clause, "ye shall surely not understand[1]": and a similar saying in Chronicles "*Believe* in Jehovah and ye shall be *confirmed*" (lit. "*Be firm* in Jehovah and ye shall be *made firm*") is rendered by the LXX "*Trust* in Jehovah and ye shall be *trusted*," perhaps meaning " ye shall be *proved trustworthy*[2]."

§ 4. "*Believing*," in Philo

[1472] Philo, being a Greek in language but a Jew in faith and theological tradition, shares in the linguistic inadequacies of the LXX (which seemed to him an inspired version of the Hebrew) but shews a Jewish sense that Abraham's "trust" was something more than Greek "believing." Traces of this appear in his frequent mention, or implication, of the instability of all other "trust" as compared with the *firmness* or *stability* of trust in God : " It is best to trust completely (πεπιστευκέναι) to God and not to the misty reasonings and the *unstable* imaginations [of men]. Abraham, at all events, trusted to God and was esteemed righteous[3]": " He [Abraham] saw into the *unfixedness* and *unsettledness* of material being when he recognised the *unfaltering stability* that attends true BEING, to which [stability] he is said to have completely trusted[4]." The praise of Abraham's faith is justified, he says, because nothing is so difficult or so righteous

---
[1] Is. vii. 9 οὐδὲ μὴ συνῆτε, Sym. διαμενεῖτε, Theod. πιστευθείητε.
[2] 2 Chr. xx. 20 ἐνπιστευθήσεσθε, comp. Sir. i. 15, xxxvi. 21.
[3] Philo i. 132 quoting Gen. xv. 6 as δίκαιος ἐνομίσθη.
[4] [1472 a] Philo i. 273 ...ἀνίδρυτον καὶ ἄστατον κατεῖδε τὴν γένεσιν ὅτε τὴν περὶ τὸ ὂν ἀνενδοίαστον ἔγνω βεβαιότητα "ᾗ λέγεται πεπιστευκέναι."

as "to anchor oneself *firmly* and *unchangeably* upon true BEING alone[1]." In the course of a long eulogy on it, he says that "the only good thing that is void of falsehood and *stable* is the faith that is toward God" or "the faith toward true BEING[2]." Elsewhere he calls this faith "knowledge," and again connects it with stability:—not that Abraham could obtain the knowledge of God's essence, he says, but he obtained clearer impressions of His Being and Providence, "Wherefore also he is said to have been the first to have '*trusted God*,' since he was the first to have an *unaltering and stable* conception, how that there exists One Cause, the Highest, providing for the world and all things therein. And, having obtained knowledge, *the most stable of the virtues*, he obtained at the same time all the rest[3]."

[1473] All these extracts bear on one passage of Scripture—that which describes the faith of Abraham. But they suffice to shew that, in the middle of the first century, a non-Christian Jew would have great difficulty in conveying to Greeks all that was meant by the Hebrew "trust" when it meant "trust in God." This difficulty would be greatly increased by the influx of so stupendous a revelation as the Incarnation; and we have now to see how the earliest Christian writers grappled with it.

Mangey prints ᾗ as the object of π.: but we might read ᾗ λέγεται "πεπιστευκέναι," "in which respect he is said to have 'believed.'" For the perf. (here and i. 132) comp. Demosth. 2 *Philipp.* § 6 οἱ θαρροῦντες καὶ πεπιστευκότες αὐτῷ and (Steph.) Philostr. *Epist.* 40 πεπίστευκας σεαυτῇ καὶ τεθάρρηκας, *i.e.* "trust absolutely."

[1] Philo i. 486 τὸ ἐπὶ μόνῳ τῷ ὄντι βεβαίως καὶ ἀκλινῶς ὁρμεῖν. This illustrates the use of ἐπί quoted above (1470 *b*) from Wisd. xii. 2.

[2] Philo ii. 39 μόνον οὖν ἀψευδὲς καὶ βέβαιον ἀγαθὸν ἡ πρὸς τὸν θεὸν πίστις, and τὴν πρὸς τὸ Ὂν πίστιν.

[3] [1472 *b*] Philo ii. 442 καὶ οὐ πρότερον ἀνῆκεν ἡ τρανοτέρας λαβεῖν φαντασίας...τῆς ὑπάρξεως αὐτοῦ καὶ προνοίας ᾗ δίκαιον. Διὸ καὶ πιστεῦσαι λέγεται τῷ θεῷ πρῶτος, ἐπειδὴ καὶ πρῶτος ἀκλινῆ καὶ βεβαίαν ἔσχεν ὑπόληψιν, ὡς ἔστιν ἐν αἴτιον τὸ ἀνωτάτω, καὶ προνοεῖ τοῦ τε κόσμου καὶ τῶν ἐν αὐτῷ. Κτησάμενος δὲ ἐπιστήμην τὴν ἀρετῶν βεβαιοτάτην, συνεκτᾶτο καὶ τὰς ἄλλας ἁπάσας.

§ 5. "*Believing*[1]," *in the New Testament, excluding the Fourth Gospel*

[1474] The Epistles to the Thessalonians and the Corinthians rarely use πιστεύω except absolutely[2], and never with "Christ," "in Christ" etc.: but the Epistle to the Galatians, before quoting the words about Abraham's "trust" and righteousness," says "We *trusted to* (εἰς) Christ Jesus that we might be made righteous (δικαιωθῶμεν) from trust in Christ (ἐκ πίστεως Χριστοῦ)" and then quotes "Abraham *trusted* God (dat.) and it was reckoned to him for righteousness[3]." The Epistle to the Romans begins by quoting the text "Abraham *trusted* God (dat.)..."; it then speaks of him as "*trusting on* (ἐπί with accus.) him that maketh righteous the ungodly," and then, "But [*having regard* or *looking*] to (εἰς δέ) the promise of God he doubted not through trustlessness but was filled with power by trust...but it was written...also for our sakes...who *trust on* (ἐπί with accus.) him that raised Jesus our Lord from the dead[4]." Later on, quoting Isaiah, "He that *trusteth* shall not make haste," the Apostle twice follows a version of the LXX in an erroneous insertion "He

---

[1] The active alone is discussed in the following pages: πιστεύεσθαι, "to be believed" or "to be entrusted with," is not considered.

[2] [1474 a] It is always absolute in these Epistles except 1 Thess. iv. 14 "If we trust that Jesus died and rose again," 2 Thess. ii. 11 "that they should trust a lie," ii. 12 "those who have not trusted the truth," 1 Cor. xiii. 7 "trusteth [in] all things (πάντα)."

[3] [1474 b] Gal. ii. 16, iii. 6. In the early portion of this chapter—for the sake of indicating the differences of Greek phrase, and the different shades of meaning of the Greek verb—πιστεύειν will be rendered "trust": π. αὐτῷ, "trust him," π. ἐπ' αὐτόν (or, rarely, αὐτῷ) "trust *on* him," π. εἰς αὐτόν, "trust *to* him." But the reader must be warned that "trust *unto*, or *into* him" would be a more adequate rendering of π. εἰς, if only it were English. It implies "looking trustfully *unto*," or perhaps sometimes "passing *into*" (**1475, 1517**).

[4] Rom. iv. 3, 5, 24.

that *trusteth on him* (dat. ἐπ' αὐτῷ)¹"; but, speaking in his own person he says, "How shall they call on him *to* (εἰς) whom they have not *trusted*²?" and he tells the Philippians³ that to them "it is given not only to *trust to* (εἰς) him but also to suffer for him⁴."

[1475] In what sense does the Apostle use "*to*," or "*into*," with "trust," contrary to Greek usage? Does he mean that, as a convert is baptized *into* Christ⁵, so, by the spiritual act of "trust," his personality *passes into* that of Christ? Or does he mean that the convert "trustfully *looks to* Christ,"—a thought that seemed to be implied in the statement that Abraham "[*looking*] *to* the promise of God...was filled with power by trust"? The latter is suggested by the Pauline noun-phrases "the *trust to* (εἰς) Christ," "the *love to* (εἰς) all⁶." It is also favoured by the Petrine expression, "*To whom*, for the moment [indeed] not seeing, yet *trusting*⁷"—which implies that "trusting" means "looking *to* Christ with the eye of trust," as also later on, "that your trust and hope may be *to God*⁸." Compare the Epistle to the Hebrews "*looking only to* (ἀφορῶντες εἰς) Jesus the chief leader and perfecter of our faith," which resembles

---

¹ Rom. ix. 33, quoting Is. xxviii. 16 (ΝAQ have this; it probably arose from conflating "not" as "to him" (779 a)), rep. Rom. x. 11.
² Rom. x. 14.   ³ Phil. i. 29.
⁴ [1474c] The First Epistle to Timothy has i. 16 "them that are destined to trust *on* (ἐπί with dat.) him *to* (εἰς) eternal life." Here the writer might use ἐπί because he was going to use εἰς in a different sense later on. But ἐπί with the dative is contrary to Pauline usage (except in quoting). The dat. is used in 2 Tim. i. 12 οἶδα ᾧ πεπίστευκα and Tit. iii. 8 οἱ πεπιστευκότες θεῷ.
⁵ [1475a] Rom. vi. 3 "as many as were baptized *into* (εἰς) Christ Jesus were baptized *into* (εἰς) his death," 1 Cor. x. 2 "they all baptized themselves (ἐβαπτίσαντο) *into* (εἰς) Moses," 1 Cor. xii. 13 "were all baptized *into* one body," Gal. iii. 27 "for as many of you as were baptized *into* Christ."
⁶ Col. ii. 5 τῆς εἰς Χρ. πίστεως, i. 4 τὴν ἀγάπην [ἣν ἔχετε] εἰς πάντας, Philem. 5 τὴν πίστιν ἣν ἔχεις εἰς (marg. πρὸς) τὸν Κύριον.
⁷ 1 Pet. i. 8 εἰς ὃν ἄρτι μὴ ὁρῶντες πιστεύοντες δὲ....
⁸ 1 Pet. i. 21 τὴν π. ὑμῶν κ. ἐλπίδα εἶναι εἰς θεόν.

the doctrine of Epictetus that we are to "*look only to* (ἀφορῶντες εἰς) God in all things great or small[1]."

[1476] In the Acts—besides occasional instances of the dative—"trust on (ἐπί)" occurs along with "trust to (εἰς)[2]." In the former, ἐπί is used, not with the dative as in Isaiah (אQ) but with the accusative. The dative would mean "*resting* on," the accusative "*coming to rest* on"; and the latter might imply "*becoming a convert*" which is perhaps the meaning in three passages. The Epistle to the Hebrews, though it very frequently uses the noun "trust" (which it defines as being "that which gives substantiality to the things one is hoping for") uses the verb only twice, once absolutely and once with ὅτι[3]—a construction apparently very rare in classical Greek[4]. The Epistle of St James indicates that Christians had begun to discuss the relation between "trust" (or "belief") and "works"; and—before quoting "Abraham believed God"—it twice uses the verb so as to warn its readers that "believing" may be non-moral: "Thou *believest* that God is one...the devils also *believe* and tremble[5]."

---

[1] [1475 b] Heb. xii. 2, Epict. ii. 19. 29. Ἀφορᾶν εἰς = "look away from [other things] to." Epictetus says about his ideal Hercules (iii. 24. 16), "For he had heard not as mere talk [but as truth] that Zeus is the Father of men: yes, he thought Him and called Him his Father, and looking only towards Him (πρὸς ἐκεῖνον ἀφορῶν) he regulated his every action (ἔπραττεν ἃ ἔπραττε)."

[2] [1476 a] In Acts ix. 42, xi. 17, xvi. 31, π. ἐπί = "become a convert," in Acts xxii. 19 "believers." In Acts x. 43 π. εἰς describes the means for remission of sins, xiv. 23 εἰς ὃν πεπιστεύκεισαν seems to express intense trust as the preparation for a dangerous enterprise, xix. 4 is doubtful, since εἰς τὸν 'I. (1) may be a resumptive repetition of εἰς ("with reference to") τὸν ἐρχόμενον, or (2) may depend on πιστεύσωσιν.

[3] [1476 b] Heb. iv. 3, xi. 6. The latter, requiring a belief that God "is" and that He "rewards," is like Philo's definition of Abraham's faith (1472) concerning the ὕπαρξις of God and concerning the fact that He προνοεῖ.

[4] [1476 c] Steph. quotes no instance of π. ὅτι, but comp. Epictet. *Fragm.* 3 εἰ βούλει ἀγαθὸς εἶναι πρῶτον πίστευσον ὅτι κακὸς εἶ, and Xen. *Hiero* i. 37 has πιστεῦσαι foll. by ὡς.

[5] Jas. ii. 19 (*bis*), 23.

[1477] In the Synoptists we have seen above (1467) that Mark is not exactly followed by Matthew or Luke in the two precepts that he attributes to our Lord, "Trust in the Gospel" and "Have trust in God." We must now add that *the Triple Tradition does not agree in a single saying of Christ, using this verb*[1]. Also, as regards the noun "trust," the only *verbatim* agreement in the Triple Tradition in the words of Christ is in the saying to the woman with the issue, "Thy *trust* hath saved thee[2]."

---

[1] [1477 a] The only triple agreement about "trusting" is in a passage where the chief priests and elders express their fear that Jesus may condemn them for not "trusting" the Baptist, Mk xi. 31, Mt. xxi. 25, Lk. xx. 5, "If we say from heaven, he will say, *Why [then] did ye not trust him?*" Other instances are peculiar to two Evangelists or to one: for example, Mk v. 36, Lk. viii. 50 "only trust" is om. by Mt. Mk xiii. 21, Mt. xxiv. 23 "trust [them] not" is om. by Lk. (the rep. in Mt. xxiv. 26 "trust [them] not" is om. by Mk as well as Lk.). At the end of the Healing of the Centurion's servant, Mt. viii. 13 "As thou hast trusted, so be it" is om. by the parall. Lk. and so is Mt. xxi. 32 "Ye did not trust him...the harlots trusted him...that ye might trust him" om. in the parall. Lk. vii. 29—30. Mt. ix. 28 "trust ye that I am able to do this?" occurs in a miracle peculiar to Mt. After the Resurrection, "trust on" occurs in a tradition peculiar to Lk. xxiv. 25 "slow of heart to trust on (π. $\dot{\epsilon}\pi\dot{\iota}$ with dat.) all that the prophets have spoken." The words "He that shall have trusted and shall have been baptized," and "these signs shall follow them that shall have trusted," are in the Mark Appendix (Mk xvi. 16—17).

[2] [1477 b] Mk v. 34, Mt. ix. 22, Lk. viii. 48. There is also an agreement, though not *verbatim*, in Mk iv. 40 "Have ye not yet *trust?*" Lk. viii. 25 has "Where is your *trust?*" and Mt. viii. 26 "O ye of little *trust.*" In Mk x. 52 (Bartimaeus), Lk. xviii. 42, "thy *trust* hath saved thee" the words are om. by the parall. Mt. xx. 34 (*two* blind men), but in *another* healing of two blind men Mt. ix. 29 has "let it be according to your *trust.*" In Mt. xv. 28 "O woman, great is thy *trust,*" the parall. Mk vii. 29 has "on account of this word, go thy way." Where Mt. xxiii. 23 has "kindness ($\check{\epsilon}\lambda\epsilon o\varsigma$) and trust" the parall. Lk. xi. 42 has "the love of God." But the Double Tradition agrees in Mt. viii. 10, Lk. vii. 9 "I have not found so great *trust*...in Israel," and Mt. xvii. 20, Lk. xvii. 6 "*trust* as a grain of mustard seed." As regards Mk xi. 22 and parall., see **1467**.

§ 6. *Antecedent probability of a restatement of the doctrine of "believing"*

[1478] Reviewing the New Testament doctrines concerning "faith," "trust," or "belief," apart from the Fourth Gospel, as they would present themselves to an Evangelist writing at the end of the first century, we see that he might naturally desire to supplement them. He might wish to guard his readers against attaching too much importance to that kind of "faith" which, in practice, produced wonderful cures of disease—as St Paul cautions the Corinthians, "Though I have faith so that I could move mountains, it profiteth me nothing[1]." Again, there was a danger that some might take the faith of Abraham to be little more than a belief that God would give him his heart's desire, quite apart from the goodness or badness of that desire[2]. To meet this, it would be well to shew what Abraham's faith really implied[3]. The Epistle to the Hebrews had defined faith, and we know from

---

[1] [1478 *a*] 1 Cor. xiii. 2: comp. Mt. vii. 22 "In thy name have we cast out devils" (uttered by those whom the Lord rejects) and see Christ's answer to the Seventy when they say (Lk. x. 17) "Even the devils are subject to us in thy name."

[2] [1478 *b*] Irenaeus parallels the faith of Abraham with that of Christians thus (iv. 21. 1) "illo quidem credente futuris quasi jam factis propter repromissionem Dei: nobis quoque similiter per fidem speculantibus eam quae est in Regno haereditatem propter repromissionem Dei." But the Jews believed that Abraham left his country as a martyr and exile at God's command in order to preserve the worship of the One God: and the Targum taught that he had been cast into a fiery furnace by Nimrod in order to make him apostatize. The trust of Abraham, then, was a trust that the kingdom of God established in his heart would be established, through his descendants, in all the world—a very different thing from the mere belief that he would have a son in his old age from his wife Sarah.

[3] Jn viii. 56 "Abraham rejoiced exceedingly in order that (**2097**) he might see my day; and he saw it and was glad."

"BELIEVING" [1479]

Clement of Alexandria[1] that some very early Christians added a second definition. Probably there were many definitions. St Paul had spoken much about the worthlessness of "works of the law," and the value of "faith," even before works[2]. St James had said that "faith without works" was "dead[3]." Both had argued truly; but they appeared to differ. The Fourth Evangelist might feel that, without arguing, a Gospel might set forth Christ's doctrine of trust in a Father in such a way as to reconcile these apparently conflicting statements.

[1479] Lastly, the writer we have in view would probably have some regard to the difficulties of Greek believers including the educated classes, and to their notions about "faith" or "belief." "Whatever we believe," said Aristotle, "comes to us through syllogism or induction[4]": how could this be reconciled with any Christian doctrine of believing? Unfortunately we have no Celsus in the first century to represent Greek scepticism. But St Paul's words, "the Jews desire signs, and the Greeks seek after wisdom[5]," and the absence or insignificance of "faith" and "believing" in the teaching of Epictetus[6], and the statement of Clement of Alexandria[7] that

---

[1] [1478 c] Clem. Alex. 432 calls it "voluntary preconception, an assent of reverence for God," πρόληψις ἑκούσιος, θεοσεβείας συγκατάθεσις. Then he adds the definition of Heb. xi. 1. Then he says (433) "But others have explained (ἀπέδωκαν) faith as a uniting assent to an unseen object (ἀφανοῦς πράγματος ἐνωτικὴν συγκατάθεσιν)." He derives faith from στάσις (? as a contraction of ἐπίστασις) calling it (629) "a settlement of our soul concerning true BEING (τὴν περὶ τὸ ὂν στάσιν τῆς ψυχῆς ἡμῶν)." By a "uniting" assent, he means "that which makes a man at one" with the Word, (635) "To trust to (εἰς) Him and through Him (δι' αὐτοῦ) is to become—being undistractedly made one (ἀπερισπάστως ἑνούμενον) in Him—a *single being* (μοναδικόν)." See Hort and Mayor on Clem. 899.

[2] Rom. iii. 20—28, iv. 2—6, ix. 11, 32, xi. 6. [3] Jas. ii. 17.

[4] Aristot. *Anal. Prior.* ii. 25 (23). [5] 1 Cor. i. 22.

[6] [1479 a] Epictetus has (*Fragm.* § 3) "If you wish to become good, first believe that you are bad," but πιστεύω does not appear in the Index. of Schweighäuser exc. as π. τί τινι in a corrupt passage (i. 26. 14).

[7] [1479 b] Clem. Alex. 432 πίστις δέ, ἣν διαβάλλουσιν, κενὴν καὶ βάρβαρον νομίζοντες Ἕλληνες.

the Greeks mocked at faith—all point to the conclusion that what Celsus said in later days against the Christian exhortation to "believe[1]" would be said by Greek philosophers in the first century as soon as they came into contact with the preachings of the Gospel. For the sake of the Greeks, then, it was needful to point out the immense difference between "believing *that*" a conclusion is logically deduced from premises, or "*that*" a fact is proved by evidence, and that other kind of belief, or trust, *in* a Person, which, as the Christians asserted, made men become the children of God.

§ 7. "*Believing,*" *in the Fourth Gospel*

[1480] It remains to consider the Johannine traditions about "believing," or "trusting." The best way of doing this will be to note the different expressions, ("trust (*absol.*)," "trust (*dat.*)," "trust *to* (εἰς)," "trust *to* (εἰς) *the name of*," "trust *that*,") in the order in which the Evangelist introduces them, and to trace their principal recurrences, so as to give an outline of his doctrine as expressed in Christ's words and in Evangelistic comments. Here it may be observed that "trust *in*" and "trust *on*" are not mentioned. The former, since it occurs only once in N.T.[2], might well not be used by John: and indeed "*abide* in," rather than "*believe* in," represents his doctrine about the highest and ultimate relation of the believer to God. "Trust *on*," also, would be inconsistent with his view, which is, that man does not "rest *on*" Jehovah as on

---

[1] [1479 c] Orig. *Cels.* i. 9 "But Celsus says that certain people discarding discussion (μηδὲ βουλομένους διδόναι ἢ λαμβάνειν λόγον) concerning the objects of their faith (περὶ ὧν πιστεύουσι) use the [cry], 'Do not examine but trust' (Μὴ ἐξέταζε ἀλλὰ πίστευσον)."

[2] [1480 a] Mk i. 15 πιστεύετε ἐν τῷ εὐαγγελίῳ, see **1467** : ἐν, written ε̄, might be so easily repeated after the final ε in πιστεύετε that we might be justified in omitting it as corrupt (with *b* and *f*) if the phrase were not so rare. Ign. *Philad.* 8 ἐν τῷ εὐαγγελίῳ οὐ πιστεύω is not an instance (Lightf.). The phrase may have been common with a certain class of early Greek Evangelists but deprecated by their successors.

the Rock of the Psalmist, but that he is "*in*" the Father—as a child is "in" his father's house, or "in" his father's heart.

[1481] The Epistle to the Hebrews, discussing "faith," begins with definition and proceeds to historical exemplification. This is the opposite of the Johannine plan, which prefers "narrowing down," that is to say, first, a broad, vague, and sometimes even inaccurate statement, afterwards corrected[1], modified, defined by reference to persons and circumstances, and finally left with the reader not as a definition but as an impression. Thus John will begin by speaking of "trusting[2]" absolutely in a context that will lead his readers to ask "through whom or what" is this "trust" to be attained. Then he will speak of those who "trusted to the name [of the Logos][3]" as receiving "authority" to become "children of God," but will leave it an open question whether they availed themselves of that authority. The first use of the word by our Lord Himself will be in a gentle reproach to an enthusiastic convert for "trusting" too easily[4]. Soon afterwards, the Evangelist, in his own person, recurring to his phrase "trusting to the name," will say,—with a play upon words—that although "many" in Jerusalem were so impressed with His "signs" that they "*trusted to* ($\epsilon\iota\varsigma$) *his name*," yet "Jesus himself *did not trust himself to* (dat.) *them*[5]"! These remarks will suffice to shew the need of careful discrimination when John varies his phrases in the following passages. We may not understand the meaning of each variation, but that each has some meaning we may feel certain.

§ 8. "*Through whom*," *or* "*what*," *do all* "*believe*"?

[1482] i. 7 "That he [the Baptist] might bear witness concerning the light that all might *trust through him* ($\delta\iota$' $\alpha\dot{\upsilon}\tau o\hat{\upsilon}$)." The meaning probably (**2302—4**) is "that all men

---
[1] Comp. iii. 22 "and he [*i.e.* Jesus] was baptizing," with iv. 2 "Yet Jesus himself was not baptizing," and see **1925**.
[2] i. 7.   [3] i. 12.   [4] i. 50.   [5] ii. 23—4.

might trust through the light," *i.e.* by seeing things clearly and truly through the pure light of the Word of God and not through the mists and twilights of their selfish fears and desires, or through the darkness of sin. Here, without supplying an object to the verb "trust," the Evangelist suggests —by mentioning the medium—that, in any case, the kind of "trust" or "belief" that his Gospel will delineate is not the trust of ignorance or superstition. It is to be the trust of those who see things as they are. Even if it could be shewn that "through him" meant "through the Baptist," it would still remain true that all men are to be led to "trust" through the Light as the higher instrument, the Baptist being the lower one.

§ 9. *"Believing in the name"*

[1483] i. 12 "But as many as received (ἔλαβον) him, to them gave he authority to become children of God, namely, to those *trusting to his name* (τοῖς πιστεύουσιν εἰς τὸ ὄνομα αὐτοῦ)." The "*he*" is the "light" previously mentioned in i. 9—11, "There-was [from the beginning] the light, the true [light], which enlighteneth every man, [by its continual] coming into the world. He was in the world and the world through him came into being, and the world recognised him not. To his own [house] (εἰς τὰ ἴδια) he came, and his own household (οἱ ἴδιοι) received him not into [their hearts] (παρέλαβον). But as many...." Compare ii. 23 "Many trusted to his name (ἐπίστευσαν εἰς τὸ ὄνομα αὐτοῦ) beholding his signs, which he was [then] doing. But Jesus himself would not *trust himself to them* (οὐκ ἐπίστευεν αὐτὸν αὐτοῖς)...."

[1484] On this last passage Origen says, "We must hold fast to *Him* rather than to *His name*, lest, while 'doing mighty works in His name,' we should [be forced to] hear His [reproachful words] uttered when men boasted about His mere name¹." On the first (i. 12) he observes that receiving "authority to become the children of God" is not the same thing as "becoming children." "Receiving authority" Origen regards apparently as a rudimentary stage belonging to those who have "merely rudimentary belief (ἁπλούστερον πιστεύοντες μόνον)." Holding fast to *Him*, as distinct from "*His name*," belongs to those who have a more perfect insight². It may be urged that these so-called "rudimentary believers" are described by the Evangelist as having been born from God (i. 13 "who were begotten, not...nor from the will of man but from God"). But Origen describes the stages of development thus: first, men receive the light, and, with it, authority to become children of God; then, "having been brought into being from God, they also hear His words³" and pass into the higher stage.

[1485] Origen's meaning becomes clearer if we remember that "to receive the light" is much the same as "to be enlightened (φωτίζεσθαι)." Now the noun "enlightenment" is mentioned by Justin Martyr in his Apology as being the name given by Christians to "baptism"; and the noun and the verb ("enlighten," "enlightenment") were probably used before the second century in the sense of "baptism" and "being baptized⁴." Moreover "baptism" is regularly con-

---

¹ Origen (Huet ii. 196) is referring to the "boast" in Mt. vii. 22—3 "In thy name have we done many mighty works," and to the reproach in the Lord's answer, "I never recognised you, depart from me."

² Origen, *ib.* ii. 324—5 διορατικώτερον κατανοοῦντες τὰ τῆς θεοσεβείας πράγματα.

³ Origen, *ib.* γενόμενοι ἐκ τοῦ θεοῦ, καὶ τὰ ῥήματα ἀκούουσιν αὐτοῦ.

⁴ [1485 a] In Heb. vi. 4 "Those who have been once *enlightened* and have tasted of the heavenly gift," the Syriac versions give (Westcott) "who have once descended to baptism" and "who have once been baptized," and the text is explained (Suicer 1490) by most Greek and Latin Fathers as referring to baptism. Comp. Heb. x. 32 "Call to mind the former days wherein *having been enlightened*, ye endured a great conflict of sufferings," *i.e.* your conversion exposed you to persecutions.

[1485 *b*] This is confirmed by Justin Martyr, who expressly says that

nected with the phrases "to the name," "in the name," in the Acts, and once in Matthew[1]. Thus a good deal of indirect evidence suggests that the Evangelist here has in mind the profession of faith or trust made in baptism. And this interpretation is adopted by Chrysostom: "Why did he say, not '*made them children of God*,' but '*gave them authority to become children of God*'? Because he was shewing us that we need all diligence to preserve, unstained and untainted—throughout our whole lives—the image of sonship by adoption *stamped upon us in our baptism*. And at the same time he made it clear that no one will be able to take from us this authority *unless we first deprive our own selves of it*."

[1486] In support of this distinction between "trusting to the name of," and "trusting to," the Lord Himself, Origen, referring to Jn iii. 18[2], says "'Trusting to His name' differs from 'trusting to Him.' Accordingly, he that is to have immunity from judgment on account of trust, has that immunity from judgment through 'trusting to Him,' not [through 'trusting] to His name.' For the Lord said, 'He that trusteth to me is not judged,' not 'he that trusteth to my name is not judged.'" And he goes on to say that "trusting to His name"

"enlightenment" was the name given by Christians to the "washing" of baptism, and then proceeds to use the noun and verb in that sense, *Apol.* 61 καλεῖται δὲ τοῦτο τὸ λουτρὸν φωτισμός...καὶ ἐπ' ὀνόματος δὲ Ἰ. Χρ....καὶ ἐπ' ὀνόματος πνεύματος ἁγίου...ὁ φωτιζόμενος λούεται, 65 κοινὰς εὐχὰς ποιησόμενοι ὑπέρ τε ἑαυτῶν καὶ τοῦ φωτισθέντος... *Tryph.* 122 ταῦτα ὑμεῖς μὲν εἰς τὸν γηόραν καὶ τοὺς προσηλύτους εἰρῆσθαι νομίζετε, τῷ ὄντι δὲ εἰς ἡμᾶς εἴρηται τοὺς διὰ Ἰησοῦ πεφωτισμένους. The Jews reply that the prophecy πρὸς τὸν νόμον λέγει καὶ τοὺς φωτιζομένους ὑπ' αὐτοῦ, and "these" (they add) "are the proselytes [of the Law]." This illustrates the fact that Jews as well as Christians applied the term to proselytes.

[1] [1485 c] Acts ii. 38 (x. 48) ἐν τῷ ὀνόματι Ἰησ. Χρ., viii. 16 (xix. 5) εἰς τὸ ὄνομα τοῦ Κυρίου Ἰησοῦ, Mt. xxviii. 19 εἰς τ. ὀ. τοῦ πατρός... Comp. 1 Cor. i. 13, 15 εἰς τὸ ὀ. Π., and εἰς τὸ ἐμὸν ὀ. The Index to Hermas gives βαπτίζω only in the phrase *Vis.* iii. 7 β. εἰς τὸ ὄνομα τοῦ Κυρίου.

[2] Jn iii. 18 ὁ πιστεύων εἰς αὐτὸν οὐ κρίνεται. ὁ μὴ πιστεύων ἤδη κέκριται ὅτι μὴ πεπίστευκεν εἰς τὸ ὄνομα τοῦ μονογενοῦς υἱοῦ τοῦ θεοῦ.

is inferior to "trusting to Him[1]." That is to say, "to trust to the name of the Son of God" avowing that trust in baptism, is only a preliminary stage in the upward progress of a Christian.

[1487] Concerning this stage the ancient Appendix to Mark says "He that shall believe and be baptized shall be saved, but he that shall not believe (ἀπιστήσας) shall be *judged guilty* (κατακριθήσεται)[2]." But, according to the Fourth Gospel as interpreted by Origen, this stage of belief, or trust, does not bring full "salvation," though the rejection of it brings condemnation. Origen's conclusion appears to be sound, and in harmony with Johannine thought and language, namely, that "to trust to the name of Jesus" implies *a lower kind of trust, a profession of belief in baptism*, which professed belief, if not followed up and developed by spiritual action, might come to nothing[3].

---

[1] [1486 a] Huet ii. 196. Chrysostom (like others in Cramer *ad loc.*) ignores the distinction between "*him*" and "*the name*," and says "He [*i.e.* the believer] is not liable to judgment *in this particular point*," *i.e.* for having rejected the Christian faith. If the believer leads an impure life, says Chrysostom, he will be punished all the more for his sins, "but on account of unbelief he is not punished because he believed once for all (ἀπιστίας δὲ ἕνεκα οὐ κολάζεται διὰ τὸ πιστεῦσαι ἅπαξ)."

[2] [Mk App. xvi. 16.]

[3] [1487 a] According to this view, ἐπίστευσεν εἰς τὸ ὄ. τοῦ Κυρίου might mean, in effect, "he became a Christian convert and was baptized." In the present tense the phrase might be used to remind "believers" of their responsibility as converts. Dealing only with π. εἰς in 1 Jn v. 10—13, we find (1) ὁ πιστεύων εἰς τὸν υἱὸν τ. θεοῦ, (2) οὐ πεπίστευκεν εἰς τὴν μαρτυρίαν ἣν μεμαρτύρηκεν ὁ θεός, and then, "These things have I written to you that ye may know that ye have eternal life—[*to you, I say,*] *that trust to the name of the Son of God*," where perhaps the meaning of the italicized words is, "you, who did not merely once for all"—ἅπαξ, as Chrysostom says—"profess baptismal faith but continuously exercise it."

[1487 *b*] 1 Jn iii. 23 is difficult, and doubtful because ℵAC and W. H. marg. read πιστεύωμεν where B and W. H. txt read πιστεύσωμεν. All have the dative, thus, "And this is his commandment that we trust the name (π. τῷ ὀ.) of his son Jesus Christ and love (ἀγαπῶμεν) one

§ 10. *Our Lord's first mention of "believing" or "trusting"*[1]

[**1488**] i. 50 "Because I said unto thee I saw thee under the fig-tree thou *believest!* Thou shalt see greater things than these." We noted above (**1481**) that the Evangelist's first use of "believing" was absolute, no object being inserted. So it is here, and the "belief" is not defined so far as this sentence goes. But it is partially defined as being a reply to Nathanael's words, "Rabbi, thou art the Son of God, thou art King of Israel." That, then, is what Nathanael "believes" and it seems definite enough, at first sight. But is it clear what precise meaning Nathanael attached to the phrase, and whether he meant "*a* king" or "*the* king" of Israel? Both of these terms are capable of conventional meanings. All that we are allowed to know for certain is (1) that Nathanael believed these to be facts about Jesus because the latter declared that He had "seen him under the fig-tree" at the moment when Philip called him, (2) that Jesus replied as above. But the tenor of the reply justifies us in inferring that this faith—which was based upon a "sign," though not a "sign" of action or of healing—was not regarded by our Lord (and consequently not by the Evangelist) as of the highest order, and that He promised Nathanael a more spiritual basis for a higher kind of belief.

---

another." Perhaps the writer substitutes the unusual dative for the preposition in order to suggest a trust that is not formal or conventional:— "that we trust [in heart as well as in word] that name [which we professed to trust in when we were baptized] and that we give effect to it by a life of brotherly love." But the text is so doubtful that nothing certain can be said about its meaning.

[1] [**1488** *a*] It will not be thought necessary to remind the reader henceforth that πιστεύω means "trust" as well as "believe." "Believe in" (not "believe on," which would better correspond to π. ἐπί) will often be used except where some special context requires the word "trust."

§ 11. *Christ's disciples "believed in him"*

[**1489**] ii. 11 "This beginning of his signs did Jesus in Cana of Galilee, and he manifested his glory, and his disciples *believed in him* (ἐπίστευσαν εἰς αὐτόν)." The word "beginning" appears to have been interpreted by Origen as denoting spiritual precedence, not chronological order. This sign, he says, performed for those who were in health, was superior to the signs performed for the sick[1]. He evidently (without denying the literal miracle) regards the wine as spiritually efficacious, and probably as an anticipation of the Eucharist. If so, it would seem to him more than a mere coincidence, that at the time when the wine passed into the bodies of the disciples, faith passed into their souls.

[**1490**] But although we may feel certain that the Evangelist records the miracle as a literal one, yet we cannot regard it as equally certain that he takes the miracle to be the cause of the "belief" of the disciples. Had their faith been of that kind, would it not have been like the faith of Nathanael above-mentioned, and like that of Nicodemus and other Jews later on, a faith not in the Lord but in His signs? And is it not (in part at least) for the purpose of dissipating such an impression that John adds "*and he manifested his glory*"? "Glory," in the Fourth Gospel, is of a spiritual nature. The Lord had recently promised Nathanael that he and all the disciples should see heaven (**646** *a*) permanently opened and the angels of God ascending and descending on the Son of man. Did not this refer to the life of the Son of

---

[1] [**1489** *a*] Huet ii. 160. According to Chrys., the disciples, "even before this, had wondered at Him: now they believed in Him," ἐπίστευσαν εἰς αὐτὸν οἱ μ. αὐτοῦ οἱ καὶ πρὸ τούτου θαυμάζοντες αὐτόν. Cramer's version adds, after αὐτόν, "because then they received some increase of their faith in Him (ὅτι περ τότε προσθήκην ἐδέξαντό τινα τῆς εἰς αὐτὸν πίστεως)." Whoever added this probably disliked the notion that the disciples now, for the first time, "believed in" Christ.

God on earth and to His words as well as His works? If even the officers of the Sanhedrin, sent to arrest Jesus, recoiled from their task with the words "Never man spake thus," might not Christ's own disciples say even more? As for the miracle, it is said by the Evangelist to have been known to the servants that drew the water, but (at the time at all events) not to the Master of the Feast and apparently to none of those that were sitting at the table. The servants, then, if any one, ought to have "believed" in consequence of the miracle. But they are not said to have believed. This "belief" is predicated only concerning His disciples, whose eyes had been so far opened that they could to some extent discern His "glory." Hence they "believed in him."

§ 12. *"Believing the Scripture"*

[1491] At this point there comes, incidentally and out of chronological order, a mention of "trusting the Scripture," thus, ii. 22 "When therefore he was raised from the dead, his disciples remembered that he meant[1] this: and they *trusted the Scripture* and the saying that Jesus said." Chronologically, this "trusting the Scripture" comes *after the Resurrection*, and after the time when the disciples had begun, in the fullest sense, to "trust *to* (εἰς) Christ." This is confirmed by xx. 9 where it is said that the beloved disciple, seeing the grave-clothes in the tomb of the risen Saviour "believed—*for not even yet did they know the Scripture that he must needs rise from the dead*[2]."

---

[1] [1491 a] "Meant," ἔλεγε. R.V. "spake," A.V. "had said," but see Tense Imperf. (**2469**). If the meaning had been "spake," the Gk should have been ἐλάλησεν; if it had been "had said," the Gk should have been εἶπεν or (xi. 13) εἰρήκει.

[2] [1491 b] There is difficulty in the unique construction, with the preposition, in the Epistle (1 Jn v. 10) " He that doth not trust God hath made God a liar because he hath *not trusted to the testimony that God hath*

[1492] Later on, the dative is used somewhat similarly in v. 46—7 "For if ye trusted Moses ye would trust me... but, if *ye trust not his writings*, how will ye trust my words?" The plural "writings (γράμματα)" denotes the five books of the Law: and in the single passage in which John uses the plural of Graphé, he perhaps wishes us to see the Pharisees (v. 39) "searching *the Scriptures*," *book by book*, and yet unable to extract their meaning. But in the passage under consideration John uses the singular, "the Scripture," without quoting any special text; and for reasons given later on, it is probable that he means "*the Scripture as a whole*," "*the Scripture as the written Word of God*," or "the revealed will of God in the Law and the Prophets." To "trust" this, in the full sense of "trusting," required the aid of the Holy Spirit[1].

§ 13. "*Believing," in the Dialogue with Nicodemus*

[1493] The preface to the Dialogue with Nicodemus says that while Jesus was in Jerusalem during the Passover "many *believed in his name* beholding his signs, which he was [daily] performing[2]." We have seen above (**1483—7**) that this probably implies that they "*were baptized in Christ's name.*"

---

testified concerning his Son (οὐ πεπίστευκεν εἰς τὴν μαρτυρίαν ἣν μεμαρτύρηκεν ὁ θεὸς περὶ τοῦ υἱοῦ αὐτοῦ)." Probably the writer uses the phrase as Ignatius speaks of (*Trall.* 2) "trusting *to* (εἰς) the death of Christ," (*Smyrn.* 6) "trusting *to* (εἰς) the blood of Christ," in order to indicate that God's testimony was of the nature of a Person to whom one looks in trust.

[1] On "The Scripture" meaning "The Scripture as a whole," see **1722** *a—l*.

[2] [**1493** *a*] ii. 23 θεωροῦντες αὐτοῦ τὰ σημεῖα ἃ ἐποίει, *i.e.* "beholding his signs, *which* he was frequently, or daily, performing" (not "beholding the signs *that* he was performing"). The relative clause adds, not defines. For want of understanding this, the text has been corrupted as follows: SS "believed our Lord because they were seeing the signs that he did *to them*": *a b* and *f* om. αὐτοῦ: *e* (besides omitting αὐτοῦ) has "signa quae faciebat in eos qui infirmi erant." See **1564** *b*.

The Evangelist appears to have assumed that, when Jesus succeeded the Baptist, the former took up the work of baptizing disciples. The Synoptists make no mention of this; but John informs us of it immediately after the Dialogue thus, iii. 22 "After these things came Jesus and his disciples into the land of Judæa; and there he was tarrying with them and was baptizing," and a little later he says that Jesus, or rather His disciples, baptized more converts than were baptized by John[1]. This is antecedently probable; for one baptized by the Baptist, as Jesus had been, would hardly have discontinued the practice of the great Prophet without some strong reason; and, if Jesus had discontinued it, would not some one of the Evangelists have mentioned the discontinuance? Supposing that Jesus, the Baptist's successor, continued to baptize, we are the better able to understand why the subject is introduced at once when Nicodemus comes to Jesus by night.

[1494] The Rabbi, it would seem, was thinking about being baptized and came to consult Jesus about the matter. He is at once warned by our Lord that baptism with water is insufficient: there must be regeneration from above and with the Spirit. This introduces the notion of "believing," but, at first, only in a general sense, believing in spiritual as distinct from material existences. When Nicodemus exclaims, "How can these things be?" Jesus replies (iii. 12) "If I told you earthly things and *ye believe not, how will ye believe* if I tell you heavenly things?" Then He concludes (iii. 14) "As Moses lifted up the serpent in the wilderness, so must the Son of man be lifted up that everyone that *believeth* may in him have eternal life."

[1495] The meaning of this allusion—so obscure to us—would be comparatively easy to a Jew familiar with the doctrine about the Serpent in the Wilderness set forth by

---

[1] Jn iv. 1—3.

Philo, Barnabas, and the Targums[1], and with Jewish thought about the Serpent as being the author of man's fall. As the first Serpent and the first Adam brought sin, so a second Serpent and a second Adam must take away sin. The first Serpent was the passion for pleasure and self; the second Serpent is to be the passion for kindness and the love of others. Thus interpreted, these difficult words teach one of the deepest of all truths, that men will never be really reformed on the lines of mere law or on the lines of mere asceticism. Never will a human being be reshaped from without, as by a sculptor's hand. He must grow from a germ of life within, his heart going up, and his desires going up with it, out of himself, into a new Man, a second Adam, the Man from heaven.

[1496] Here, according to the best interpretation, the Dialogue ends; and the Evangelist proceeds with a comment of his own. Comparing Christ's first utterance about belief (to Nathanael) with this, His second utterance (to Nicodemus), we find Him in the former promising Nathanael a vision of "greater things," but here implying that Nicodemus and his friends would fail to believe "the heavenly things." But in neither case does the Lord define "belief." Only by the allusion to the Brazen Serpent, along with the mention of regeneration by the Spirit, we are led to ask what is meant by "believing," and what are to be its processes and objects.

[1497] The passage that follows has been taken by many as a part of Christ's own utterance; but it contains expressions ("only begotten Son," "believe in the name of," "do truth") used elsewhere by the Evangelist and not used

---

[1] [1495 *a*] See Philo i. 79, 82, 315, Barn. xii. 7, Targ. on Numb. xxi. 6—9—all full of interest, but not possible to discuss here. This is our Lord's first mention of "*life*" in this Gospel. Comp. Numb. xxi. 9 "when he looked unto the serpent of brass *he lived*."

elsewhere by our Lord; it speaks of Redemption in the past tense as an Evangelist would speak after Christ's death; and the tone of the passage is like that of other Evangelistic comments in this Gospel[1]. It answers the question "*To what are we to trust?*" suggested by the words, "in order that *he that trusteth* may in him have eternal life."

[**1498**] iii. 16—18 "For God so loved the world that he gave his only begotten Son that everyone that *trusteth to him* might not perish but might have eternal life...*He that trusteth to him* is not under judgment (οὐ κρίνεται). He that *trusteth* not is already judged [guilty] because he hath not *trusted to the name of the only begotten Son of God*[2]." The comment of Barnabas on the healing efficacy of the Serpent may be of use here: "When any of you shall be bitten (saith the Scripture) let him come to the Serpent that is hanging on the tree and let him *hope and believe that it, though dead, is able to make alive* and straightway he shall be saved (*i.e.* healed)[3]." This is a very rudimentary and erroneous definition of "trusting": but it helps us to understand why John does not attempt to *define*, and prefers to *suggest*. And his suggestion here is that we are to trust— not *in* a "dead" person or "thing," nor *that* a person or thing can "make alive," but—*to* (εἰς) an "only begotten Son," who will make us alive (as will be shewn hereafter) not in spite of the fact that He has died, but *because* He has died (as the seed dies to live and to give life).

---

[1] [1497 a] These arguments are alleged by Westcott for the conclusion that iii. 16—21 is "a commentary on the nature of the mission of the Son." To these may be added (**2066**) the frequent use of γάρ. Also ὁ θεός (nom.)—which occurs here in iii. 16, 17—is very rarely used by our Lord as compared with ὁ Πατήρ, but in the Epistle it occurs about 12 times.

[2] Comp. 1 Jn iv. 9 "Herein was the love of God manifested in us that God hath sent his only begotten Son into the world that we might live through him."

[3] Barn. xii. 7 ἐλθέτω ἐπὶ τὸν ὄφιν...καὶ ἐλπισάτω πιστεύσας ὅτι αὐτὸς ὢν νεκρὸς δύναται ζωοποιῆσαι καὶ παραχρῆμα σωθήσεται.

[1499] The metaphors for describing this giving of eternal life through the uplifted Son of man upon the Cross are various. Life may be regarded negatively as deliverance from sin. In that aspect, our burden of sin may be described as falling from our shoulders as we kneel before the Cross, or as taken from us and nailed to it with the Crucified One. But John probably looks at life positively, as a union with Christ, who, when we look to Him with the eye of faith, draws us to, or into, Himself, or passes into us that we may pass into Him.

[1500] Greek philosophers, as we have seen, condemned Christian faith as irrational; and in modern times some might liken it to that "fancy," or imaginative love, which is "engendered in the eye." Probably John would have accepted this comparison, only asking us to remember what the eye of the soul is and what is the object of the soul's vision. He would have admitted that no man can come to the Father unless he is, so to speak, "enamoured" with—or as Jesus said, "drawn by"—the ideal Sonship. No water can suffice to cleanse away sin. The pure fire, and passion, of the Spirit can alone drive out the impure fires and passions of the flesh.

§ 14. *After the Baptist's last words*

[1501] iii. 36 "He that *trusteth to* the Son hath eternal life; but he that refuseth to obey the Son shall not see life, but the wrath of God abideth on him." This is part of a comment by the Evangelist on the last words of the Baptist "He must increase but I must decrease"; and it shews why, even as compared with the greatest of prophets, the Son "*must* increase" while their claims on humanity decrease, because, while they represent God's messages, He represents God's Fatherhood. "Refuseth to obey," or "rebelleth," is closer than R.V. ("obeyeth not (*marg.* believeth not)") to the Biblical use of ἀπειθεῖν, which denotes stubborn disobedience to, or rebellion against, parents, or God, or obvious truth[1].

[1502] Here, then, "*trusting to*" is indirectly defined, by being contrasted with "*rebelling against*"; and thus the notion of "loyalty to," "allegiance to," is connected with the former. The words are parallel to the above quoted Evangelistic comment (iii. 18) " He that trusteth not [to the Son] *is already judged*," where the meaning was "is already condemned." This is now more emphatically expressed: "the wrath of God remains permanently on him." The Evangelist has in view a "rebel" answering to the appeal of the Gospel of God, "I will not believe that thou art my Father," to which the reply must be, "Then thou dost thyself make me remain thy Judge."

§ 15. *In Samaria*

[1503] iv. 21 " *Trust me* (πίστευέ μοι) woman, *that* the hour cometh when neither in this mountain nor in Jerusalem shall ye worship the Father."

iv. 39—42 "Now from that city many *trusted to him*, [many, I mean] of the Samaritans, on account of the word of the woman, when she testified, 'He told me all that ever I did'... (40) and he abode there two days and many more *trusted* because of his [own] word, and they said to the woman, 'No longer on account of thy speaking *do we trust*. For we ourselves have heard and know that this is truly the Saviour of the world.'"

[1504] The second of these passages may be conveniently taken first, because its motive is clear, namely, to emphasize

---

[1] [1501*a*] See Rom. x. 21 quoting Is. lxv. 2 and Rom. ii. 8 "*rebel against* the truth." The adj. occurs in Rom. i. 30, 2 Tim. iii. 2, "rebellious against parents," also in Lk. i. 17, Acts xxvi. 19, Tit. i. 16, iii. 3. The verb occurs nowhere in the Gospels except here.

the importance of *personal* trust in Christ. But the statement is not quite consistent. For let us suppose that fifty ("many") "believed on account of the word of the woman," and that a hundred and fifty ("many more") "believed on account of his (*i.e.* Christ's) word." How could the hundred and fifty say to the woman "*no longer* do we believe on account of thy speaking[1]"? The Diatessaron and SS try to meet the difficulty by dropping "more" ("many believed because of his word "). Codex *e* has "*much more* (multo amplius) did they believe because of his word." This makes admirable sense; but it is unfortunately not supported by other authority[2]. And, had it been the original, why should it have been altered? Probably the text is correct and the meaning, though not logically expressed, is this : "Some (say, fifty) believed because of the woman's word; but many more (say, a hundred) believed for the first time, *or (as regards the fifty) had their belief strengthened*, because of Christ's word: and all these came to the woman saying, 'The beginning of our belief came from you: but now we have heard Him for ourselves and we believe because of His word[3].'"

---

[1] [1504 a] Even supposing that fifty of the hundred and fifty had first believed "on account of the word of the woman" and were now strengthened in their belief "on account of Christ's word," yet the fact would remain that a hundred had never owed their belief to the woman, and could not use such language to her.

[2] [1504 b] Codex *e* seems to have read πλειονεπιστεγcan. This could easily arise from πλειονεcεπιcτεγcan: and πλείονες and πλείους are found as v.r. in Acts xxvii. 12, 1 Cor. xv. 6. Elsewhere in N.T. πλείονες (nom.) is found of persons four times (Acts xxvii. 12, xxviii. 23, 1 Cor. xv. 6, Heb. vii. 23) and πλείους (nom.) thrice (Acts xix. 32, xxiii. 13, 21). Both Origen and Heracleon read "many more" (Huet ii. 244, 248).

[3] [1504 c] Heracleon (according to Origen, Huet ii. 248 B) wished to supply μόνην after λαλιάν ("No longer do we believe because of thy speaking alone "). This, however, taken strictly, would indicate that he regarded all the speakers as being originally indebted to the woman for their faith.

[1504 d] Origen says (Huet ii. 245 E) Ἡ μὲν οὖν ἀρχὴ τῶν ἀπὸ τῆς

[1505] We are not obliged to suppose that the Samaritans first described as having "trusted to" the Lord received this faith, before seeing and hearing Him, on the mere report of the woman. The "fifty" may have been so far prepared by the woman to believe that, as soon as they entered His presence, they actually and genuinely believed in Him, but with a rudimentary belief. The Evangelist appears to recognise a lower and a higher faith, even while describing the lower by the phrase hitherto applied to the faith of the disciples and true believers ("*trusting to him*"). Thus a new shade of distinction is introduced, belief varying according to what the Greeks call the διὰ τί, or "*Why?*" In the former case, the answer to the *Why?* is "Because of the word of the woman"; in the latter, "because of His word."

[1506] Let us now return to our Lord's own saying about "belief," or "trust," early in the story. Under ordinary circumstances, and in an ordinary speaker, we might suppose the words "*Trust me*, woman, *that* the hour cometh......," to have been merely an asseveration meaning "I assure you that it is so." But we must have regard to the fact that this is an utterance of Christ, the third passage in which He mentions "trusting"; and the Gospel has hitherto appeared to be carrying us from stage to stage in the development of a doctrine about "trusting." We have also to consider the conclusion of the narrative, and the way in which it seems to point a moral about "trusting" and different kinds of "trust." The result should convince us that we are bound to try first of all to make sense of our Lord's words in their literal and

---

Σαμαρείας πιστευόντων ἦν πολλῶν λόγος ὁ τ. γυναικὸς μαρτυρούσης...ἡ δὲ αὔξησις καὶ πληθυσμὸς τῶν πολλῷ πλειόνων πιστευόντων οὐκέτι διὰ τὸν λόγον τ. γυναικὸς ἀλλὰ διὰ τὸν λόγον αὐτοῦ, where, for ἦν πολλῶν, we should perh. read τῶν πολλῶν contrasted with τῶν πολλῷ πλειόνων. Origen's antithesis "The *beginning*...but the *increase and multiplication*," may be intended to convey a suggestion that the increase *extended to the "belief,"* *and not only to the number of those "believing."*

weighty meaning by taking them as a precept, "Trust me." Taken thus, they call on the woman (to whom afterwards He vouchsafes the unique revelation of His Messianic nature) to "trust Him" that the House of Worship is not Jerusalem or Gerizim but Spirit and Truth. These, He says in effect, are the true Temple.

[1507] The Evangelist has already described Him as meaning "the Temple" when He mentions Himself[1]. So, here, the incarnate Temple of God is described as taking compassion on this poor Samaritan woman—who, amidst all her temptations of the flesh, has this additional peril, namely, that her idea of God is a Person much quarrelled about by learned Jewish and Samaritan Rabbis—and He asks her[2] to "trust" Him, when He assures her that prayer is not a

---

[1] ii. 21 "He was saying [this] (2469) concerning the temple of his body," better perhaps "meant this to refer to the temple etc."

[2] [1507 a] He does not speak as one commanding (aorist, πίστευσον), but rather as one requesting (pres. πίστευε). In this Gospel, Christ never uses the authoritative imperative of this verb. Neither does Mk v. 36 "Fear not, only *believe* (πίστευε)." But the parall. Lk. viii. 50 has πίστευσον: and so has Acts xvi. 31. Some Christians abused it, according to Celsus (Origen, *Cels*. i. 9) Φησὶ δέ τινας μηδὲ βουλομένους διδόναι ἢ λαμβάνειν λόγον περὶ ὧν πιστεύουσι, χρῆσθαι τῷ "Μὴ ἐξέταζε ἀλλὰ πίστευσον καὶ ἡ πίστις σου σώσει σε" (printed by Dindorf as two sayings, the second being, "Thy faith will save thee").

[1507 b] The aorist imper. occurs, however, in Soph. *Oed. R.* 646 πρὸς θεῶν...πίστευσον τάδε, where it seems to imply the urgency of entreaty rather than authoritative command. In Eurip. *Hel*. 710 λόγοις δ' ἐμοῖσι πίστευσον τάδε, it is authoritative. In these, and in two other instances quoted by Steph., π. is connected with a neut. accus. Herodian viii. 3. 22 τὸ δὲ παράδοξον τῆς ἀποβάσεως ποιεῖ πάντα πιστεῦσαι, Aristot. *Prior. Analyt.* ii. 23 Πιστεύομεν γὰρ ἅπαντα ἢ διὰ συλλογισμοῦ ἢ δι' ἐπαγωγῆς. Comp. Habak. i. 5 ἔργον ἐγὼ ἐργάζομαι...ὃ οὐ μὴ πιστεύσητε, where the antecedent of ὅ is prob. "the doing of the deed," not "the deed": but Acts xiii. 41 quoting this repeats ἔργον before ὅ. In N.T. this neut. accus. occurs thrice, Jn xi. 26 πιστεύεις τοῦτο, 1 Cor. xi. 18 μέρος τι πιστεύω, xiii. 7 πάντα πιστεύει. It is probably of a semi-adverbial character like Eurip. *Or*. 1103 γυναιξὶ πιστεύω βραχύ. Steph. gives no instance of a non-neuter accus. with πιστεύω.

sectarian or provincial business. Nathanael had been gently reproached by the Lord for "trusting" before he had seen the "greater things"; Nicodemus had been warned that "he that trusteth" must look upward to the Son of man "lifted up" in order that he "might have in him eternal life"; now the woman of Samaria is bidden to "trust *Him*," in the assurance that worship (which is the "looking upward" of the heart) will be effectual wherever it is offered "in spirit and truth." This cosmopolitan subordination of local worship ("Jerusalem," "Gerizim") prepares the way for the sublime confession at the end of the story—based, not upon faith but upon knowledge, and not on seeing but on hearing—"We have *heard* him ourselves and *know* that this is indeed the Saviour of *the World*."

§ 16. *The nobleman's "believing"*

[1508] iv. 48 "Except ye see signs and wonders *ye will assuredly not believe* (οὐ μὴ πιστεύσητε)!" Compare this with iv. 50 "Go thy way, thy son liveth. The man *believed the word that Jesus had spoken*," from which it appears that he *did* "believe," in some sense, *before* he had seen any "signs and wonders." It follows that we must take the words "ye will assuredly not" like similar words in xviii. 11 ("I am assuredly not to drink it!" (**933—6, 1007**)) and like many other exclamations of Jesus, as being of a semi-interrogative nature (**2236**). The utterance, though addressed *to* the nobleman, is not *about* the nobleman alone. The pronoun is not "*thou*" but "*ye*," and the full meaning of this condensed sentence might be paraphrased in modern English thus: "I know the ways of your class, the Herodians, the courtiers, the men of the world. None of you, as a rule, will believe without seeing signs and wonders! Is it to be so with you also?" It is exclamatory as regards the class but interrogative as regards the individual.

[1509] At the same time the Evangelist takes pains to shew that the man passes through stages of belief. He "believed," *in some sense*, at once: but he merely believed "the word that Jesus had spoken," namely, "thy son liveth." Afterwards, when he ascertained that his son had actually recovered in the hour of this utterance, then (iv. 53) "*he believed*—he himself and his household." What he *now* "believed" we are not told. But we are led to infer (1) that it was a belief, or trust, "in," or "to" Jesus Himself, (2) that it was, even now, not a perfect belief, for it had been caused in part by a "sign and wonder." We perceive in this narrative—which contains the fourth utterance of Jesus about "trusting" or "believing"—a recognition of two facts: first, that a certain class of people will not "trust" without "signs and wonders," and, secondly, that the Lord, while sometimes working such "signs," endeavours to raise them to a trust that is above "signs[1]."

§ 17. *"Believing" the testimony of the Father*

[1510] Hitherto, except in the Dialogue with the Samaritan Woman ("trust me") our Lord has never mentioned the object of trust. Now, it is brought before the reader in the course of a controversy with the Jews arising from an act of healing on the sabbath. Jesus asserts that He "sees" His Father performing such acts as these, that He, the Son, does them because the Father, who has sent Him, has given

---

[1] [1509 *a*] The Nobleman in Jn is, in some respects, parallel to the father of the "lunatic" in Mk. The former, when he hears the words "ye will not believe," does not deny the weakness of his belief but says, in effect, "Come down at all events and do what you can for my child before it is too late." This is not unlike the father's "*If thou canst*," in Mk. Only, in Mk, the father frankly avowed the mixed nature of his feeling "I believe, help thou mine unbelief." All this beautiful tradition of Mk's is left out by Mt. and Lk. Jn gives something corresponding to it.

them to Him to do, and that they are His Father's "testimony": (v. 24—47) "He that heareth my word *and trusteth him* (dat.) *that sent me* hath eternal life and cometh not into judgment, but hath passed out of death into life.... (38) and ye have not his word (or, Logos) abiding in you, because whom he sent, *him* (dat.) *ye trust not*.... (44) How can ye *trust* (πιστεῦσαι), receiving glory from one another and the glory that is from the only God ye seek not!.... (46) If ye *trusted Moses* (dat.), ye would *trust me* (dat.), for he wrote concerning me. But if ye *trust not his writings* (dat.) how will ye *trust my words* (dat.)?"

[1511] Here, "trust" means "*believe the testimony of*," and it is implied that if the Jews had thus trusted Moses, they would have trusted the Son, and if they had trusted the Son they would have trusted the Father. And concerning this last "trust" it is said that the man possessing it "hath eternal life." The section is mainly of a negative character. Even the strong phrase "hath eternal life" is followed by the negative "cometh not into judgment"; and life is regarded as being in its commencement ("hath passed out of death into life"). The context teaches that those who do not possess within their hearts, in any degree, the Word or Logos of God, having no affinity with the law of moral harmony and order, cannot revolve about His "glory," but make their own "glory" the centre of their actions. Having broken loose from the attractive force of God's overruling and universal Fatherhood, they no longer look to Him, or trust Him, as Father, but look always to themselves.

§ 18. *After the Feeding of the Five Thousand*

[1512] The Feeding of the Five Thousand is almost expressly said by our Lord to have failed in producing "trust" even in the hearts of those who received the bread. "Ye seek me," He says to them, "not because ye saw signs but because ye ate of the loaves and were filled. Work not [for] the food that perisheth but for the food that abideth unto life eternal.... This is the work of God *that ye trust*[1] *to him* whom God [hath] sent.... The bread (or, loaf) of God is the One[2] that cometh down from heaven and giveth life to the world... I am the bread of life. He that cometh to me shall surely not hunger and he that *trusteth to me* shall surely not thirst at any time. But I [have] said to you that ye have both (καί) seen [? me][3] and do not *trust*."

[1513] These words of Christ, and those of the Jews which are interspersed between them, present great difficulty because of the apparent blending of the literal and the spiritual. In particular, the last sentence has perplexed commentators because Jesus is nowhere recorded to have said "ye have both seen me and do not trust." But the words may be intended to sum up all that Jesus has just said, thus: "Your notion of the Bread of Life is greedy enjoyment; but the true Bread is *trust in God.* You say, 'How must we work the works of God?': I reply, 'The one work of God is to *trust to his Messenger.*' You say, 'What doest thou (ποιεῖς), or workest thou (ἐργάζῃ), that we may see and trust thee[4]?,' and you point to the Manna as being 'bread from heaven': I reply, 'The Manna was not the Bread from Heaven. That is a thing of the past. But the true Bread is now being offered to you, every day and every hour, by

---

[1] vi. 29 ἵνα πιστεύητε. On the distinction between this and πιστεύσητε, see 2524—5.

[2] [1512 a] vi. 33 ὁ γὰρ ἄρτος τ. θεοῦ ἐστὶν ὁ καταβαίνων, where ὁ καταβαίνων is taken by the Jews as meaning "the *bread* (or, *loaf*) that cometh down," but it may mean "the *man* that cometh down." "One" is an attempt to represent this ambiguity.

[3] [1512 b] vi. 36. W. H. bracket με, which is omitted by SS, as well as אA and most Latin MSS. But its difficulty explains (without justifying) its omission; and there is no satisfactory way of explaining how it could be erroneously inserted.

[4] vi. 30 (dative), but Jesus had used (vi. 29) the preposition "to."

the Father. The Bread is not anything that I 'do ($\pi o\iota\hat{\omega}$) or work ($\grave{\epsilon}\rho\gamma\acute{a}\zeta o\mu a\iota$).' It is I myself. I am the Bread. You ask for a sign that you may 'see and believe.' *You have seen me, and I have been telling you this, and yet you do not believe*[1].' "

[1514] If that is the meaning, Jesus is reproaching the Jews for not seeing the divine facts of human life, somewhat as Epictetus reproaches cultured Greeks for denying the existence of Demeter at the very moment when they were eating bread[2]. According to Johannine doctrine, the Bread of Life is not to be sought above the clouds but wherever we see good men and women, who diffuse peace and trust around them. Jesus was the incarnation of such goodness.

[1515] An underground stream of Jewish thought, coming to the surface in Mark's Gospel but not in Matthew's and Luke's, is possibly reappearing here—a tradition about the spontaneousness of God's kindnesses and about the calm and trustful spirit in which they are to be received. Mark says that the Kingdom is like a man that sows seed "and *sleeps* and rises night and day" and the seed grows "he knows not how," and "the earth *of itself*[3] bringeth forth fruit." This tradition about God's *giving to men in their sleep* appears in the Psalmist's contrast between worrying drudgery and trustful work, "Except the Lord build the house, they labour but in vain that build it; except the Lord keep the city, the watchman waketh but in vain. It is vain for you that ye rise up early, and so late take rest and eat the bread of

---

[1] vi. 26—36. [2] Epict. ii. 20. 32.
[3] [1515 a] Mk iv. 28 αὐτομάτη, so Philo, on Isaac (the self-taught, αὐτομαθής) i. 571—2 ἔστι δὲ καὶ τρίτος ὅρος τοῦ αὐτομαθοῦς τὸ ἀναβαῖνον αὐτόματον (that which cometh up of itself). Comp. also Clem. Rom. 22—3, on "the faith that is in Christ," in connexion with trustful acceptance of God's mercies ending with words that (Lightf.) "strongly resemble Mk iv. 26 sq."

anxiety. *He giveth unto his beloved in sleep as [abundantly as to you]*[1]."

[1516] So here, Christ's principal saying appears to be a protest against that faithless kind of work which might be called "dead works," the craving for which might lead some to accumulate not only purifications but even almsgivings, not from love for man but from faithless dread of God. In answer to the question put by the Jews, "What are we to *do* that we may work the works of God?" Jesus replies in effect, "*Do*, in the first instance, nothing—nothing, at least, that *you* would call '*doing*.' Simply *trust to* God's Messenger."

[1517] As regards the metaphor implied in "*trusting to*," we observe that it occurs in different contexts that may imply different shades of meaning. "He that cometh to me shall surely not hunger and he that *trusteth to* me shall surely not thirst at any time[2]" implies *approach to*. "This is the will of my Father that every one that beholdeth the Son and *trusteth to him* should have eternal life[3]" implies *looking to*. But does not this "beholding" correspond to "beholding the Serpent lifted up in the Wilderness"? And, if so, does it not mean that kind of "looking to" Jesus on the Cross which *draws* the sinner *to*, or *into* Jesus, so that he can exclaim with the Apostle, "I have been crucified with Christ[4]"?

---

[1] [1515 *b*] Ps. cxxvii. 1—2. On "in sleep," see Gesen. 446 *a*; "as abundantly" Gesen. 486 *a*. For the latter, Targ. has "convenienter et recte," but it takes "sleep" as the object (as A.V. and R.V. txt). The Targ. also takes "bread of cutting cares" as "the bread of the miserable for which they have toiled," thus "In vain will ye labour for yourselves, ye that rise up early to practise robbery for yourselves, ye that delay and sit quiet to perpetrate crime, devouring the bread of the miserable for which they have toiled." The first verse of the next Psalm (cxxviii. 1) appears to paint the opposite picture of trustful toil. "Blessed is every one that feareth (*i.e.* reverences) the Lord, that walketh in his ways. For thou shalt eat the labour of thine hands and happy shalt thou be."

[2] vi. 35.   [3] vi. 40.
[4] Gal. ii. 20, comp. Rom. vi. 6.

The Evangelist himself suggests this in the context; for he adds (as words of Christ) "No man is able to come unto me except the Father draw him," and, later on, "I, if I be lifted up, will draw all men unto me[1]."

[1518] Another aspect of the spiritual union expressed by saying that men are "drawn" towards Christ may be described by saying that Christ is taken into men as their food. Accordingly, this Dialogue goes on to speak first of "trusting to" the Son, and then of "eating the flesh of" the Son, as implying the possession of eternal life[2].

[1519] The conclusion of the section dissipates any literalistic impressions that might be derived from these intense verbal efforts to represent invisible truths so as to force upon us their reality. The disciples are warned by our Lord that "It is the spirit that giveth life, the flesh profiteth nothing: the *words* that I have spoken to you, [these] are spirit and [these] are life[3]"; and Peter bases his allegiance to the Lord, and his confession at the close of the narrative, not on the miracle of the loaves and fishes, but on Christ's *words*: "Lord, to whom shall we go? Thou hast *words* of *eternal life*[4]." Similarly the Samaritans said, "We have *heard* [him] and know that this is of a truth the Saviour of the world." And Peter, moved by the "words," now says, " *We trust completely* ($\pi\epsilon\pi\iota\sigma\tau\epsilon\acute{\upsilon}\kappa\alpha\mu\epsilon\nu$) (**2442**) *and know* that thou art the Holy One of God[5]."

§ 19. "*Not believing*"

[1520] Hitherto the Evangelist has made no mention, in his own person, of any actual refusal to believe, or "not

---

[1] vi. 44, xii. 32.
[2] [1518 a] Comp. vi. 47 "He that *trusteth* hath eternal life" (where $\epsilon\mathrm{i}\varsigma$ $\dot{\epsilon}\mu\acute{\epsilon}$ though rightly omitted by W. H. from txt has to be supplied, in thought, from the preceding words), and vi. 54 "He that eateth my flesh ...hath eternal life."
[3] vi. 63.   [4] vi. 68.   [5] vi. 69, see **1629**.

believing[1]." But now, after the "scandal" created by the Doctrine of Bread, when many of the Lord's disciples deserted Him, John tells us that (vii. 5) "Not even his own brethren *were disposed to trust* (or, *were [then] trusting*) *to him* (**2466**)." And at the end of the chapter the chief priests and Pharisees ask triumphantly (vii. 48) "Has any one of the rulers *trusted to* him, or [any one] of the Pharisees?" This implies a general "not believing," and Nicodemus, "one of the rulers," who is present, does not say anything to the contrary.

[1521] On the other hand, it is said that "many of the multitude trusted to him," alleging the number of His signs[2] —according to which standard Elisha would be called twice as great a prophet as Elijah, since he worked fourteen signs to his Master's seven! There can be little doubt that the Evangelist does not intend his readers to magnify this kind of "belief," or "trust." It is divided by an immense interval —this arithmetical belief—from that genuine spiritual dependence on the Messiah implied in our Lord's words following not long afterwards (vii. 37—8) "If any man thirst, let him come unto me and drink. *He that trusteth to me*,... rivers shall flow from his belly, [rivers] of living water." This carries His doctrine a stage beyond the previous announcement, "*He that trusteth to me* shall surely never thirst": for it implies that the believer will satisfy not only his own thirst but also that of others. The faithful convert will convert others to faith[3].

---

[1] [1520 *a*] It has occurred, but only in Christ's words *e.g.* iii. 12, v. 38 etc.: but there is an approximation to an Evangelical statement in vi. 64 "He knew...who they were that did not believe."

[2] vii. 31 "The Messiah, when he shall come, will he do more signs than this [man] hath done?"

[3] [1521 *a*] In vii. 39, the aorist participle probably includes future believers (**2499**), who were destined to receive the Spirit after having "trusted to him."

§ 20. "*Believing witnesses*"

[1522] A large part of the next chapter (viii. 1—46) treats of "trusting" as illustrated by the Law about "*two witnesses.*" The Father and the Son are declared to testify conjointly[1]. Apparently the meaning is that Christ's words and acts of healing, by diffusing physical as well as spiritual health among men, testify that they are in accordance with the Laws of Nature, or in other words, with the words of God the Father. In this chapter, the dative is twice used by our Lord, because the meaning is "*trust the evidence of*" *a witness*, and because He speaks negatively, blaming the Jews because they will *not even trust Him as a witness*, much less *trust to Him as their Deliverer*[2]. He also once uses (again with a negative) the phrase "trust *that*," as follows (viii. 24) "Except ye *trust that* I AM [HE], ye shall die in your sins." This is discussed elsewhere (**2223**), and an attempt is made to shew that it means, unless ye trust in God's purpose to make Man one with Himself.

[1523] Another passage, not in Christ's words but in narrative, distinguishes between (1) "many," who "*trusted to* him," and (2) "those who had *trusted him*, [being] Jews[3]." The latter are described as shortly afterwards becoming Christ's bitter opponents, then as "liars," and as "children of the devil." This is one of the most cogent of many passages indicating that John sometimes denotes great differences of meaning by slight differences of word, and that he takes pains to shew that the word "believe" might represent a transient emotion, or might have a non-moral significance.

---

[1] viii. 18.

[2] viii. 45—6 (*bis*) οὐ πιστεύετέ μοι.

[3] viii. 30—1 πολλοὶ ἐπίστευσαν εἰς αὐτόν... τοὺς πεπιστευκότας αὐτῷ Ἰουδαίους. On this, see **2506**.

§ 21. *After the Healing of the Blind Man*

[**1524**] A new phase of "trusting" is introduced by our Lord when He says to the blind man, whom He has healed, ix. 35 "*Thou [at all events] dost trust to* (σὺ πιστεύεις εἰς) *the Son of man*[1]?" To Nathanael, stimulating him to a higher trust, Jesus had said that he should see "the angels ascending and descending on the Son of man." He had also said to Nicodemus, "The Son of man must be lifted up that every one that *trusteth* may in him have eternal life[2]"—which implied *some* connexion between "trusting" and the Son of man: but Jesus had never, up to this time, expressly connected "trust" and "the Son of man," as He does here.

[**1525**] The phrase seems to denote a trust in, so to speak, the humanity of God, a trust in Man with all his physical and intellectual imperfections[3], as being a revelation of God superior to the revelation of Him contained in the heavens. The blind man has been battling for his Healer against the logic and brow-beating of the Sanhedrin, and has been cast out of the Synagogue. Now he receives his reward. The Saviour, finding him, does not say to him as to the impotent man of Bethesda, "Sin no more," but "Thou [I am sure] dost trust to the Son of man." The sequel illustrates the Johannine conception of faith, and, it may be added, the

---

[1] [**1524** *a*] On the reasons for taking this as a statement in interrogative tone, see **2242**. It corresponds to the interrogative statement made to the nobleman iv. 48 "Ye will surely not believe" (**1508**). The meaning is, "Though all the rulers of Jerusalem refuse to believe, thou at all events, I am sure, dost believe."

[2] i. 51, iii. 14.

[3] [**1525** *a*] Ps. viii. 3—5 "The Son of man," in John, is never "the Son of man" as conceived in Daniel seated on the clouds. It is rather the ideal of the Psalmist, as also the ideal suggested in Mk ii. 10 ("the Son of man hath authority upon earth to forgive sins") and ii. 28 ("the Son of man is lord also of the Sabbath...").

real nature of faith. The man does not even know the meaning of the phrase; yet he has in his heart the conception of the *Person*, and is already, virtually, a believer, "Yea, and who is he, Lord, that I may *trust* to him?" and then, "Lord, I *do trust.*"

[1526] As a contrast, the unbelief of the Jews is more and more emphasized. Far from "believing," in the Christian sense, because of the cure of blindness, they are confirmed in their belief that the Healer is a "sinner[1]." Jesus, in Solomon's porch, makes one more appeal to them, asking for a lower kind of faith than He had hitherto mentioned. He does not now say "trust *to* me," nor "trust *me*," but "trust works" (x. 37—8): "If I am not doing the works of my Father, trust me not: but if I am doing [them], even if ye be not trusting me, *trust the works.*" He seems to mean, "Only trust that the works are *kind* as well as wonderful. Only trust in their *motive*. Then you may go on from that to something higher." For, after "*trust the works,*" He adds, "that ye may recognise, and grow in the recognition (**2511**), that in me is the Father and I in the Father."

[1527] This section concludes with the statement that Jesus, after the Jews had attempted to stone Him in the Temple, went away again beyond Jordan "and abode there" and "many *trusted to* him there[2]." The adverb "there" occurs seldom in John at the end of a sentence, and still more seldom at the end of a section. Possibly it is emphatic and is intended to contrast the safety of the Lord, and the multitude of believers, beyond Jordan, with the persecution and unbelief in Jerusalem[3].

---

[1] The only mention of "believing," in the Evangelist's words, at this stage, is (ix. 18) "The Jews therefore *did not believe* concerning him that he had been blind and recovered sight until they called his parents...."

[2] x. 40, 42.

[3] [1527 a] Ἐκεῖ is certainly emphatic in Jn xi. 8 "Goest thou again *there* [of all places]?" meaning "the very place where they sought to stone thee."

§ 22. *The Raising of Lazarus*

[1528] "Trusting" is repeatedly mentioned in the Raising of Lazarus as, in part, the cause of the miracle, or of the manner in which it is performed. When our Lord prays aloud at the grave, He says (xi. 42) "For the sake of the multitude that standeth around I said [it] that they may *trust that* thou didst send me"; and previously, to the disciples (xi. 14—15) "Lazarus is dead, and I rejoice on account of you—*in order that ye may trust*—that I was not there." The latter passage is obscure (2099): but it seems to include the meaning that the Lord's absence has been ordained in order that the belief of the disciples in Him may be strengthened by the sequel *i.e.* the Raising of Lazarus. Nevertheless, "in order that ye may trust" (aorist) is grammatically remarkable if it means "that ye may grow in trust," or "that ye may continue to trust me." It would most naturally mean "that ye may become believers"; but, in that sense, it could not be applied to those who were already Christ's most devoted disciples[1].

[1529] Difficulty is also presented by the contrast between (1) the words uttered by our Lord to Martha and (2) what is commonly interpreted as His subsequent reference to them:

(1) (xi. 23—6) "Thy brother shall rise again... I am the resurrection and the life. He that *believeth in* (εἰς) *me*, even though he die (or, be dead), shall live; and every one that is living and *believing in me* shall assuredly never die. Thou *believest this*[2]?"

---

[1] For the difference between πιστεύσητε and πιστεύητε, see 2524—5.

[2] [1529 *a*] xi. 26 πιστεύεις τοῦτο. On this construction, rare in N.T. see 1507 *b*. It is a short way of saying, "Thou believest me as to this?" "Believe" has advantages over "trust" in the rendering of this passage.

(2) (xi. 40) "Said I not unto thee[1], 'If thou shalt *believe* ('Ἐὰν πιστεύσῃς) thou shalt see the glory of God'?"

To the disciples our Lord had said that the sickness of Lazarus was to be for the glory of God and of the Son of God[2]; but not to Martha. And there is nothing in Christ's first utterance to her to suggest that He is looking forward to any "rising" of Lazarus from the dead before that general "rising again" which He Himself mentions to her. Nor is there anything in it to indicate to Martha that her "believing" was to be a condition of her "seeing" her brother raised from the dead. On the contrary, the story shews that Martha was quite ready to believe that Jesus could have saved Lazarus from death, and could, even now that he was dead, restore him to life[3]. But any expectation of this kind would naturally be suppressed in her by Christ's mention of the "rising again" in general terms, applying to all believers[4].

[1530] But may He not have uttered these words to Martha on a previous occasion? Bearing in mind the saying of Jesus to Nathanael, "Thou shalt see greater things than these," we ought to find no difficulty in supposing that He uttered similar sayings to other converts. To Martha, therefore, at some time before the Raising of Lazarus, perhaps at

---

[1] [1529 *b*] Or as W. H. (ὅτι ἐάν) "that, if thou shalt believe, thou shalt see." But it is more in accordance with Johannine usage to print ὅτι 'Ἐάν as above. See ὅτι "recitativum (2189—90)."

[2] xi. 4 "This sickness is not unto death but for (ὑπέρ) the *glory* of God in order that the Son of God may be *glorified* through it."

[3] xi. 21—2 "If thou hadst been here my brother had not died. Even now I know that whatsoever thou shalt ask God, God will give thee."

[4] [1529 *c*] xi. 23—4 "'Thy brother shall (or, will) *rise again* (ἀναστήσεται)'...'I know that he will *rise again in the rising again* (ἀναστήσεται ἐν τῇ ἀναστάσει) in the last day...'" The following words "I am *the rising again* (ἀνάστασις) and the life. He that believeth in me shall live even if he be dead, and every one that liveth and believeth in me shall never die," seem expressly intended to include *all* "believers," and to exclude all expectation of a material or special revivification for her brother.

her conversion, He may have said, "If thou shalt believe, thou shalt see the glory of God[1]," no doubt in a spiritual sense—as Origen interprets the saying to Nathanael and the disciples[2]—meaning that she should see the mysteries of the divine Love. But, in such a saying, "the glory of God" would include that particular "glory" which accrued to the Father in heaven from the signs worked by the Son on earth—a "glory" that the Pharisees did not discern because they did not "believe."

[1531] Assuming the relation between Jesus and the family of Lazarus to be as John records it, we are confronted, in the death of Lazarus, with a crisis in the Christian Church—the first death in a family of "believers." Many years afterwards, the Thessalonians were startled by the death of a believer as being something disappointing and unsettling. They seem to have expected that the Lord would come from heaven and take all the saints up to His presence before death could touch them. How much more might the death of a friend of Jesus cause a chill to fall on the faith of some, in our Lord's lifetime, who "supposed that the kingdom of God was immediately to appear[3]"!

[1532] According to this view, Jesus, face to face with a threatening crisis for some of His dearest friends, is here strengthening the faith of one of them by referring to some

---

[1] [1530 a] Comp. Mk iv. 11 "To you is given the mystery of the kingdom of God" (where Mt.-Lk. have "to *know* the mysteries..."; and "to *see* the mystery" would make good sense) also Mk ix. 1 "There are some of those standing here that shall not taste of death till they *see* the kingdom of God having come in power" (Mt. xvi. 28 "the Son of man coming in his kingdom," Lk. ix. 27 simply "the kingdom of God").

[2] [1530 b] Orig. *Cels.* i. 48 τοῦτο δὲ τὸ ἀνοιχθῆναι τοὺς οὐρανοὺς προλέγων τοῖς μαθηταῖς ὁ σωτὴρ ἐσόμενον ὀψομένοις αὐτό... Καὶ οὕτως Παῦλος ἡρπάγη εἰς τρίτον οὐρανὸν πρότερον ἰδὼν αὐτὸν ἀνοιχθέντα... "I do not suppose," he says (*ib.*), "that the *sensible* heaven has been opened and its *material frame* (σῶμα) divided by opening in order that Ezekiel might record such a thing."

[3] Lk. xix. 11.

previous utterance to her, not recorded in the Gospel. Strange though this may seem, it is the explanation adopted by Westcott of words uttered by Jesus on another occasion, "But I said to you ' *Ye have both seen [me] and did not believe*[1]'": and its adoption there is more difficult than here, because here there is some antecedent probability that our Lord would have made to Martha the same sort of promise that He made to Nathanael and others.

[1533] Reviewing all the mentions of "believing" in the Raising of Lazarus, we are led to see some similarity between the attitude of Christ here and His attitude in the Synoptic Gospel when preparing for an act of healing where "belief," or "faith," cannot be expected from the person to be healed or revivified. The Synoptists describe our Lord as stimulating the faith of the parents, or as being moved by it to perform a cure ("Only believe," "'If thou canst,' all things are possible to him that believeth," "O woman, great is thy faith[2]"): so, in the Johannine healing of the nobleman's son, the father is stimulated (**1508**) by the words "Ye will not believe[3]": and so, in this critical conflict, John describes the Lord as, so to speak, marking out the field of battle and strengthening the weakness of His friends and allies, that their faith may, in the order of the Father's purposes, enable the Son to perform the coming miracle.

[1534] Even though we may be obliged to reject some of the details of the Raising of Lazarus as unhistorical, we may be able to accept the fact that our Lord did occasionally restore to life those who would ordinarily be described as "dead." And the first death among His disciples might well cause questioning to the Saviour. Was He to raise up the dead in this case? If so, was He to do so afterwards in every case? He might feel sure from the beginning, that the

---

[1] vi. 36.   [2] Mk v. 36, Lk. viii. 50, Mk ix. 23, Mt. xv. 28.
[3] iv. 48.

sickness of a particular sufferer was to be "for glory" and not "for death": but whether the "glory" included deliverance from physical death, might not be revealed to Him at first; and the strain on the faith of His disciples and friends might profoundly affect Him, even at the very time when He taught Martha that the Son of Man Himself, in His unity with the Father, was "the Rising Again and the Life[1]"— and that no man, once joined to the Father through the Son, could ever die.

[1535] The sudden departure of Martha from Jesus, after her profession of faith in Him[2], may be supposed to have prevented her from receiving any of those suggestions (of a miraculous revivification) which had been thrown out by Him to the disciples. And they are no more than suggestions. Jesus says, at first, "I go to wake him," and is understood literally: but afterwards "He said plainly, Lazarus is dead," and makes no mention of any purpose to raise him from the dead. Without much straining of the narrative, we may suppose that our Lord did not receive the full revelation of the divinely purposed rising again of Lazarus till He stood near the grave, with His disciples and Martha and Mary, all believing in Him, and all prepared to believe in Him—whatever He might do or not do.

[1536] Whatever uncertainty may attend the traditions concerning "believing" in connexion with Martha, the Evangelist leaves us under no doubt as to the effect of the miracle on the "believing" of the Jews and as to its general consequence: "Those that came to Mary believed in him"; but the chief priests and Pharisees said (xi. 48...53) "If we let him [continue] thus, all *will believe* in him, and the Romans will come and take away our [holy] place and

---

[1] The same word is practically repeated in "Thy brother shall *rise again*" and "I am the *rising again*" (xi. 23, 25).

[2] xi. 28 "Having said this she went away."

our nation... From that day therefore they took counsel to kill him." Thus, like all the public signs of Jesus, the sign of the Raising of Lazarus produces a mingled harvest, tares and wheat, belief and unbelief. Or, to take the metaphor preferred by John, the increasing light produces in some souls a shadow of increasing darkness.

§ 23. *"Believing in the light"*

[1537] In the next chapter the darkness just mentioned is described as becoming darker than ever—and this, as an indirect consequence of "believing." That the chief priests should "take counsel for" the death of Jesus, dealing with Him as a magician, was at all events from their point of view not an immoral act; but now they purpose the death of a man against whom they bring no charge (xii. 11): "They took counsel to kill Lazarus also, because, on his account, many of the Jews...*began to believe in* (ἐπίστευον εἰς) *Jesus*[1]."

[1538] Perhaps the imperfect tense ("they *began* to believe") and *the fact that these "Jews" did not believe in Jesus on account of Himself, but "on account of Lazarus,"* and the emphasis laid by the Evangelist on the great part played by the "sign" in winning for Jesus a welcome from "the multitude," are all intended to prepare the reader for finding that this "belief" will speedily end in nothing; and that more real importance is to be attached to the quiet approach of the Greeks to our Lord, through the mediation of Philip, "Sir, we would see Jesus[2]." At all events "the multitude" is soon afterwards mentioned—for the last time in the Gospel—as taking the Voice of the Father from Heaven to be thunder, or, at best, the voice of an angel; and their last words to the Son of man,—who had lived and

---

[1] Or, "believed from time to time," *i.e.* now some, now others. But "began to believe," or "were disposed to believe," is more probable.

[2] xii. 20—21.

was about to die, for their sake—are "Who is this Son of man[1]?"

[1539] This was darkness indeed, as a conclusion of a Gospel of light: and the rest of this section treats of "believing," or rather "not believing," under the metaphor of darkness and light. In this connexion, there are two sayings of Jesus about believing. The first of these is addressed to the multitude after they have asked the question "Who is this Son of man[2]?" He no longer bids them believe in the Son of man, nor in Himself, but in "the light." The Epistle says "He that loveth his brother abideth in the light"; and "He that saith he is in the light and hateth his brother is in the darkness[3]." This appears to be the predominant thought here. As light was the first created thing in the creation of the world, so what corresponds to it, namely, love, is the first principle in the spiritual world, the medium through which God is discerned by man. Christ's hearers were in danger of losing the last spark of this spiritual faculty through their subservience to conventional religion and through their conventional desire to persecute non-conformity. In the presence of these spiritual weaklings Christ abates His claim. He does not say "Believe in me, or Believe in the Son, that ye may become the sons of God," but "Believe at all events in the light, so far as[4] ye have it still with you, that ye may become sons of light."

---

[1] xii. 34.

[2] [1539 a] Jesus had said nothing here about a "Son of man." His words were, "And *I*, if I be lifted up from the earth, will draw all men unto me." But His doctrine to Nicodemus had mentioned "the lifting up of the Son of man," and perhaps the Evangelist wishes to describe the "multitude" as rebelling against this new term (which they had heard from Jesus on previous occasions) and as preferring the familiar and (for them) conventional term "Christ" or "Messiah": "We have heard from the Law that the Christ abideth for ever, and how sayest thou that *the Son of man* must be lifted up? Who is this *Son of man*?"

[3] 1 Jn ii. 9—10.

[4] xii. 36 "So far as." On ὡς, as distinct from ἕως, see 2201.

[1540] This expression "sons of light" is followed by an evangelistic comment indicating that the appeal was vain; and the language suggests that the light, henceforth, was hidden from the Jews. "These things spake Jesus, and he went away and *was hidden* (**2538**) *from them.*" Then the Evangelist sums up his account of the national unbelief. "Though he had done so many signs," he says, "they *did not believe in him*[1]." Their unbelief was a judicial retribution predicted by Isaiah: "For this cause *they were not able to believe*[2] because again Isaiah said, 'He hath blinded their eyes....'" Then turning from the nation as a whole to their "rulers," he concludes with an astonishing remark. In spite of the general unbelief we should not have been surprised to hear that "a few," or "some" of the rulers believed: but John says: "Nevertheless, however, *of the rulers also many believed in him*[3]; but on account of the Pharisees they would not confess [him] in order that they might not be put out of the synagogue; for they loved the glory of men rather than[4] the glory of God."

[1541] This remarkable statement may be perhaps best explained by supposing that these "many rulers" had not only made formal profession of belief in Jesus (having been perhaps baptized by His disciples) but had also believed in Him with some degree of genuine conviction, and with attachment, calling themselves His disciples—but, like Joseph of Arimathæa, "secretly, for fear of the Jews[5]." If so, it would seem that John deliberately uses the phrase "believed in him" in order to shew how even such "believing" might come to naught without "confession[6]." He is more severe

---

[1] xii. 37 οὐκ ἐπίστευον, see **2466**, perh. "they were not disposed to believe in him."   [2] xii. 39.
[3] xii. 42 ὅμως μέντοι καὶ ἐκ τῶν ἀρχόντων πολλοὶ ἐπίστευσαν εἰς αὐτόν.
[4] xii. 43 "Rather than," μᾶλλον ἤπερ, almost = "and not," see **2092**.
[5] xix. 38.
[6] Comp. Rom. x. 9—11 "If thou shalt confess with thy mouth Jesus [as] Lord, and shalt believe in thy heart that God raised him from

on them here than on Joseph of Arimathæa later on. Joseph's motive for secrecy, says the Evangelist, was "fear of the Jews"; the motive of these "many" was "the love of the glory of men rather than of the glory of God." But he infers this "love of glory" from the fact that they feared to be "cast out of the synagogue."

[**1542**] Many people, now-a-days, would consider this an austere inference. A man may "love the glory of God" more than "the glory of men," and yet may be deterred from doing what is right, if his love of God's glory is weaker than his fear of being cast out from friendship, from social intercourse, and from community of worship, with his neighbours and kinsmen. All the more reasonable is it to suppose that John, when concluding his history of the growth of belief and unbelief among the Jews during Christ's preaching of the Gospel, wishes to brand with the stamp of inferiority, or spuriousness, that sort of faith in Christ which might be called "belief in Him" and yet did not lead to public confession.

[**1543**] We now come to the last saying of our Lord about "believing,"—the last, that is to say, in His public teaching: xii. 44—6 "Jesus cried aloud and said, *He that believeth in me believeth not in me but in him that sent me*, and he that beholdeth me beholdeth him that sent me. I, light[1], have come into the world in order that *everyone that believeth in me may not abide in the darkness*." This is not said to have been addressed to any class in particular. It is a warning to all the world that "belief" in Christ is not really

---

the dead, thou shalt be saved: for with the heart man believeth unto righteousness; and with the mouth confession is made unto salvation. For the Scripture saith, Whosoever believeth on him shall not be put to shame." Perhaps John implies that if these rulers had "confessed," they would not have been "put to shame," nor would they have been afterwards ashamed of Christ crucified.

[1] On the force of this appositional construction, see **1933**.

belief in Him unless it is belief also in Him that sent Christ, nor is it true belief if the believer "abide in darkness" *i.e.* in doubt, or fear, or unbrotherly feeling towards his fellowmen.

[**1544**] The announcement is to be read along with the description of the "belief" of the rulers, many of whom—once, at all events—"believed in him." There are degrees of "darkness." Some of these "rulers" had perhaps so far turned against their Master that they now agreed with Caiaphas that "one man must die for the people"; these were "abiding in the darkness" of midnight. Others, like Joseph, had not voted with Caiaphas[1]; but Joseph is not recorded to have spoken or voted against Caiaphas, and these, too, may have kept silent "through fear of the Jews." The conduct of this second class was typified by Nicodemus, of whom it is twice said that "he came to Jesus by night[2]." It was not the blackest of the "night"—the "night" associated with Judas[3]: but still it was the night or twilight of men "abiding in darkness" and not "believing,"—not at least in the full sense of the term. With these warnings against false or formal or fearful belief, and with these commands to "believe in the light," the public teaching of Christ is brought to its close.

§ 24. *The Last Discourse*

[**1545**] After the Washing of Feet and the exhortation to the disciples to imitate their Lord's action, the discourse

---

[1] Lk. xxiii. 51.
[2] Jn iii. 2, xix. 39.
[3] [**1544** *a*] Jn xiii. 30 "Having received the sop, therefore, he went out. *Now it was night.*" The only other mention of "night" in the Evangelist's words (apart from Christ's) refers to the disciples on the night before Peter returned to our Lord through the water (xxi. 3) "*In that night they took nothing.*"

turns on the "stumbling[1]" that would be caused by the impending betrayal and death of Christ; and the only mention of believing in this chapter is (xiii. 19) "From henceforth[2] I say [it] to you before it come to pass, *that ye may believe*, when it hath come to pass, *that I am [he]*." The aorist subjunctive, which is probably the correct reading, may denote that the verb refers to "believing" the particular prediction just mentioned, so that the words mean "*that ye may believe that I am he [concerning whom it has been written 'He that eateth my bread...']*[3]." This is Origen's explanation; and, if it is correct, the passage describes our Lord as endeavouring to strengthen the faith of the disciples to meet a particular emergency (as in the Raising of Lazarus[4]).

[1546] Finding that they are still weak and their hearts full of trouble, He presently recurs to the thought of "trusting" or "believing," and now in a general sense (xiv. 1) "*Ye believe* (or, *Believe*) *in God. Believe in me also*," and (speaking to Philip) (xiv. 10) "*Believest thou not that I am in the Father and the Father in me?*" Then He addresses all the disciples, (xiv. 11—12) "*Believe me that I am in the Father and the Father in me: but, if* [ye can] not [believe me, *i.e.* my mere word], *believe on account of the works [by] themselves*," "*He that believeth in me*, the works

---

[1] The *word* "stumbling" is not used till xvi. 1 "These things have I spoken unto you *that ye may not be caused to stumble* (ἵνα μὴ σκανδαλισθῆτε)." But the *thought* of "stumbling" extends from xiii. 19 onwards.

[2] [1545 a] "From henceforth" may perhaps mean, that Christ had not said it before, because He desired to give Judas the opportunity of repenting during the Washing of Feet. But there had been no repentance, and this had been indicated by the words (xiii. 10—11) "Ye are not all clean." Since therefore the treachery could not be averted, the Saviour says that "from henceforth" He will not conceal it.

[3] [1545 b] So Origen *ad loc.* Huet ii. 394 E ἵνα...πιστεύσητε ὅτι ἐγώ εἰμι περὶ οὗ ταῦτα πεπροφήτευται. Origen comments at great length on this passage (Huet ii. 394—8). In the first three quotations of it, the text has πιστεύσητε, but in the three following ones πιστεύητε, see 2524.

[4] xi. 15 ἵνα πιστεύσητε, see 2525.

that I do he also shall do; and greater works than these shall he do because I go to the Father." He concludes by declaring that He has carried out the intention, mentioned above, to warn the disciples before the evil falls upon them (**1545**), "*I say* [*it*] *to you before it come to pass* (πρὸ τοῦ γενέσθαι) *that ye may believe* (πιστεύσητε) *when it shall have come to pass, that I am he.*" These words He repeats, except the last clause, saying (xiv. 29) "*And now I have said* [*it*] *to you, before it hath come to pass* (πρὶν γενέσθαι) *that, when it shall have come to pass, ye may believe* (πιστεύσητε)." The object of belief ("that I am he") is not repeated, but presumably it is omitted merely for brevity; and the aorist subjunctive here, as above, indicates a particular, not a general, belief—a belief that Christ's sufferings were foreordained and prophesied. The main object of belief mentioned in this section is of a general character, the Unity of the Father and the Son ("I in the Father and the Father in me[1]"), implied by a belief in the Father inseparable from a belief in the Son ("Ye believe (*or*, Believe) in God. Believe in me also[2]").

[**1547**] In all these exhortations and strengthenings, "belief," in its various forms, is not regarded as an end or ultimate object. It is merely an imperfect condition, a process of passing into unity with the Father in the Son, so as to "abide" in love. "Abiding" not "believing," "peace" not "faith," are the ultimate objects. Hence, in the chapter that describes Christ as the Vine, and the disciples as the branches that "abide" in the Vine (xv. 1—27), there is no mention of "believing." But the following chapter once more takes up the task of strengthening the disciples against the trials of "persecution": and now Jesus explains that these persecutions arise from unbelief for which the world will be condemned. The Paraclete will convict

---

[1] xiv. 11. [2] xiv. 1.

the world of sin, He says, "*because they believe not in me*[1]." This harmonizes with what He told the Jews: "This is the work of God, that ye believe in him whom he [*i.e.* the Father] sent[2]." The "work" of God being "belief," it follows (for those who accept Christ's teaching about a devil) that the "work" of the devil, or "sin," is unbelief or disbelief. And the object of the unbelief is the same as the object of the belief, "he whom God hath sent," that is to say, God's messenger or representative in every age and society, those men and women who are, as Plato says, "most like God."

[1548] This high and pure "belief," which the world had not, the disciples had, (xvi. 27) "For the Father [of] himself loveth you because ye have loved me and *have believed that I came forth from [the house of] the Father.*" But the disciples themselves, even while possessing this precious belief, appear to confuse it with one of a baser and less enduring metal—belief based upon the evidence of signs: for, because Jesus has read their thoughts, they say to Him (xvi. 30) "Now we know that thou knowest all things... *hereby* (ἐν τούτῳ) *we believe that thou camest forth from God.*" This mischievous complacency in the possession of a definite religious belief based upon definite evidential proof—the root of how many evils to Christendom!—Christ hastens to destroy: "*For the moment ye believe!* Behold the hour cometh and hath come for you to be scattered, each to his own, and to leave me alone."

[1549] This is the last mention of "believing" made by our Lord in His teaching to the disciples, before the Resurrection: and it is of the nature of a warning against making "belief" one's end, and, so to speak, "believing in believing." We are not to aim at believing but at "peace," and this, a peace, not gained through conformity with the selfish world, but through believing in the unselfish Messenger,

---

[1] xvi. 9.   [2] vi. 29.

whom the Father has sent to conquer the selfishness of the world. This we are taught by the last words of the Last Discourse (xvi. 33) "These things have I spoken to you *that in me ye may have peace.* In the world ye have tribulation. But be of good cheer, I have conquered the world."

§ 25. *The Last Prayer*

[1550] Our Lord, in His Last Prayer, prays for the unity of the disciples, but not that they may "believe," or "have faith." The latter petition He here reserves for "the world." Concerning the disciples—in spite of His warning that their belief will not prevent them from deserting Him— He says (xvii. 8) "*They believed that thou didst send me.*" Both for them and for those whom He calls (xvii. 20) "the believers through their word"—that is, the converts made by the Apostles—He prays that they may be "all one," one with the Father, and with the Son, and with each other. But in connexion with "the world" He mentions the word "believing" as an object to be attained hereafter, thus (xvii. 21) "In order that they also [*i.e.* the Church] may be in us, *in order that the world may grow in the belief* ($\pi\iota\sigma\tau\epsilon\dot{\upsilon}\eta$) *that thou didst send me.*" The verb is in the present (not the aorist) (**2524** *foll.*) and the prayer is that the world may receive a living and growing belief, not a mere formal one, that Jesus of Nazareth was sent by God—a belief, not based on signs and wonders but on the unity of the Church with the Father and the Son, through the Spirit, in brotherly love.

§ 26. *After the Death and Resurrection*

[1551] There remain—besides an utterance of our Lord, which will be considered last of all—four statements about "believing" made by the Evangelist. The first of these attests the flow of blood and water from the side of Jesus on the Cross: (xix. 35) "And he that hath seen hath testified, and his testimony is true; and he (**2383**) knoweth that he saith true *that ye also may grow in belief* (πιστεύητε)." If W. H. are right, as they probably are, in reading the present subjunctive, the belief is of a general and vital kind, including a belief in the Lord as "the fountain for sin and for uncleanness[1]."

[**1552**] Next comes the earliest mention of "believing" after the Resurrection: (xx. 8) "Then therefore entered in the other disciple also, he that came first to the tomb, and *he saw and believed* (εἶδεν καὶ ἐπίστευσεν): for not even yet did they know the scripture, [how] that he must rise from the dead." Apparently this disciple "believed" in Christ's resurrection, simply on the evidence of the open tomb and the grave clothes—although the open tomb suggested to Mary Magdalene something quite different, namely, that the Lord's enemies had taken away the body. With this must be taken the reply of Thomas to the assertion of the disciples that they had "seen" the Lord, (xx. 25) "Except I see in his hands the print of the nails...*I will assuredly not believe.*" From the sequel it would seem that Thomas and the beloved disciple were alike in one respect, since both "*saw and believed.*" What our Lord says about this will be considered later on.

[**1553**] The fourth Evangelistic mention of "believing" describes the object of the Gospel (xx. 31) "But these things have been written *that ye may grow in the belief* (πιστεύητε) that Jesus is the Christ the Son of God, and that, *believing* [*this*] (πιστεύοντες), ye may have life in his name." Accepting once more W. H.'s reading, the present subjunctive, we interpret it as denoting the object to be not the profession of faith on the part of converts, but the growing faith, or

---

[1] [**1551** *a*] Zech. xiii. 1. If the aorist were read the meaning might be belief in this special fact, or that "ye might become believers," but more probably the former.

abiding faith, of those already converted. But why does the writer introduce the words "in his name" ("life in his name") since we have seen above (**1483—7**) that Origen is probably correct in supposing "believing *in his name*" to be an inferior stage of belief to "believing *in him*"? The answer is that he does not speak here of "*believing in the name*" *of Jesus*, but of "*having life in his name*." And "name" here, as in the Epistle[1], is connected with the word "Son," implying that life is found in the divine Sonship of Christ. There is, therefore, no reference here to the rudimentary or initial faith professed at baptism. The writer is addressing believers already baptized in the name of Jesus Christ the Son of God, and he says to them, in effect, "I write unto you, children of God, in order that you may grow in the faith that Jesus is the Messiah, the Son of God, and that, growing in this faith, you may have life in His Sonship."

[**1554**] Last comes the saying of our Lord (xx. 29) "Because thou hast seen me thou hast believed! *Blessed [are] they that [shall] have not seen and [yet] [shall] have believed*," to be considered along with the statement that "the other" disciple "*saw and believed*," and that Thomas said "except I *see*...I will assuredly not *believe*[2]." Both Origen and Chrysostom appear to take the aorist participles as referring to future believers ("those after the apostles")[3].

---

[1] [**1553** *a*] 1 Jn iii. 23 "*the name of his Son*," v. 13 "*the name of the Son of God*." In 1 Jn ii. 12 "*on account of his name*" follows the words "I write unto you, *little children* (τεκνία), because your sins are forgiven," and appears to mean that both the "childhood" and the "forgiveness" are "on account of" the divine Sonship of Christ. These are the only instances of "name" in the Epistle.

[2] Μακάριοι οἱ μὴ ἰδόντες καὶ πιστεύσαντες, comp. xx. 8 καὶ εἶδεν καὶ ἐπίστευσεν, and xx. 25 ἐὰν μὴ ἴδω...οὐ μὴ πιστεύσω.

[3] [**1554** *a*] Origen blames those who thought that a superior blessing was pronounced on those who had "not seen," because, he says, "according to their interpretation *the successors of the apostles* (οἱ μετὰ τοὺς ἀποστόλους) are more blessed than the apostles themselves" (Huet ii. 195 C).

The aorist participle might have that meaning even if the time of the "blessing" had been defined as present by the insertion of "*are*," as in the Sermon on the Mount "*Blessed are ye* when men *shall revile you*[1]"; and it may much more easily have this meaning where the time of the blessing is left undefined. Antecedently, it seems likely that this reference to future believers should be at all events included, and very unlikely that it should be restricted to, say, a score of unmentioned persons, thus:—"blessed are those who, in the course of the last week, have believed [on the strength of the testimony of those who saw me at the beginning of the week], and who have not [themselves] seen [me]."

[**1555**] But are we to suppose that those who believe without having seen are *more* "blessed" than those who believe *because* they have seen? Origen earnestly maintains that this is unreasonable. The meaning is, he says, that the former class *also* is "blessed," not that it is *more* "blessed." In that case, however, is not the statement a truism? And what is the force of making the statement to Thomas, unless it suggests a gentle reproach of some kind, *e.g.* that *some* of those who will believe without seeing are more blessed than *some* of those who believe after seeing? Moreover, is no contrast intended between the beloved disciple, who "*saw and believed*," but without asking to "see," and Thomas who "*saw and believed*," but not till he had refused to believe unless he was allowed to feel as well as to see?

[**1556**] Chrysostom, at all events, recognises such a contrast as likely to occur to his readers. His words are as follows, "And yet, some one may say[2], the disciples 'saw

---

Chrysostom even paraphrases the aorist by the future "He pronounces a blessing not on the disciples alone but also on those who shall believe after them (τοὺς μετ' ἐκείνους πιστεύσοντας)."

[1] Mt. v. 11 μακάριοί ἐστε ὅταν ὀνειδίσωσιν ὑμᾶς (sim. Lk. vi. 22).

[2] [**1556***a*] The Latin translation in Migne gives "inquies" for φησίν. But it might mean "the sacred writer says." This is the general meaning of φησίν in quotations.

and believed.' [True,] but they sought no such thing [as Thomas sought] (οὐδὲν τοιοῦτον ἐζήτησαν), but on the evidence of the napkins (ἀλλ' ἀπὸ τῶν σουδαρίων) they straightway accepted the word concerning the resurrection, and before they had beheld the body [of the risen Saviour] they exhibited the belief [that He had risen] in completeness."

[1557] These words call attention to yet one more difficulty in the context. For the Gospel says "*he*," i.e. "the other disciple" (not Peter), "saw and believed," and it suggests that Peter, though he had seen, had *not* "seen and believed." *But Chrysostom assumes that both the disciples "saw and believed."* So, too, says an ancient Greek commentary in Cramer: "When *these, having beheld the linen cloths, and having believed*, departed to their homes in amazement." And SS reads the plural "*they* saw and believed[1]."

[1558] These readings are not in the least surprising. What is surprising is that any MS. has been allowed to preserve the present reading, which implies unbelief, or slowness of belief, in Peter as compared with "the other disciple." Yet this, by reason of its difficulty and the consent of all the uncial MSS., must be accepted as the true reading. And it raises a question similar to that which is suggested by Chrysostom, Does not the Evangelist mention *two* kinds of "seeing and believing"? The beloved disciple "saw and believed" on the mere evidence of what was to be seen in the open grave. He did not "seek" what Thomas sought: he did not say, "Until I have *seen* the mark of the nails in his hands I will assuredly not believe"; he "saw" much less than Thomas demanded to see, and yet he "believed"; surely the Lord would pronounce him "blessed"!

Accepting the text, as it stands, concerning the two disciples (without Chrysostom's alteration "*they* believed,"

---

[1] [1557 *a*] The Latin MSS. have "*he* saw and believed," but some of these agree with ℵ in carrying on the sing. thus "for not even yet did *he* know the Scripture."

and without the Latin alteration "*he* knew") we arrive at the following probable inferences concerning the Evangelist's meaning and motive.

[1559] (1) He regards "belief" upon detailed ocular evidence as inferior to that kind of "knowledge" which is given to us by the Spirit interpreting the Scripture as a whole[1]—that is to say, by the Spirit of God interpreting the history of man in the light of the Incarnation. Yet both "belief" and "knowledge" must play their several parts. The beloved disciple, he says, "*believed*" on slight ocular evidence. Afterwards he "*knew*," and "*knew*," too, that things "*must be*" thus and thus, *i.e.* "knew" as confidently as men of science "*know*," though in a different sphere, and with a different sense (a faculty that some would call "feeling" rather than "knowing").

[1560] (2) He wished to shew that there were many different roads to this "knowledge" of the risen Saviour. Peter, in one sense, was the first to approach to it. Peter entered the tomb first, and was the first to see the signs of the Resurrection, but he did not at once "believe." For him, this revelation was to come later and through "appearing," in accordance with the traditions of the Church: "He appeared to Cephas, then to the Twelve[2]," and "The Lord is risen indeed and hath appeared unto Simon[3]." The tradition of the manifestation near Gennesaret said that Peter came first to Jesus through the waters[4]—perhaps the waters of repentance—"but the other disciples" came soon afterwards, "for they were not far off[5]"; yet the beloved disciple had been the first to say "It is the Lord[6]," recognising Him by the voice, before Peter and the rest had recognised Him by vision. Again, Mary Magdalene did not "believe" so soon as the beloved disciple. After he had "believed," she re-

---

[1] For this, the Johannine meaning of "the Scripture" (sing.) see 1722 *l*.
[2] 1 Cor. xv. 5.   [3] Lk. xxiv. 34.   [4] Jn xxi. 7—8.
[5] xxi. 8.   [6] xxi. 7.

mained "weeping[1]." Nor did she *see and believe.* On the contrary, she "*saw*" without "*believing*"; for she "supposed it was the gardener." But she was the first to "*hear.*" And when the Shepherd, risen from the dead, "called" the first of the flock "by name," she was the first to hail Him, and the first to "see" as well as the first to "hear." She, too, like Thomas, desired to "touch." But the refusal of her request did not shake her faith, or rather, we should say, cancel her knowledge. Thomas, latest of believers, insisted on "touching" as well as on "seeing," as a condition of "believing." It is not stated that he "touched." But the Lord said to him, apparently in the way of gentle reproof[2], "Because thou hast seen me thou hast believed!" Then He did not add, "Blessed are thine eyes because they have seen[3]," but "Blessed are they that have *not seen and believed.*"

[1561] (3) This is the last of the Lord's many utterances about "believing" in the Fourth Gospel; and, if it is read in the light of His other sayings, illustrated by the Evangelist's own remarks and narratives bearing on the same subject, it confirms the conclusion that "believing" is to be regarded, in different aspects, not as a consummation or a goal, but as a number of different stages, by which different individuals pass, in accordance with their several individualities, toward the one centre, "Jesus, the Christ, the Son of God" in whom they are to "have life[4]."

---

[1] xx. 11.

[2] [1560 *a*] Yet, as it is said, of the woman, (Lk. vii. 47) "her sins, which are many, are forgiven because she loved much," so here the narrative says, in effect, concerning Thomas, "His doubt, which was great, became blessed because he believed much." It was reserved for the doubter to say, with inspired conviction, "My Lord [is] also my God." On the reasons for this rendering, see 2049—51.

[3] Comp. Mt. xiii. 16, Lk. x. 23.   [4] Jn xx. 31.

CHAPTER II

"AUTHORITY"

§ 1. *"Authority," in the Triple Tradition of the Synoptists*

[1562] All the Synoptists agree in saying that our Lord taught "as one having *authority*," or that "his word was with *authority*," and, later on, that the Pharisees asked Him "by what *authority*" He acted: and in five of these six passages R.V. and A.V. agree in using the word "*authority*" to express ἐξουσία[1]. But in a much more important passage, where Jesus Himself says, "that ye may know that the Son of man hath *authority* on earth to forgive sins," the texts both of A.V. and R.V. have "*power*," although R.V. has "*authority*" in its margin[2]. Clearly our Lord used the word here in a good sense. It is very commonly found with "*give*," and it generally means "power that is delegated," that is to say, not tyranny that is seized, but a right lawfully given, or an office or magistracy duly and lawfully appointed. Throughout the Synoptic Gospels, in most cases if not in all, "authority" is the best translation. In Mark, R.V. gives

---

[1] Mk i. 22, Mt. vii. 29, Lk. iv. 32; Mk xi. 28—33, Mt. xxi. 23—7, Lk. xx. 2—8. In Lk. iv. 32 "his word was with *authority*," A.V. has "*power*."

[2] Mk ii. 10, Mt. ix. 6, Lk. v. 24, see **1594** *c*.

"*authority* to cast out devils," and "*authority* over the unclean spirits"; and similarly in Matthew, "All *authority* hath been given unto me in heaven and earth": but in these three passages A.V. has "power[1]."

§ 2. "*Authority*," in the Apocalypse

[1563] In the Apocalypse, this delegated power or "authority" is most frequently applied to messengers of God commissioned to punish (vi. 8) "There was given unto them [*i.e.* to Death and Hades] *authority* over the fourth part of the earth to kill..." R.V. naturally shrinks from using the word when it is applied to "locusts" (from the smoke of the pit) to which "*authority* (R.V. *power*) was given as the scorpions of the earth have *authority* (R.V. *power*)," "and in their tails is their *authority* (R.V. *power*) to hurt men five months[2]." Yet even there the context indicates that these supernatural "locusts" (like the terrestrial) have a "*permitted* power," so that "power" alone does not quite express the meaning. And certainly "authority" is better in the description of the two Witnesses, who "have the *authority* to shut the heaven that it rain not during the days of their prophecy, and they have *authority* over the waters...[3]." There R.V. has, twice, "power"; but it returns to "authority" in the following, "Now is come the salvation and the power, and the kingdom of our God, and the *authority* of his Christ[4]."

[1564] It might be supposed, from this, that R.V. goes on the principle of rendering "delegated power" to reward and "delegated power" to punish by two different words, calling the former "authority" and the latter "power." But R.V. uses "authority" repeatedly concerning the Dragon

---

[1] Mk iii. 15, vi. 7, Mt. xxviii. 18.
[2] Rev. ix. 3, 10, comp. ix. 19.
[3] Rev. xi. 6.
[4] Rev. xii. 10.

and the Beast[1], and then returns to "power," when describing the angel that "came out from the altar, he that hath *authority* over the fire[2]." Very rarely is the word connected with God as in the following, "They blasphemed the name of the God that hath the *authority* over these plagues[3]." R.V. uses "authority" of evil powers in the following: "The ten horns...are ten kings...they receive *authority* (A.V. *power*) as kings with the beast for one hour...they give their...power and *authority* (A.V. *strength*) unto the beast[4]," but of a good angel "coming down out of heaven having great *authority*[5] (A.V. *power*)." An alternative is given by R.V. in describing the blessings of those who have part in the first resurrection, "Over these the second death hath no *authority* (so R.V. marg., but R.V. txt and A.V. "*power*"), but they shall be priests of God[6]." The following instance is particularly noteworthy, "Blessed are they that wash their robes that their *authority* may be (?) over the tree of life[7]," R.V. "that they may have *the right* (A.V. *have right*)[8]."

---

[1] [1564 *a*] Rev. xiii. 2—12 "the dragon gave him...great *authority* (so A.V.)...and they worshipped the dragon because he gave his *authority* (A.V. *power*) unto the beast...and there was given to him *authority* (A.V. *power*) to continue forty and two months...and there was given to him *authority* (A.V. *power*) over every tribe and people and tongue and nation...and he exerciseth all the *authority* (A.V. *power*) of the first beast in his sight."

[2] Rev. xiv. 18.

[3] [1564 *b*] Rev. xvi. 9 τὸ ὄνομα τοῦ θεοῦ τοῦ ἔχοντος ἐξουσίαν. This was, perhaps, intended to represent *the heathen polytheistic thought* about "*the god that* has authority over these plagues." But it might mean "the name of *the* [*one*] *God, who* has authority" (R.V. "of the God which hath," A.V. "of God, which hath"). A.V. and R.V. often use "the ...*which*" where Shakespeare would have used "the...*that* (2273 *a*)."

[4] Rev. xvii. 12, 13. [5] Rev. xviii. 1. [6] Rev. xx. 6.

[7] [1564 *c*] Rev. xxii. 14 ἵνα ἔσται ἡ ἐξουσία αὐτῶν ἐπὶ τὸ ξύλον τῆς ζωῆς, A.V. "right to the tree of life," R.V. "the right [to come] to the tree of life." See 1594 *b*.

[8] All the instances in Rev. have been given above, except Rev. ii. 26 "He that overcometh...to him will I give *authority* over the nations," which is capable of a twofold interpretation.

§ 3. *Luke's view of "authority"*

[1565] The two following parallel passages in the Double Tradition (318 (ii)) exhibit Luke alone as using the word "authority." Perhaps Luke, in both, means "authority" in a bad sense, or rather "authority" given by God for the purpose of punishing evil, as in the Apocalypse. The first passage gives the words of Satan in the Temptation thus:

Mt. iv. 9	Lk. iv. 6—7
"All these things will I give thee if thou wilt fall down and worship me."	"To thee will I give all this *authority* and their[1] glory, because they have been delivered to me, and to whomsoever I will I give it. If thou therefore wilt worship before me it shall be all thine."

The second is from the Preparation of the Twelve Apostles, where they are warned by our Lord, to fear, not destruction of body but destruction of soul:

Mt. x. 28	Lk. xii. 4—5
"And be not ye afraid of them that kill the body but are not able to kill the soul: but be afraid rather of him *that is able* ($\delta\upsilon\nu\acute{\alpha}\mu\epsilon\nu o\nu$) to destroy both body and soul in hell."	"But I say unto you, [being] my friends, Be not afraid of them that kill the body, and, after these things, have nothing beyond to do: but I will point out to you whom to fear. Fear him that—after killing—hath *authority* to cast into hell. Yea, I say unto you, fear him."

Compare the "casting," in Luke here, with "Lest the Judge deliver thee to the *Exactor* ($\pi\rho\acute{\alpha}\kappa\tau o\rho\iota$) and *the*

---

[1] "*Their* glory," *i.e.* the glory of (Lk. iv. 5) "all the kingdoms of the world."

Exactor cast thee into prison[1]." It seems probable that Luke attributes the "*casting into hell*" (or "*into the prison*") to Satan acting as God's instrument of punishment.

[1566] In the first passage of Luke this "authority" does not extend to "*destroying in* hell," but only to "*casting into* hell." In the second passage (Lk. xii. 58—9) it is said that the prisoner will not come out "until" he has paid "the uttermost farthing"—which may imply that ultimately he will come out. According to this view, Satan and his angels would seem to be, like the angels in the Apocalypse, the instruments of God's justice, having "authority" from the Judge to punish man's sins; and Luke's interpretation of Christ's saying is, "Do not fear *earthly enemies*; but fear your *spiritual enemy*, who, if you sin, has authority from God to cast you into Gehenna." Matthew, however, seems to have taken the precept as meaning "fear *God*, the *Judge*"; and this, from very early times, appears to have been the view of the Christian Fathers, who, even when following Luke's version, have substituted "*is able*" for "*hath authority*," so as to suggest God rather than Satan[2].

[1567] Elsewhere, Luke uses the word "authority" in several passages peculiar to himself, of which the most notable are Christ's words to the Seventy, "Behold I have given you *the authority* (R.V. om. "*the*," A.V. "*power*") to

---

[1] Lk. xii. 58=Mt. v. 25 "and the Judge to the Officer (ὑπηρέτῃ) and thou be cast into prison."

[2] [1566 a] Justin Mart. *Apol.* 19, as Lk., but "is able," δυνάμενον, Clem. Hom. xvii. 5. 4 mostly Lk., but "fear him that *is able* to cast both body and soul into the Gehenna of fire," Clem. Alex. 972 (*Exc. Theod.*) δυνάμενον...εἰς γέενναν βαλεῖν, but 981 (freely) τὸν δυνάμενον...ἐν γεέννῃ ἀπολέσαι. On the other hand Iren. iii. 18. 5, quoting Mt. mostly, ends with Lk., thus, "timete autem magis eum qui *habet potestatem* (=hath authority) et corpus et animam mittere in gehennam." Clement's *Ancient Homily* § 5 (Lightf.) has, "Fear him that, after you are dead, hath authority over soul and body to cast into the Gehenna of fire."

tread upon serpents and scorpions[1]," and His utterance at the moment of being arrested where (as a parallel to Mark's "but that the Scriptures might be fulfilled") Luke has "But this is your hour, and the *authority* of darkness[2]."

[1568] This last expression, "the authority of darkness," occurs in the Epistle to the Colossians where it is said that the Father "delivered us from the *authority of darkness* and removed us to the kingdom of the Son of his love[3]." There, the antithesis between "authority" and "kingdom" suggests that the writer uses the former in the sense of temporary power, delegated and misused. In this sense, and hence in the sense of blind "despotism" ("doing and saying what one likes") it is used sometimes by the later Greek writers, as also in English poetry[4],

---

[1] Lk. x. 19.

[2] [1567 a] Lk. xxii. 53. Comp. Lk. xii. 11 "When they bring you before the synagogues and the *rulers* (ἀρχάς) and the *authorities* (A.V. *powers*)," xx. 20 "to deliver him up to the *rule* (ἀρχῇ) *and to the authority* (so R.V., but A.V. *the power and authority*) of the governor," Lk. xxiii. 7 "in Herod's *jurisdiction*" (so R.V. and A.V. and this transl. is necessary here).

[3] Col. i. 13.

[4] [1568 a] The English poets vary in their use of the word, according to temperament, perhaps. Milton, for example, would probably never apply the word "authority" to the angels of God's chastisements, because he regards them as (*Comus*) "slavish instruments of vengeance" in the hands of "the Supreme Good." In his poems, such phrases as "true authority in men," "reason and authority," "authority usurp'd," "the authority which I deriv'd from heaven," generally shew, by their context, the meaning of the ambiguous word. Milton is followed by Cowper, who mostly uses the word in a good sense except where "authority grows wanton," or "sleeps." But Shakespeare lays great stress on the evil of "the demi-god Authority," on "art made tongue-tied" by it, and on the hypocrisies of "authority and shew of truth." Shelley is even more vehement against "the supine slaves of blind Authority." Wordsworth's *Prelude* describes "blind Authority beating with his staff the child that might have led him," but it would be hasty to infer that he condemns Authority in the abstract. For the context mentions "Decency and Custom starving Truth," and no one could suppose that Wordsworth

though mostly in such context as to make the meaning clear¹.

[1569] In the plural, "ruling powers" and "authorities" are frequently mentioned together in N.T., referring to human or to angelic powers,—sometimes in a good sense, sometimes in a bad one².

---

condemns "decency." Tennyson's use is perhaps best exemplified by the line in *Morte d'Arthur* "Authority forgets a dying king." Pope's poems (excluding the Translations) do not contain the word. These facts bear on the various uses of the word in N.T. They also serve as a general warning against applying to N.T. writers the rule, "Ab uno disce omnes."

¹ [1568 b] In the instances quoted by Lightf. on Col. i. 13, Demosth. 428 inserts ἄγαν, Xenoph. *Hiero* § 5 τῆς εἰς τὸ παρόν, Plut. *Vit. Eum.* 13 ἀνάγωγοι ταῖς ἐ. ib. *Alex.* 33 τὴν ἐ. καὶ τὸν ὄγκον τῆς Ἀ. δυνάμεως, Herodian ii. 4 ἀνέτου.

² [1569 a] Lightf. on Col. i. 16 refers to Lk. xii. 11, Tit. iii. 1 (comp. Lk. xx. 20). Angelic powers are meant, good, in Eph. iii. 10, Col. i. 16, ii. 10, but bad in Eph. vi. 12, Col. ii. 15. Lightf. adds "in one passage at least (1 Cor. xv. 24) both [good and bad] may be included."

[1569 b] In Rom. xiii. 1, ὑπερεχούσαις ἐξουσίαις, "*higher authorities*" (R.V. "*the* higher powers," but there is no article) the epithet might be added, in part, to distinguish them from "*evil*," or "*lower*," authorities, and it might be rendered "*supreme*," as in 1 Pet. ii. 13 "to the king, as *supreme*." Ὑπερέχω, when an object is not expressed or obviously implied, appears to mean "preeminent *among things of its own kind*," so that the word in Rom. would not mean "higher than we subjects are" but "preeminent *among authorities.*" In Wisd. vi. 5 οἱ ὑπερέχοντες means rulers of the highest kind, and the context includes "kings." In 1 Pet. ii. 13, the writer passes from "the king *as supreme*" to "governors" "sent from time to time (πεμπόμενοι)" to punish evildoers and reward well-doing. In Rom. xiii. 1, after "supreme authorities," the writer goes on to speak of "the rulers," and he says that "there is no *authority* except [ordained] by God" and recommends "doing good" as the way "not to fear the *authority.*"

[1569 c] The context of Rom. xiii. 1 indicates that St Paul has in view the Imperial authority of Rome—to which he was more than once indebted for deliverance from Jewish persecution—and its adequate representatives throughout the empire. He wrote before the Neronian persecution, at a time when he might fairly say that "supreme authorities" in the empire deserved obedience. He adds "There is no [real]

[1570] "AUTHORITY"

[1570] Luke in his Gospel—not in his Acts—seems to favour the view expressed in an early saying of Jewish Tradition that governors were essentially bad, and that one should not "make oneself known to the government[1]." In the following three versions of our Lord's doctrine on true government and true greatness, it will be observed that Mark guards himself—while Luke does not—against being supposed to attack *all* "ruling" and *all* "authority." Mark

---

authority (or, "no [such] authority") that is not [ordained] by God." Such a protest might be needful against Talmudic views of "authority" (1570 a) among the Jewish members of the Roman Church. Though it is conceivable that the Apostle would have included even Herod Antipas, Pilate, Felix, Festus, and Caiaphas among "authorities" to whom "subjection" was due, he would probably not have included them among "supreme authorities." And it is certain that he would not have said of the murderer of John the Baptist, "For the rulers are not a fear to the good work but to the evil."

[1569 d] On Col. i. 13 "from the authority of the darkness" Chrys. says, "It is a grievous thing to be under the devil *at all* ($ἁπλῶς$): but to be thus *with authority*, this is still more grievous ($τὸ\ δὲ\ καὶ\ μετ'\ ἐξουσίας\ τοῦτο\ χαλεπώτερον$)." This may imply a distinction between (1) those who are attacked by the prince of darkness without having committed any special sin that makes them subject to him, (2) those whom the prince of darkness has received "authority" to "cast into prison" because, for example, they have refused to agree with the adversary (Lk. xii. 58 quoted above). Job would be an instance of the former class.

[1] [1570 a] *Aboth* i. 11 "Shemaiah said, 'Love work; and hate lordship [Rabbanuth]; and make not thyself known to the *government*,'" paraphrased thus by Dr Taylor "Avoid growing great and coming under the notice of the 'rashuth' ($=ἐξουσία$, concretely) in such a way as to excite jealousy or suspicion." Comp. *Aboth* ii. 3 "Be cautious with *those in authority*, for they let not a man approach them but for their own purposes." The feeling that a poor magistrate or governor may be much more dangerous than a rich king perhaps underlies Prov. xxviii. 2—3 "For the transgression of a land many are the princes thereof...a poor man that oppresseth the poor is like a sweeping rain, which leaveth no food": and Caesar, in later times, might be a refuge against a Pilate, a Felix, or a Festus. The words "*danger*" and "*dungeon*" are etymologically—and very naturally—derived from "*dominium*" i.e. lordship.

"AUTHORITY" [1571]

inserts, 1st "*they that seem* to rule," or, "*are reputed* to rule," 2nd "they that use authority *to the utmost*[1]":

Mk x. 42	Mt. xx. 25	Lk. xxii. 25
"...they that *are reputed* to rule the nations *lord it* (κατακυριεύουσιν) over them and *their*'great ones[2]' use authority *to the utmost* over them."	"...the rulers of the nations *lord it* over them and the great ones use authority *to the utmost* over them."	"The kings[3] of the nations are lords (κυριεύουσιν) (1594 d) over them and those who use authority over them are called benefactors."

[1571] Luke appears to be alluding to the name *Euergetes*, or Benefactor, assumed by several Eastern kings, one of whom, it is said, was called by the Alexandrians *Kakergetes*, or Malefactor[4]. It seems antecedently improbable that so bitter and pointed a saying as Luke's, if actually uttered by our Lord in this context, could have been dropped by Matthew as well as Mark, in their report of it. As Luke appears to be

---

[1] [1570 b] Mk x. 42, 1st, δοκοῦντες ἄρχειν, 2nd, κατ- before ἐξουσιάζουσιν. Mt. omits δοκοῦντες but has κατ-. Steph. gives no other instance of κατεξουσιάζειν. Lk. has 1st, βασιλεῖς, and 2nd, ἐξουσιάζοντες. The LXX has ἐξουσιάζειν freq. but κατεξουσιάζειν nowhere.

[1570 c] Κατ' appears to mean "to the utmost," "oppressively," perhaps with allusion also to the idiom "have authority *against* (κατά with gen.)." This idiom occurs in Jn xix. 11. Comp. the use of κατα- in 1 Cor. vii. 31 R.V. "those that use the world as not *abusing it* (marg. *using it to the full*, καταχρώμενοι)," ix. 18 "so as not to *use to the full* (so R.V. but A.V. *abuse*) my authority (μὴ καταχρήσασθαι τῇ ἐξουσίᾳ)." A similar abuse or excess is implied by Mk-Mt. in κατακυριεύουσιν.

[2] [1570 d] "*Their* 'great ones'" *i.e.* those whom *they call* "great ones." Mark, not long before, has recorded a discussion on the question (ix. 34) "Who is the greatest?" Matthew has missed the force of "*their*," as well as "*reputed*."

[3] [1570 e] Lk.'s "kings" goes still further away than Mt.'s "rulers" from Mk's "reputed to rule." Comp. Col. i. 13 "*authority* of darkness ...the *kingdom* of his Son," on which see **1568**.

[4] [1571 a] Wetstein (Lk. xxii. 25) quoting Athenaeus xii. p. 549 E. Wetst. gives abundant instances of this title.

deviating from the exact tradition in other details mentioned above, we may perhaps take this detail as a paraphrase (or misunderstanding of a Semitic original). But in any case, regarded all together, Luke's divergences from Mark and Matthew indicate a disposition in his Gospel to interpret *official* "authority" in a bad sense.

§ 4. *Christ's "authority," how defined by the Synoptists*

[**1572**] Mark and Luke agree, though not *verbatim*, in associating their evangelistic statements about our Lord's "authority" with authority over devils, *i.e.* the power of casting out unclean spirits, an instance of which they give, in detail, immediately afterwards—together with the comment of the multitude:

Mk i. 22—7	Lk. iv. 32—6
"And they were amazed at his teaching: for he was teaching them as one having *authority* and not as the scribes…. 'What is this? A new teaching! With *authority* doth he command even the unclean spirits…!'"	"And they were amazed at his teaching, because his word was in *authority*…. 'What is this word, that in *authority* and power he commandeth the unclean spirits…[1]!'"

[**1573**] Matthew altogether omits this instance of exorcism and all reference to its "authority." But he inserts the tradition—in Mark's fuller form, with the phrase "and not as the scribes"—immediately after the Sermon on the Mount, thus (Mt. vii. 27—9) "'…and great was the fall thereof.' And it came to pass, when Jesus had finished these words, the multitudes were amazed at his teaching: for he was teaching them as one having *authority* and not as their scribes."

[**1574**] Two distinct kinds of "authority" might be signified by the two clauses in Mark. The first is authority of doctrine. Christ taught "*not as the scribes*," who appealed to

---

[1] Or "What is this word! Because (*i.e.* For) in authority.…"

previous traditions and interpretation of the Law; He appealed to the consciences of His hearers and to the purity and high morality of His precepts ("Ye have heard that it hath been said to them of old....but I say unto you"). The second is authority over the minds and souls of men, manifesting itself especially in the casting out of devils ("*With authority doth he command even the unclean spirits*"). Matthew refers here only to the first ("*not as the scribes*")[1], Luke only to the second ("*the unclean spirits*").

[1575] In the healing of the paralytic, a spiritual "authority" of the highest kind is distinctly claimed by our Lord in the words "The Son of man hath *authority* upon earth to forgive sins[2]." But here the evangelistic records of the comments of the multitude in Mark and Luke are singularly disappointing. In these two Gospels the multitude say nothing about the "authority" to forgive, but merely "We have never seen [things] thus" or "We have seen strange things to-day[3]"—commenting only on what they had "seen," namely, the cure of the disease. Matthew alone has something more to the point, a brief indication that the multitude did actually comment on Christ's assertion that the Son of man had "authority to forgive." "They glorified God, *who had given such authority to men*[4]." In Mark, the multitude does not even repeat its previous exclamation "A new teaching!" And Mark and Luke leave the impression that, when this particular "Son of man" had passed away, the "authority to forgive" would, or might, simul-

---

[1] [1574 *a*] But, immediately after this mention of Christ's "authority," Matthew places the healing of the centurion's servant at a distance, with the words of the centurion (viii. 9) "I also am a man under *authority* having under myself soldiers." The centurion evidently supposed that as he and his soldiers were severally subject to authority, so diseases were subject to the authority of Christ, who had only to say "Go," and the disease would go. [2] Mk ii. 10, Mt. ix. 6, Lk. v. 24.
[3] Mk ii. 12, Lk. v. 26. [4] Mt. ix. 8.

taneously pass. But Matthew's version suggests that *a new "authority" had been sent down from heaven to remain among "men,"*

§ 5. *"Authority," in the Fourth Gospel*

[1576] "Authority" in the Fourth Gospel may be regarded first in the Evangelist's order, illustrating the way in which he develops his doctrine about it. Thus treated, the subject begins with what Matthew, as above quoted, calls the "authority" given to "men." The Logos was not received by His own, but (i. 12) "As many as received him, to them gave he *authority* to become children of God." Then comes the authority given to the Son, which is thrice mentioned, (v. 26—7) "As the Father hath life in himself, even so gave he to the Son also to have life in himself; and he gave him *authority to do judgment* (κρίσιν ποιεῖν) because he is Son of man," (x. 18) " No one taketh it [*i.e.* my life] away from me, but I lay it down of myself; I have *authority* to lay it down and I have *authority* to take it again. This commandment received I from my Father," (xvii. 2) "Thou [*i.e.* the Father] gavest him *authority* over all flesh, that—*all that thou hast given him, to them he may give eternal life.*"

[1577] The last mentions of the word are in a dialogue between our Lord and Pilate, thus (xix. 10—11) "Speakest thou not unto me? knowest thou not that I have *authority* to release thee and have *authority* to crucify thee?" to which the reply is, "Thou wouldest have no *authority* against me except it were given thee from above: therefore he that delivered me unto thee hath the greater sin." The detailed meaning of our Lord's reply (**1390—2**) may be uncertain, but it is clear that He is correcting a false notion of authority, which Pilate regarded as meaning "despotism," the power of ruling over others as one likes. The Gospel takes the Pauline view (**1569** *b*) that "supreme authorities" are ordained by God.

[1578] Deferring the consideration of the above-mentioned "authority" given to men to "become children of God," and reviewing the mentions of the "authority" given to Christ, we find that the latter includes (1) "doing judgment," (2) "laying down life and taking it again," (3) "authority over all flesh" for the purpose of "giving eternal life" to "all that the Father has given" to the Son.

§ 6. *"Authority" to become "children" of God*

[1579] Against Pilate's notion of "authority" as being the power to do as one pleases the Evangelist tacitly protests at the very beginning of his Gospel by connecting it with the word "children (τέκνα)." This at once implies obedience and willingness to obey and love the Father. But it also implies adoption into the whole family of the Father, whence follows an obligation, or rather a spontaneous impulse, to love and help the other children. This corresponds to the Synoptic doctrine "become as a little child (παιδίον)," or "receive the kingdom of God as a little child." The Synoptic Tradition of our Lord's answer to the question, "Who is the greatest?" is that He replied "He that is the least," meaning "He that makes himself as the least and humblest of the family in serving the rest." In one Synoptic passage, our Lord likens this service to His own service, "Even as the Son of man came not to be ministered unto but to minister and to give his life a ransom for many[1]." This teaches that "to become a child of God" means to become naturalised in self-sacrifice: and this is the Johannine conception of the "authority" bestowed upon men by the Son of God, preeminence in child-like imitation of the Father in heaven.

[1580] As compared with the Synoptic doctrine in which the authority given to men consisted in the power of driving

---

[1] Mk x. 45, Mt. xx. 28, Lk. diff., see **1275—88**.

out evil spirits[1], the Johannine doctrine is expressed more amply and more permanently. The latter bears some resemblance to the tradition peculiar to Matthew (**1575**) namely that God had given unto men authority to forgive sins. But "authority to forgive" might be interpreted by a man of Pilate's nature as being "the power of giving immunity from punishment according to one's own pleasure." Hence the advantage of the Johannine doctrine ("become children"), which teaches that "authority" goes hand in hand with spiritual childhood. The true "authority" to forgive rests with those childlike souls that can see and hear the Father in heaven forgiving before they themselves pronounce the words of forgiveness on earth. According to John, human authority at its highest implies perpetual and voluntary dependence upon divine will.

§ 7. *The "authority" of the Son to "do judgment"*

[**1581**] It is a remarkable fact that the first mention of "authority" in connexion with the Son—whether uttered by our Lord or by the Evangelist—is in the statement that "the Father judgeth no one" but gave the Son "*authority to do judgment* because he is Son of man[2]"; and yet the Evangelist has previously said (iii. 17) "God *sent not the Son into the world to judge the world* but that the world through him should be saved." Other statements about "judging" are (v. 30) "As I hear I judge and my judgment is true," and

---

[1] [**1580** *a*] See Mk iii. 15 (parall. Mt.-Lk. om.) "authority to cast out the devils," vi. 7 "authority over (genit.) the unclean spirits," Mt. x. 1 "authority over (genit.) unclean spirits so as to cast them out and to heal every disease and every sickness," Lk. ix. 1 "power and authority over (ἐπί w. accus.) all the devils and to heal diseases." See also Lk. x. 19 (to the Seventy) "I have given you the authority to tread upon (ἐπάνω) serpents," probably denoting powers of evil.

[2] v. 22—27. Both v. 26—7 and v. 21—3 might be evangelistic comments (**2066** *b*).

(viii. 15) "I judge no man: yea, and if I judge, my judgment is true: because I am not alone, but I and the Father that sent me." Elsewhere, using a different noun (κρίμα instead of κρίσις) Jesus says (ix. 39) "For judgment came I into this world that those who see not may see and that those who see may become blind."

[1582] These verbal inconsistencies must have perplexed readers restricting their conception of Christ's judgment to an image of Him, on a future day, seated on a cloud, detached from those whom He is judging. ·Probably they were meant to perplex and to force men to enlarge their conception. To the same conclusion tend other Johannine sayings, one, for example, that declares the judgment to be *already* in action, (iii. 18) "He that believeth not *is judged already*," and another that defines judgment thus (iii. 19) "Now *this is* the judgment that light hath come into the world and *men loved darkness rather than light*." Elsewhere Christ says that not He Himself but His word will judge: (xii. 47—8) "I judge him not...he...hath one that judgeth him: the word that I spake, the same shall judge him in the last day[1]," (xvi. 8—11) "He [*i.e.* the Paraclete] shall convict the world concerning *judgment*...concerning *judgment* because the prince of this world *hath been judged.*"

[1583] In one aspect, the "judgment" here contemplated seems to be described almost impersonally, as a Law of the spiritual world by which the souls that love the light are divided from those that hate it. When the Son of man is uplifted on the Cross to save the world, those that see and reject Him are by the very act of rejecting "judged already." Those that trust in Him pass out of the sphere of judgment into life and unity with Him. The others, by their own act, pass into darkness. It suggests the action of light in attracting some creatures while repelling others; or it may be likened

---

[1] Comp. viii. 50 "There *is* (emph.) he that seeketh and judgeth."

to the power of the sun to harden clay while it melts wax. Such illustrations have this objection, they at once raise questions about necessity and free will. These problems are recognised by the Evangelist, but their solution is not attempted. He assumes that human souls are not by unalterable nature divisible into "clay" and "wax[1]." Unbelief is sin, and sin divides unbelievers from believers. Their own sin judges, in some sense, the sinners. In another sense, the Son of man judges them. But His object is, not to "judge" but to "save."

[1584] In another aspect, "doing judgment" is perhaps intended to be distinguished from "judging." The former is used in O.T., sometimes along with "doing righteousness," but sometimes by itself, to mean "righting the wrongs of the oppressed[2]." It occurs in the famous appeal of Abraham to God in behalf of Sodom: "That be far from thee...to slay the righteous with the wicked....Shall not the Judge of all the earth do *right*?" A reason is given for the entrusting of this "authority to do judgment" to the Son, and it is "because he is Son of man." That is to say, not because He is God and knows all secrets, but because He is man and has felt all human sufferings, "a man of sorrows and acquainted with griefs." In raising up the oppressed, the Champion of Justice must also cast down the oppressor: but the result is good for both in Plato's sense of justice— "doing the best for all."

[1585] Mark never uses the word "judgment." Matthew and Luke use the phrase "in the day of judgment," or "in

---

[1] [1583 *a*] Comp. Rom. ix. 21 "Hath not the potter *authority* over the clay...?" where the "authority" depends on the knowledge of the potter to do what is best with every kind of clay: but the parallel is between the "potter" and the all-wise Creator rather than between "man" and "clay."

[2] Deut. x. 18, Sir. xxxii. (xxxv.) 18 etc. For "do righteousness and judgment," see Gen. xviii. 19 etc.

the judgment," to mean a day, or season, in which condemnation will be pronounced. John's definition of "the judgment," as given above, and his accumulation of apparently deliberate verbal inconsistencies as to the Person judging, indicate a desire on the part of the beloved disciple to separate the conception of His beloved and adored Master from that of a Judge with flaming fire taking vengeance on His enemies—and to lead his readers to see His "authority to do judgment" in other aspects. When the Evangelist says "the word that I spake shall judge him," we are reminded of the "still small voice" that questioned Elijah, and akin to this, perhaps, is the saying that the Comforter, or Holy Spirit, will "convict the world concerning judgment[1]." Both of these passages, and others in this Gospel, suggest that human conscience is to play a part in ratifying the judgment that is pronounced with "authority" by the Logos.

§ 8. *"Authority" in connexion with "life"*

[1586] The previous section bore on the saying "He [*i.e.* the Father] gave authority to him [*i.e.* the Son] to do judgment," which is preceded by the words "As the Father hath life in himself, so also to the Son he gave to have life in himself"—thus connecting the gift of "life in oneself" with the gift of "authority to do judgment." We have now to consider two sayings that connect "authority" still more closely with "life." Both of them are in the first person so that they are certainly to be taken as proceeding from our Lord Himself, and not—like the saying in the last section—possibly from the Evangelist.

---

[1] [1585 *a*] Jn xvi. 11. "The day of judgment" is not mentioned in the Gospel. The nearest approach to it is (v. 29) "resurrection of judgment" contrasted with "resurrection of life." "The day of the judgment" occurs once in the Epistle, not in connexion with "adversaries," or "the wicked," but with ourselves (1 Jn iv. 17) "that we may have confidence in *the day of the judgment*."

[1587] The first occurs in the Parable of the Good Shepherd, which is really a discourse on good rulers. It describes the natural king, the king called by God, as ruling by his voice, not by coercion. He does not drive the sheep, he leads them. He calls them each by name; they hear him and follow. The secret of this success is, that this ideal Shepherd is ready to lay down his life for the sheep: (x. 17—18) "Therefore doth the Father love me because I lay down my life that I may take it again. No one taketh it away from me, but I lay it down of myself. I have *authority* to lay it down and I have *authority* to take it again. This commandment received I from my Father."

[1588] No one "has *authority*" to lay down his life except that he may, in some sense, take it again, any more than the Sower has "authority[1]" over "the grain of wheat" to throw it into the fire. No one "has *authority*" to lay down his life for his own sake alone, that is, for his own honour or pride or to secure eternal happiness—without any regard to others. If life is to be "laid down" with "authority," it must be laid down out of "love" for others— love for the Father and His children, not for the Father alone. The "army of martyrs" is "noble," but not unless it is ennobled by "love": "Though I give my body to be burned and have not love, I am nothing." But the man that lays down his life in the harvest field of humanity to bring forth fruit, the true Martyr, does not, and cannot, do this in his own strength, but because he has been ennobled and strengthened to do it, and has received high rank and "authority" in the kingdom of Heaven. He does it, in one sense spontaneously, but, in another, obediently, saying in the moment of martyrdom, "This commandment received I from my Father."

---

[1] The Sower might be said to have "authority" over the seed as "the Potter" has (**1583** *a*) over the clay, but authority based on knowledge of Law, and obedience to Law.

[**1589**] This, the Johannine view of "authority," is a wholesome antidote against complacency and a strong stimulant to well-doing. "Even the devils are subject to us in thy name," say the Seventy to Jesus, in a tradition peculiar to Luke. But their Lord's reply warns them against rejoicing in this authority, and bids them rejoice rather that their names were written in heaven[1]. Much more, we may be sure—from what He said in the Triple Tradition—would He have bidden them rejoice in making themselves lords over their own passions for the sake of being servants of mankind in the spirit of Him who "gave his life for the sheep." While it discourages selfish asceticism and artificial self-humiliations —which perhaps St Paul meant by his term "voluntary humiliation"—the Johannine doctrine keeps the eye of the possessor of "authority" fixed on the source of all authority, namely, the Father, whose "commandment" cannot be "obeyed" without perpetual regard to His children.

[**1590**] The next passage connecting "authority" with "life" occurs in the beginning of the Lord's last prayer, (xvii. 1—2) "Father, the hour is come, glorify thy Son, that the Son may glorify thee: even as thou gavest him *authority over all flesh*—that, all that thou hast given unto him, to them he should give eternal life," where the italicized words may be compared with those peculiar to Matthew describing the sending forth of the Apostles to preach the Gospel to the world, "*All authority hath been given unto me in heaven and earth*, Go ye, therefore, and make disciples of all the nations[2]....." It cannot be supposed that the author of this tradition in Matthew meant that "all authority...in earth" had been given to the Saviour in such a way as to necessitate the immediate conversion of the whole "earth" to Christianity. The meaning must be that the Son had been appointed by the Father to be Lord of men *de facto* in heaven and *de jure* on earth.

---

[1] Lk. x. 17—20.   [2] Mt. xxviii. 18.

[**1591**] This limitation is expressed in John by the words "all that thou hast given him." The phrase (**2444**) denotes the Church on earth. The whole sentence and the context recognise that "all flesh" will *not* own the "authority" of the Son. Even among the Apostles, one, "the son of destruction," must be "destroyed[1]," or "lost": the Son Himself acknowledges this. But He also acknowledges that the "glorifying" of the Father consists in giving "eternal life," and that the Son has "authority over all flesh" to offer this gift, whether accepted or not. The impression left upon us is, that although the "destruction" of "the son of destruction" must take place that the Scripture, that is, the will of the Father, may be fulfilled, and although "all flesh" will not at once accept the gift of life, yet, in the end—whether by ultimate acceptance or not we are not told—by some means God will be fully "glorified." And there the Evangelist leaves the insoluble problem of sin.

[**1592**] As regards "authority," it is defined by the term, unusual in N.T., "all flesh," a term used repeatedly in O.T. to describe the destruction of all animate nature with the exception of Noah and his companions, in the deluge[2]. It is also used by Luke in his Gospel and in the Acts in quotations from Isaiah and Joel describing the vision of glory, or the outpouring of the Spirit, in the kingdom of God[3]. In both these senses it may be intended here to denote that the authority of the Messiah is to extend to Gentiles as well as to Jews, and to dominate human nature.

[**1593**] The last mention of "authority" in the Fourth Gospel is in a dialogue that serves the purpose of summing up the Evangelist's doctrine about it by contrasting the

---

[1] Jn xvii. 12.

[2] Gen. vi. 12, 17, 19, vii. 15, 16 etc.

[3] Lk. iii. 6 (Is. xl. 5), Acts ii. 17 (Joel ii. 28). It is also in 1 Pet. i. 24 (Is. xl. 6). It does not occur elsewhere in N.T. without negative, "no flesh" Mk xiii. 20 etc. (**2260—3**).

wrong with the right conception. It exhibits the nominal Ruler, who has the semblance of authority, and is proud of it, sitting in judgment on the real Ruler. The former is a mere slave. Of his own will, he would release Jesus. But the crowd cries "Thou art not Caesar's friend," and Pilate "*therefore* brought Jesus forth." Again the "Governor" struggles for permission to release the innocent, and again the crowd cries "We have no king but Caesar." "Then, *therefore*," Pilate "delivered him unto them to be crucified[1]." Yet this same man had just said to his prisoner, "Knowest thou not that *I have authority* to release thee and *I have authority* to crucify thee[2]?"

[1594] Jesus, in His reply, contents Himself with pointing to the responsibility that attaches itself to "authority." It is "given," He says, "from above." As for the true meaning of the term, Pilate—who asked "What is truth?"—was no more competent to receive it than were the Pharisees to whose question ("By what authority[3]?") Christ had refused to answer. To grasp the conception of true "authority" we must be able to grasp the conception of the Good Shepherd: and to do this—so the Gospel tells us—the Jews were absolutely unable. They said "We see," but they were blind. Jesus spoke to them about the Shepherd, but they could not touch the fringe of His meaning. "They did not know what the things were (**1721** *a*) that he was speaking to them[4]." In that Parable, Christ had virtually replied by anticipation to Pilate's boast "*I have authority.*" The false Ruler says to the true, "I have *authority* to take thy life": the true Ruler replies, "I have *authority* to lay it down[5]."

---

[1] xix. 12—16.   [2] xix. 10.   [3] Mk xi. 28 etc. (**1562**).
[4] ix. 39—x. 6.
[5] [**1594** *a*] The mischief that might arise from regarding the "authority" of Christ as a magical power of casting out evil spirits, or of imparting the Spirit of Holiness—a power limited to the Twelve in Mark, and to the Twelve and the Seventy in Luke—is seen in the request

of Simon Magus in the Acts (viii. 19) to be allowed to purchase "this *authority*," namely, to impart the Spirit. A protest against superstitious or servile views of it seems also to underlie several passages in the Epistles to the Corinthians where St Paul refuses to use certain material apostolic privileges that had come to be connected with apostolic "authority" (1 Cor. ix. 1—5) "Am I not an *apostle?*...Have we no *authority* to eat and drink [at the cost of the Churches]...even as *the rest of the Apostles...?*" There was, perhaps, a danger that some of the large number called Apostles or Missionaries in the first century, while saying (1 Cor. vi. 12) "*I have authority* (ἔξεστιν) to do all things," might forget to say (*ib.*) "But I will not be *brought under the authority of any* (οὐκ ἐξουσιασθήσομαι ὑπό τινος)." That is to say, they might be tempted to rule over converts in the spirit of Pilate rather than in the spirit of Christ (Mk x. 42, 1 Pet. v. 3) "exercising lordship to the utmost (κατακυριεύοντες)." Comp. *Didach.* xi. 12 "But whosoever shall say in the spirit, 'Give me money, or other things,' ye shall not listen to him."

[1594 *b*] As regards Rev. xxii. 14 (quoted in **1564** *c*) ἡ ἐξουσία αὐτῶν ἐπὶ τὸ ξύλον, the interpretation is complicated by the fact that Rev. has (1) accus. also in vi. 8 ἐδόθη αὐτοῖς ἐ. ἐπὶ τὸ τέταρτον τ. γῆς, xiii. 7 ἐδόθη αὐτῷ ἐ. ἐπὶ πᾶσαν φυλήν, xvi. 9 τοῦ θεοῦ τοῦ ἔχοντος τ. ἐ. ἐπὶ τ. πληγὰς ταύτας, but (2) genit. in ii. 26 δώσω αὐτῷ ἐ. ἐπὶ τῶν ἐθνῶν, xi. 6 ἐ. ἔχουσιν ἐπὶ τ. ὑδάτων, xiv. 18 ὁ ἔχων ἐ. ἐπὶ τ. πυρός. Perhaps ἐπί with accus. may imply "*extending over*," suggesting "extending *to.*" Or, if criticism decides that the book is composite, that might explain the variation.

[1594 *c*] In Mk ii. 10, Mt. ix. 6, Lk. v. 24 (referred to in **1562**) Lk. (and sim. Mt.) has ἐ. ἔχει ἐπὶ τῆς γῆς (whereas Mk has ἐπὶ τῆς γῆς at the end of the Lord's words) thus suggesting the meaning "hath *authority over the earth*," as in Revelations (**1563—4**). There is great variation in the Latin versions between "in terra," "in terram," and "super terram." In LXX, ἐξουσία with ἐπί is very rare (Sir. xxx. 28 (xxxiii. 19) φίλῳ μὴ δῷς ἐ. ἐπὶ σέ, Dan. iii. 97 (LXX, not Theod. nor Heb.) ἐ. δοὺς ἐφ' ὅλης τῆς χώρας) : but ἐξουσιάζω ἐπί with accus. is in Neh. v. 15, ix. 37, 1 Mac. x. 70 (of oppressive authority).

[1594 *d*] Lk. xxii. 25 (**1570**) probably avoids κατακυριεύω, not because he wishes to soften the word, but because, outside the LXX, it meant "*overcome*," as in the only instance mentioned by Steph., Diod. xiv. 64 "*having overcome [in a naval engagement]*."

CHAPTER III

JOHANNINE SYNONYMS

§ 1. *The use of synonyms in this Gospel*

[1595] In the Introduction (**1436—7**) it was pointed out that the Dialogue in the Fourth Gospel between our Lord and Peter, after the Resurrection, interchanged the words "love (ἀγαπᾶν)" and "like (φιλεῖν)" in a manner hardly capable of being briefly and literally expressed in any English Version, and not expressed by our Revised Version except by a marginal note stating that the two Greek words for "love" are different. The whole of this Gospel is pervaded with distinctions of thought, represented by subtle distinctions of word or phrase—words and phrases so far alike that at first the reader may take the thought to be the same, though it is always really different. In discussing the word "trust" or "believe," for example, it appeared that "trust to the name of," "trust to," and "trust," signified different things. Again, the word "authority" was shewn to mean a different thing in most Synoptic passages from what it means in the Fourth Gospel; and, even in the Fourth, Pilate uses it in one sense and our Lord in another. If the writer thus emphasizes the various shades of meaning in the same words ("trust" and "authority") we must anticipate that he will do the same thing in using different (though synonymous) words, and that his play upon "loving" and "liking" will have many parallels in his Gospel.

[1596] Some of these will be hard to detect. For example, the word φιλέω, or "take as a friend," which is for the most part (**1728** *m—p*) a lower word than ἀγαπάω, is applied by our Lord Himself (on the very first occasion on which it occurs in this Gospel) to the love of the Father for the Son, thus (v. 20) "For the Father *taketh as a friend* the Son and sheweth him all that he himself doeth." Codex D and a few other authorities alter this to "loveth." A most natural alteration! But if we compare what Christ says later on where He declares that henceforth He will call His disciples "friends" because He intends to tell them all His secrets[1], we shall find that the meaning is, not that the Father "*loveth*" the Son (which is assumed) but that the Son, to speak in metaphor, is of age to be a fellow-counsellor with the Father, who *treats Him as a friend, and* "*sheweth him all that he himself doeth*." These remarks will suffice as an introduction to a discussion of some of the most important of the Johannine synonyms.

§ 2. "*Seeing*"

[1597] A distinction between "seeing" and "beholding" is clearly implied in the saying of Jesus to the disciples (xvi. 16) "A little [while] and ye no longer *behold* me (θεωρεῖτέ με), and again a little [while] and ye *shall see* me (ὄψεσθέ με)." The disciples repeat the saying in perplexity. It is repeated again by Jesus in His reply to their questionings with one another. In each of the three cases the same distinction is observed, apparently indicating that "behold"

---

[1] [**1596** *a*] xv. 14—15. So, in Genesis (xviii. 17), God refuses to hide His plans from Abraham, His (Jas. ii. 23) "friend." The same meaning is probably intended in Jn xvi. 27. On the other hand, in xx. 2 "the disciple whom Jesus *loved*" (ἠγάπα in xiii. 23, xix. 26, xxi. 7, 20) is perhaps called "the disciple whom Jesus (**1436**) *still loved* (ἐφίλει)," because he had not yet "believed," so that he is regarded as under a cloud.

means "behold with the bodily eye" but "see" means "see spiritually[1]."

(i) Θεωρεῖν.

[1598] This distinction is pretty regularly maintained. Ὄψεσθαι is repeatedly used of spiritual promise (i. 39) "Come and *ye shall see*[2]," (i. 50) "*thou shalt see* greater things," (i. 51) "*ye shall see* the heaven opened and the angels of God," (xi. 40) "*thou shalt see* the glory of God," and thrice in the passage referred to above, concerning the resurrection of Jesus. This makes seven mentions. Then occurs the thought that our "*seeing*" Christ depends on Christ's "*seeing*" us, just as man's "knowing" God is sometimes identified both in N.T. and in O.T. with God's "knowing" man[3]. The seven

---

[1] [1597 a] Comp. Philo i. 578 "that which receives the divine apparition (τ. θείαν φαντασίαν) is the eye of the soul. For, else, what the mere bodily eyes *behold* (θεωροῦσι) they apprehend with the cooperation of light (συνεργῷ φωτὶ χρώμενοι καταλαμβάνουσιν)...." (i. 579) "Whenever you hear that God *appeared* (ὀφθέντα) to men, understand that this takes place apart from material light (φωτὸς αἰσθητοῦ)."

[1597 b] Ὀφθῆναι, "appeared," or "was seen," is the word regularly used by St Paul to describe the manifestations of Christ after the Resurrection (1 Cor. xv. 5—8). Jn xxi. 1, 14 uses ἐφανερώθη "was manifested" or ἐφανέρωσεν ἑαυτόν "manifested himself" (Mk App. [xvi. 12, 14] ἐφανερώθη). But in predicting His self-manifestation, Jesus (xiv. 21) uses ἐμφανίζω, saying that He will "make himself manifest" to the believer and not to the world because He and the Father will "come to him and make an abiding place in his heart (παρ' αὐτῷ)." This illustrates what Philo says, that, whenever God has "appeared to" (or "been seen by") men, it has been "apart from material light." It is unfortunate that in English we render ὤφθη in two ways, (1) "was seen by," (2) "appeared to." If it is rendered "was seen by," we must remember that the sight is (in many cases) *not received by the bodily eye*. If it is rendered "appeared to," we must remember that the thing seen is to be regarded as *real and objective*, though spiritual.

[2] [1598 a] Some inferior MSS. read "Come and see," assimilating the phrase to the ordinary Rabbinical formula (on which see Wetst., Schöttg. and *Hor. Heb. ad loc.*) expressed in Jn i. 46 "Come and see."

[3] [1598 b] Comp. Gal. iv. 19, where St Paul, after saying "But now, *having known God*," corrects himself and adds—"or rather *being known by God*," i.e. being taken into the family circle of God and being recognised as His children.

promises, therefore, of "*seeing*" are summed up in a promise of "*being seen*," (xvi. 22) "*I will see you* (ὄψομαι ὑμᾶς) and your joy no man shall take from you." On the other hand θεωρεῖν, at all events at the outset of the Gospel, is used of unintelligent, superficial, or at least inferior "beholding." People (ii. 23) "behold" Christ's signs, but Jesus does not trust them; the Samaritan woman asserts that she (iv. 19) "beholds" (in a mere feeling of wonder) that Jesus is "a prophet": the multitude that (vi. 2) "beholds" Christ's signs is avoided by Him because they unintelligently desire to make Him a king by force; the disciples (vi. 19) "behold" Jesus walking on the water—"and feared." When a higher signification exists, it seems derived from a special context, as in vi. 40 "Everyone that beholdeth the Son and *believeth*," and so (xii. 44, 45) "He that believeth on me...believeth on him that sent me...(45) and he that [*thus, in a spirit of belief*] beholdeth me beholdeth him that sent me." Or else, a better meaning is derived from antithesis, as when the world's "beholding" with coarse material vision is contrasted with the rudimentary spiritual "beholding" which Jesus appears to acknowledge in the disciples even before the Resurrection, (xiv. 17—19) "The Spirit of truth, which the world cannot receive because it does not *behold* it (θεωρεῖ) nor so much as have an understanding of it (οὐδὲ γινώσκει); ye have an understanding of it...(19) Yet a little while and the world *beholdeth* me no more; but *ye* (emph.) *behold* me: because I live, ye shall live also," *i.e.* "the world shall cease to behold my visible and material body, but ye shall still behold me with the faith of affection[1]."

---

[1] [**1598** *c*] This should be compared with the higher standard of spiritual vision adopted later in xvi. 16—19, "Ye *behold* (θεωρεῖτε) me no more," *i.e.* ye shall rise above the beholding in the flesh, and also above the beholding in mere half-faith. Literally, the Evangelist (as often) contradicts himself. He appears to do it with a deliberate purpose (**1925**).

[1599] In the post-resurrection narrative, there appears a remarkable and systematic distinction between "verbs of seeing," intended apparently to lead up to the words of Jesus that even *any kind of mere "seeing"* is inferior to believing (xx. 29 "Blessed are they that have *not seen* (ἰδόντες) and have believed[1]")—although "believing" itself is only a preparation for "abiding" in the Son.

[1600] The Resurrection is regarded as a mystery. Insight into it is gradually bestowed on the disciples in three different stages[2]. First Mary Magdalene "notes (βλέπει)" the stone removed from the tomb. Then the two disciples run towards it. The disciple whom Jesus loved (1596 a) reaches the tomb first. He "glances in (παρακύψας[3])" and "notes (βλέπει)" something more than Mary—the linen swathing bands that had (xix. 40) once "bound" the body, now discarded. He does not venture, however, to enter the darkness of the sepulchre. Peter is the first to do this, and there he "beholds (θεωρεῖ)"—steadfastly and in perplexity, but still not as yet in faith—the napkin, which had confined the head of Jesus, now discarded. Then (as a third stage) the beloved disciple is described as passing through three

---

[1] [1599 a] Mere usage may sometimes cause a change from one verb to another even where the meaning is the same. For example, ἰδών is the regular word for past "seeing" (βλέψας being very rare), and βλέπε, not ἴδε, is used, especially by Mk, to mean "look to it," "take heed." Ἑώρακα, used by Mary Magdalene (xx. 18) "*I have seen* the Lord," implies probably more than mere material seeing, and perhaps not material seeing at all. It is very unlikely that the Evangelist supposes that Caiaphas, had he been standing by the side of Mary, would have seen the Saviour. See **1601**.

[2] [1600 a] Comp. Schöttg. ii. 76 (quoting Tanchum. 77 a) "When God reveals His Shechinah to the Israelites, it is not done in a moment"; "Come and learn [a mystery] from the case of Joseph, who did not for many years reveal himself to his brethren. So therefore God revealed Himself by degrees and slow degrees."

[3] [1600 b] On παρακύπτω, which occurs in N.T. only here (xx. 5, 11), possibly in Lk. xxiv. 12 and certainly in Jas. i. 25, 1 Pet. i. 12, see **1798—1804**. In the Epistles it has a spiritual meaning.

processes: he "entered in" and "saw (εἶδεν)" and "believed." We are not told that he "saw" anything but the grave-clothes and the empty grave: but it is implied that he "saw" the truth of the Resurrection.

[1601] The two depart, and Mary is left alone. Twice she is mentioned as "weeping." Then she, too, "glanced into (παρέκυψεν εἰς)" the tomb, and "beholds (θεωρεῖ)" two angels; but still there is no faith. Twice is the question put to her, "Why weepest thou?" In the second case, it is put by Jesus, and the word θεωρεῖ is repeated. She "beholds" Him, but not intelligently: she mistakes Him for some one else. Not till she is "*called by her name*[1]" does she recognise and answer. Thus her faith is apparently caused not by sight but by *hearing*; and, although she really has seen Jesus, and, in her report to the disciples, she says, "I *have seen* (ἑώρακα) the Lord[2]," the intention appears to be to emphasize the spiritual truth that the mere "*beholding*" (θεωρία) of an image of the risen Saviour is not a true "*seeing*" (ὅρασις). Philo lays stress on the statement that the children of Israel "*saw* the *voice* of the Lord (ἑώρα τὴν φωνήν)[3]." So Mary's vision was caused by a "voice." She only *beheld* (θεωρεῖ) the form, but may be said to have *seen* (ἑώρακε) the voice, of Jesus. Thomas refused to believe unless he might touch the Lord, Mary is forbidden to "touch" Him: nor is it said that He "shewed her his hands and his side" in order to convince her (as He is said to have convinced others) that He was not "the gardener." In one sense, then, she might be said to have believed, like the beloved disciple, because she discerned the truth, though she had not "seen" with the outward eye the body of Jesus: and perhaps Mary and the beloved

---

[1] Comp. Jn x. 3—4 "He *calleth* his own sheep *by name* and leadeth them out...and the sheep follow him for they know his voice."

[2] xx. 18.   [3] Philo i. 443, quoting Ex. xx. 18.

disciple are both included in the blessing pronounced upon those who have "*not* seen (ἰδόντες)¹ and believed."

[1602] In the third and last and specially sacred manifestation of Jesus to the Seven, this notion—*i.e.* of revelation, not through sight, but through some other cause—is still further developed. While the disciples are fishing, Jesus suddenly "stood on the beach." The disciples do not recognise Him by sight, nor even by voice, when He calls them "children" and directs them towards success. It is not till they have obeyed His word and have been rewarded, that the beloved disciple exclaims to Peter, "It is the Lord." Then—with a repetition quite needless but for the writer's desire to insist on belief through *hearing*—the narrative describes how "Simon Peter, *having heard that it was the Lord*," plunged into the sea and hastened towards Him². And even while the disciples are participating in the sacred meal of the Loaf and the Fish they are (so it is implied) unable to recognise Him by *sight*, but only by *knowledge*, "None of the disciples dared to question him, 'Who art thou?' *knowing* that it was the Lord³." If they had recognised Him by sight, where was the need to "question"? The writer indicates that their knowing—though it was "absolute *knowledge*" (εἰδότες)—proceeded *not from sight but from inward conviction*.

[1603] Being thus used to express a rudimentary stage of "seeing" spiritual truth, θεωρεῖν is not used at all in the Epistle metaphorically, and only once literally⁴.

---

¹ [1601 *a*] xx. 29. Note that the Evangelist does not, and could not, write οἱ μὴ ἑωρακότες. In that spiritual sense, Jesus could not pronounce a blessing on "those who have not seen": for ὅρασις means "true vision."

² xxi. 7.   ³ xxi. 12.

⁴ [1603 *a*] 1 Jn iii. 17 θεωρῇ τ. ἀδελφὸν αὐτοῦ χρείαν ἔχοντα, *i.e.* stolidly beholding one's brother in need and doing nothing to help him.

(ii) Θεᾶσθαι.

[1604] This word, being connected with "theatre" and with the notions of a spectacle and a multitude, will be rendered here "contemplate"—a rendering inadequate but intended to distinguish it[1] from θεωρεῖν "behold." It is used twice of Jesus. The first instance is when He "contemplates" His two earliest disciples (i. 38) "following" Him. These are the beginning of the Church. It is used again when He (vi. 5) lifts up His eyes to heaven and "contemplates" the great multitude coming to the Feast of the Bread from heaven. These represent the developed Church. Elsewhere it is used of disciples, or believers, contemplating some manifestation, not of God, but of the glory of God (i. 14, 32, iv. 35, xi. 45) and so in 1 Jn i. 1, iv. 12 ("No man hath contemplated God"), 14.

(iii) Ὁρᾶν.

[1605] John's use of this verb is confined to the future

---

[1] [1604 a] Θεᾶσθαι cannot perhaps be expressed in English so as to distinguish it from θεωρεῖν. "Contemplate" is quite inadequate, and so are "gaze at" and "survey." In N.T., θεᾶσθαι is almost always connected with *a number of people* either as "seeing" or as "being seen," *e.g.* with the multitudes going out to "see the sight" of John the Baptist (Mt. xi. 7, Lk. vii. 24), or with the king coming in to see the assemblage of his guests (Mt. xxii. 11). In the Synoptists, the only exception to this is Lk. v. 27 where Jesus watches Levi engaged in his public occupation (parall. Mk ii. 14, Mt. ix. 9 εἶδεν). But Mk App. [xvi. 11] ἐθεάθη ὑπ' αὐτῆς is applied to Jesus seen by Mary Magdalene alone after the Resurrection.

[1604 b] In Jn (i. 32) it is applied once to the Baptist seeing the Holy Spirit descend on Christ. In Rom. xv. 24 it probably means that the Apostle wishes to have the joy of beholding the assembly of the whole of the Roman Church. It is perhaps impossible to say confidently how the writer differentiates Jn i. 18 θεὸν οὐδεὶς ἑώρακεν πώποτε from 1 Jn iv. 12 θεὸν οὐδεὶς πώποτε τεθέαται. The former would most naturally apply to the revelation of God received individually by Patriarchs and Prophets, the latter to that received by the saints of the collective Church. The absolute God has been seen by none, whether singly or collectively.

ὄψομαι and the perfect ἑώρακα[1]. Ἑώρακα, in John, means that kind of "having seen" which has produced a permanent result enabling the man that "hath seen" to "bear witness." There are few exceptions to the letter, and none to the spirit, of this rule. It is possible, however, to "have seen"—so far as the bad can "see"—and to "disbelieve," or even to "have seen" and to "hate," not only the Son but even "the Father": and the mention of "the Father" shews that spiritual sight, not material, is contemplated[2]. It is characteristic of the writer that, while he says "God no one *hath seen* at any time[3]," he represents Jesus as apparently blaming the unbelieving Jews for not having "seen" the "form" of the Father ("Ye have neither heard his voice *nor seen his form*, and ye have not his word abiding in you[4]"). Jesus also says: "Not that any one *hath seen* the Father except him who is from the Father," and "He that hath seen me *hath seen* the Father[5]." The object is to shew that the pure in heart must needs "*have seen*" the Father in the Son.

[1606] Ἑωρακώς is applied to "*having seen*" (through divine revelation) the fountain of blood and water that gushed from the side of Jesus. Here, too (as in i. 34, iii. 32), "witnessing" follows close on "*having seen*": (xix. 35) "He that *hath seen hath borne witness*[6]."

---

[1] [1605 a] It would be interesting to ascertain the motives that led the writer to dispense with the present. (In Philo the pres. is freq., especially of Israel "seeing God." In the LXX it is often used as a noun, *e.g.* 2 S. xxiv. 11 "David's *seer* (τὸν ὁρῶντα (A +τὸν) Δαυείδ).") In Jn vi. 2, many MSS. read ἑώρων: but probably the scribes cancelled the first two letters of the original εθεωρων (for -ογν).

[2] vi. 36, xv. 24 "They have both seen and hated me and my Father."
[3] i. 18.   [4] v. 37.   [5] vi. 46, xiv. 9 (comp. xiv. 7).
[6] [1606 a] Besides these two passages there is iv. 45, "The Galileans received him, *having seen* (ἑωρακότες) all the things that he did in Jerusalem." Although the writer may intend to correct the very unfavourable impression given of the Galileans by Luke (iv. 29), yet, in a context describing such transient faith or "receiving" as this, we should rather expect θεωρεῖν than ὁρᾶν. In vi. 2 ἑώρων in some MSS.

(iv) Βλέπειν.

[1607] Βλέπειν is used of material sight, especially in connexion with the healing of blindness (ix. 7—25, five times). In the same connexion it means (with a play on the word (ix. 39—41)) spiritual seeing. It is also used of "looking" in ordinary life (xiii. 22 "they looked on one another")[1]. Only by a rare metaphor is the word used of the Son of God, in heaven (v. 19) "looking at" the deeds of the Father (in which sense Philo also uses it of the Eldest Son of the Father in heaven "looking at (βλέπων)" the acts of the Father as patterns for His own action)[2].

(v) Αἴρειν ὀφθαλμούς etc.

[1608] The act of "raising the eyes" or "looking up" is regarded by Philo (on Gen. xviii. 2, P. A. 242) as symbolical[3]. Jesus uses it in a symbolical sense when He bids the disciples (iv. 35) "lift up" their "eyes" and behold the spiritual harvest. But it is also thrice used by the Evangelist concerning Jesus. In the first case, (vi. 5) it precedes the sign of the Bread of Life. In the second, it precedes (xi. 41) the raising of Lazarus. In the third (xvii. 1) it introduces the last prayer of the Son to the Father; and there, as if a climax was intended, the Evangelist writes, not simply "lifting up," but "*lifting up to heaven.*"

(vi) Ἰδεῖν etc.

[1609] The thought implied by this verb often differs according to its grammatical form owing to considerations

---

has wrongly supplanted ἐθεώρουν (1605 a). Possibly, here too, after πάντα, stood an original τεθεωρηκοτες which has been altered to εωρακοτες.

[1] Comp. i. 29, xi. 9. In xx. 1, 5, xxi. 9, 20 it refers to things "seen" or "noted" after the Resurrection.

[2] [1607 a] Philo i. 414 Τοῦτον μὲν γὰρ πρεσβύτατον υἱὸν ὁ τῶν ὄντων ἀνέτειλε πατήρ, ὃν ἑτέρωθι πρωτόγονον ὠνόμασε, καὶ ὁ γεννηθεὶς μέντοι μιμούμενος τὰς τοῦ πατρὸς ὁδούς, πρὸς παραδείγματα ἀρχέτυπα ἐκείνου βλέπων, ἐμόρφου εἴδη.

[3] See also Philo i. 95, 299, 645, ii. 13.

other than grammatical. In the participle and the subjunctive, this is the customary verb to express ordinary seeing, so that its use implies no special meaning. But in Gen. i. 31 it is used in the past indicative (εἶδεν) concerning the Creator surveying His work and pronouncing it good, and this stamps that tense as likely to be used by Philo and his school to express that kind of "sight" which precedes some spiritual utterance or process. Also, in Rabbinical writers, "Come and see" is commonly used as a preface to the statement of some profound mystery[1], and this is hinted at in the reply of Philip to Nathanael (i. 46) "Come and see (ἴδε)," as if, in answer to Nathanael's incredulous words, "Can any *good* come out of Nazareth?" God replied through the mouth of the unconscious instrument, Philip, "Come and see [*the mystery of mysteries, the Supreme Good*][2]." Another use of this formula is where the Jews themselves invite Jesus to "come and see" the apparent triumph of death, unconsciously inviting Him to the highest manifestation of His own divine and life-giving power in triumphing over death (xi. 34): "'Where have ye laid him?' They say unto him, 'Sir, *come and see*.' Jesus wept[3]."

---

[1] See *Hor. Heb.* on Jn i. 47 (R.V. i. 46).

[2] In the Johannine Epistles this vb. occurs thrice, 1 Jn iii. 1 ἴδετε ποταπὴν ἀγάπην δέδωκεν..., v. 16 ἐάν τις ἴδῃ τ. ἀδελφόν, 3 Jn xiv. ἐλπίζω... σε ἰδεῖν.

[3] [**1609 a**] "Come and *see*" must be distinguished from (i. 39) (R.V.) "Come and *ye shall see* (ὄψεσθε)" (A.V. "Come and see" reading ἴδετε), which is not a Rabbinical precept but a Messianic promise. The context there is full of emblematic meaning. It contains the very first utterance of Christ, "*What seek ye?*"—which is, according to Philo (i. 196 commenting on Gen. xxxvii. 15), the utterance wherein Elenchos (*i.e.* the Convicting Logos or Spirit) addressing the wandering soul, asks it what is the object of its existence.

[**1609 b**] The two seekers after truth reply, "Rabbi...where *abidest* thou?," unconsciously asking the Son to tell them of His eternal Abiding-place, the "Eternal Home," "the bosom of the Father." The Saviour does not say to *them* (see Chrysostom) as He says, in effect, to the

[1610] In the indicative, εἶδον is used of the disciples (i. 39) "coming and seeing" where Jesus "abides"; Abraham also (viii. 56) "saw," prophetically, the glory of the Messiah, and Isaiah (xii. 41 "saw") is probably represented as seeing it in the same way. When the beloved disciple entered the tomb of Jesus, he "saw" and "believed" (**1552—60**). Applied to Jesus it occurs thrice to describe His mysteriously "seeing" Nathanael under the fig-tree[1], the blind man to whom He gives sight, and Mary to whom He restores Lazarus from the dead[2].

[1611] Philo, commenting on the statement (Gen. i. 31) that "God *saw* (εἶδεν) his works," deprecates the literal meaning, and apparently implies that the words indicate a *transference* of knowledge or intellectual "sight" from Himself to His creatures[3]. Certain it is that in each of these last two cases, when Jesus "saw (εἶδεν)" a human being, the act is a prelude to a *transference* from Him of (1) sight, (2) life : and, in the case of Nathanael, the threefold εἶδεν prefaces a transference of spiritual life.

§ 3. "*Hearing*"

[1612] A difference between the Johannine and the Synoptic view of "hearing," as a means of receiving the

---

Scribe (Mt. viii. 20, Lk. ix. 58) "Foxes have holes—but the Son hath no abiding-place." On the contrary, He promises that, if they will "come," they shall "see" the abiding-place.

[1] i. 47—50 "Jesus *saw* (εἶδεν) Nathanael coming...I *saw* (εἶδον) thee... Because I said to thee I *saw* (εἶδον) thee...."

[2] ix. 1, xi. 33. In the latter, it is said that "when he *saw* her weeping and the Jews that had come with her weeping he...troubled himself." In the healing of the impotent man the participle is used (v. 6) Τοῦτον ἰδὼν ὁ Ἰ..., and also in xix. 26 Ἰ. οὖν ἰδὼν τὴν μητέρα....

[3] [1611 a] Philo i. 442 Λέγεται γὰρ ὅτι (Gen. i. 31) Εἶδεν ὁ θεὸς τὰ πάντα ὅσα ἐποίησεν, οὐκ ἴσον τῷ, ὄψιν ἑκάστοις προσέβαλεν, ἀλλ' εἴδησιν καὶ γνῶσιν καὶ κατάληψιν ὧν ἐποίησεν. That this represents God as "teaching," appears from the following words, Εἶχε τοίνυν εὐπρεπὲς ὑφηγεῖσθαι καὶ διδάσκειν καὶ δεικνύναι....

revelation of Christ, is perceptible in their different ways of representing the last part of the following passage of Isaiah—which is quoted by Jesus Himself in the Three Gospels, and by the Evangelist in the Fourth. The Hebrew is (R.V. txt) (Is. vi. 9—10), "Go and tell this people, Hear ye indeed, but understand not, and see ye indeed, but perceive not. Make the heart of this people fat, and make their ears heavy, and shut their eyes: *lest they see with their eyes, and hear with their ears, and understand with their heart, and turn again and be healed.*"

Mk iv. 11–12 (lit.)	Mt. xiii. 13	Lk. viii. 10	Jn xii. 39–40
"…in parables. That seeing (βλέποντες) they may see and not perceive (ἴδωσιν), and hearing they may hear and not understand, lest at any time they should turn and it should be forgiven them."	"…in parables. Because seeing they do not see and hearing they do not hear, neither do they understand[1]."	"…in parables, that seeing they may not see and hearing they may not understand."	"For this cause they could not believe, for that Isaiah said again, He hath blinded their eyes and he hardened their heart; lest they should see with their eyes and perceive (νοήσωσιν) with their heart, and should turn and I shall (*i.e.* should) heal them."

[1613] This is not the place to discuss all the differences of these four versions, but merely to indicate that John, in quoting this prophecy, consistently drops all that refers to hearing ("make their *ears heavy*," "lest they…*hear with their ears*"). Did he do this because it seemed superfluous, the

---

[1] Mt. continues, "And there is being utterly fulfilled for them the prophecy of Isaiah saying, 'By hearing ye shall hear…lest at any time… they should turn, and I shall (*i.e.* should) heal them'"—quoting the LXX version of the whole of the prophecy given above.

metaphor of the "eyes" being sufficient? It is probable that he deemed no word in Scripture superfluous. But he may have had regard to the whole tenor of his own Gospel—the revelation of the incarnate Word. How could the Word be heard by those whose "ears" have been "made heavy" by God? To modern readers it will occur at once that this difficulty is no greater than that which is suggested by the parallel question, "How could the Light of the World be seen by those whose 'eyes' have been 'blinded' by God?" Logically, that is true. But under the influence of traditions about the (Ps. lviii. 4) "deaf adder that stoppeth her ear," and (Jer. viii. 17) "adders that will not be charmed," some might reserve this particular metaphor (of "deafness") to denote incurable spiritual defect.

[1614] It is a remarkable fact that John does not relate a single instance of the cure of the deaf. He does not even mention the word "deaf" in the whole of his Gospel. Using the word "hear" in two senses, (1) "perceiving by the sense of hearing," (2) "hearkening to" or "obeying¹," he represents

---

¹ [1614 a] 'Ακούω with accus. = "*perceive by hearing*," with genit. = "*hearken to*," or "*obey.*" The following passages illustrate the difference between the two constructions.

[1614 b] (1) 'Ακούω with accus. iii. 8 "thou *hearest* its voice," but knowest not its home, object, and meaning; v. 24 "He that *heareth* my word and believeth...," *i.e.* not merely hears; v. 37 "Ye have never [*so much as*] *heard* his voice," much less understood and obeyed it; viii. 43, 47 (1614 d); xix. 8 "When therefore Pilate *heard* this *word* (λόγον)"—to be contrasted with xix. 13 "Pilate therefore, *giving ear to these words* (λόγων)," *i.e.* intimidated by them and obeying them.

[1614 c] (2) 'Ακούω with genit. v. 25—8 "the [spiritually] dead shall *hearken to* the voice (φωνῆς) of the Son of God and they that hearken shall live...all that are in the tombs shall *hearken to* his voice," and shall obey by coming forth to judgment, whether for good or ill; (vii. 40) "having *hearkened to* these words, said, 'This is truly the prophet,'" x. 3, 16, xviii. 37, of those "*hearkening to*" the voice of the Good Shepherd, or "my voice," xii. 47 "Every one that shall *hearken to* my words and not observe them," *i.e.* understand them, and either not obey them, or *obey them for a time, but "not keep* (φυλάξῃ) *them.*"

Jesus as saying to some of the Jews that they were unable to "hear" His word, even in the former sense. The context implies that they were of the nature of "the deaf adder"—which will not hear the voice of (vii. 24, comp. Ps. lviii. 1) "righteous judgment"—the Serpent or Slanderer: "Why do ye not *recognise the meaning of* (γινώσκετε) my speech? *Because ye are not able to hear* my word[1]. *Ye are from your father the devil.*"

[1615] The importance attached by John to "hearing" as compared with "seeing" appears in several passages and not only in the rebuke to Thomas. When Mary Magdalene returns from the tomb to the disciples, "I have seen the Lord" is not the whole of her tidings. She adds that "He said these things to her": and it has been shewn above (**1601**) that she believed in the Resurrection, not because she "saw," but because she heard. The Prologue of the Gospel, it is true, mentions what we have called above (**1604**)—most inadequately—"contemplating." "And the Word became flesh and tabernacled among us and we *contemplated* his glory." But if this is compared with what may be called the Epilogue, that is to say, the Epistle, it will appear that this "contemplation of," or "gazing on," the earthly form and life of the Logos, was but a rudimentary and transient manifestation. The higher manifestations are described as "*hearing*" and "*seeing*," both of them in the perfect:—"what we *have heard* [and retain in our hearts]," "what we *have seen* [and keep in our minds]." In contrast to this the "contemplating" is spoken of in the past, along with the "handling"—"we contemplated," "our hands handled."

[1616] The whole passage in the Epistle[2] is well worth study for the light it throws on John's use of synonyms and

---

[1] [1614 *d*] Jn viii. 43. In antithesis, it is said (viii. 47) "He that is from God perceives-by-hearing the words (ἀκούει τὰ ῥήματα) of God,' *i.e.* he has the faculty of perceiving the voice of God. Sir. xii. 13 ("Who will pity a snake-charmer?") shews that "deaf adders" were frequent. They represent unjust rulers in Jer. viii. 17. See *Ency.* 4394.

[2] 1 Jn i. 1—5.

for other reasons. "*We have heard*" is repeated thrice, and so is "*we have seen.*" On the other hand, "we *bring tidings*" (ἀπαγγέλλομεν) is repeated twice, and then the verb occurs a third time, slightly varied—"we *publish tidings*" (ἀναγγέλλομεν). The first words in the Prologue are, "*In the beginning was the Word*"—which implies "hearing." The first words in the Epilogue are "*That which was from the beginning, that which we have heard.*" Then the writer says "*that which we have seen with our eyes.*" Why did he not also say "that which we have heard with our ears," in parallelism, and after the manner of Isaiah? This is one of many questions (arising out of Johannine style) to which the answer must be that the author had *some* motive, but that we do not know what it is. We may however fairly conjecture that the motive is connected with his omission of Isaiah's clause about "*hearing*," to which attention was called above (**1613**).

[**1617**] The Epistle continues in aorists, "That which we contemplated and our hands handled." It seems to mean "saw and touched in the flesh"—transient facts, but facts on which the permanent "*having* heard" and the permanent "*having* seen" are based. And the writer does not make these earthly manifestations two ("that which *we* contemplated, that which *we* handled") but only one. "Handling,"—perhaps, better, "feeling in the dark"—may well allude to doctrine—such as Paul utters but not of necessity distinctively Pauline—that God placed men on the earth "if perchance they would *handle him* and find him[1]." According to this view, the Epistle teaches us that what men's hands handled "concerning the Word of life," was a rudimentary though necessary manifestation. It was preparatory for something higher, just as the "contemplation" or "spectacle" of the glory of the Incarnation was preparatory for the higher "seeing," or "vision," of the glory of God.

---

[1] Acts xvii. 27. Ψηλαφάω (Steph.) almost always means "*feel in the dark.*"

[1618] After saying that the subject of this hearing, seeing, contemplating and touching was "the Word of life," the writer repeats himself thus: "And the life was manifested, and we *have seen* and bear witness and bring tidings to you." He then breaks off to define the subject of the tidings as being "the eternal life that was with ($\pi\rho\acute{o}\varsigma$) the Father and was manifested to us." Then he repeats himself once more, "That which we *have seen and have heard* we bring tidings of to you also."

[1619] Why "to you also"? Because of a feeling of "fellowship." And this leads him to think of the "fellowship" of the Father (whom he has just mentioned) with the Son (whom he has not yet mentioned but mentions now) as follows, "in order that ye also may have fellowship with us. Yea, and our fellowship is with the Father and with his Son Jesus Christ."

[1620] Another way of saying "for the sake of fellowship" would be "for the sake of making men feel joy together in brotherly love." Accordingly, the writer defines his object a second time in connexion with "joy" and with "light," the type of joy, "And these things we write unto you in order that our[1] joy may be fulfilled [by your fellowship therein]. And this is the tidings ($\dot{\alpha}\gamma\gamma\epsilon\lambda\acute{\iota}\alpha$) that we have heard from him and *publish as tidings* ($\dot{\alpha}\nu\alpha\gamma\gamma\acute{\epsilon}\lambda\lambda o\mu\epsilon\nu$) to you, that God is light and in him is no darkness at all." Thus gradually the writer has led us on from stage to stage; and from "that which was from the beginning" we have been brought down to "fellowship." Now he is fairly on the way to apply his high theology concerning "fellowship" in heaven to practical morality about "fellowship" on earth, and here we must leave him. But we shall have examined this passage to little purpose if we have not perceived that every stage is carefully considered, every word weighed, and every repetition de-

---

[1] V.r. "your joy."

liberate. In particular, we are to note the threefold repetition of "hearing" and "seeing" and the prominence given to the former. "*That which we have heard*" begins, and "*the tidings that we have heard*" concludes, these reiterations of the avenues by which the Logos has revealed itself to men. In harmony with this doctrine, Mary Magdalene believes because she "hears," though she does not "see," or sees amiss—and it is "hearing" that elicits the Samaritan confession, "This is the Saviour of the world[1]."

§ 4. "*Knowing*"

[1621] The verbs of "knowing" are οἶδα and γινώσκω. Οἶδα means "I know," or, in a popular sense, "know all about": γινώσκω means "I acquire knowledge about," "come to know," "understand," "recognise," "feel."

(i) Οἶδα.

[1622] It is only in a popular sense that man can be said to "know (all about) (οἶδα)" God, or even about a human being (for the soul, in the strict sense, is beyond human knowledge). In the last words of Jesus (xvi, xvii), οἶδα is not used at all. In the Epistle it is never used with a personal object, but, generally, only about the "facts" of revelation. Yet by some of the prophets (Is. v. 13 (LXX), xlv. 5, Jer. iv. 22, ix. 6) it is brought as a charge against the people, or their leaders, that they neither "know" (οἶδα) nor wish to "know" God; and Jeremiah (xxiv. 7, xxxi. 34) predicts a time when all shall "know" Him. Many of the Jews may have assumed that they, having discarded idolatry, the sin of their forefathers, were not only distinguished from (Is. lv. 5) "the nations" (*i.e.* Gentiles) that "knew not God," but were also entitled to say that they themselves "knew God." The Evangelist exhibits Jesus as denouncing this assumption and as declaring that the Jews are entirely ignorant of Him.

[1623] Their ignorance proceeded from their attempt to

---

[1] See **1503—7, 1560, 1601.**

rise to the conception of God through a written Law, and not through God's Creation as a whole, including the Law but also including Man. As there was no humanheartedness in their conception of God, so there was nothing divine in their conception of Man. If, therefore, many of the Jews thought they "knew all about" God, when they affixed to Him the labels authorised by Moses and the Prophets, much more would they suppose that they "knew all about" man. And, of course, Jesus would be no exception to their rule of universal knowledge. According to them, it was enough to say that they "knew all about" the "father and mother" of Jesus, and it followed that they "knew all about" Him. The Messiah Himself would be no Messiah to them if they knew "whence he is": He must needs come from some incomprehensible source: else He has no title to allegiance.

[1624] With manifest irony the Evangelist makes the Jews say to one another (vi. 42) "Do not we (*emph.* ἡμεῖς) *know* his father and his mother [too]?" Later on, they say (vii. 27) "As to this man, we *know* (οἴδαμεν) whence he is; but as to the Messiah, when he is to come, no one is to *understand* (γινώσκει) whence he is." Jesus repeats their assertion (**2236**) half as an assertion of theirs, half as an exclamation of His own, and then points out its falseness (vii. 28) "'Both me do ye know and ye know whence I am!' [So ye say] and [yet] I am not come from myself; but he that hath sent me is true, whom ye (ὑμεῖς) [being false] *know* not: I (ἐγώ) *know* him...," and again (viii. 14) "I *know* whence I came (ἦλθον) and whither I return; but ye (ὑμεῖς) *know* not whence I come (ἔρχομαι)[1] or whither I return," and (viii. 19) "Ye neither

---

[1] [1624 *a*] A distinction appears to be drawn between "I came" and "I come" (or "am coming"). The Logos "*came*" from the Father (**1637**) when He (i. 11) "*came*" in the special act of the Incarnation: but the Logos is also constantly "*coming*" from the Father to the created world, in a myriad of non-special acts or sustaining processes. Even in this lower and less personal sense—as the source of the "ever coming" Logos—the Father is not known to the Jews.

know me nor my Father; if ye *had known* (ἤδειτε) me, ye *would have known* my Father also (ἂν ἤδειτε)." Now for the first time γινώσκειν is applied to "God," as object, in order to introduce a solemn protest, in which Jesus thrice repeats the word οἶδα in connexion with the Father, (viii. 55) "Ye have had *no understanding of* (ἐγνώκατε) him; but I *know* (i.e. *have absolute knowledge of*, οἶδα) him; and if I say that *I know* (οἶδα) him not, I shall be a liar like unto you: but I *know* (οἶδα) him[1]."

[1625] Henceforward, this popular use of οἶδα, in the words of Jesus, applied to "the Jews," is dropped, with the single exception of xv. 21 ("They *know* not him that sent me"). But the Jews—having above asserted (vii. 27) "We *know* this man whence he is," now say (ix. 29): "But this man we *know not* whence he is." They mean, apparently, that they do not know with what authority He comes. But they are intended by the Evangelist to testify unconsciously against themselves, "We know not the Living God." For "God" is the "whence he is."

(ii) Γινώσκω.

[1626] Even when used in the perfect, this verb is quite distinct in meaning from οἶδα. Strictly speaking, we ought not to say that the Father, or the Eternal Son, γινώσκει "comes to know," "understands," or "feels": but the Evangelist, after applying the word to the Good Shepherd, who (x. 14) "understands (γινώσκει)" and is understood by, His sheep, delights in applying it, in a spiritual metaphor, to the Father and the Son (*ib.* 15): "Even as the Father *understands* me and I *understand* the Father": and he has previously used it of Jesus entering into and "understanding" the

---

[1] [1624 *b*] For other instances of οἶδα and γινώσκω in the same sentence, see **1626** and comp. Jn xxi. 17 "Lord, thou *hast absolute knowledge of* (οἶδας) all things, thou *understandest* (or, *feelest*, γινώσκεις) that I still love thee" (where the meaning seems to be that the All-knowing must have sympathy enough to understand the sincere though imperfect love of a sinful but penitent creature).

weaknesses of those who "believed on his name[1]." He sometimes (1624 b) uses the word so as to imply "sympathy"; and we may then render it by "feel." The present tense is especially frequent. Note the contrast with the aorist in the following distinction (x. 38) "Even if ye do not now believe in me, believe in my works, that ye may *come to know definitely by evidence* (γνῶτε) and that ye *may continue in the ever growing knowledge* (γινώσκητε) that the Father is in me." Here the aorist (γνῶτε) means "ascertain," the present (γινώσκητε) "feel by constant experience[2]." In several passages there is a contrast between γινώσκω and οἶδα: (xiii. 7) "What I do thou hast no *knowledge* of (οἶδας) now[3]: but thou shalt *understand* (γνώσῃ) hereafter." Note also the distinction between ᾔδειτε and ἐγνώκειτε in the two following sentences, the former addressed to the Pharisees, the latter to the disciples.

(i) (viii. 19) "If you had *known all about* (ᾔδειτε) me, [as you assumed], you would have *had absolute knowledge of* (ᾔδειτε ἄν) the Father."

(ii) (xiv. 7) "If you had *learned to understand and sympathize with* (ἐγνώκειτε) me, you would also *have had absolute knowledge of* (ᾔδειτε ἄν) the Father: from henceforth, [understanding me] you *feel and understand* (γινώσκετε) him and [indeed] have seen him[4]."

---

[1] Jn ii. 24—5 "Jesus would not trust himself to them because he [by] himself *could understand* all [men] (διὰ τὸ αὐτὸν γινώσκειν πάντας)... for he [by] himself *could understand* (αὐτὸς γὰρ ἐγίνωσκεν) what was in man."

[2] [1626 a] Comp. the distinction between the aorist and the present subjunctive of πιστεύω. Both in πιστεύω and in γινώσκω the pres. subj. expresses a *living* and *growing* faith or knowledge (2524).

[3] [1626 b] *With a negative*, οἶδα and ἔγνωκα need not mean "I have not a perfect knowledge," "I have not a perfect understanding." They may mean simply "I have no knowledge, or no understanding," *e.g.* xiv. 9: "So long a time have I been with thee, and *hast thou no understanding of* (οὐκ ἔγνωκας) me, Philip?"

[4] [1626 c] The writer seems to take a pleasure in varying his terms,

[1627] It is interesting to observe how the Evangelist, while always using the *perfect* of "see" (ἑώρακα) prefers the *present* of "come to know" (γινώσκω): naturally, because— whereas a thing "seen" is sometimes taken in at a glance— "knowing," if it is genuine "knowing," is in constant growth; (xiv. 17) "The world doth not behold (θεωρεῖ) it [*i.e.* the Spirit] nor *grow in the understanding of* [γινώσκει] it: ye (emph.) *grow in the understanding of* (ὑμεῖς γινώσκετε) it because it abideth with you." Note the contrast between (xiv. 31) ἵνα γνῷ ὁ κόσμος and (xvii. 23) ἵνα γινώσκῃ ὁ κόσμος: the former means, "in order that the world may *learn once for all* [from the crucifixion and sacrifice of Christ]"; the latter, "in order that the world *may gradually learn* [from the spectacle of the divine unity of the Church]." The present is also found in the definition of eternal life (xvii. 3) "This is life eternal that they should *grow in the knowledge of* (γινώσκωσι) thee, the only true God." The same thing is expressed in the Epistle, where the writer speaks of this special "knowledge" as the result of a special "intellect" or "understanding (διάνοια)," which God gives us, (1 Jn v. 20) "The Son of God hath come and hath given us an *understanding* (διάνοιαν), that we may *have the living and growing knowledge of* (γινώσκομεν) (*sic*) him that is true."

[1628] In the Epistle, γινώσκω is constantly used for the spiritual instinct by which we feel, or recognise, spiritual truths, (1 Jn ii. 3) "Hereby we *understand* (γινώσκομεν) that we *have reached a perfect understanding of* (ἐγνώκαμεν) God." Comp. 1 Jn ii. 5, 18, 29; iii. 19, 24; iv. 2 etc., and especially iv. 6—7 "He that *feeleth*, or *understandeth*, (γινώσκων) God, giveth ear to us; he that is not from God giveth not ear to us:

---

not for the sake of variation, but for the sake of detaching his reader from fixed formulae: xv. 21 "These things will they do because they *know* (οἴδασιν) not him that sent me," xvi. 3 "These things will they do because they did not *recognise* (or, *did not receive the knowledge of*) (ἔγνωσαν) the Father or me."

from this we *feel*, or *understand*, the Spirit of truth and the Spirit of error.... Everyone that loveth is born of God and *feeleth* (γινώσκει) God...; he that loveth not *never felt* (οὐκ ἔγνω) God."

[1629] In the Gospel (vi. 69) the Confession of St Peter places belief before knowledge—as if the former prepared the way and the latter followed, the former being the more rudimentary and the latter the higher development—"We *have a perfect belief* (πεπιστεύκαμεν), and we *have a perfect knowledge* (ἐγνώκαμεν), that thou art the Holy One of God." On the other hand, 1 Jn iv. 16, reversing the order, says, "We *have a perfect knowledge* and we *have a perfect belief* [as to] the love that God hath in us." In the former the meaning seems clear, "We believe, nay more, we know." But in the latter (ἐγνώκαμεν καὶ πεπιστεύκαμεν τὴν ἀγάπην), the accusative appears to be governed by the compound verb "know and believe," since πιστεύω could not have an accusative of the object (1507 b) unless it were neuter—and the question arises, What is the reason for so harsh a construction? Possibly the writer had in mind the beautiful saying in the Ephesian Epistle (iii. 19) "to *know* the love of Christ which passeth knowledge." When St Paul has used the phrase "having recognised God," he corrects it into "or rather having been recognised by God (1598 b)." So here, the writer perhaps began to say "we know the love that God hath," and then broke off into "believe," as though to imply that it is "beyond knowledge" unless the "knowing" daily grows in conjunction with "believing[1]."

---

[1] [1629 a] There is great difficulty in Jn xvii. 25, (lit.) "O righteous Father, on the one hand (καί) the world recognised (ἔγνω) thee not: but I recognised (ἔγνων) thee...." Does this mean (1) that the pre-incarnate Son "recognised" the Father from the beginning, or (2) that the incarnate Son recognised the Spirit of the Father when He was baptized and sent forth to preach the Gospel? Chrysostom tries to explain it, but soon falls into a change of tense that breaks the antithesis, ἐγὼ μέν

§ 5. "Coming"

[1630] The First Epistle to the Corinthians, after "the salutation of me Paul with mine own hand," has "If any man loveth not the Lord let him be anathema. *Maran atha.*" "Maran atha" is explained by R.V. margin as "*Our Lord cometh*[1]." This proves that the two Aramaic words were used to Corinthians, about the middle of the first century, by an Apostle familiar with them, as a kind of watchword. Like many other watchwords, it was misunderstood at an early period. The earliest epitaph known to contain it quotes as follows "If any of our own [folk] ($\tau\hat{\omega}\nu$ $\grave{\iota}\delta\acute{\iota}\omega\nu$) or other person, dare to deposit a body here, besides us two, may he give account to God and let him be anathema *maranathan* (sic)[2]." This inscription is said by the Editor to be of the fourth or fifth century: but it is highly probable that at a very much earlier period Greeks took the phrase to be a kind of curse, as it is taken popularly now and has been for centuries. The juxtaposition of "anathema" in St Paul's Epistle would facilitate the misinterpretation. Nor would it be corrected by the knowledge,—which a few Greeks might retain and transmit to a gradually diminishing number—that the word had some connexion with the "Lord coming." "That"—the misinterpreters might say—"justifies our view. The Lord *is* 'coming'—to smite sinners with a curse."

$\sigma\epsilon$ $o\tilde{\iota}\delta\alpha$ $\ddot{\alpha}\lambda\lambda o\iota$ $\delta\acute{\epsilon}$ $\sigma\epsilon$ $o\dot{\upsilon}\kappa$ $\underline{\ddot{\epsilon}\gamma\nu\omega\sigma\alpha\nu}$. It happens that $\ddot{\epsilon}\gamma\nu\omega\nu$ is followed by $\kappa\alpha\acute{\iota}$, and ϵΓΝῶΚΑΙ might arise from a corruption of ϵΓΝωΚΑΚΑΙ, which is the reading of D. More probably, however, the aorist is used for antithesis in contrasting the Son with the World: and perhaps the words are meant to suggest the *two* forms of recognising above mentioned.

[1] 1 Cor. xvi. 22.

[2] [1630 a] Boeckh *Inscr. Gr.* 9303. Hastings *Dict.* renders $\tau\iota\varsigma$ $\tau\hat{\omega}\nu$ $\grave{\iota}\delta\acute{\iota}\omega\nu$ "private person": but the above seems to make better sense. There is of course no punctuation in the Epitaph.

[**1631**] Yet there are good reasons for thinking that it does not mean "the Lord is come, or coming," but "Come, Lord[1]." In any case it was certainly used in the second century, and probably in the first, as a part of the Eucharistic Liturgy, where "cursing" is out of the question: "Let grace come (ἐλθέτω) and let this world go (παρελθέτω)[2]. Hosanna to the Son of David. If anyone is holy, let him come (lit. be a comer, ἐρχέσθω) [to the Lord]. If anyone is not [holy] let him become repentant (μετανοείτω). *Maran atha.* Amen." If the phrase is imperative, then this invocation is singularly apt and impressive after receiving the sacred bread and wine: "COME, LORD, [into our hearts]!" Of course the prayer may also have reference to another "coming," namely, "on the clouds"; and the latter, which might easily overshadow the former, might be taken to mean "Come, Lord, to avenge thy saints," and nothing else. The formula, as used at the close of the Apocalypse, "Yea, I come quickly: Amen, *come, Lord Jesus*" seems to refer to the "coming on the clouds[3]." Yet, in the same book, the preceding invitation to "come" suggests a spiritual meaning: "And the Spirit and the Bride say, *Come.* And he that heareth, let him say, *Come.* And he that is athirst, *let him come*[4]," very much resembling the combination of "If any one is holy let him come," and "Come, Lord," in the *Didaché.*

[**1632**] In the account of the Baptism, all the Gospels agree in assigning to John the Baptist the word "*cometh*" in connexion with the Deliverer whom he heralded. Moreover Matthew and Luke represent the Baptist as using the word in a message sent to Christ, "Art thou *he that cometh*?

---

[1] [**1631** *a*] *Enc.* and Hastings' *Dict.* ("Maranatha") both take this view.

[2] [**1631** *b*] *Didach.* x. 6. It is difficult to express ἐλθεῖν and παρελθεῖν exactly: "pass into our hearts" and "pass away," or "appear" and "disappear," might express one aspect of the play on the words.

[3] Rev. xxii. 20.   [4] Rev. xxii. 17.

or look we for another[1]?" Taken together, the two traditions demonstrate that "he that cometh," as a title of the Lord Jesus, would be known to His followers in Galilee before any thought of Him as "coming on the clouds of heaven" had entered their minds.

[1633] Apart from the utterances of the Baptist, all the Gospels agree that when Jesus rode into Jerusalem the crowd welcomed Him with the words, " Blessed is *he that cometh*!" This is a quotation from the Psalms, and the words might be addressed to any pilgrim entering the City; but, if "he that cometh" was already a Galilæan title for the new Deliverer, the successor of David, then it becomes almost a certainty that the multitude used the phrase in the sense of "prince" or "king": and accordingly all the Evangelists insert some paraphrase of this kind[2]. This confirms our view of "he that cometh" as a technical Jewish term. According to Matthew and Luke these words are quoted by our Lord Himself in a warning to Jerusalem: "Ye shall assuredly not see me [Mt. + henceforth] until ye shall say, Blessed is *he that cometh* in the name of the Lord." But Luke places these words long before the Entry into Jerusalem, apparently taking the prediction to be fulfilled on that occasion. Matthew places them after the Entry (when the Lord is bidding farewell to the Temple) apparently looking forward to a second coming[3].

[1634] Except in the Entry into Jerusalem there appears in the Triple Tradition little or nothing to indicate a desire to use the word "cometh" about Jesus in a technical or mystical manner to suggest a Messiah or Deliverer. But there is perhaps an allusion to a "coming" of a different kind. The warning to "watch," and the words "in an hour that ye think

---

[1] Mt. xi. 3, Lk. vii. 19.
[2] [1633 a] Mt. xxi. 9 "the son of David," Lk. xix. 38 "king," Jn xii. 13 "king of Israel," Mk xi. 10 adds a whole clause "Blessed is the coming kingdom of our father David."
[3] Lk. xiii. 35, Mt. xxiii. 39.

not, the Son of man *cometh*," are followed, not long afterwards, by a threefold "coming" of Christ to the disciples at Gethsemane, each time finding them asleep. Matthew here thrice applies the historic present "*cometh*" to Jesus. In Mark (who does the same) this is not surprising, as he uses the historic present freely. But the fact that Matthew here, and here alone, applies this form to Jesus[1], suggests that on this special occasion he may have retained Mark's tradition as having a symbolical association. The connexion between "*he that cometh*," and a "king," pointed out above (**1633**), is illustrated by the prophecy of Zechariah "Behold *thy king cometh*": and Matthew is the only Synoptist that quotes this[2].

[**1635**] Passing to the Fourth Evangelist we may note first the fact—and it is a most important one considering how seldom he agrees with the Synoptists in quoting the same passages from Scripture—that he too, like Matthew, quotes from Zechariah, in connexion with the Entry into Jerusalem, the prophecy, "Behold, thy king *cometh*." Moreover, throughout his Gospel, he seems to take a pleasure in using the words "cometh," or "he that cometh," about Christ, as though to suggest that He is the realisation of the popular title of the Deliverer, even though the people do not receive Him. That He is *ever* "*coming*," like the sunlight, is suggested in the Prologue[3]. In the Triple Tradition, the Baptist's words about

---

[1] [**1634** *a*] Mk applies ἔρχεται to Jesus in iii. 20, vi. 1, 48, x. 1, xiv. 17, 37, 41, Mt. only in xxvi. 36, 40, 45. Mt. also thrice repeats ἔρχεται in the previous warning (where Mk and Lk. have it only once and twice respectively) xxiv. 42—4 "ye know not on what day your Lord *cometh*... if he had known...in what watch the thief *cometh*...at what hour ye think not the Son of man *cometh*."

[2] [**1634** *b*] Mt. xxi. 5, quoting Zech. ix. 9. Matthew's fondness for this particular word in connexion with "the last day" may perhaps be illustrated by Mt. xvii. 11 "Elijah indeed *cometh*" (where the parall. Mk ix. 12 has "having come") and certainly by Mt. xxv. 19 "But after a long time the lord of those servants *cometh* and maketh reckoning with them."

[3] i. 9, where "coming into the world" should be connected with "light."

the Messiah ("cometh, or coming, after me") seem to indicate discipleship. "After me" is omitted by Luke. But John retains the phrase, and interprets it so as to testify to the Messiah, whom the Baptist "seeth *coming* unto him[1]"; and, later on, speaking in his own person, he describes the Lord not as "he that came," but "*he that cometh* from above......*he that cometh* from heaven[2]." The Woman of Samaria with very misty views of the Messiah, the Five Thousand (who wish to make "the prophet" Jesus a king), the Jews in their discussions about the Messiah's birth-place, all use this word "cometh"—ignorant that the Messiah is always coming and had actually come[3].

[1636] The present tense is also introduced into the narrative of the Raising of Lazarus[4], as though in sympathy with the "coming" Deliverer concerning whom Martha says, "Thou art the Christ, the Son of God, that *cometh* into the world[5]," and similarly in the Entry into Jerusalem, "having heard that Jesus *cometh*," which prepares the way for "Blessed is he that *cometh*" and "Behold thy king *cometh*[6]." In the sacramental washing of feet, also, Jesus "*cometh* to Simon Peter[7]." After the Resurrection, there are three instances of "coming." The first is in the past tense[8], perhaps to denote that Jesus, on this first occasion, had come from the Father (to whom He had ascended) in a kind of second spiritual incarnation. The second is in the present tense though the context is

---

[1] i. 15, 27, 29, 30.   [2] iii. 31.
[3] iv. 25 "I know that Messiah *cometh*," vi. 14 "This is of a truth the prophet that *cometh* into the world," vii. 27 "When Christ is to come (ἔρχηται)," vii. 41 "*Cometh* Christ from Galilee?" vii. 42 "Christ *cometh* from Bethlehem."
[4] xi. 20, 38.
[5] xi. 27.   [6] xii. 12, 13, 15.   [7] xiii. 6.
[8] xx. 19 "And, the doors having been shut...*there-came* Jesus and stood in the midst." On the past tense used to express the "coming" in the Incarnation, see **1637**.

similar to that in the first[1]. The third is also in the present, but the context is quite different. It describes Jesus as first saying ["Come] hither! break your fast," and then as Himself coming. "There *cometh* Jesus and taketh the bread and giveth to them[2]."

[1637] In our Lord's own words, the Aorist is generally used to describe His coming, or being sent, from the Father, and the Perfect to describe His arrival in the world, as though He said, "I *came* (or, was sent) from heaven; I *am come* to earth." The Evangelist also prefers the Aorist to describe the former aspect. For this reason, "*come forth*" is always in the Aorist when describing the Incarnation[3]. In the Last Discourse Jesus thrice uses the Present "I am coming," to express His future coming to the Disciples, even where it is joined with a Future: "I *am coming* to you and *will* receive you to myself[4]." Once, He uses the Future "*We shall come*"

---

[1] xx. 26 "*There-cometh* Jesus, the doors having been shut, and stood in the midst."

[2] [1636 a] xxi. 12—13. Perhaps the disciples are to be regarded as first obeying the Lord by coming and reclining around the "(one) loaf" and the "(one) fish"; and then the Lord "comes" and gives them "the loaf" and "the fish" (τὸ ὀψάριον). In the Washing of Feet Jesus "comes" to Peter separately. So, perhaps, He comes round to each in turn here.

[3] [1637 a] viii. 42 "I *came forth* (ἐξῆλθον) from God and *am come* (ἥκω); for indeed I *have not come* (ἐλήλυθα) from myself but he *sent* me." Ἥκω is also in Ps. xl. 7—8 "Lo, *I am come*...I delight to do thy will," quoted as a Messianic utterance in Heb. x. 7, 9, "Behold *I am come* (ἥκω) to do thy will." Ἐξῆλθον is similarly used in Jn xiii. 3, xvi. 27, 28, 30, xvii. 8. In Jn i. 11, "He came (ἦλθεν) to his own," it cannot be said that the notion of coming from the Father predominates; but it does in viii. 14 "I know whence I *came*." And the Aorist is also used when the "coming" is regarded as a Mission—the Son being sent by the Father in order to do something—ix. 39 "For judgment I *came* into this world," x. 10 "I *came* that they might have life," xii. 47 "For I *came* not to judge the world." This seems to be the meaning of ἐλθών in 1 Jn v. 6, "This is he *that came* through water and blood," *i.e.* that came from the Father to redeem mankind.

[4] xiv. 3, comp. xiv. 18, 28.

to describe the joint visit of the Father, the Son, and the Spirit to the soul of the believer[1].

[1638] His last use of the verb is in the Present, twice repeated, and it is very significant. "If I will that he [*i.e.* the beloved disciple] remain *while I am coming*, what is that to thee? Follow thou me." The words would most naturally mean "during the short interval, *while I am coming*," as we use the phrase in English, meaning, "I am on the point of coming," and as it is used in Greek, in the First Epistle to Timothy[2]. But they lend themselves to an inner meaning that would harmonize with Origen's view concerning the "beloved disciple" who, he says, was in the bosom of the Son spiritually even as the Son was "in the bosom of the Father[3]."

[1639] According to this view we might suppose that the author of the Fourth Gospel, accepting the old traditional Johannine name of God, "He that IS and WAS and IS COMING[4]," wished to differentiate it from the merely grammatical associations of Past, Present, and Future, and therefore laid stress, consistent stress throughout the whole of the Gospel, on the claim of the Logos to be called COMING not as being future, but as being *ever present to come and save*. Hence in the Prologue of his Gospel, he describes the Light, from the beginning, as "*coming* into the world." Now, at its close, after describing the Son as, in one sense, *having* come, and as having prepared "the beloved disciple" to wait for Him, and to represent Him, on earth, he suggests that, in a second sense, the Son is still "coming" to help such a disciple, and in a third sense, that He will hereafter "come" to make those who thus wait one with Himself[5].

---

[1] [1637 *b*] xiv. 23. Is this intended to emphasize the fact that (vii. 39) "there was *not yet* the Spirit because Jesus had not yet been glorified"?

[2] 1 Tim. iv. 13, see 1735 *a*.

[3] Orig. on Jn xxi. 20 foll. (Huet ii. 405—6).   [4] Rev. i. 4.

[5] [1639 *a*] A comparatively unimportant use of ἔρχεται may be noted

§ 6. "Worshipping"

(i) Προσκυνέω, in the Samaritan Dialogue.

[1640] In the Dialogue with the Samaritan Woman, Jesus is represented as using προσκυνέω twice with dative, twice with accusative, and, in two more instances ("ye worship *that which* (ὅ) ye know not, we worship *that which* (ὅ) we know") with construction that must remain doubtful because the antecedent may have been intended to be either dative or accusative[1]. The accusative is certainly employed at the end, iv. 23—4 (R.V. but see **2167, 2398**) "For such doth the Father seek to be *his worshippers* (τοὺς προσκυνοῦντας αὐτόν). God is Spirit and *they that worship him* (οἱ προσκυνοῦντες αὐτόν) must worship in spirit and truth." When we ask what is the meaning of "*such*," we are led back to the preceding sentence "The true worshippers shall *worship* (*to*) (dat.) the Father in spirit and truth." The question arises

in the Johannine phrase "the hour *cometh*," or "the hour *cometh and now is*," where the Synoptists say "the days *will come*." Similarly when two men are waiting for the same train, one, looking at the station-clock, may say "The train *will soon be coming*," while the other, at the same moment, catching sight of the train itself some two or three miles away, may say, "The train *is coming*." John represents Christ in the latter way, speaking as a Seer. Ἔρχεται is used by John thus seven times (**1891**). On the last occasion, instead of "and now is," there is added the Perfect (xvi. 32) "The hour *cometh* and *hath come*."

[1639 *b*] "The hour *hath come*" occurs thrice: (1) (xii. 23) "There cometh Andrew and Philip and they tell Jesus [about the desire of the Greeks to see Him]. But Jesus answered them saying, *The hour hath come* that the Son of man should be glorified," (2) (xvi. 32) "Behold the hour cometh and *hath come* that ye should be scattered each to his own and leave me alone; and yet I am not alone because the Father is with me," (3) (xvii. 1) "Father, *the hour hath come*, glorify thy Son." In the context of the first instance occur the words (xii. 27) "Father, glorify thy name." We may, therefore, say that in each of the three instances the Son is regarded as in close communion with the Father who sees the accomplishment of the fore-ordained future as though it were past.

[1] Orig. Comm. (Huet ii. 213 B) indicates that Heracleon (ᾔδεσαν τίνι προσκυνοῦσι) took the antecedent to be dative.

what was meant by the variation of case, and the attempt to answer it necessitates an examination of the general use of the word προσκυνέω.

(ii) Προσκυνέω, outside N.T.

[1641] From Herodotus[1] downwards, it was recognised that "to worship (προσκυνεῖν)" a king by prostration was a slavish or barbaric custom unworthy of Greeks. The Spartans said, and the other Greeks agreed with them, that it was not in accordance with law and custom (ἐν νόμῳ) to "worship a man." The Greeks did not suppose that such "worship" implied a belief that the man so worshipped was a god—any more than Jack Cade supposed himself to be a god when he said that his people were to "worship" him as "their lord[2]." But whereas Englishmen felt that a vassal might "worship" his "lord," Greeks, before the Christian era, felt that they could not "worship" any human being. In almost all cases—the exceptions perhaps being where they desired to emphasize the attitude of worship—the Greeks used προσκυνέω, in this sense, with the accusative[3].

---

[1] Steph. quoting Herod. vii. 136, viii. 118, Demosth. 549. 16 πρ. τοὺς ὑβρίζοντας ὥσπερ ἐν τοῖς βαρβάροις. See also L. S.

[2] [1641 a] 2 *Hen. VI.* iv. 2. 81 "I thank you, good people, there shall be no money : all shall eat and drink on my score : and I will apparel them all in one livery, that they may agree like brothers and *worship me their lord.*"

[3] [1641 b] See Wetst. (on Mt. ii. 2) who quotes Aelian *V. H.* i. 21 as using the dative *when he is going to describe the posture in detail*, Ἰσμηνίας αἰσχύνης χωρὶς πῶς Περσῶν βασιλεῖ προσεκύνησεν, but the accusative when he merely states that one could not have audience of the king πρὶν ἢ προσκυνῆσαι αὐτόν. Wetst. quotes Lucian *Navig.* § 30 with the accus.; and in *ib.* § 37 προσκυνείτωσαν ἡμῖν Reitz reads ὑμῶν gov. by ἄρξω. The Index to Lucian gives no instance with the dative, but several with the accusative. Also in Polyb. v. 86. 10, quoted by Wetst. with dat., Steph. follows Reisk. in reading προσκλίνουσι for προσκυνοῦσι. Steph. adds "Apud Josephum plurima sunt utriusque structurae exempla libris interdum dissentientibus": in *Ant.* vi. 7. 5 the accus. and dat. are in consecutive lines ("God" being, in both cases, the object) (see **1642** b), but in vii. 5. 5, ix. 13. 3, xx. 3. 1, the accus. is used.

[1642] The canon. LXX uses προσκυνέω more than a hundred times with the dative to represent "bowing down to" Jehovah, or to false gods, or to great men, and the dative represents the Hebrew "to." The accusative occurs only six or seven times, and then in connexion with some special circumstances, mostly implying contempt, after the manner of the Greeks[1]. The coincidences of meaning in these cases are too striking to be accidental and they indicate that a Jewish writer might exceptionally use προσκυνέω in the Greek style, with the accusative, to denote exceptional "worship" (like that of the sheaves) or "worship" that ought not to be paid except by slaves (like the "worship" paid by Pharaoh's servants and by the princes of Joash and refused by Mordecai), or even ordinary idolatry[2].

(iii) Προσκυνέω in N.T.

[1643] Passing to N.T. we find a striking instance of the juxtaposition of the two constructions in the Temptation, where Satan uses the verb with the dative but our Lord in His reply uses it with the accusative. In the Satanic verbal demand for mere "*prostration*" the Lord discerns a latent demand for "*worship*": and He answers the latter, not the

---

[1] [1642 a] In Gen. xxxvii. 7, 9, it describes the "sheaves" and the "stars" worshipping, in Joseph's dream. In Ex. xi. 8, Moses says that the servants of Pharaoh will come "beseeching" him (προσκυνήσουσί με) (lit. "bowing down to me"). In 2 Chr. xxiv. 17 the princes "came and *bowed down* to (accus.) the king [Joash]. Then the king hearkened unto them and they forsook the house of the Lord...and served the Asherim." In Is. xliv. 15 it means worshipping idols; and the Epistle of Jeremiah, in consecutive verses, uses the accusative for the worship of false gods, and the dative for that of Jehovah (προσκυνοῦντας αὐτά...σοὶ δεῖ προσκυνεῖν). A Greek insertion in Esther has the accus. twice in a single verse (iv. 17) "As to my refusal to worship the haughty Haman...I will worship no man"—which is quite in Greek style.

[2] [1642 b] It would be interesting to ascertain the usage of Josephus, and whether it varies in *Ant.* and in *Wars*. The instances given (1641 b) by Steph. are too few to be of much value; but so far as they go, they indicate that Josephus favoured the accus. and that *Ant.* vi. 7. 5 τῷ θεῷ is a corr. of τὸ θεὸ (966 a).

former. We may suppose Satan to be saying "All that I ask is that thou wilt *bow down to me* [Luke, *before me*]—a mere gesture, nothing more"; whereto the Lord replies "Thou demandest, in effect, *worship*. And it is written, Thou shalt *worship* the Lord thy God." In any case it can hardly be doubted that some distinction is intended, especially as Luke, while deviating slightly from Matthew in Satan's utterance, agrees with Matthew, against both the Hebrew and the Greek of Deuteronomy, in differentiating the construction of the verb in our Lord's reply[1].

[1644] In Mark, προσκυνέω with the accusative is once used—where the parallel Luke has "fell down before him"—perhaps to represent the demoniac as actually worshipping Jesus, since he calls Him "the Son of the Most High[2]." Matthew—apart from the quotation in the Temptation—never uses it with the accusative. Apart from the Temptation, Luke never has προσκυνέω at all, except in a possible interpolation describing the disciples as "worshipping" Christ after the Resurrection. There it is used with the accusative[3]. The dative is once used by Mark to describe the mock homage paid to Christ in the Passion[4]; and several times by Matthew to describe people prostrating themselves before Jesus[5], or

---

[1] **[1643 a]** Mt. iv. 9 πρ. μοι, Lk. iv. 7 πρ. ἐνώπιον ἐμοῦ : Mt. iv. 10, Lk. iv. 8 κύριον τὸν θεόν σου πρ. : Deut. vi. 13 "Thou shalt *fear* the Lord thy God," φοβηθήσῃ (but A προσκυνήσεις). Codex A corrupts the text again in Deut. x. 20, presumably influenced by the Christian Gospels.

[1643 b] Antecedently we might have supposed that the Greek Churches would frequently have altered the Hebrew "fear" (in "fearing God") into some word less likely to suggest servile terror, *e.g.* "reverence": and, if that had been the case, it might have explained προσκυνεῖν in this quotation. But in the LXX such alterations (*e.g.* Jonah i. 9 σέβομαι) are almost non-existent.

[2] Mk v. 6 (but Tisch. αὐτῷ), Lk. viii. 28 προσέπεσεν αὐτῷ (Mt. om.).

[3] Lk. [[xxiv. 52]].

[4] Mk xv. 19, Mt.-Lk. om.

[5] Mt. viii. 2, ix. 18, xiv. 33, xv. 25. The dative in Mt. ii. 2, 8, 11 describes homage or worship to be paid to the infant Christ.

(once) before other superiors[1]. One of these instances describes the women prostrating themselves before Christ after the Resurrection[2]. In two instances Matthew uses it absolutely, once when describing the mother of Zebedee's children petitioning Jesus, and once describing the disciples of Christ worshipping after the Resurrection[3].

[1645] Reviewing the Synoptic use of προσκυνέω we see that Matthew is alone in using the dative to describe people as prostrating themselves before Jesus. Mark never uses it thus except to describe an act of mockery, and Luke never at all—his reason perhaps being indicated by Peter's words to Cornelius, when the latter had fallen and "worshipped" in the Acts, "Rise up, I also am a man[4]." The Epistles avoid the word: it is not used in any of them (outside quotations) except once to describe a man suddenly converted "He will fall down on his face and worship God[5]." On the other hand, we have found the accusative used once by Matthew and Luke to describe the actual worship of God; once by Mark, probably, to describe the worship of the Son of the Most High; once by an early tradition in Luke to describe the worship of the risen Saviour.

[1646] These facts, so far as they go—suggesting that the Synoptists reserve the accusative for the worship due to God or to God's Son—contrast with the use in the LXX illustrated above, and still more with the use in Revelation which remains to be mentioned. The accusative is used in that book no less than six times to denote the worship of "the Beast" or of devils[6]. Both grammar and history, on this point, might be

---

[1] Mt. xviii. 26.   [2] Mt. xxviii. 9.
[3] Mt. xx. 20, xxviii. 17.
[4] [1645 a] Acts x. 25: Προσκυνέω occurs also in Acts viii. 27, xxiv. 11 (absol.) of going up to Jerusalem to "worship," and vii. 43 προσκυνεῖν αὐτοῖς (an addition to Amos v. 26) of idolatry.
[5] 1 Cor. xiv. 25. In Heb. i. 6, xi. 21 it is either quoted or allusively used.
[6] Rev. ix. 20 "devils," xiii. 8, 12, xiv. 9, 11, xx. 4.

illustrated by a letter from Tiridates to Nero, who is generally supposed to have been "the Beast" mentioned in Revelation: "I came unto thee, [as being] my God, to worship thee even as the [God] Mithras[1]." The Greeks would speak of the worship of the Emperor in the Greek form (*i.e.* with the accusative) and the author of Revelation (or of portions of it) might sometimes adopt the Gentile phrase in speaking of Gentile idolatry, while at other times he might employ the construction most usual in Jewish Greek.

(iv) Προσκυνέω in John.

[1647] Coming to the use of the word in the Fourth Gospel, we find it with the dative describing the man born blind "worshipping" Jesus[2], and used absolutely concerning "Greeks," who "went up to worship at the feast[3]." In the Samaritan narrative, where the verb is frequent, it has been noted above (1640) that the accusative comes twice after two instances of the dative. That passage also attributes to Jesus language ("salvation," "the Jews," "we worship that which we know") quite inconsistent with His character and language as elsewhere represented in this Gospel. It would seem to be more appropriate to the Samaritan woman mimicking the dogmatism of Jewish Rabbis: "Ye [Samaritans] worship that which ye know not: we [Jews] worship that which we know, because salvation is from the Jews." Origen's long discussion of the context, and his brief allusion[4] to the views of a writer earlier than Heracleon, shew that in

---

[1] [1646 a] Wetst. (on Jn xx. 28) "Dio 63. Tiridates ad Neronem, ἐγὼ πρός σε ἦλθον τὸν ἐμὸν θεόν, προσκυνήσων σε ὡς καὶ τὸν Μίθρην."

[2] Jn ix. 38 (D αὐτόν).

[3] Jn xii. 20. The verb is also used absolutely in the Samaritan dialogue, iv. 20 (*bis*), 24.

[4] [1647 a] Huet ii. 211 D Πολὺ δέ ἐστι νῦν παρατίθεσθαι τοῦ Ἡρακλέωνος τὰ ῥητά, ἀπὸ τοῦ ἐπιγεγραμμένου Πέτρου Κηρύγματος παραλαμβανόμενα... διόπερ ἑκόντες ὑπερτιθέμεθα, ταῦτα μόνον ἐπισημειούμενοι.... This appears to mean "*It is [too] much at this point to quote* from Heracleon the [exact] sayings, alleged from the [work] entitled Peter's Preaching... wherefore we deliberately pass them over, noting these alone...." The Latin, instead of "[too] much" has "longe melius."

very early times indeed the whole of the passage caused difficulty. Origen's words even suggest that Heracleon had before him (or thought he had) some tradition that interpreted "*Ye* [worship that which ye know not]" as "*ye Jews*[1]."

---

[1] [1647 *b*] Origen's text at this point is full of corruptions as indicated by Huet's margin, and Heracleon's views do not come out very definitely. But Origen clearly accuses Heracleon of having "accepted the word ὑμεῖς in an eccentric way and inconsistently with the context (ἰδίως καὶ παρὰ τὴν ἀκολουθίαν τῶν ῥητῶν...ἐκδεξάμενος)." Then follow these words, in which I bracket what appear to be corrupt: Τὸ, Ὑμεῖς ἀντὶ τοῦ Ἰουδαῖοι, [ἐθνικοί], διηγήσατο· οἷον δέ ἐστι πρὸς τὴν Σαμαρεῖτιν λέγεσθαι, ''Ὑμεῖς οἱ Ἰουδαῖοι' [ἢ πρὸς Σαμαρεῖτιν, Ὑμεῖς οἱ ἐθνικοί]; "He explained the word 'You' as being instead of the word Jews [Gentiles]. But how absurd it is that it should be said to the Samaritan, Ye Jews [or to a Samaritan, Ye Gentiles]!"

[1647 *c*] All this confusion can be explained on the hypothesis that Heracleon had before him a tradition arranging the words as part of the Samaritan's speech thus "Our fathers worshipped in this mountain and ye say, [that] '*In Jerusalem is the place where one must worship. Ye [Samaritans] worship ye know not what, we [Jews] worship that which we know, because salvation is from the Jews.*'" Heracleon regarded the words "Ye worship" as uttered by the Samaritan, not in the character of a Jewish Rabbi but in her own person against the Jewish Rabbis. "Ye" therefore seemed to him to stand "*in the place of the word Jews* (ἀντὶ τοῦ Ἰ.)." [Comp. Eustath. on *Iliad* i. 117, τὸ "ἢ ἀπολέσθαι" ἀντὶ τοῦ "ἤπερ."] This was very natural—so far. And, if we read on and ask how Heracleon explained "salvation to come from the Jews," we find him saying that salvation (Huet ii. 213 B—C) "came to pass in the Judaean [land] but was *not in [the Jews] them[selves]* (ἀλλ' οὐκ ἐν αὐτοῖς)," and also "From that nation salvation *came forth* and the Word [came] into the world." In other words, he seems to say that salvation did *not* belong to the Jews but "*came forth from them*" *in order to pass to others.*

[1647 *d*] It is not at all certain that this is Heracleon's meaning, or that Origen represents Heracleon rightly, or that Origen's present text represents Origen rightly. But the hypothesis of transposition of persons goes some way toward explaining the undoubted fact that Origen discerns in Heracleon's rendering of "ye" "inconsistency with the context." As for the words I have bracketed in Origen, they appear to have been added by some editor that took ἀντί to mean "*instead of*" in the sense of "*a mistake for*," so that a blank seemed to need filling ("He interpreted the word 'ye' as meaning, instead of Jews——"). Then he filled the blank suitably by adding "Gentiles" and adapted the context.

[1648] A very ancient tradition is quoted by Heracleon from the Preaching of Peter to this effect: " Peter taught that one ought not to worship after the manner of the (?) Greeks[1]... serving stocks and stones, nor to pay one's devotions to the Divine Being after the manner of the Jews since they, *while supposing themselves to be alone in the knowledge of God*, are ignorant of Him, serving angels, and the month, and the moon[2]." Heracleon seems to have quoted this as bearing on the words in the Samaritan Dialogue " *We* (ἡμεῖς)—*i.e.* we as distinct from others—worship that which we know." In any case, this extract certainly confirms the view that the words "*we* know" were uttered by the Samaritan in the character of a Jewish teacher and not by our Lord in His own person[3]. The extract also illustrates the possibility of a reference to twofold worship, suggested by the twofold construction of the verb, in the passage under consideration.

[1649] The Jews thought it essential to prostrate themselves before God in Jerusalem, the Samaritans in Mount Gerizim: Jesus—who, even when He prays, is not described in this Gospel as " praying (προσεύχομαι) " or as using the word " pray "—cuts at the root of all local worship and even of all rules about external attitudes of worship, by first denying the claims of both mountains, and then indicating that the Person worshipped is " the Father " towards whom " prostration " would be out of place: " Believe me, woman, that the hour cometh when neither in this mountain nor in Jerusalem shall

---

[1] [1648 a] Huet ii. 211 E. Πέτρου διδάξαντος μὴ δεῖν καθελεῖν ἃς (marg. κατ' ἐθνικούς, I suggest καθ' Ἕλληνας) προσκυνεῖν τὰ τῆς ὕλης πράγματα ἀποδεχομένους, καὶ λατρεύοντας ξύλοις καὶ λίθοις, μήτε κατὰ Ἰουδαίους σέβειν τὸ θεῖον, ἐπείπερ καὶ αὐτοὶ μόνοι οἰόμενοι ἐπίστασθαι θεὸν ἀγνοοῦσιν αὐτόν, λατρεύοντες ἀγγέλοις καὶ μηνὶ καὶ σελήνῃ.

[2] [1648 b] "The month." Comp. Gal. iv. 10 "ye observe days and months," Col. ii. 16 " Let no man judge you...in respect of a feast day or a new moon or a sabbath."

[3] Comp. Rom. ii. 17 "Thou bearest the name of a Jew...and gloriest in God and *knowest* his will."

ye prostrate yourselves before the Father." Then He continues[1], still using the Jewish idiom, but qualifying it so as to non-literalise its meaning: "Nay, the hour cometh, and now is, when the true worshippers shall prostrate themselves before the Father [not in Gerizim or Jerusalem and not in any literal sense, but] in spirit and truth."

[1650] Now, having extended the area of what was once mere Jewish and Samaritan "prostration" in Jewish and Samaritan sanctuaries, and having made it coequal with the area of "spirit and truth," the Dialogue proceeds, as in the Temptation, to drop the Jewish phrase (with the dative) and to take up the Greek or cosmopolitan one (with the accusative). Only the Evangelist has to bear in mind that the Greek phrase with the accusative was frequently applied to the polytheistic worship of "a god" or "gods." Hence, he not only repeats "the Father" but also defines "the [one] God," as being "Spirit," thus: "For such doth the Father seek to worship him (accus.). The [one] God is Spirit [not limited by place nor one that requires prostrations at his feet] and they that worship him (accus.) must worship in spirit and truth."

[1651] According to this view, there is here, as also in the Temptation, a deliberate differentiation of two Greek constructions capable of representing various distinctions according to the nationality or individuality of the writer. But both in the Temptation and in the Samaritan Dialogue

---

[1] [1649 a] "Continues," *i.e.* if the words "Ye worship...from the Jews" are transposed (as above suggested) and assigned to the Samaritan as personating a Jewish character. Origen says (Huet ii. 209 B—C) "The phrase, '*The hour cometh*' is written twice, and, in the first instance, '*and now is*' is not added: but in the second *the Evangelist says 'Nay the hour cometh and now is.*'" But I do not understand him to mean that these last words (iv. 23—4) are Evangelistic comment. If they were, the accusative might be explained on that ground, as proceeding from the Evangelist and not from Jesus, and as being in a different style. But there are many reasons against this.

the Evangelists appear to use προσκυνέω with the accusative as meaning such worship as ought to be paid to God alone, *i.e.* not prostration but "reverence," which the Hebrews called "fear"—"Thou shalt *fear* the Lord thy God and him alone shalt thou serve." This verb "fear" had been actually paraphrased (**1643** *a*) by Matthew and Luke as "worship" (in the Greek idiom). Possibly John has in mind the Deuteronomic saying about "fear" and its Evangelistic paraphrase as "worship": and this is all the more probable as he says that "perfect love casteth out fear[1]." But in any case we are safe in asserting that John is here using two different forms of the same phrase with differences of meaning, in an attempt to represent the Lord as raising men's hearts from formal to spiritual worship.

§ 7. "*Going away (or, back),*" *and* "*going (on a journey)*[2]"

(i) Ὑπάγω *and* πορεύομαι.

[**1652**] The importance of the distinction between these two words consists mainly in their application by our Lord to

---

[1] 1 Jn iv. 18.

[2] [**1652** *a*] Ὑπάγω, in Jn, mostly = "go back (or, home)": πορεύομαι = "go (on a journey)." In contexts specifying an errand or place, ὑπάγω, in Jn, means simply "go away," as in (ix. 7) "*Go away,* wash in the pool of Siloam" (rep. ix. 11) and perhaps in xxi. 3 ὑπάγω ἁλιεύειν (unless it implies *resuming* a former occupation). Elsewhere "home" may be implied in "going back," as in (iv. 16) "*Go home,* call thy husband," (vi. 67) "Do ye also desire *to go to your homes?*" (xviii. 8) "Let these *go to their several homes,*" (xi. 44) "Loose him and let him *go home.*" In vi. 21 "to the land to which *they were making their way* (ὑπῆγον)" may refer to Capernaum as a home, or simply to the Western coast to which they were "going back." In vii. 3 "*Go* (ὕπαγε) into Judaea," the meaning may be "go back," as it certainly is in xi. 8, "*Dost thou go back* (ὑπάγεις) again there," *i.e.* into Judaea.

[**1652** *b*] In xii. 11 (R.V.) "By reason of him [*i.e.* Lazarus] (δι' αὐτόν) many of the Jews *went away* (ὑπῆγον) and believed (ἐπίστευον) on Jesus," the meaning of ὑπῆγον depends on the meaning of δι' αὐτόν. If δι' αὐτόν,

Himself, ὑπάγω, "go away," being frequently thus used throughout the whole of the Gospel, but πορεύομαι, "go on a journey," being sometimes used by Him along with ὑπάγω in His Last Discourse. The question is, What distinction, if any, is intended to be drawn between them[1]?

(ii) Why Luke avoids ὑπάγω.

[1653] The first point to notice is that ὑπάγω, both in the LXX and in the Synoptic Gospels, appears to have been what may be called a "debateable" word, *i.e.* a word preferred by some and disliked and deliberately altered by others. In canon. LXX it occurs only once[2] (Ex. xiv. 21) "The Lord *caused* the sea *to go* [*back*]," ὑπήγαγεν. But in Tobit, ℵ has it four times in the sense of "go home," whereas B has, in one of these instances, πορεύομαι, and in others no certain equivalent[3]. Precisely the same phenomenon, only on a larger scale, meets us in the Synoptists. In the first four

in Jn, could mean "by reason of something *in the past* concerning him," then it might mean here "on account of the raising of Lazarus," and ὑπῆγον κ. ἐπίστευον might be rendered "were in the habit of going away to their several homes and believing as a consequence of a visit to Lazarus in Bethany." But διά τινα in Jn appears generally (**1884** *a*, *b*) to mean "for the sake of a person, with reference to the *future*": and in the preceding context (xii. 9), διὰ τὸν Ἰησοῦν, "*for the sake of* Jesus," means "*for the sake of seeing* Jesus." Hence xii. 11 must probably be rendered "Many, for the sake of [seeing] him [*i.e.* Lazarus], *used to go away* [*from their party*, or, *from Jerusalem*]...." In xii. 9 it is said that "many *came* (ἦλθαν)...to see Lazarus"; now it is implied that although the rulers of the Jews discouraged visits to Bethany the temptation to see Lazarus was so great that "many" from time to time slipped away, or deserted their party for the sake of seeing him, and, if they did see him, they always used to believe.

[1] [1652 *c*] Before the Last Discourse our Lord never says πορεύομαι, except in the preface to the Raising of Lazarus, where the words (xi. 11) "I *go* to awake him [*i.e.* Lazarus]" presumably refer (at least primarily) to a literal journey into Judaea.

[2] Setting aside Jerem. xxxvi. 19 (ℵ*) ὑπάγεις for ὑμεῖς.

[3] [1653 *a*] Tob. viii. 21 ὕπαγε ὑγιαίνων πρὸς τὸν πατέρα σου, B πορεύεσθαι μετὰ ὑγείας, x. 11 and xii. 5 (ℵ) ὑγιαίνων ὕπαγε (B om.), x. 12 ὕπαγε πρὸς τὸν πενθερόν σου (B τίμα τοὺς π. σου).

instances where Mark uses ὑπάγω (followed twice by Matthew) Luke has severally ἀπελθών, πορεύου, ὑπόστρεφε, and πορεύου[1]. In the Riding into Jerusalem, Luke, for once, follows Mark[2] (and that too, against Matthew); but afterwards Luke substitutes severally εἰσελθόντων and πορεύεται[3]. The last of these instances is of particular importance because it is uttered by our Lord about Himself, "The Son of man *goeth home* (or, *back*) (ὑπάγει) even as it is written concerning him," where Luke has, "The Son of man *goeth* (πορεύεται) according to that which is decreed[4]."

[1654] The reasons for Luke's dislike of the word may be inferred from any good Greek Dictionary; for it would shew that, when intransitive, ὑπάγω may mean quite opposite motions, such as "go back," "go quietly, or slowly, away," "go on," or "come on" (in the sense of our vernacular "come up!" or "cheer up!"). All these are exclusive of its transitive meanings. Luke, therefore, may have been quite justified in altering a word endeared to some by its use in the vernacular Greek Gospel, but liable to ambiguity and perhaps not used among the educated as Mark uses it. The naturalness of such an alteration confirms the conclusion suggested by the agreement of Mark and Matthew, namely, that our Lord was reported in the earlier Greek Gospels to have said about Himself "The Son of Man *goeth away, goeth back*, or *goeth home* (ὑπάγει)" and that Luke changed this into "goeth (on a journey) (πορεύεται)."

(iii) Ὑπάγω, "*go home.*"

[1655] John's first use of ὑπάγω is in a saying of our Lord about the New Birth (iii. 8), "thou knowest not whence it cometh nor whither it *goeth away*, or *goeth back* (ὑπάγει)." He is speaking about the *Pneuma*, Breath, or Holy Spirit. Playing on the word as though it were God's breath on earth,

---

[1] Mk i. 44, ii. 11, v. 19, 34 and parall. Mt.-Lk.
[2] Mk xi. 2 (where Mt. has πορεύεσθε).   [3] Mk xiv. 13, 21.
[4] Mk xiv. 21, Mt. xxvi. 24, Lk. xxii. 22.

the wind, He says "It breatheth, or bloweth, where it willeth, and thou hearest the voice, or sound, thereof." So far it might mean "wind"—though *Pneuma* would very rarely be used in this sense. But then, after describing its mysterious motion, He says, "So, *i.e.* equally mysterious to thee, is every one that is begotten of the *Pneuma*"—and the Rabbi at once perceives that Jesus means "Spirit" now, and perhaps meant it before. Probably He included the two meanings, since men live amid the motions and voices of *Pneuma* in both senses and are equally ignorant of their sources and tendencies. Compare this passage with (vii. 33) "I *go back* (ὑπάγω) to him that sent me," and with (viii. 14) "I know whence I came and whither I *go back* (ὑπάγω), but ye know not whence I am coming and whither I *go back*." It appears from these passages that as the Breath or Spirit of God may be regarded as exhaled when it comes forth to men and inhaled when it goes back to God, so the Word or Son of God is regarded as "coming" when He is manifested to men as beginning to do a work appointed by the Father, and as "going back" to the Father when He is manifested to men as having accomplished the work[1].

[1656] In the First Epistle of John it is said, "He that

---

[1] [1655 *a*] We might speak similarly of the "waters" of God, which "come" as rain and "go back" partly as clouds, partly as trees, grass, corn. These, in turn, in the shape of decaying vegetation, "go back" directly to their Mother. Or else, as pasture, they "go back" indirectly, helping the animal world to "go back" in a corresponding way, *i.e.* to make its return, or pay its offering, to Nature. Comp. Is. lv. 1—11 "Come ye to the waters...as the rain cometh down and the snow from heaven and returneth not thither but watereth the earth and maketh it bring forth and bud and giveth seed to the sower and bread to the eater, *so shall my word be that goeth forth out of my mouth: it shall not return unto me void, but it shall accomplish that which I please, and it shall prosper in the thing whereto I sent it.*" In Ps. civ. 29—30 the same Hebrew word "spirit" or "breath," LXX πνεῦμα, is repeated, "Thou gatherest *their spirit*, they die...thou sendest forth *thy spirit*, they are created."

hateth his brother is in the darkness and walketh (περιπατεῖ) in the darkness and knoweth not where he *goeth* [*to his goal*] (ὑπάγει)[1]"; and the Gospel appears to suggest a similar ignorance of the "goal" of man's life as being implied in the inability of the Pharisees to understand where the Son is "going home," or "going to his goal." Perhaps their minds were fixed on another notion of "going home" which is set forth thus in the Jewish Prayer Book: "Know whence thou camest and whither thou art going, and before whom thou wilt in future have to give account and reckoning. Whence thou camest:—from a putrefying drop; whither thou art going:—to a place of dust, worms and maggots; and before whom thou wilt in future have to give account and reckoning:—before the Supreme King of kings, the Holy One, blessed be he[2]."

[1657] But a Jewish Teacher of the first century, commenting on the question of the Angel to Hagar, "*Whence comest thou and whither goest thou* (πορεύῃ)?" says that it is the voice of Conviction and that it is a reproach addressed to the wandering soul that has deserted the service of the Higher and Sovereign Purpose. And he adds expressly that this poor vagrant's "*going* (πορεύομαι)" is indefinite: "Thou art chasing after uncertainties, rejecting acknowledged truths[3]." John, in the Gospel as well as in the Epistle, seems to distinguish this mere "going (πορεύομαι)" from the "going home (ὑπάγω)" of a child of God, begotten of God and returning to God. The "home" is the love of God, and the way to it is the love of man. Those who will not receive the Spirit of God have no conception of the "home" or the

---

[1] [1656 a] 1 Jn ii. 11. So Westc. *ad loc.*, "the final goal (*knoweth not whither*) to which life is directed." But I cannot reconcile this with a note of his on the same page, "ὑπάγει, *goeth*. The idea is not that of proceeding to a definite point (πορεύεσθαι) but of leaving the present scene."

[2] Jewish Prayer Book, ed. Singer pp. 190—1, quoting *Aboth* iii. 1.

[3] Philo i. 576.

way to it. Concerning these Jesus says, at the close of His Gospel, what perhaps is, in effect, (xii. 35) " He that walketh in the darkness knoweth not *his way home* ($\pi o\hat{v}\ \dot{v}\pi\acute{a}\gamma\epsilon\iota$)." Concerning Jesus Himself, His Gospel having been now preached, the Evangelist says, first, "Now before the feast of the Passover, Jesus, knowing that the hour had come that he should pass away ($\mu\epsilon\tau a\beta\hat{\eta}$) from this world to the Father," and then, " Knowing that the Father had given all things into his hands and that from God he had come forth, and to God *he was going home* ($\dot{v}\pi\acute{a}\gamma\epsilon\iota$)[1]"—and then follows the account of the Washing of Feet, the legacy of Christ's example bequeathed to the Disciples.

[1658] We see then that in this last passage the Evangelist, after describing the impending death in his own words as a " passage to the Father," adds clauses to shew the full trust reposed by the Father in the Son, and concludes with the word used previously by our Lord about Himself (*"he was going home"*). From henceforth, Christ is represented as using the word repeatedly, at first without any suggestion of the goal or object of the "going back" or "going home," and as it were provoking the Disciples to ask Him what the goal may be. "Whither I *go home* ye cannot come," "Whither I *go home*, ye know the way," " I *go home* and I come to you[2]." Towards the end of the Discourse, He becomes more definite: " But now I *go home* unto him that sent me[3]," and, strangely enough—though one of the Disciples has expressly uttered the question " Whither goest thou home?[4]"—He says, " None of you asketh me, Whither goest thou home?[5]" Finally He declares, " I *go home* to the Father[6]."

(iv) Ὑπάγω applied to the Disciples.

[1659] Before comparing these passages with others (in

---

[1] xiii. 1—3.   [2] xiii. 33, xiv. 4, 28.   [3] xvi. 5.
[4] xiii. 36.   [5] xvi. 5.   [6] xvi. 10.

the same Discourse) in which Jesus speaks of "going" to the Father, it will be well to mention one in which ὑπάγω is used by Him about the Disciples, (xv. 16) "Ye chose not me but I chose you and set (ἔθηκα) you *that ye may go* (ἵνα ὑμεῖς ὑπάγητε) and may bear fruit and that your fruit may remain." On this Chrysostom says, "*I set you*, that is, planted (ἐφύτευσα)"; and then, "*That ye may go* (he still keeps the metaphor of the vine), that is, that ye may be stretched out (ἐκταθῆτε)[1]." But this rendering "*stretched out*," i.e. "*may grow*," "*make progress*," is against the regular Johannine usage, of which, as we have seen, there are many instances. Hence most modern commentators render it "That ye *may go away from me* and bear fruit," *i.e.* may go forth as missionaries. But does this, as Chrysostom says, "still keep the metaphor"? Is it not contrary to the whole drift of Johannine thought, which represents the Disciples as unable to "bear fruit" unless they "*abide in*" Christ, or "*abide in*" the Vine? If ὑπάγω had to be taken of literal motion, would it not mean in this Gospel, not "go abroad," but "go away to your homes," as it means when Jesus says to the Twelve "Do ye also desire to *go away* from me?" Lastly, would it not be a curious mixture of metaphor ("bear fruit") and literalism ("go away to the cities of Israel")?

[1660] For these reasons the best explanation is perhaps a modification of Chrysostom's, based, not solely on the metaphor of the Vine, but also on the whole Johannine conception of "*going home*" *as being the appointed errand of the grain of corn, and the vine-branch, and the human soul, and the Incarnate Logos.* All these "came forth from God" and are bound by the Law of their Nature to "go back home to God." As the Spirit (**1655**) "goes home," so they that are

---

[1] [1659 a] Chrys. refers to Ps. lxxx. 11 "she stretched out (ἐξέτεινε) her branches." On τίθημι, "set," and very probably interpreted correctly by Chrys. as "plant," see **1336** *e*. It might include "grafting."

born of the Spirit "go home" when they have done their work on earth. Yet, even before they are "at home with the Lord" (as St Paul says) in heaven, they are "at home" with Him on earth, "abiding in" the Vine. There *is*, therefore, a confusion of metaphor in a literal sense, but it is a deliberate confusion, such as we find in the statements that the Father "is in" the Son and the Son "is in" the Father. The meaning probably is, not, "that ye may go away from me to Joppa, Antioch, or Ephesus," but "that ye may *go home* with me by the way of the Cross to the Father in heaven."

(v) Πορεύομαι substituted for ὑπάγω.

[1661] There remains the most difficult passage of all, in which the Saviour gives up, for a time, ὑπάγω, and substitutes πορεύομαι, "*go (on a journey)*." Most unfortunately, the interpretation of it is complicated by the context, in which the words ordinarily rendered "I should have said [it] to you *because*" (εἶπον ἂν ὑμῖν ὅτι) may mean—and (it will be maintained later on) probably do mean—"I should have said to you *that*." Moreover the passage is full of emotion that is reflected in the style. As Jesus elsewhere says that He came not to judge the world but adds "Yea, and even if I should judge (καὶ ἐὰν κρίνω δὲ ἐγώ), my judgment is true[1]," so here, He seems to say "I do not admit that I am going from you; I do not admit that there is any need to prepare a place for you in my Father's House where I have supreme authority and where there is room for all. I am not '*going on a journey* (πορεύομαι),' I am *going home* (ὑπάγω)." Then, like a mother with very young children, He instructs their ignorance by dropping into their way of speaking: "But even if I should '*go on a journey*,' and even if I should '*prepare a place for you*,' yet where is the harm? I will come again and receive you to myself[2]."

[1662] From this point onward, to the close of the

---

[1] viii. 16.   [2] xiv. 2—3. See **2186** foll.

Discourse, Jesus occasionally uses πορεύομαι, "I go (on a journey)," and ἀπέρχομαι, "I go away" in His efforts to comfort and fortify the Disciples against the impending assault[1]. This "going (on a journey)," He says, "will be profitable" for them. It will strengthen the believer: (xiv. 12) "Greater works than these shall he do because I *go* (πορεύομαι) to the Father," (xiv. 28) "Ye have heard that I said to you 'I *go home* (ὑπάγω) and come [again] to you. If ye loved me ye would have rejoiced that I *go* (πορεύομαι) to the Father, for the Father is greater than I," (xvi. 5—7) "I *go home* (ὑπάγω) to him that sent me: and none of you asketh me 'Where *goest thou home*?' But, because I have said these things to you, the sorrow [thereof] hath filled your heart. But I tell you the truth: it is profitable for you that I *go away* (ἀπέλθω). For, if I go not away, the Paraclete will assuredly not come unto you. But if I *go* (πορευθῶ) I will send him unto you"; (xvi. 28—9) "I came forth from the Father and have come into the world: again I leave the world and *go* (πορεύομαι) to the Father."

[1663] This is the Lord's last word about "going" or "going home," and it will be noted that He ends with the former, the word (so to speak) of the Disciples, not the word that He generally chooses for Himself. On hearing it, the Disciples joyfully exclaim (xvi. 29) "Now speakest thou plainly" as though now they understood everything. But He at once dashes down their joy: "Do ye now believe? Behold the hour cometh and hath come that ye should be scattered every man to his own and leave me alone." Clearly, if Christ intended to strengthen the Disciples by predicting to them the immediate future and by preparing them to stand by His side before Pilate as fellow-martyrs, He did not succeed. But the impression left on us by these mysterious interchanges of

---

[1] So perhaps St Paul says that he, like a nurse, uses babe language to the new converts, 1 Thess. ii. 7, reading νήπιοι.

synonymous phrases of departure is that the Evangelist felt that the departing was partly objective, partly subjective, and that the Lord Himself could not succeed, and did not wish to succeed, in doing more than prepare the Disciples ultimately to realise the nature of the "going" and of the "going home" and the "profitableness" of the "going away."

[1664] Logically, or spiritually, one might argue that, if Peter had not denied his Master but had faced Caiaphas and Pilate by His side, there would have been, in one sense, no "going away" of the Lord, no severance (for him) from his Master, not even when Jesus breathed His last upon the Cross. For the eye and ear and hand of faith, Jesus would still have been present, still speaking, still to be "handled." But this was not decreed. It was not given to any man to pass into the higher life save through the shadow of death; and this shadow was to be cast, partly on the minds of the Disciples, partly on the Logos Himself, so there was indeed an actual "*going away*" as well as a "*going home*[1]."

On the difference between ἀγαπάω and φιλέω, see **1716** *d—f* and **1728** *m—p*; ἀληθής and ἀληθινός, see **1727** *d—i*; ἀποστέλλω and πέμπω, see **1723** *d—g*; διάκονος and δοῦλος, see **1717** *d—g* and **1723** *i*; πράσσω and ποιέω, see **1772** *b*; and for other synonyms see Verbal Index in Part II.

---

[1] [1664 a] In the Acts of John (§ 12) (ed. James) the beloved disciple, weeping on the Mount of Olives, is represented as actually hearing Christ's voice there, while He is hanging on the Cross below: but this is obtained by a complete surrender of reality in the Passion. The passage illustrates early Gnostic thoughts, of which the beginnings were probably often present to the mind of the author of the Fourth Gospel: "John"—says the Lord's voice—"unto the multitude down below in Jerusalem I am being crucified and pierced with lances and reeds, and they are giving me gall and vinegar to drink: but unto thee I am speaking, and hearken thou to what I say."

BOOK II

JOHANNINE AND SYNOPTIC DISAGREEMENTS

CHAPTER I

JOHANNINE DEVIATIONS FROM SYNOPTIC VOCABULARY

§ 1. *Introductory remarks*

[**1665**] In order to use to the best advantage the following English alphabetical list placed here for future reference as well as for an immediate cursory glance, the reader should bear in mind that this Vocabulary deals almost entirely with such words as are *common to the Three Synoptists* but omitted or rarely used by John[1]. It omits, for example, the words "blessed," "confess," "devil[2]," "judge," because they are not used by Mark. These must be deferred till we discuss the vocabulary of the Double Tradition of Matthew and Luke in its relation to that of John.

[**1666**] This greatly restricts the scope of the present list which, at the first glance, seems to teach us little but what we knew before, namely, that John excludes from his Gospel a great deal that may have interested the Churches in Galilee and Jerusalem in the last half of the first century much more

---

[1] Occasionally the Vocabulary will give a typical word used by two of the Synoptists and not by Jn, *e.g.* "to make common," used by Mk-Mt. but not by Lk. See **1671** *c*.

[2] [**1665** *a*] *i.e.* διάβολος, "*the* devil." Δαιμόνιον "*a* devil," in the sense of an "unclean spirit," is freq. in Mk. "Blessed," μακάριος (not εὐλογημένος etc.) is denoted above.

than it appealed to the churches of Asia Minor, and to the Roman world in general—and perhaps, in particular, to fairly educated inquirers after moral truth, such as the followers of Epictetus—at the beginning of the second century. Under the heading "devils," for example, we note without surprise that John omits all reference to "casting them out." Many, too, will be prepared to find in his Gospel no mention of several forms of disease such as "leprosy," "deafness," "dumbness," and "paralysis." His desire to subordinate the individuality of John the Baptist to his instrumentality in testifying to Christ will also explain why he is silent about "Herod Antipas" and his brother "Philip." For this, and for other reasons, "divorce" and "adultery" (which are connected directly with the names of these two princes and indirectly with the murder of John the Baptist) are nowhere mentioned by him. Even the distinctive names of "Sadducees," "Scribes," and "Publicans"—so important to Jews—nowhere find mention in his cosmopolitan Gospel.

[1667] At these omissions we cannot be surprised, and we learn comparatively little from them. We learn more from the absence of words denoting special sins or temptations—for example, "hypocrite" and "hypocrisy," "rich," "riches," "possessions," "money," "treasure," and the word "temptation" itself. And, as we proceed in our examination, we find omissions of such a kind as to convince us that they do not in all cases indicate omission of the subject but only variation in the manner of expressing it. For example, it has been pointed out that the Fourth Gospel does not contain the words "repent," "repentance," "forgiveness," "watch" and "pray." But who can believe that the author did not recognise the necessity of these things, and the necessity that every Gospel should indirectly, if not directly, inculcate them?

[1668] It would not be easy always to distinguish those things which John really omits from those things which he expresses variously; still less would it be possible to assign in each case his motive for the omission or variation of expression. But an attempt has been made in several instances to indicate, in footnotes to the following lists, the Johannine substitute for a Synoptic word, and, in some few instances, to suggest the motive. Generally, we may say that John prefers to pass over local distinctions of sects, classes, and rulers, material distinctions of physical evil, and moral distinctions of various sins, in order to concentrate the mind on the elements of the spiritual world, light and darkness, spiritual life and death, truth and falsehood. Comparisons and discussions as to "greatest" or "least," and even the mention of the "little ones" so common in the Synoptic Gospels, are absent here. The word "righteous" is never used except in the words, "O righteous Father." The Synoptists contrast the "old" and the "new": the latest Gospel never uses the word "old." The Synoptists frequently represent Jesus as "rebuking," "commanding," "having compassion," "being filled with indignation": John dispenses with these words, mostly thinking it enough to say that Jesus "said," or "spake," or "did" this or that, and leaving the words and deeds of the Messiah to speak for themselves[1].

[1669] Apart from these general Johannine equivalents, it is occasionally possible to point out the definite Johannine equivalent of a Synoptic term. For example, instead of the word "parable ($\pi\alpha\rho\alpha\beta o\lambda\eta$)" John uses "proverb ($\pi\alpha\rho o\iota\mu\iota\alpha$)," (rendered by some, "dark saying"); and instead of "mighty works ($\delta\upsilon\nu\alpha\mu\epsilon\iota\varsigma$)" he uses "signs ($\sigma\eta\mu\epsilon\hat{\iota}\alpha$)." In the footnotes to these terms in the several English Vocabularies in which they appear the reader will find explanations of these

---

[1] [1668 a] In the case of Lazarus, the Lord's "friend," John describes an affection and a mysterious "self-troubling" of the Lord accompanied with tears; and on two other occasions he mentions "trouble" (1727 b); but this is exceptional.

deviations. The motive, in both cases, seems to have been a desire to prevent spiritual truth from being buried under religious technical terms or obscured by heated discussions that had attached themselves to special terms. And in making the second of these two changes (the change of "mighty work" to "sign") John is consistent throughout his Gospel. For he avoids the word δύναμις not only when meaning a "mighty work," but also in the sense of "power." He abstains also from the kindred word "powerful," and from the synonymous words "strength" and "strong." He seems to desire to shew that heavenly power is far above mere "might" and deserves a higher name. Accordingly, he calls it by the term discussed in a previous chapter (**1562-94**), "authority."

[**1670**] These remarks will suffice to guard the reader against being misled by a mere statistical and superficial view of the words and numbers in the appended Vocabulary. The words are sometimes grouped together to prevent such a danger. For example, under the head of "faith" it will be found that, although John never uses this noun, he compensates for it by using the verb, "have faith," or "believe," far more often than the Synoptists. Similarly, lest the reader should be misled by being told that Luke never uses the noun "Gospel (εὐαγγέλιον)," it will be pointed out that he uses the verb "evangelize," or "preach the Gospel (εὐαγγελίζω)" with a compensating frequency.

[**1671**] As a rule, where a word is only once or twice used by one Evangelist and often used by other Evangelists, the one or two passages are quoted in a footnote. Thus, under the word "angels," a footnote, giving the three instances of Johannine use, shews that it is only once used in an utterance of our Lord, and there about angels "ascending and descending on the Son of man"—a different aspect from any mentioned by the Synoptists. So, another note on "children," giving all the Johannine uses of the word, suggests a parallelism between John's tradition about "becoming children of God" and Matthew's tradition about "turning and becoming as children." On every page, facts will be alleged, and passages quoted, to shew how unsafe it is to draw an inference from rarity of usage in one Gospel, and from frequency of usage in others, without some reference to the passages themselves[1].

---

[1] [1671 a] The need of discrimination in dealing with the statistical results of the following Vocabulary may be illustrated by the facts collected under the words (1) "Astonish(ment)" and (2) "Twelve, the."

(1) Several of the words used by the Synoptists apparently in a good sense to express the amazement or astonishment of the multitude at Christ's miracles are altogether omitted by Jn; and he nowhere applies any such word to our Lord Himself (as the Synoptists do). Jn does use one of these words ($\theta\alpha\nu\mu\acute{\alpha}\zeta\omega$) rather frequently. But *it will be shewn that he appears to use it in a bad sense, to describe unintelligent surprise.*

[1671 b] (2) "The Twelve" are mentioned—as will be shewn by the note—four times by Jn, but always in connexion with some mention of treachery, possible desertion, or unbelief. Again, whereas Matthew (x. 40, and sim. Lk. x. 16) represents Jesus as saying, apparently to the Twelve, "He that receiveth *you* receiveth me," Jn, in the corresponding saying, instead of "*you*," has (xiii. 20) "*whomsoever I shall send.*" Also, while omitting the names of many of the Twelve as given (with some variations) by the Synoptists, Jn records the calling of Nathanael, and his subsequent presence at the Eucharist of the Seven, in such a way as to suggest that he must have been if not identical, at all events on a level, with one of the Synoptic Twelve. These facts seem to point to *some* consistent purpose, although its exact nature (whether supplementary, or corrective, or both) may be difficult to determine. In any case the fact remains that the Johannine mentions of "the Twelve" are divergent from those of the Synoptists, except where the latter use the phrase "Judas one of the Twelve."

[1671 c] As the first Vocabulary is constructed largely for the purpose of giving an English reader a general view of the Gospel words that Jn does *not* use, I have inserted in it some words that do not occur in all three Synoptists. So, too, in the later Vocabularies, matter will be occasionally inserted that may not fall strictly under their several headings, if it will be useful for further reference, and if it can be given with such numeral statistics, or annotations, that the reader cannot possibly be misled. See, in particular, **1838.**

SYNOPTIC WORDS COMPARATIVELY SELDOM OR NEVER USED BY JOHN[1]

English	Greek	Mk	Mt.	Lk.	Jn
[1672] Add[2]	προστίθημι	1	2	7	0
Adultery, adulterous, etc.	μοιχαλίς, μοιχάομαι, μοιχεία, μοιχεύω, μοιχός	5	12	4	0
Afar	μακρόθεν	5	2	4	0
Age, world [apart from the phrase εἰς τὸν αἰῶνα][3]	αἰών	2	7	5	1
And (Hebraic)[4]	καί	c. 400	c. 250	c. 380	c. 100
Angel or messenger[5]	ἄγγελος	6	20	25	3
Angry, s. Indignant	ἀγανακτέω	3	3	1	0
Anxiety, s. Care	μέριμνα	1	1	2	0
Apart, privately[6]	κατ' ἰδίαν	7	6	2	0
Apostles (i.e. the Twelve)[7]	ἀπόστολοι	2	1	6	0

---

[1] [1672*] "Chri." opposite to any word signifies "in Christ's words," and "narr." signifies "in narrative." Thus "body" (Chri.) is put down as occurring twice in Mk, but Mk uses it also twice in "narr." By "narr." (unless called "strict narr.") is meant "outside Christ's words." "Narr.," therefore, would include words assigned to the Baptist, Pharisees, disciples, etc. ("Strict narr." excludes such words.) For Addenda see **1885** (i) foll.

[2] "Add" is Hebraic in Lk. xx. 11, 12 (lit.) "he *added* to send," R.V. "he sent *yet*."

[3] [1672 a] "Age," "World." Jn ix. 32 R.V. "Since the world began (ἐκ τοῦ αἰῶνος)." For Jn's use of αἰών elsewhere, always in the phrase εἰς τὸν αἰῶνα "for ever," see **1712** d.

[4] "And" ("in oratione historica ex simplici Hebraeorum narrandi modo," Bruder (1888) p. 456). The numbers are roughly given. See **2133**.

[5] "Angel." The instances in Jn are i. 51 "Ye shall see...the *angels* of God ascending and descending on the Son of man," xii. 29 "an *angel* hath spoken to him," xx. 12 "she beholdeth two *angels*."

[6] [1672 b] "Apart, privately," freq. applied by Synoptists to Christ's teaching. Contrast Jn xviii. 20 "I have spoken openly to the world. I ever taught in synagogue and in the temple...and in secret spake I nothing."

[7] "Apostles." Jn xiii. 16 "nor is an *apostle* greater..." means "anyone sent" and is not confined to one of the Twelve.

FROM SYNOPTIC VOCABULARY [1673]

English	Greek	Mk	Mt.	Lk.	Jn
Arise	ἀνιστάναι (in intrans. forms)	17	6	29	4
,, [used of the sun, clouds etc.]	,, ,,	2	3	1	0
Ask, i.e. question[1]	ἐπερωτάω (not ἐρωτάω)	25	8	17	2 or 1
[1673] Astonish(ment)[2]	ἐκθαμβέομαι	4	0	0	0
	ἐκπλήσσομαι	5	4	3	0
	ἔκστασις	0	2	1	0
	ἐξίσταμαι	4	1	3	0
	θάμβος, θαμβέομαι	3	0	2	0
	θαυμάζω	4	7	13	6

[1] [1672 c] "Ask," i.e. question. Jn ix. 23 "He is of age, *ask* him" (marg. ἐρωτήσατε), xviii. 7 "He *asked* them, Whom seek ye?" see also "pray" (1688) and "ask," ἐρωτάω (1708). N.B. "2 or 1" indicates v.r.

[2] [1673 a] "Astonish(ment)." In Jn, θαυμάζω is used twice in narrative. In iv. 27 "they [the disciples] *began to marvel* that he was talking with a woman," it implies a shock of surprise at Christ's unconventional conduct. In vii. 15, "the Jews therefore *began to marvel* saying, How knoweth this man letters," the context seems to shew that the "marvel" was not that of receptive awe, but that of perplexed hostility. In iii. 7, v. 28, "*marvel* not," Jesus rebukes "marvel," as implying want of insight, and in vii. 21, in answer to the Jews, who say "Thou hast a devil," He says "I have done one work and ye all *marvel*," i.e. stare at it in unspiritual amazement. So far, Jn's use suggests that he takes the word *in a bad sense* (which it has generally in the Canonical LXX).

[1673 b] There remains Christ's reply to the Jews that (v. 18) "sought the more to kill him" after the mighty work of healing accomplished by Him on the sabbath. To these would-be murderers, blind to the divinity of beneficence, Christ replies (v. 20) "Greater works than these will he [the Father] shew him [the Son]—that ye *may go on marvelling* (ἵνα ὑμεῖς θαυμάζητε)." If "marvel" is here in a bad sense, as in O.T., this is akin to the famous saying of Isaiah quoted elsewhere by John (xii. 38—40) that God "blinded" the eyes of men "*that they might not* (ἵνα μή) see with their eyes." So here the meaning would be that the Father will shew the Son still greater works—and all that *ye*— the pronoun is emphatic—ye, blind and resolute enemies of the light, may go on persisting in your *marvel*.

[1673 c] It is not surprising that Mr Burkitt's Syriac text (SS is illegible) renders this difficult passage "*And do not* wonder," adding, "that I have said [it] to you." But the comparison of Jn xii. 40 makes the meaning consistent with the language of Isaiah, as well as with the

English	Greek	Mk	Mt.	Lk.	Jn
Baptism	βάπτισμα	4	2	4	0
Baptist[1]	βαπτιστής	2	7	3	0
Bartholomew	Βαρθολομαῖος	1	1	1	0
Beat (1)	δέρω	3	1	5	1
Beat (2)	τύπτω	1	2	4	0
Bed, couch (1)	κλίνη	2	2	3	0
Bed, couch (2)[2]	κράβαττος	5	0	0	4
Beelzebul	Βεελζεβούλ	1	3	3	0

Johannine use of the verb "marvel"—which, in the Fourth Gospel, is *not a virtue but a vice, quite distinct from "awe" or "reverence."*

[1673 d] Mk vi. 6 has "And he *marvelled* (ἐθαύμασεν) because of their unbelief" (in the visit to Nazareth) where the parall. Mt. xiii. 58 (? Lk. iv. 16—24) has no such statement. But Mt. viii. 10, Lk. vii. 9 have "But having heard it Jesus *marvelled* (ἐθαύμασεν)," *i.e.* at the belief of the centurion. In the former case, the word is equivalent to "shocked" as in Gal. i. 6 (which means that the Apostle is "shocked" at the Galatian instability); in the latter, it implies wondering admiration.

[1673 e] It appears from Boeckh's *Greek Inscriptions* (4768 foll.) that ἰδὼν ἐθαύμασα, or εἶδον καὶ ἐθαύμασα, was the regular phrase in use among tourists in the second century to record their impressions after visiting the underground tombs at Thebes, "I saw and *wondered*." If the phrase had already become hackneyed in that sense, John may have had an additional reason for disliking θαυμάζω as a word to express Christian wonder or awe. An interpolated but very early tradition in Lk. xxiv. 12 says that Peter, after visiting the empty tomb "went away (ἀπῆλθεν) to his home (πρὸς αὐτὸν) *wondering* at that which had come to pass." The interpolation somewhat resembles Jn xx. 8—10 which says that one at all events of the two disciples "*saw and believed*," and then that they "went away again to their homes (ἀπῆλθον οὖν πρὸς αὐτούς)." Possibly Jn's "*saw and believed*" contains an allusion not only to the general hackneyed phrase "*saw and wondered*," but also to some particular Christian application of it, such as appears in the interpolation—which is regarded by W. H. as being of very early date.

[1] [1673 f] "Baptist," in the Synoptists, distinguishes John the son of Zacharias from John the Apostle. In the Fourth Gospel, John the Apostle is never mentioned by name, though probably implied in "the disciple that Jesus loved," and in other phrases. The Fourth Gospel mentions a John as father of Peter but only in Christ's words ("Simon, son of John").

[2] "Bed." κράβαττος (Mk ii. 4—12, Jn v. 8—11, also pl. Mk vi. 55) is a term condemned by the Grammarian Phrynichus.

FROM SYNOPTIC VOCABULARY [1674]

English	Greek	Mk	Mt.	Lk.	Jn
[1674] Begin[1]	ἄρχομαι	26	13	31	1
Behold! (1)[2]	ἰδού (not ἴδε)	8	61	55	4
Behold! (2)	ἴδε	9	4	0	15
Believe, believing, s. Faith					
Beloved[3]	ἀγαπητός	3	3	2	0
Beseech, etc.[4]	παρακαλέω	9	9	7	0
Bethphage	Βηθφαγή	1	1	1	0
Bird[5]	πετεινόν	2	4	4	0
Blaspheme, blasphemy[6]	βλασφημέω, -ία	7	7	4	2
Bless, blessed[7]	εὐλογέω, -ητός	6	5	15	1
Body (Chri.)	σῶμα	2	11	9	0
Branch[8]	κλάδος	2	3	1	0

[1] [1674 a] "Begin," only once in Jn (xiii. 5) "He *began* to wash the feet of the disciples." This unique use of the word in Jn (as contrasted with its frequent use in the Synoptists) is very noteworthy and may have been among the reasons that led Origen (*ad loc.* Huet ii. 380 B) to interpret it as meaning that Jesus "*began*" the purification *now* and completed it *afterwards*. In such a writer as John, "began" must be assumed here to have some definite meaning, and not to be used as in Mark.

[2] [1674 b] "Behold!" Jn iv. 35 and xvi. 32 (Chri.), xii. 15 (quot. Zech. ix. 9), xix. 5 (Pilate) "*Behold*, the man!" Mk and Jn never use it in narr.: Mt. and Lk. freq. use it in narr., and five times agree in using it (352) against the parall. Mk.

[3] "Beloved," always with "son" exc. Mt. xii. 18 (quoting Is. xlii. 1 ἐκλεκτός). But see "love," ἀγαπάω (1716 d foll., 1728 m foll., and 1744(i)foll.).

[4] "Beseech." Παρακαλέω in Mk and parall. Mt.-Lk. is used of "beseeching" addressed to Jesus; outside the Triple Tradition it sometimes means "comfort," "exhort," *e.g.* in Mt. ii. 18, v. 4, Lk. iii. 18, xvi. 25.

[5] "Bird." Mt. xxiii. 37, Lk. xiii. 34 have ὃν τρόπον ὄρνις ἐπισυνάγει... Ὄρνις is not used by Jn.

[6] "Blaspheme" etc., in Jn, only x. 33 ἀλλὰ περὶ βλασφημίας, uttered by the Jews, x. 36 ὑμεῖς λέγετε ὅτι, Βλασφημεῖς, by Christ replying to the Jews.

[7] "Bless," in Jn, only xii. 13 εὐλογημένος ὁ ἐρχόμενος..., the cry of the multitude quoting Ps. cxviii. 26. For μακάριος, "blessed," see 1859 e.

[8] "Branch," κλάδος. But Jn has κλῆμα, "branch" in his Parable of the Vine xv. 2, 4, 5, 6.

[1675] JOHANNINE DEVIATIONS

English	Greek	Mk	Mt.	Lk.	Jn
[1675] Break (bread)[1]	κλάω	3	3	2	0
Bring word, s. Tell[2]	ἀπαγγέλλω	3	8	11	1
Build, s. also House[3]	οἰκοδομέω	4	8	12	1
Call, *i.e.* name[4]	καλέω	1	15	29	1
Call, *i.e.* summon, invite[5]	καλέω	3	11	14	1
Call anyone to (oneself)	προσκαλέομαι	9	6	4	0
[1676] Care[6]	μέριμνα	1	1	2	0
Cast out, s. Devils					
Centurion	Mk κεντυρίων, Mt.-Lk. ἑκατοντάρχης	3	4	3	0

[1] [1675 a] "Break (bread)." The Synoptists never use this word except in connexion with the Feeding of the Five Thousand (where Jn omits it) and at the Eucharist. Mk and Mt. use it also in the Feeding of the Four Thousand, which Lk. and Jn omit.

[2] [1675 b] "Bring word," ἀπαγγέλλω, in Jn, only xvi. 25 "*I will bring word to* (R.V. tell) you plainly about the Father." Ἀπαγγέλλω in the Gospels, apart from quotations, should never be rendered "tell" (as in R.V. Mk v. 14, 19, vi. 30 etc.) but almost always "bring word" (as in R.V. Mt. ii. 8, xxviii. 8) or "report." Epictetus ii. 23. 2 condemns those who asserted that there was no "reporting power (δύναμις ἀπαγγελτική)" in the senses (comp. Steph. quot. Sext. Pyrrh. i. 197 οὐκ ἀπαγγελτικῶς). There is a "spirit," he says, infused in the eyes, which goes forth from them and returns to them with an impression of the things seen, and no "messenger" is "so swift." The Sibyl (vii. 83) calls the Logos "a *reporter* (ἀπαγγελτῆρα) of logoi," and Steph. quotes Euseb. *Dem.* v. 202 B θεοῦ λόγον ἐν ἀνθρώπῳ τῆς τοῦ πατρὸς εὐσεβείας ἀπαγγελτικόν. The word is therefore appropriate to the Spirit of the Son in heaven, "reporting" to man on earth.

[3] [1675 c] "Build," in Jn, only ii. 20 "In forty-six years was this temple built." Comp. Mk xiv. 58, xv. 29 parall. to Mt. xxvi. 61, xxvii. 40 about the building of a new Temple (not mentioned in Lk.).

[4] "Call," *i.e.* name. Mk xi. 17, "*shall be called* a House of Prayer," quoting Is. lvi. 7 ; Jn i 42 "*thou shalt be called* Cephas."

[5] "Call," *i.e.* invite, summon. In Jn, only ii. 2 "Now Jesus also *was invited*, and his disciples."

[6] "Care." Mk iv. 19 "the *cares* of the world" parall. to Mt. xiii. 22, Lk. viii. 14. The verb μεριμνᾶν "be anxious (or, careful)" is in Mt. (7), Lk. (5), Mk (0), Jn (0).

FROM SYNOPTIC VOCABULARY [1676]

English	Greek	Mk	Mt.	Lk.	Jn
Charge	παραγγέλλω	2	2	4	0
Child[1]	τέκνον	9	15	14	3
Child (little)[2]	παιδίον	12	18	13	3
Child (infant)	νήπιος	0	2	1	0
Children (babes, pl.)	βρέφη	0	0	1	0
Chosen, masc., i.e. the elect[3]	ἐκλεκτός	3	5	2	[? 1]
City (Chri.)	πόλις	1	13	12	0
City (narr.)	πόλις	7	13	27	8
Cleanse, make clean, purify etc.[4]	καθαρίζω	4	7	7	0
Clothe[5]	περιβάλλω	2	5	2	1
Cloud	νεφέλη	4	4	5	0

[1] [1676 a] "Child," τέκνον. Jn i. 12 "He gave them authority to become *children* of God," viii. 39 "If ye are *children* of Abraham," xi. 52 "...that he might gather...the *children* of God." To "*become children of God*" is apparently equivalent to being (Jn iii. 3) "*born from above*," without which, it is said, a man "cannot see the kingdom of God": and the two expressions together appear to resemble the tradition peculiar to Matthew (xviii. 3) "Except ye turn and become as little children ye shall in no wise enter into the kingdom of heaven." Τεκνία (pl.) is in Jn xiii. 33.

[2] [1676 b] "Child (little)," παιδίον. Jn iv. 49 "Come down before my *child* die," xvi. 21 "But when she is delivered of the *child*, she remembereth no more the anguish," xxi. 5 "*Children*, have ye (R.V.) aught to eat?" In the Synoptists, "(little) children" may be called a "fundamental word" of doctrine. In Jn it is never used except vocatively, and hence, in the Preface (p. ix) it is said to be omitted. On xxi. 5, see **2235** *c*.

[3] [1676 c] "Chosen," masc. Jn i. 34 (SS) "*the chosen [one]* of God," W. H. "son" (**593** a). Comp. Lk. xxiii. 35 "the Christ of God *the chosen [one]*." Elsewhere the word is masc. pl. as in the Epistles, "the elect [ones]." Jn has "choose" five times—Mk (1), Mt. (0), Lk. (4)—and always in the words of Christ, concerning His choice (exc. Jn xv. 16 "Ye did not choose me").

[4] "Cleanse," used by the Synoptists mostly of "cleansing" from leprosy, which (**1666**) Jn never mentions.

[5] [1676 d] "Clothe," in Jn, only xix. 2 "they *clothed him with* (περιέβαλον αὐτόν) a purple garment," probably written (**1805-6**) with allusion to Synoptic parallels, including Lk. xxiii. 11 "Having *clothed him* in gorgeous apparel (περιβαλὼν ἐσθῆτα λαμπράν)."

[1677] JOHANNINE DEVIATIONS

English	Greek	Mk	Mt.	Lk.	Jn
[1677] Colt[1]	πῶλος	4	3	4	1
Come to[2]	προσέρχομαι	5 or 6	51	11	1
Command (1)	ἐπιτάσσω	4	0	4	0
Command (2)	κελεύω	0	7	1	0
Command (3)	προστάσσω	1	2	1	0
"Common," make[3]	κοινόω	5	5	0	0
Compassion, com- passionate, pity etc.[4]	⎧ ἔλεος ⎨ ἐλεέω ⎩ σπλαγχνίζομαι	0 3 4	3 8 5	6 4 3	0 0 0
Condemn[5]	κατακρίνω	2	4	2	0
[1678] Confess[6]	ἐξομολογέομαι	1	2	1	0
Country, the c. round about	περίχωρος	1	2	5	0
Cross (Chri.)	σταυρός	1	2	2	0
Crucify (Chri.)[7]	σταυρόω	0	3	0	0
Crucify with (Jesus)	συνσταυρόω	1	1	0	0

[1] "Colt," in Jn, only xii. 15, quoting Zech. ix. 9. Jn lays much less stress than the Synoptists lay on the Finding of the Colt. He uses the word "ass," where Mk-Lk. use "colt," while Mt. uses "ass and colt" (1861 *b*).

[2] [1677 *a*] "Come to," in Jn, only xii. 21, of the Greeks, who "*came to* Philip" saying, "Sir, we would see Jesus." In the Epistles, it occurs only in 1 Tim. vi. 3 (?), Heb. (7), 1 Pet. ii. 4, and always of approaching a source of grace.

[3] [1677 *b*] "Common," *i.e.* unclean. All these instances occur in Mk vii. 2—23 and the parallel Mt. (Lk. omits the whole). Mk vii. 2, 5 also has (*bis*) κοινός (adj.) in the phrase κοιναῖς χερσίν.

[4] [1677 *c*] "Compassion." The Synoptic words meaning "pity" sometimes correspond to the Heb. חסד, which also means "kindness," or "*loving-kindness*." This might sometimes be expressed by "love," which occurs in Jn more frequently than in all the Synoptists taken together.

[5] [1677 *d*] "Condemn." Jn, however, uses κρίνω, "judge" freq. (19)— Mk never, Mt.-Lk. seldom (1714 *d—f*)—and often where the context indicates "condemn," as Jn iii. 17, 18 (where A.V. has "condemn" thrice).

[6] [1678 *a*] "Confess." Mk i. 5, Mt. iii. 6 "*confessing* their sins," Mt. xi. 25, Lk. x. 21 "I *make confession*, or *acknowledgment*, to thee, Father." Lk. xxii. 6 (act.) ἐξωμολόγησεν, "[Judas Iscariot] *made an agreement*." Jn (1861 *a*) has ὁμολογέω but not of "confessing sins" (exc. in Epistle).

[7] "Crucify" (Chri.) Mt. xx. 19, xxiii. 34, xxvi. 2 (1206).

166

FROM SYNOPTIC VOCABULARY [1679]

English	Greek	Mk	Mt.	Lk.	Jn
Crucify with (another)[1]	συνσταυρόω	0	0	0	1
Cup[2]	ποτήριον	6	7	5	1
Damsel	κοράσιον	5	3	0	0
Daughter[3]	θυγάτηρ	5	8	8	1
[1679] David[4]	Δαυείδ	7	17	13	2
Deaf or dumb	κωφός	3	7	4	0
Death, put to[5]	θανατόω	2	3	1	0
Deny utterly[6]	ἀπαρνέομαι	4	4	4	0
Desert, desolate (adj.)	ἔρημος	5	3	2	0
Destroy[7]	καταλύω	3	5	1	0
Devils (plur.)	δαιμόνια	8	6 or 8	16	0
Devil(s), cast out	ἐκβάλλω δ.	7	6 or 7	7	0
Devil(s), possessed with[8]	δαιμονίζομαι	4	7	1	1
Disease[9]	νόσος	1	5	4	0
Diseased[9]	κακῶς ἔχων	4	5	2	0

[1] [1678 b] "Crucify with [another]." This occurs in Jn xix. 32. But the Johannine context so differs from the Synoptic as to make the meaning in Jn "crucified with *the first malefactor*," not "crucified with *Jesus*." Lk. omits the word altogether. See 1817 c.

[2] [1678 c] "Cup." Lk. omits Mk x. 38—9, Mt. xx. 22—3 "Are ye able to drink the *cup*...?" Jn's single instance is (Jn xviii. 11) "The *cup* that the Father hath given me..."

[3] [1678 d] "Daughter," in Jn, only xii. 15, quoting Zech. ix. 9 "*Daughter* of Zion."

[4] [1679 a] "David." Both Jn's instances are in vii. 42 "Did not the Scripture say that from the seed of *David*, and from Bethlehem the village where *David* was, the Christ is to come?"

[5] "Death, put to." Lk. xxi. 16 (diff. from parall. Mk xiii. 12, Mt. x. 21) "they shall *put to death* some of you," comp. Jn xvi. 2 "he that killeth (ἀποκτείνας) you." For "death," see 1710 c—d.

[6] "Deny utterly." Jn has "deny," ἀρνέομαι, concerning Peter's Denial xiii. 38, xviii. 25, 27, and i. 20 "confessed and denied not."

[7] [1679 b] "Destroy." But, corresponding to καταλύω used concerning the temple or its stones (Mk xiii. 2, xiv. 58 etc.), Jn ii. 19 has λύσατε.

[8] [1679 c] "Devil(s), possessed with," in Jn, only x. 21 "Others said, these are not the works of *one possessed with a devil*." But Jn has—always in dialogue—δαιμόνιον ἔχω (5) and δαιμόνιον (1).

[9] [1679 d] "Disease." Jn has ἀσθένεια (2) and ἀσθενέω (8). The former is used once in Mt. (viii. 17 "took our infirmities") but that is in a quotation from the Heb. (not LXX) of Is. liii. 4.

[1680] JOHANNINE DEVIATIONS

English	Greek	Mk	Mt.	Lk.	Jn
Distant (also means "enough," "have in full")[1]	ἀπέχω	2	5	4	0
Divide	μερίζω	4	3	1	0
Divide asunder[2]	διαμερίζω	1	1	6	1
Divorce[3]	ἀπολύω (R.V. "put away")	4	9	2	0
Drink, give to drink	ποτίζω	2	5	1	0
[1680] Ear[4]	οὖς	5	7	7	0
Earthquake[5]	σεισμός	1	4	1	0
Eat[6]	ἐσθίω	11	11	12	0
Elders	πρεσβύτεροι	7	12	5	0
Elect, s. Chosen					
Elijah[7]	Ἠλείας	9	9	7	2
End[8]	τέλος	3	5	4	1
Enemy[9]	ἐχθρός	1	7	8	0
Enough (see note above on Distant)	ἀπέχω	2	5	4	0

[1] "Distant etc." The numbers include the three meanings.

[2] "Divide asunder," in Jn, only xix. 24, quoting Ps. xxii. 18 about the division of Christ's garments.

[3] "Divorce." These numbers do not include ἀπολύω = "release," "send away" etc.

[4] "Ear." Jn xviii. 10, 26 has ὠτάριον (1), ὠτίον (1), both about the ear of Malchus.

[5] [1680 a] "Earthquake." Mk xiii. 8 (parall. Mt. xxiv. 7, Lk. xxi. 11) predicts earthquakes in the Last Days. Mt. viii. 24 σεισμὸς μέγας ἐγένετο ἐν τ. θαλάσσῃ means "tempest," Mt. xxviii. 2 mentions an earthquake at the time of the Resurrection (not in Mk-Lk.-Jn).

[6] [1680 b] "Eat." This does not include (a) φαγεῖν and (b) τρώγειν. Φαγεῖν is freq. in all the Synoptists, and fairly freq. in Jn. Τρώγειν occurs only in Mt. (1) (xxiv. 38 "*eating* and drinking") Jn (5) always of eating Christ's flesh, exc. in xiii. 18, quoting Ps. xli. 10, (Heb.) "he that *eateth* my bread." Ἐσθίω, the pres. tense, occurs in discussions about eating with sinners, and in the narrative of the Eucharist etc.

[7] "Elijah," in Jn, only i. 20, 25.

[8] [1680 c] "End," in Jn, only xiii. 1 "He [Christ] loved them to the *end* (2319—23)." There is nothing in Jn about "the end" as meaning the Last Day etc. See 1715 a.

[9] "Enemy." Mk xii. 36, only in quotation (Ps. cx. 1) parall. to Mt. xxii. 44, Lk. xx. 43 (**1856**).

FROM SYNOPTIC VOCABULARY [1681]

English	Greek	Mk	Mt.	Lk.	Jn
Enter, go into	εἰσπορεύομαι	8	1	5	0
Exceedingly (1)	λίαν	4	4	1	0
Exceedingly (2)	ἐκπερισσῶς	1	0	0	0
Exceedingly (3)	περισσῶς	2	1	0	0
Exceedingly (4)	σφόδρα	1	7	1	0
[1681] Face[1]	πρόσωπον	3	10	14	0
Faith, or, belief (**1670**)	πίστις	5	8	11	0
Faith, have, in, i.e. believe	πιστεύω	10	11	9	c. 100
Faithful, believing[2]	πιστός	0	5	6	1
Faithless (-ness), unbelieving (-belief)[2]	ἀπιστέω (-ία, -ος)	3	2	4	1
Fall (Chri.)[3]	πίπτω	5	11 or 13	14	1
Fall (narr.)	πίπτω	3	6	3	2
Fall against, fall down before	προσπίπτω	3	1	3	0
Fast, fasting	νηστεία, νῆστις, νηστεύω	7	9	5	0
Fear (n.)[4]	φόβος	1	3	7	3
Fear (vb.) (Chri.)[5]	φοβέομαι	2	8	11	1
Fear (vb.) (narr.)	φοβέομαι	10	10	12	4

[1] [1681 a] "Face." In apparent reference to a passage where the Synoptists use (Mk i. 2, Mt. xi. 10, Lk. vii. 27) πρὸ προσώπου, Jn iii. 28 uses ἔμπροσθεν.

[2] [1681 b] "Faithful," "faithless," in Jn, only xx. 27 "Be not unbelieving (ἄπιστος) (R.V. faithless) but believing (πιστός)." In idiomatic English, "*faithless*" now means "not keeping faith," and is applied to breaking one's word, breach of trust etc. Jn does not mean this.

[3] "Fall" (Chri.), in Jn, only xii. 24 "Except the grain of corn *having fallen* (πεσών) into the earth die."

[4] [1681 c] "Fear" (n.). In Jn, always in a bad sense, and in the phrase (Jn vii. 13, xix. 38, xx. 19) "because of the *fear* of the Jews," *i.e.* because they were afraid of the Pharisees. Mk iv. 41 and Mt.-Lk. freq. use φόβος in a good sense, to mean "*awe*." Comp. the only passage mentioning fear in the Epistle, 1 Jn iv. 18 "There is no *fear* in love, but perfect love casteth out *fear*, because *fear* hath punishment."

[5] [1681 d] "Fear" (vb.). Jn vi. 20 "It is I; *fear* not." In Christ's words it is always used thus negatively in Mk (2), and almost always in Mt.-Lk. In Mt.'s narrative it is once used by an angel Mt. xxviii. 5 "*Fear* not ye."

JOHANNINE DEVIATIONS

English	Greek	Mk	Mt.	Lk.	Jn
Few (plur.)	ὀλίγοι	2	6	4	0
Field	ἀγρός	8	16	10	0
[1682] Fire[1]	πῦρ	4	12	7	1
First (adj. or noun, not adv.) (Chri.)[2]	πρῶτος	5	11	7	0
Flee[3]	φεύγω	5	7	3	2
Forgive, forgiveness[4]	ἀφίημι, ἄφεσις	12	18	17	2
Gain (vb.)[5]	κερδαίνω	1	6	1	0
Gather[6]	ἐπισυνάγω	2	3	3	0
Generation	γενεά	5	13	15	0
Gentile, s. Nations					
Gift[7]	δῶρον	1	9	2	0
Go before[8]	προάγω	5	6	1	0
Go before[8]	προπορεύομαι	0	0	1	0
Go before, go forward[8]	προέρχομαι	2	1	2	0

[1] [1682 a] "Fire," in Jn, only xv. 6 "They gather them and cast them into the *fire*," in the metaphor, or parable, of the Vine. Mt. twice uses "fire" in connexion with "Gehenna," or "hell" (v. 22, xviii. 9) which does not occur in Jn.

[2] [1682 b] "First." Jn omits all discourses about "who shall be *first*," as also about "who shall be the *greatest*" (1683 b—c).

[3] [1682 c] "Flee," in Jn, only x. 5, 12, of the sheep "fleeing" from the stranger, and the hireling from the wolf.

[4] [1682 d] "Forgive." This does not include ἀφίημι meaning "leave," "suffer." "Forgiveness" occurs nowhere in Jn, "forgive" only in xx. 23 "Whose soever sins ye *forgive*, they are *forgiven* unto them." See also (1690) "Remission of sins."

[5] [1682 e] "Gain." Comp. "reward," μισθός, Mt. (10), but Mk (1), Lk. (3), Jn (1).

[6] [1682 f] "Gather." Jn xi. 52 (ἵνα καὶ τὰ τέκνα τοῦ θεοῦ...συναγάγῃ εἰς ἕν) uses συνάγω in a sense similar to that of ἐπισυνάγω in (a) Mt. xxiii. 37, Lk. xiii. 34, ποσάκις ἠθέλησα ἐπισυναγαγεῖν (Lk. ἐπισυνάξαι) τὰ τέκνα σου (where, however, Jn speaks of the scattered children of God generally, but Mt. Lk. refer to the children of Jerusalem), and in (b) Mk xiii. 27, Mt. xxiv. 31 ἐπισυνάξει (Mt. -ξουσιν) τοὺς ἐκλεκτοὺς αὐτοῦ ἐκ τῶν τεσσ. ἀνέμων. All use συνάγω, Mt. more freq. than Mk Lk. and Jn taken together.

[7] [1682 g] "Gift." See "gain," and "reward," freq. in Mt. Jn has the form δωρεά once (iv. 10) "If thou knewest the *gift* of God."

[8] [1682 h] "Go before, or, forward." Jn generally prefers simple

FROM SYNOPTIC VOCABULARY [1683]

English	Greek	Mk	Mt.	Lk.	Jn
Good [applied to a person][1]	ἀγαθός	3	6	6	1
Gospel	εὐαγγέλιον	7	4	0	0
Gospel, preach the (lit. speak gospel)[2]	εὐαγγελίζω, -ομαι	0	1	10	0
Governor[3]	ἡγεμών	1	10	2	0
Grass	χόρτος	2	3	1	1
[1683] Great[4]	μέγας	15	20	26	5
Great, sufficient	ἱκανός	3	3	10	0
how great, how much, how many	πόσος	6	8	6	0
Greater (of persons)[5]	μείζων	1	6	6	7

verbs with prepositions to compound verbs. Comp. Jn xiv. 2 "I go to *prepare* (ἑτοιμάσαι) a place for you." This implies "going before."

[1] "Good," appl. to a person, in Jn, only vii. 12 "Some said, He [*i.e.* Jesus] is *good*."

[2] [1682 *i*] "Gospel, preach." See also "preach," "proclaim," *i.e.* κηρύσσω, which Jn never uses. On the other hand, Jn uses λαλέω, "speak," more freq. than Mk and Lk. taken together.

[3] [1682 *j*] "Governor," or ruler. Each of the Synoptists uses the word once in Christ's prediction that the disciples will be tried before "*rulers* and kings." The other instances of Mt. and Lk. (except Mt. ii. 6) refer to Pilate.

[4] [1683 *a*] "Great" is never applied by Jn to persons as it is in Mk x. 42—3 and parall. Mt., (Lk. "greater"). Jn applies it (μέγας) only to (vi. 18) "wind," (vii. 37, xix. 31) "day," (xi. 43) "voice," (xxi. 11) "fishes."

[5] [1683 *b*] "Greater," of persons. Mk's only instance is Mk ix. 34 "They had conversed with one another in the way [on the question], Who is the *greatest* [lit. *greater*] (τίς μείζων)?" Mk represents Jesus, in His reply, as saying "Whosoever of you desireth to be *first*," but Mt. and Lk. both in the parallel and elsewhere assign to Jesus the word "*greater*" concerning "persons"—in particular about the Baptist (Mt. xi. 11 οὐκ ἐγήγερται...μείζων...ὁ δὲ μικρότερος...μείζων, and sim. Lk. vii. 28).

[1683 *c*] Jn assigns to the Samaritan woman the words (iv. 12) "Art thou *greater* than our father Jacob?" and to the Jews (viii. 53) "Art thou *greater* than our father Abraham?" But when the word is used by Jesus it is either used *with a negative* (xiii. 16) "the bond-servant is not *greater* than his master *nor* the apostle *greater* than the [apostle's] sender" (comp. xv. 20), or else applied to the Father as "greater" than

[1684] JOHANNINE DEVIATIONS

English	Greek	Mk	Mt.	Lk.	Jn
Hand (Chri.)	χείρ	5	9	9	5
Hand (narr.)	χείρ	19	15	16	10
Have (in full) (see note above on Distant)	ἀπέχω	2	5	4	0
Heal (1)[1]	θεραπεύω	5	16	14	1
Heal (2)[2]	ἰάομαι	1	4	11	3
Hell, s. Fire	γέεννα	3	7	1	0
Here (Chri.)	ὧδε	6	12	12	1
Here (narr.)	ὧδε	4	6	3 or 4	4
Herod (the Great)	Ἡρώδης	0	9	1	0
Herod (Antipas)	Ἡρώδης	8	4	13	0
Herodians	Ἡρωδιανοί	2	1	0	0
Herodias	Ἡρωδιάς	3	2	1	0
High	ὑψηλός	1	2	1	0
Highest	ὕψιστος	2	1	7	0
[1684] House (1)[3]	οἰκία	19	26	24	5
House (2)	οἶκος	12	9	32	3
House-master	οἰκοδεσπότης	1	7	4	0
Hunger (vb.)[4]	πεινάω	2	9	5	1

the Son (xiv. 28) or "greater" than all things (? x. 29 W.H. marg.). John assumes that all that is great and good in men comes to them from their being in the Father (or the Father in them) so that arithmetical comparisons between man and man are out of place. Comp. Plato 69 A (*Phaed.* 13) which declares that the balancing of μείζω πρὸς ἐλάττω is not "the right exchange with a view to virtue."

[1] [1683 d] "Heal" (1), in Jn, only v. 10 "The Jews therefore began to say to him *that had been healed* (τῷ τεθεραπευμένῳ)," *i.e.* the man that had been (Jn v. 5) "in his infirmity."

[2] [1683 e] "Heal" (2). Mt. xiii. 15, Jn xii. 40 are quotations from Is. vi. 10. Jn v. 13 ὁ δὲ ἰαθείς (Tisch. ἀσθενῶν) is called ὁ τεθεραπευμένος in Jn v. 10. Jn iv. 47 "that he would come down and *heal* his son," is a request to Jesus. It will be seen that Jn never uses θεραπεύω or ἰάομαι in his own person except participially to describe people that have been healed.

[3] [1684 a] "House" (1). It means "household" in Jn iv. 53 and perh. in viii. 35 ("doth not abide in the house for ever"). It means "the Father's house" in xiv. 2, and the house of Martha and Mary in xi. 31 and xii. 3. See also "build."

[4] "Hunger," in Jn, only vi. 35 "He that cometh unto me shall assuredly not *hunger*."

FROM SYNOPTIC VOCABULARY [1685]

English	Greek	Mk	Mt.	Lk.	Jn
Husbandman[1]	γεωργός	5	6	5	1
Hypocrite, hypocrisy	ὑποκριτής, -ισις	2	14	4	0
Increase, grow[2]	αὐξάνω	1	2	4	1
Indignant, become[3]	ἀγανακτέω	3	3	1	0
Inherit, inheritance, inheritor	κληρονομέω, -ία, -ος	3	5	5	0
Isaac[4]	Ἰσαάκ	1	4	3	0
Israel[5]	Ἰσραήλ	2	12	12	4
James (son of Alphaeus etc.)[6]		4	3	3	0
James (son of Zebedee or brother of John)[6]		10	3	5	0
Jericho		2	1	3	0
John (son of Zebedee)		10	3	7	0
Just, justify etc., s. Righteous					
[1685] Kingdom[7]	βασιλεία	19	56	45	5
Know, recognise[8]	ἐπιγινώσκω	4	6	7	0

[1] "Husbandman," in Jn, only xv. 1 "My Father is the *husbandman*."

[2] "Increase," in Jn, only iii. 30 "He must *increase* but I must decrease."

[3] [1684 b] "Indignant, become." Ὀργίζομαι, "be angry," occurs Mt. (3), Lk. (2), but Mk (0), Jn (0), and therefore is not in this vocabulary.

[4] "Isaac." In Mk, only xii. 26, quoting Ex. iii. 6.

[5] [1684 c] "Israel." Jn iii. 10 "Art thou the teacher of *Israel* and knowest not these things?" appears to contain a shade of irony. It is the only Johannine instance of the use of "Israel" in the words of the Lord. The others are i. 31, 49, xii. 13. Of Lk.'s instances, 7 are in his Introduction.

[6] [1684 d] "James." These names and numbers are given as in Bruder (1888). But the distinctions are doubtful. The important fact is that "James" does not occur at all in Jn.

[7] [1685 a] "Kingdom." "The kingdom of God, or, of heaven etc.," occurs more than 80 times in the Synoptists. In Jn it occurs only in the Dialogue with Nicodemus, iii. 3, 5, "the k. of God," and in xviii. 36 "my kingdom" (thrice repeated, ἡ β. ἡ ἐμή).

[8] [1685 b] "Know, recognise." For γινώσκω, and οἶδα, see **1715**.

[1686] JOHANNINE DEVIATIONS

English	Greek	Mk	Mt.	Lk.	Jn
Lame[1]	χωλός	1	5	3	1
Lamp, lampstand[2]	λύχνος, -ία	2	3	8	1
Last (excluding "last day")[3]	ἔσχατος	5	10	6	0
Lawful, it is[4]	ἔξεστιν	6	10	5	2
Lead astray, go astray, err	πλανάω	4	8	1	2
Lead away	ἀπάγω	3	5	4	0
Leave	καταλείπω	4	4	4	0
Leaven (n. and vb.)	ζύμη, -όω	2	5	3	0
Leper, leprosy	λεπρός, -α	3	5	5	0
[1686] Liken, compare[5]	ὁμοιόω	1	8	3	0
Little ones[6]	μικροί	1	4	1	0
Manifest, known (adj.)[7]	φανερός	3	1	2	0
Market-place	ἀγορά	3	3	3	0
Marry, marriage[8]	γαμέω, -ίζω, -ος etc.	5	18	13	2
Marvel, s. Astonish					

---

[1] [1685 c] "Lame," in Jn, only v. 3 "A multitude of them that were infirm, blind, *lame*, withered."

[2] [1685 d] "Lamp," λύχνος. The only instance in Jn is v. 35 "He [*i.e.* John the Baptist] was the *lamp*."

[3] [1685 e] "Last" is not applied to persons etc. in Jn, but "the *last* day," *i.e.* the Day of Judgment, ἐσχάτη ἡμέρα, occurs 7 times in Jn and never in Synoptists.

[4] "Lawful, it is," in Jn only v. 10 "*It is not lawful* for thee to take up thy bed," xviii. 31 "*It is not lawful* for us to kill anyone."

[5] [1686 a] "Liken," Mk iv. 30. "Like," ὅμοιος, is also freq. in Mt. (9), Lk. (9) (but abs. from Mk) in connexion with parables. In Jn ὅμοιος occurs twice, Jn viii. 55 "*like* you," ix. 9 "*like* him."

[6] [1686 b] "Little ones," in Triple Tradition, only in Mk ix. 42, Mt. xviii. 6, Lk. xvii. 2 "one of these *little ones*" [Mk+"*that believe*," Mt.+"*that believe in me*"]. The most reasonable explanation of Lk.'s omitting "that believe in me" and of Mk's omitting "in me" is that the bracketed words were early glosses explaining or defining "little ones."

[7] [1686 c] "Manifest." The vb. φανερόω, however, occurs Mk (1+[2]), Mt. (0), Lk. (0), Jn (9). Besides Mk iv. 22 it occurs in Mk App. xvi. 12, 14 concerning the Resurrection. In Jn xxi. 1 (*bis*), 14 it refers to the Resurrection. See **1716** *i, j*.

[8] [1686 d] "Marriage," γάμος occurs in Jn ii. 1, 2 of the "marriage" at Cana.

FROM SYNOPTIC VOCABULARY [1687]

English	Greek	Mk	Mt.	Lk.	Jn
Mary (mother of the Lord)[1]	Μαρία(μ)	1	5	12	0
Matthew	Ματθαῖος	1	2	2	0
Mercy, s. Compassion					
Middle, midst	μέσος, ἐν μέσῳ, εἰς τὸ μέσον etc.	5	7	14	4
Might, mighty work[2]	δύναμις	10	13	15	0
Mighty (possible, able) (1)	δυνατός	5	3	4	0
Mighty (2)[3]	ἰσχυρός	3	3	4	0
Mock[4]	ἐμπαίζω	3	5	5	0
Money, silver[5]	ἀργύριον	1	9	4	0
Mountain	ὄρος	11	16	12	4
[1687] Nations (plur.)[6], i.e. Gentiles	ἔθνη	4	12	9	0
Near, be or draw near (vb.)[7]	ἐγγίζω	3	7	18	0
Neighbour[8]	πλησίον	2	3	3	0

[1] "Mary." Mk vi. 3 "Is not this the carpenter, the son of *Mary*?"

[2] [1686 e] "Mighty work." Instead of δυνάμεις, "mighty works," which is the usual Synoptic word for Christ's miracles, Jn uses σημεῖα, "signs." To express "power," in a certain sense, he freq. uses ἐξουσία, where R.V. gives "*power*" in txt. but sometimes "*right*," sometimes "*authority*," in margin. "*Authority*" would perhaps be the best word in almost every case (1562—94).

[3] [1686 f] "Mighty" (2). Note that in Mk i. 7, Mt. iii. 11, Lk. iii. 16, John the Baptist says, concerning Jesus, "*Mightier* (ἰσχυρότερος) than I": whereas Jn i. 27 gives the context but omits these words.

[4] "Mock," in Mk x. 34, xv. 20, 31 concerning the "mocking" in the Passion, predicted or practised, and so in Mt.-Lk. exc. Mt. ii. 16, Lk. xiv. 29.

[5] "Money." Mk xiv. 11 "They promised to give him [Judas Iscariot] *money*." Jn ii. 15 has κέρματα "(copper) money."

[6] [1687 a] "Nations." The sing., however, ἔθνος occurs 5 times in Jn (1718 f) and also in Mk xiii. 8, Mt. xxiv. 7, Lk. xxi. 10 "*nation* against *nation*," Mt. xxi. 43 "a *nation*," Lk. vii. 5, xxiii. 2 "our *nation*."

[7] [1687 b] "Near." The adv. ἐγγύς "near," occurs Mk (2), Mt. (3), Lk. (3), Jn (11).

[8] [1687 c] "Neighbour." In Jn πλησίον occurs only in Jn iv. 5 "Sychar, *near* to the parcel of ground..."

JOHANNINE DEVIATIONS

English	Greek	Mk	Mt.	Lk.	Jn
O !	ὦ	1	2	2	0
Oath (s. also Swear)	ὅρκος	1	4	1	0
Oil	ἔλαιον	1	3	3	0
Old[1]	παλαιός	3	3	3 or 5	0
Olives (Mt. of)	ἐλαιῶν (al. -ών)	3	3	4	0
Other, another[2]	ἕτερος (not ἄλλος)	[1]	10	34	1
Parable[3]	παραβολή	13	17	18	0
Paralytic	παραλυτικός	5	5	1	0
Pass, pass by (1)	παρέρχομαι	5	9	9	0
Pass, pass by (2)[4]	παράγω	3	3	0	1
Pay, render, requite[5]	ἀποδίδωμι	1	18	8	0
People[6]	λαός	2	14	37	2
Philip (founder of Caesarea)	Φίλιππος	1	1	1	0
Philip (husband of Herodias)	Φίλιππος	1	1	0	0
Physician	ἰατρός	2	1	3	0
Pity, s. Compassion					
Plant (vb.)	φυτεύω	1	2	4	0
Poor (Chri.)[7]	πτωχός	3	4	8 or 9	1
Power, s. Might					
Pray, prayer	προσεύχομαι, -ή	13	19	22	0
Preach, proclaim	κηρύσσω	12	9	9	0
Prepare[8]	ἑτοιμάζω	5	7	14	2

[1] [1687 d] "Old." Compare, however, 1 Jn ii. 7 about the "*old* commandment" (*bis*).

[2] [1687 e] "(An)other," in Jn, only xix. 37 "Again *another* Scripture saith...." As it occurs only in Mk App. [xvi. 12] (as indicated by the bracketed [1]), and not in Mk, it ought not, strictly, to come in this list.

[3] "Parable," παραβολή, is, in Jn, παροιμία. See **1721** *c—d*.

[4] "Pass by" (2), παράγω, in Jn, only ix. 1 "And, *passing by*, he saw a man blind from birth."

[5] "Pay, render," in Mk only xii. 17 "*Render* therefore to Caesar...." See "Render (**1691**)."

[6] [**1688** a] "People," in Jn, only in the saying of Caiaphas (xi. 50, xviii. 14) that "one man" was to "die for *the people*." In Mk vii. 6 it is in a quotation from Is. xxix. 13 ; in Mk xiv. 2 it is in a saying of the chief priests ; in Mk xi. 32 W.H. have ὄχλον.

[7] [**1688** b] "Poor" (Chri.), in Jn only xii. 8 "The *poor* ye have always," om. by SS and D.

[8] [**1688** c] "Prepare," ἑτοιμάζω, in Jn, only xiv. 2—3 (*bis*) "I go to *prepare* a place." Also κατασκευάζω occurs Mk (1), Mt. (1), Lk. (2), Jn (0).

FROM SYNOPTIC VOCABULARY [1689]

English	Greek	Mk	Mt.	Lk.	Jn
Prepared, ready[1]	ἕτοιμος	1	4	3	1
Prevent, hinder	κωλύω	3	1	6	0
Priest[2]	ἱερεύς	2	3	6	1
Prison[3]	φυλακή	2	8	6	1
Privately, apart[4]	κατ' ἰδίαν	7	6	2	0
[1689] Publican	τελώνης	3	8	10	0
Put on (a garment), (mid.) be clothed in[5]	ἐνδύω	3	3	4	0
	περιβάλλω	2	5	2	1
Ransom	λύτρον, -όω, -ωσις	1	1	3	0
Read (scripture)[6]	ἀναγινώσκω	4	7	3	0
Ready, s. Prepared	ἕτοιμος	1	4	3	1
Reason[7]	διαλογίζομαι, -ισμός	8	4	12	0
Rebuke	ἐπιτιμάω	9	7	12	0
Receive[8]	δέχομαι	6	10	16	1
Recline, lie, sometimes cause to lie[9]	ἀνακλίνω	1	2	3	0
	κατακλίνω	0	0	5	0
Recline with[9]	συνανάκειμαι	2	2	3	0

[1] "Prepared," "ready," in Jn, only vii. 6 "but your time is always *ready*."

[2] "Priest," in Jn, only i. 19 "*priests* and Levites."

[3] "Prison," in Jn, only iii. 24 "For John was not yet cast into *prison*." The numbers above do not include φυλακή meaning "watch," for which see **1696**.

[4] "Privately," see "Apart" (**1672** *b*).

[5] "Put on," see "Clothe" (**1676**).

[6] [**1689** *a*] "Read (scripture)," Jn has ἀναγινώσκω once, but not of scripture, xix. 20 "This title, therefore, the Jews *read*."

[7] [**1689** *b*] "Reason," when used in the phrase "reasoned among themselves," is sometimes synonymous with "murmur," γογγύζω, which occurs Mk (0), Mt. (1) (in parable), Lk. (1), Jn (4)—or with διαγογγύζω which occurs in Lk. alone (2).

[8] [**1689** *c*] "Receive," δέχομαι, in Jn, only iv. 45 "the Galilaeans *received* him": but λαμβάνω, "receive *i.e.* welcome (a person)," occurs Mk (0), Mt. (0), Lk. (0), Jn (11) (**1721** *f—g*). Παραλαμβάνω occurs Mk (6), Mt. (16), Lk. (6), Jn (3), always of persons except in Mk vii. 4, but not always of friendly reception.

[9] [**1689** *d*] "Recline" (almost always at meals). Ἀνάκειμαι and ἀναπίπτω, in a similar sense, occur in all the Four Gospels.

[1690] JOHANNINE DEVIATIONS

English	Greek	Mk	Mt.	Lk.	Jn
Reed[1]	κάλαμος	2	5	1	0
[1690] Remission of sins[2]	ἄφεσις ἁμαρτιῶν	1	1	3	0

[1] [1689 e] "Reed." Mk xv. 19, 36, Mt. xxvii. 29, 30, 48, Lk. om., of the "reed" mentioned in the Passion: Mt. xi. 7, Lk. vii. 24 (the only instance) "a *reed* shaken by the wind": Mt. xii. 20 (quoting Is. xlii. 3) "a bruised *reed*."

[2] [1690 a] "Remission of sins," ἄφεσις ἁμαρτιῶν, is connected by Mk i. 4 and Lk. iii. 3 with the Baptist's preaching, but the parall. Mt. iii. 2 omits it and mentions "the kingdom of heaven" [Mt. xxvi. 28, however, inserts "for the remission of sins" in the account of the Eucharist where Mk-Lk. omit it]. The following facts bear on ἄφεσις in LXX and on Jewish traditions about the Hebrew original of the word.

[1690 b] (i) Apart from a few unimportant exceptions, ἄφεσις, in canon. LXX, means *the "release" of the Sabbatical Year, or of Jubilee*, and is not connected with atonement except once in a passage describing the scape-goat that is (Lev. xvi. 26) "*for Azazel.*" Josephus speaks of Jubilee as the year (*Ant.* iii. 12. 3) "wherein debtors are *freed from their debts* and slaves are *set at liberty*"; and he says that "the name denotes *Aphesis.*" Isaiah lxi. 1—2 connects "*liberty* (ἄφεσιν) to the captives" with "*the acceptable year of the Lord,*" which (Ibn Ezra says) means "the Year of Remission": and this forms part of the text, so to speak, of our Lord's first sermon in Luke (iv. 17—19). Debtors sometimes sold themselves or their children into slavery; so that remission of servitude and remission of debt would naturally often go together.

[1690 c] (ii) Part of the observance of *Aphesis* consisted in "releasing" the land from service by abstaining from agriculture for a whole year and allowing the poor to partake of such fruits or crops as grew of themselves. That this institution was observed shortly before, and shortly after, our Lord's birth, we know from the testimony of Josephus *Ant.* xiv. 16. 2, xv. 1. 2, Philo in Eus. *Praep. Evang.* viii. 7 and Tac. *Hist.* v. 4. Josephus says that it caused great distress when Herod besieged Jerusalem (as well it might), and he quotes (*Ant.* xiv. 10. 6) a decree of Julius Caesar remitting tribute for every Sabbatical Year.

[1690 d] (iii) That inconvenience was caused by the "remission" of debts in the Sabbatical Year as late as the birthtime of Christ, we know from the Mishna, which tells us that Hillel (probably about the beginning of the Christian era) introduced a legal means of evading the Law because people entertained the (Deut. xv. 9) "base thought" of refusing to lend in view of the approaching *Aphesis*. But the Gemara (*J. Shebiith* x. 4) adds (Schwab ii. 428) " Mais est-ce que cet acte [de

Hillel] a pour origine la Torâ ? Non ; seulement lorsque Hillel l'a institué, il l'a basé sur une allusion biblique."

[1690 e] (iv) In Jeremiah (xxxiv. 13—15) the act of "proclaiming *Aphesis*" is shewn by the context to mean, or include, freedom from servitude ; and both that prophet and Nehemiah (Neh. x. 31 "that we would forgo *the seventh year and the exaction of every debt*") contended against the wealthy for that very observance of *Aphesis* which Hillel practically abrogated. Hillel was the greatest and best of the Pharisees and acted (no doubt) from perfectly pure motives ; but the Pharisees of the next generation were called a "generation of vipers" by the Baptist, and he refused to give them baptism. It is antecedently probable that peasants and fishermen would dislike the evasion of the Law, and that the Baptist, the last of the prophets, who bade those that had "two coats" to "give to him that had none," would with still more force insist on the observance of the statute Law of the Nation, which no Pharisee could abrogate.

[1690 f] (v) Josephus tells us that the Baptist (*Ant.* xviii. 5. 2) insisted that his disciples, before being baptized, should be "thoroughly purified beforehand by *righteousness*," and he distinguishes "*righteousness towards one another*" from "piety to God." Luke iii. 12, 14 tells us that the publicans and soldiers said to the Baptist "*What shall we do?*" and were told how to exercise "righteousness" according to their ability. These two witnesses convert the above-mentioned probability to a certainty, that the Baptist would make rich men and Pharisees "*do*" something before he gave them baptism : and the least they could do (according to the view of a Prophet) would be to observe the written Law in all its requirements for the good of the poor.

[1690 g] (vi) Both in Greek and in Hebrew, "release" means also "forgive." In Aramaic (1181) "debt" and "sin" may be represented by the same word. Hence "*forgive* us our *sins*" might be interchanged with "*release* us from our *debts*." The conditional prayer, "Release us from our debts as we release those that are indebted to us" might have a twofold meaning.

[1690 h] (vii) The fact that Matthew reads "*debts*" for "*sins*" in the Lord's Prayer should be considered in this connexion. And many other kindred questions deserve discussion, although they cannot be discussed here, for example, whether John the Baptist did not intend something like a compulsory socialism, and whether Jesus of Nazareth did not intend to convert this into what should ultimately become a voluntary socialism. Possibly it may appear that such an incident as the death of Ananias and Sapphira was one of many signs that might reveal to the Apostles and their successors the evil of importing into the Church what was (practically) a compulsory socialism twenty centuries or more before the Church was ready for even any form of voluntary socialism.

[1691]   JOHANNINE DEVIATIONS

English	Greek	Mk	Mt.	Lk.	Jn
[1691] Render, requite, pay[1]	ἀποδίδωμι	1	18	8	0
Repent, repentance	μετανοέω, -οια	3	7	14	0
Report, bring word to, s. Tell	ἀπαγγέλλω	3	8	11	1
Reproach	ὀνειδίζω	1	3	1	0
Rest, the	λοιπός	2	4	6	0
Retain, seize, take hold of[2]	κρατέω	15	12	2	2
Reward, wages[3]	μισθός	1	10	3	1
Rich, riches[4]	πλούσιος, πλοῦτος	3	4	12	0
Right, on the[5]	ἐκ δεξιῶν (μου) or ἐν τοῖς δεξίοις	6	7	4	0
Righteous, just (appl. to men)	δίκαιος	2	c. 15	10	0
Righteous (appl. to God)[6]	δίκαιος	0	0	0	1

[1] "Render," see "Pay" (1687), and the note on "Reward" below.

[2] [1691 a] "Retain etc." Jn uses κρατέω twice, but only in one passage, and metaphorically (xx. 23) "Whose soever [sins] ye *retain* they are *retained*." The meaning is obscure. See 2517—20.

[3] [1691 b] "Reward," "wages." The two instances in Mk and Jn are Mk ix. 41 "He *shall* surely *not lose his reward*," Jn iv. 36 "*Already... is taking his reward*." The former regards the reward as future, the latter regards it as present.

[4] [1691 c] "Rich," see "Poor" (Chri.) which is shewn (1688 b) to occur only once in Jn (where D and SS om. the mention).

[5] [1691 d] "Right, on the." Jn makes no distinction of "right" and "left" between the malefactors crucified with the Saviour. Also, he never speaks of the Son as "*at the right hand*" of the Father, but as "*in*" the Father, or "*one*" with the Father, and similarly of the disciples as being "*in*" the Son. Jn xxi. 6 "on the right side" is not included in the list above because "side (μέρη)" is added.

[6] [1691 e] "Righteous" applied to God occurs in Jn xvii. 25 "O *righteous* Father." Applied to things, it occurs Mk (o), Mt. xx. 4 "Whatsoever is *righteous* (i.e. *just*) I will give you"; Lk. xii. 57 "Why, even of yourselves, judge ye not *that which is righteous* (τὸ δίκαιον)?" i.e. judge *justly*; Jn v. 30 "My judgment is *righteous*," vii. 24 "Judge *righteous* judgment." Jn and Mk never use δικαιόω "justify," "make righteous," which occurs Mt. (2) Lk. (5). On "righteousness," which occurs Mk (o) Mt. (7) Lk. (1) Jn (2), see 1854 b. The facts suggest that Jn uses the adjective and noun in the Platonic sense of "just" and "justice" rather than in the technical Hebrew meaning, "observant of the requirements of the Law [of Moses]." On "judging justly," see 1714 d—g.

FROM SYNOPTIC VOCABULARY [1692]

English	Greek	Mk	Mt.	Lk.	Jn
Rock[1]	πέτρα	1	5	4	0
Root	ῥίζα	3	3	2	0
[1692] Sadducee	Σαδδουκαῖος	1	8	1	0
Sake of, for the[2]	ἕνεκα	4	7	5	0
Salt	ἅλας	3	2	2	0
Sanhedrin, council[3]	συνέδριον	3	3	1	1
Satan[4]	Σατανᾶς	5	3	5	1
Satisfy[5]	χορτάζω	4	4	4	1
Save[6]	σώζω	14	15	17	6

[1] "Rock," in Mk, only xv. 46 "Hewn out of *rock*."

[2] [1692 a] "Sake." Jn however uses ὑπέρ in xiii. 37, 38 (A.V.) "*for* thy, my, *sake*," (R.V.) "*for* thee," "*for* me." Comp. Jn xv. 21 "These things will they do unto you *because of* (διά) my name," (A.V. and R.V.) "*for* my name's *sake*." Jn xii. 30 "*for* your *sakes*" has διά, Jn xvii. 19 "*for* their *sakes*" has ὑπέρ. For the difference between the Johannine and the Synoptic view, see 1225—6. On the Johannine "sake," διά, see 1721, and 1884 *a—b*.

[3] "Sanhedrin," etc. Lk. xxii. 66, Jn xi. 47.

[4] [1692 b] "Satan," in Jn, only xiii. 27 "Then (*i.e.* at that moment, τότε) entered into him *Satan*," i.e. into Judas Iscariot; Lk. xxii. 3 ("But *Satan* entered into Judas") places the "entering" earlier.

[5] [1692 c] "Satisfy," in Jn, only vi. 26 "Because ye ate from the loaves and were *satisfied*," lit. fed as beasts with grass—probably used by Jn in a bad sense, but not so by Mk vi. 42, Mt. xiv. 20, Lk. ix. 17 etc.

[6] [1692 d] "Save." In the words of Christ, "*save*" is used by the Synoptists in the phrase "Thy faith hath *saved* thee" (after acts of healing), "he that will *save* his soul (*i.e.* life) shall lose it," etc. But there is no Synoptic statement that Christ came to "*save*" except in the story of Zacchaeus peculiar to Luke (Lk. xix. 10) "For the Son of man came to seek and to *save* the lost."

[1692 e] Mt. xviii. 11 (R.V. marg.) has "Many authorities, some ancient, insert, 'For the Son of man came *to save* that which was lost'": Lk. ix. 56 (R.V. marg.) has, besides another insertion supported by "some ancient authorities," the following one supported by "fewer": "For the Son of man came not to destroy men's lives but *to save* [*them*]." But W.H. omit both of these without marginal alternative. And they are omitted by SS.

[1692 f] Jn iii. 17 "God *sent* not *the Son* into the world that he should judge the world but that the world *should be saved* through him," is probably, as Westcott argues at some length, a comment of the Evangelist, not an utterance of Christ: but the necessity for so long an argument shews how easily comment on Christ's words might be taken

JOHANNINE DEVIATIONS

English	Greek	Mk	Mt.	Lk.	Jn
Scourge, i.e. painful disease	μάστιξ	3	0	1	0
Scribe	γραμματεύς	22	19	14	0
Scriptures, the (pl.) (1722)	αἱ γραφαί	2	4	3	1
Seed (lit.)	σπέρμα, σπόρος	3	5	2	0
Seed (metaph.)[1]	σπέρμα	4	2	2	3
Seize, retain, take hold of[2]	κρατέω	15	12	2	2
Sell (Chri.)	πωλέω	1	4	5	0
Sell (narr.)[3]	πωλέω	2	2	1	2
Set before[4]	παρατίθημι	4	2	3	0

as part of Christ's words, and illustrates the growth of the interpolations mentioned in the last paragraph.

[1692 g] The Johannine version of the words of Christ certainly represents Him as saying (a) Jn v. 34 "These things I say that *ye may be saved*," (b) Jn x. 9 "Through me if anyone enter in *he shall be saved*," (c) xii. 27 "Shall I say, 'Father, *save* me from this hour?'" (**933—40**), (d) xii. 47 "*I came not that I might judge the world but that I might save the world.*" The 1st, 2nd, and 4th of these clearly imply spiritual "saving."

[1] [1692 h] "Seed" (metaph.). Jn vii. 42 "From the *seed* of David," viii. 33 "We are Abraham's *seed*," viii. 37 "I know that ye are Abraham's *seed*." Jn xii. 24 has κόκκος for "grain (of wheat)," to suggest the soul dying that it may live.

[2] "Seize." See above, "Retain" (1691 a).

[3] "Sell" (narr.). All these relate to the casting out of them that "sold" in the Temple.

[4] [1692 i] "Set before," i.e. set food before, Mk vi. 41, Lk. ix. 16, in the Feeding of the Five Thousand; and Mk viii. 6 (*bis*), 7 in the Feeding of the Four Thousand. But Mt. in the parall. to these three passages of Mk omits παρατίθημι. Mt., when using this word, applies it *to spiritual food, or teaching by parables*, xiii. 24, 31 "Another parable he *set before* them."

[1692 j] Lk. has x. 8 "Eat the things *set before* you," xi. 6 "I have nothing to *set before* him," but also uses the middle to mean (xii. 48, xxiii. 46) "entrust," "commend." Comp. Acts xiv. 23 "*commended* them to the Lord," but xvi. 34 (act.) "*set before* them a table," i.e. fed them, xvii. 3 "opening [the Scriptures] and *setting before them* [*the doctrine*] that it behoved the Christ to suffer." The word has these various meanings in the Epistles also: 1 Cor. x. 27, 1 Tim. i. 18, 2 Tim. ii. 2, 1 Pet. iv. 19.

FROM SYNOPTIC VOCABULARY [1693]

English	Greek	Mk	Mt.	Lk.	Jn
Seven, seven times	ἑπτά, -κις	8	11	8	0
Shed blood	ἐκχύννω αἷμα	1	2	2 or 3	0
Sick, s. Diseased	κακῶς ἔχων	4	5	2	0
[1693] Sidon	Σιδών	3	3	3	0
Silent, be (1)	σιγάω	0	0	3	0
Silent, be (2)	σιωπάω	5	2	2	0
Sinner, sinful[1]	ἁμαρτωλός	6	5	17	4
Sit (1)	καθέζομαι	0	1	1	3
Sit (2)	κάθημαι	11	19	13	4
Sit (3)	καθίζω	7	8	8	2
Sleep (1)	καθεύδω	8	7	2	0
Sleep (2)[2]	κοιμάομαι	0	2	1	2
Smite (1)	πατάσσω	1	2	2	0
Smite (2)	τύπτω	1	2	4	0
So, in the same way	ὡσαύτως	2	4	2 or 3	0
So as to, so that[3]	ὥστε	13	15	4	1
So to say, as it were, about[4]	ὡσεί	1	3	8	0
Sodom (1671 c)	Σόδομα	0	3	2	0
Sow[5]	σπείρω	10	16	6	2
Spit on[6]	ἐμπτύω	3	2	1	0
Straightway (1 a) (**1910** foll.)	εὐθύς	c. 40	7	1	3
Straightway (1 b) (**1914** foll.)	εὐθέως	0	11	6	3

[1] "Sinner" occurs in Jn only in the dialogue about the man born blind, four times, Jn ix. 16, 24, 25, 31 (**1371 b**).

[2] [1693 a] "Sleep" (2). Κοιμάομαι means the sleep of death in Mt. xxvii. 52 "the saints that *slept* arose." In Jn xi. 11 "Lazarus has *fallen asleep* (κεκοίμηται)," the disciples take the verb literally and comment on it thus (xi. 12) "If he *has fallen asleep* he will recover (**1858**)."

[3] [1693 b] "So as to," "so that," occurs in Jn only in iii. 16 "*so that* he gave his only begotten Son," a comment of the Evangelist, not a saying of Christ's. See "save" above (**1692 f**).

[4] [1693 c] "So to say," "about" occurs in Mt. xiv. 21, parall. Lk. ix. 14 "*about* five thousand," but Mk and Jn, who also mention "five thousand," do not thus qualify it.

[5] "Sow," in Jn, only iv. 36—7, of spiritual sowing.

[6] [1693 d] "Spit on," referring to the Passion, does not occur in Jn; but πτύω, "spit," occurs in Mk vii. 33, viii. 23, Jn ix. 6 in connexion with healing. See **1737 b**.

English	Greek	Mk	Mt.	Lk.	Jn
Straightway (2)[1]	παραχρῆμα	0	2	10	0
Strength, strong	ἰσχύς, ἰσχυρός	4	4	5	0
Strong, be[2]	ἰσχύω	4	4	8	1
Stretch out the hand(s)[3]	ἐκτείνω χεῖρα(ς)	3	6	3	1
[1694] Stumble, make to stumble, stumbling-block[4]	σκανδαλίζω, σκάνδαλον	8	19	3	2
Substance, possessions, living	βίος	1	0	5	0
	ὑπάρχοντα	0	3	8	0
	κτήματα	1	1	0	0
Suffer	πάσχω	3	4	6	0
Sufficient (marg. worthy), great	ἱκανός	3	3	10	0
Sun	ἥλιος	4	5	3	0
Swear (s. also Oath)	ὀμνύω	2	13	1	0
Swine	χοῖρος	4	4	4	0
Synagogue[5]	συναγωγή	8	9	15	2

[1] [1693 e] "Straightway" (2). Παραχρῆμα is not strictly entitled to a place here, but it is inserted to explain that Lk.'s deficiency in respect of εὐθύς and εὐθέως may be compensated by his excess in respect of another word of similar meaning. Παραχρῆμα, both in Mt. and Lk., is connected with miraculous results in the context exc. (a) Lk. xix. 11 "that the kingdom of God was destined to come *immediately*," (b) Lk. xxii. 60 "And *immediately*, while he was yet speaking, the cock crew." In (a), the meaning is, perhaps, "come by special miracle"; in (b), attention seems to be called to a miraculous coincidence.

[2] [1693 f] "Strong, be" occurs in Jn only in xxi. 6 "They were no longer strong [enough] to draw it [*i.e.* the net]." On Jn's non-use of "strong," "mighty" etc., see the latter (1686 f).

[3] [1693 g] "Stretch out the hands," in Jn only xxi. 18 "Thou shalt *stretch out thy hands*," to which is added, "Now this he spake signifying by what manner of death he [*i.e.* Peter] should glorify God," *i.e.* by stretching out his hands on the cross.

[4] [1694 a] "Stumble" etc. Jn has only the verb, vi. 61 "Doth this *make you to stumble?*" xvi. 1 "This have I said to you that ye be not *made to stumble.*"

[5] [1694 b] "Synagogue," in Jn, only vi. 59 (R.V.) "These things said he in [the, *or*, a] *synagogue* (ἐν συναγωγῇ) as he taught in Capernaum," xviii. 20 "I ever taught in [the, *or*, a] *synagogue* (ἐν συναγωγῇ) and in the temple." Perhaps "in synagogue" (like our "in church") would be the best rendering in both passages.

FROM SYNOPTIC VOCABULARY

English	Greek	Mk	Mt.	Lk.	Jn
Take hold of, s. Retain	κρατέω	15	12	2	2
Teacher, Master (voc.)[1]	διδάσκαλε	10	6	12	2
Tell (R.V.), bring word[2]	ἀπαγγέλλω	3	8	11	1
[1695] Tempt, temptation[3]	πειράζω, -ασμός	5	8	8	1
Testimony[4]	μαρτύριον	3	3	3	0
That (i.e. in order that)[5]	ὅπως	1	17	6	1
Then (i.e. after all)	ἄρα	2	7	6	0
Then (i.e. at that time)	τότε	6	88	14	10
Third[6]	τρίτος	2	6	9	1

---

[1] [1694 c] "Teacher," voc., in Jn, only i. 38 'Ραββεὶ ὃ λέγεται μεθ. Διδάσκαλε, xx. 16 'Ραββουνεὶ ὃ λέγεται Διδάσκαλε. Jn viii. 4, where δ. occurs without the Aramaic, is an interpolation. For "Rabbi" see 1815.

[2] [1694 d] "Tell (R.V.)," in Jn, only xvi. 25 "I will *tell* you plainly concerning the Father" (see 1675 b). Jn also has ἀγγέλλω (not used by Synoptists) in xx. 18 "then cometh Mary Magdalene *telling* the disciples."

[3] [1695 a] "Tempt," in Jn, only vi. 6 "But this he said *tempting* him," of Jesus "tempting" Philip.

[4] [1695 b] "Testimony." In Mk-Mt., only in the phrase εἰς μ. αὐτοῖς (or, τοῖς ἔθνεσι) which seems to mean "as a testimony *against* them" (Mk i. 44, vi. 11, xiii. 9, Mt. viii. 4, x. 18, xxiv. 14) or "a testimony with regard to them in case they should disbelieve." Lk. ix. 5 (parall. to Mk vi. 11) has εἰς μ. ἐπ' αὐτούς, but Lk. v. 14 εἰς μ. αὐτοῖς. Lk. xxi. 13 has ἀποβήσεται ὑμῖν εἰς μ. absolutely. This must be carefully distinguished from μαρτυρία, a freq. Johannine term (1726).

[5] [1695 c] "That," i.e. in order that, Mk iii. 6 (Mt. xii. 14) ὅπως αὐτὸν ἀπολέσωσιν, Jn xi. 57 ὅπως πιάσωσιν αὐτόν. It is noteworthy that the only instance of ὅπως in Mk-Jn refers to attempts to destroy or arrest Jesus. Comp. Mt. xii. 14 ὅπως αὐτὸν ἀπολέσωσιν, xxii. 15 ὅπως αὐτὸν παγιδεύσωσιν ἐν λόγῳ, xxvi. 59 ὅπως αὐτὸν θανατώσωσιν. Lk. vi. 11 (parall. to Mk iii. 6, Mt. xii. 14) has τί ἂν ποιήσαιεν τῷ 'Ι. These figures have nothing to do with ἵνα "in order that" (1726).

[6] [1695 d] "Third," in Jn, only ii. 1 "On the *third* day there was a marriage in Cana." "*On the third day*" in Mt.-Lk. always refers to Christ's Resurrection; but Mk has "*after three days*" (1297).

185

English	Greek	Mk	Mt.	Lk.	Jn
Third time, the (adv.)[1]	τρίτον, ἐκ τρίτου	1	1	1	3
Throne (1671 c)	θρόνος	0	5	3	0
Time, season [2]	καιρός	5	10	13	3
To-day	σήμερον	1	7	12	0
Torment	βασανίζω, -ος	2	4	3	0
Touch [3]	ἅπτομαι	11	9	10	1
Tradition (1671 c)	παράδοσις	5	3	0	0
Treasure, treasure-house, lay up treasure	θησαυρίζω, -ός	1	11	5	0
Tree	δένδρον	1	12	7	0
Turn, turn back [4]	ἐπιστρέφω	4	4	7	1
Twelve (disciples, or apostles), the [5]	(οἱ) δώδεκα (μαθηταί, ἀπόστολοι)	11	8	7	4
Tyre		3	3	3	0
Unclean	ἀκάθαρτος	11	2	6	0
Understand, understanding	συνίημι, σύνεσις, συνετός	6	10	6	0
[1696] Verily (1)[6]	ἀμήν	14	c. 30	6	0
Verily verily (2)[6]	ἀμὴν ἀμήν	0	0	0	26

[1] [1695 e] "Third time" (adv.). This occurs in Mk xiv. 41, "cometh *the third time*," Mt. xxvi. 44 "prayed *a third time* (ἐκ τρίτου)." In Lk. xxiii. 22, Jn xxi. 14, 17 (*bis*) there is no parallelism. Jn xxi. 14 τοῦτο ἤδη τρίτον ἐφανερώθη refers to a "third" manifestation of the Resurrection.

[2] [1695 f] "Time," "season," in Jn, only vii. 6—8 "my *time* (*bis*)... your *time*."

[3] [1695 g] "Touch," in Jn, only xx. 17 "*Touch* me not." In the Synoptists it almost always refers to Jesus touching the diseased or the diseased touching Him or His garments.

[4] [1695 h] "Turn," in Jn, only xxi. 20 "Peter, *turning about* (ἐπιστραφείς)." The active is applied to Peter in Lk. xxii. 32 "When once thou hast *turned again* (ἐπιστρέψας)."

[5] [1695 i] "Twelve, the," never mentioned by Jn except in connexion with the treachery of Judas (vi. 70, 71) or some suggestion of desertion in the context (vi. 67) "Will ye also go away?" or some unbelief (xx. 24) "Thomas, one of the Twelve."

[6] [1696 a] "Verily." No one has been able hitherto to explain why the Three Gospels never use ἀμήν doubly, and the Fourth never singly, in reporting the sayings of Christ. Lk. also has ἀληθῶς thrice (ix. 27, xii. 44, xxi. 3) with λέγω, a combination peculiar to him.

FROM SYNOPTIC VOCABULARY [1696]

English	Greek	Mk	Mt.	Lk.	Jn
Villages (pl.)[1]	κῶμαι	4	2	3	0
Vineyard	ἀμπελών	5	10	7	0
Wallet	πήρα	1	1	4	0
Watch (vb.)	γρηγορέω	6	6	2	0
Watch, a (of the night)	φυλακή	1	2	2	0
Way, road[2]	ὁδός	16	22	20	4
Wealth, s. Riches					
Well-pleased, good pleasure	εὐδοκέω, -ία	1	4	4	0
Widow	χήρα	3	1	9	0
Wife (not "woman")	γυνή	10	16	16	0
Wind	ἄνεμος	7	9	4	1
Wisdom, wise[3]	σοφία, σοφός	1	5	7	0
Within	ἔσωθεν	2	4	3	0
Without, outside	ἔξωθεν	2 or 3	3	2	0
Witness[4]	μάρτυς	1	2	2	0
Woe	οὐαί	2	13	14	0
Wonder, s. Astonish					
Zebedee	Ζεβεδαῖος	4	6	1	1

[1] **[1696 b]** "Villages" (pl.). All the Evangelists use κωμή (sing.), Jn (3) referring to (vii. 42) Bethlehem or (xi. 1, 30) "Bethany."

[2] **[1696 c]** "Way." Jn mentions "the Way" in only two passages, one (i. 23 quoting Is. xl. 3) describing John the Baptist as bidding men "make straight" *the way* of the Lord, the other (xiv. 4, 6) describing Christ as saying "whither I go, ye know *the way*," and "I am *the way*."

[3] **[1696 d]** "Wisdom," "wise." In Mk, "wisdom" occurs only in Mk vi. 2 (parall. Mt. xiii. 54) "What is this *wisdom* that is given to this man?" Mk nowhere uses "wise." Mt.-Lk. use also φρόνιμος Mk (0), Mt. (7), Lk. (2), Jn (0).

[4] **[1696 e]** "Witness." Mt. xxvi. 25 (parall. Mk xiv. 63), also Mt. xviii. 16 (alluding to Deut. xix. 15) ἐπὶ στόματος δύο μαρτύρων ἢ τριῶν σταθῇ πᾶν ῥῆμα. Comp. Jn viii. 17 "Yea, and it is written in your law, that of two men the testimony is true δύο ἀνθρώπων ἡ μαρτυρία ἀληθής ἐστιν)." In Rev. ii. 13, xi. 3, xvii. 6 μάρτυς = "martyr" (even R.V. is obliged to render it thus in txt. of xvii. 6) and prob. also (of Jesus) in i. 5, iii. 14 (meaning "*testifying* by one's death"). Possibly this technical sense of μάρτυς in some Christian circles at the beginning of the 2nd century caused John to abstain from it.

CHAPTER II

SYNOPTIC DEVIATIONS FROM JOHANNINE VOCABULARY

§ 1. *Introductory remarks*

[1697] In the following list of words characteristic of the Fourth Gospel and comparatively seldom (or never) used by the Synoptists, one of the most noteworthy among many noteworthy facts is that Mark only once mentions the word "*Father*," as expressing God's fatherhood in relation to men[1]. The noun "*love*," too, never occurs in Mark. Matthew uses the word once in a prediction that "the *love* of the many shall wax cold." Luke speaks once of "the love of God" where the parallel Matthew omits it[2]. Mark's deficiencies are to some extent filled up by the two later Synoptists: but if we put ourselves in the position of an early evangelist trying to convert the world with nothing but Mark's Gospel in his hands, we shall be all the better able to understand the attitude of John towards Christian doctrine in general and Mark's version of it in particular. Mark, for example, mentions God as the Father of men once, and God the Father, in all, four

---

[1] Mk xi. 25. Mk viii. 38, xiii. 32, xiv. 36 mention the word in relation to the Son of man, but not in relation to men in general.

[2] Mt. xxiii. 23 "Ye have left [undone] the weightier matters of the Law namely, [righteous] judgment and kindness and faith," Lk. xi. 42 "Ye pass by [righteous] judgment and the love of God."

times: John uses the term a hundred and twenty times. Mark abundantly uses the term Gospel, or Good News, but nowhere tells us what the "good news" is: John nowhere uses the term, but everywhere exhibits the Son of God as bringing to mankind the best of good news, namely, that God is a loving Father, and that men can find an eternal home in His love.

[**1698**] Where the Synoptists speak of a Kingdom, there John implies a Family. That is the great difference between the Three Gospels and the Fourth. The latter nowhere mentions the Kingdom of God except to represent Jesus as warning a great Rabbi that it cannot be seen or entered except after a new birth; and in the first of these warnings, the words "born from above" indicate that one must become a child of the Family of Heaven. Something of this kind appears to be latent in the Synoptic doctrines about "little children" and "little ones." In this connexion the Synoptists inculcate two distinct duties. One is the duty of "receiving" *little children*; the other is that of "receiving the Kingdom of God *as a little child*," meaning, apparently, with an innocent, pure, and sincere heart. A great deal is implied in each of these precepts, and both are liable to be misunderstood. The second, for example, might encourage some to suppose that they were to become "as a little child" *in understanding*; and these would require the Pauline warning, "In malice be ye babes, but in understanding be ye men[1]." Against an error of this kind, men would be fortified by the Johannine doctrine that "little children" meant "the children of God," and that this was a title of "authority"—but authority in a new sense, the "authority to lay down one's life" for others (**1586—94**).

[**1699**] John teaches that, as there is an eternal unity in the divine Family, namely, the Father, the Son and the

---

[1] 1 Cor. xiv. 20.

Spirit, so there is a foreordained unity for the human Family (namely, those who receive the Spirit of the Father by receiving the Son). Into that Family they must first be "born" from above. Then they must "abide" in it. Or, from another point of view, it must "abide" in them. They must "eat the flesh" of the Son, so that the Son may be in them, even while they are in the Son. They must also "drink" His "blood." Other metaphors describe the members of this Family as eating the "bread" that "descends from heaven," the "bread of life," as "drinking" of the "water of life," as "coming to the light," and as "walking in the light." In a family, "prayer" from the children to the father is out of place. Hence John never uses the word "pray." The Son speaks always of "requesting" or "asking," and He bids the disciples "ask" what they will in His name. The Father's "will" is the sole "law" for Him. If the Fourth Evangelist mentions the Law, it is as being the Law of the Servant ("the law of *Moses*") or the Law of the Jews ("*your* law" etc.). The Son never says, in this Gospel, "I have come to fulfil the Law" but "I have come to do the will of him that sent me."

[1700] Instead of a Kingdom and instead of the laws of a King, the Fourth Gospel proclaims Nature; only, of course, not materialistically, not a mere machinery, but, as we might put it, Mother Nature. According to Epictetus, "Nature is of all things the most powerful in man and draws him to her desire[1]"; and he says elsewhere that there is nothing to which man is so much drawn as to the Eu-Logon[2]; and man is by

---

[1] [1700 *a*] Epict. ii. 20. 15. He is arguing against Epicurus, who, he says, desired to eradicate the belief in (*ib.* ii. 20. 6) "natural human fellowship (τὴν φυσικὴν κοινωνίαν ἀνθρώποις πρὸς ἀλλήλους)" and yet was forced by Nature to act inconsistently with his own theory.

[2] [1700 *b*] Epict. i. 2. 4 τὸ εὔλογον. "That which is reasonable" does not fully express the Greek. It might be rendered "good Logos" (as τὸ εὐτυχές might be rendered "good fortune," τὸ εὐγενές "good birth" etc.) so as to give play to the many meanings of Logos.

Nature created for "fellowship." John represents the Eu-Logon, or Good Logos, as one with the Father in the Spirit of Fellowship. But he also represents Him as incarnate and as revealing the Spirit of Fellowship at a height never before reached. The beast dies for the herd fighting against wolves, and man dies for his country against foreigners. Both are inspired by Mother Nature, the Spirit of Fellowship. But the incarnation of the Good Logos dies as a Jew, crucified by Jews, for "*all men*" alike, with the prediction, "I, if I be lifted up, will draw *all men* unto me"—*i.e.* I will draw all men into harmony with Nature.

[1701] These remarks may be of use in preparing the reader for a prominent feature in the following Vocabulary, namely a predominance of simple terms such as a child might use to describe family life. The one term wanting is "*brother*." This, in the Fourth Gospel, is merged in the relationship between the Father and His children, and it is not used till after the Resurrection: "But go unto my *brethren*, and say unto them I ascend unto my Father and your Father."

[1702] Where the Fourth Gospel deals with history, it is in a cosmopolitan spirit. Not only do the Synoptic distinctions of "publicans," "sinners," "scribes," and "Sadducees," disappear, but, instead of the old fundamental demarcation between "the people," *i.e.* Israel, and "the nations," *i.e.* the Gentiles, we find the term "Jews" used, almost as Tacitus uses it, as the embodiment of narrow hostility to all that is humane and truthful[1]. Both the Romans and the Greeks —never mentioned by the Synoptists—are introduced by John, the former as destined to "take away" the "place" of the unholy "nation[2]," the latter as exemplifying the devout and

---

[1] [1702 a] On the corrupt attribution to Jesus of the words, "Salvation is from the Jews," see 1647—8. On the other hand John alone uses (i. 47) "*Israelite*" as synonymous with "*upright*."

[2] xi. 48.

intelligent world awakening to the truth—the "coming" of the "isles," as Isaiah[1] predicted, to the light of God's glory[2].

[1703] Since the Johannine Gospel deals with Nature (in the higher sense) and not with books or written codes of laws, it naturally speaks of things that can be seen and known by any one that will use his natural powers. The three Greek words most commonly used to mean "*know*" and "*see*" (οἶδα, γινώσκω, and ὁράω) are used more often in the Fourth Gospel than in the Three taken together[3]. The same statement applies to the word "*testify*" or "*bear witness*" (μαρτυρέω). The Evangelist regards the Gospel not as a message proceeding from a prophet, but as a "testimony" to what the Son of God "*sees*" the Father doing in heaven; and what He sees He can enable all the children of God to see. Hence comes a great insistence on "the *truth*," a word *never used by the Synoptists in the modern and Johannine sense of truth in the abstract.* By "knowing truth," John means a correspondence of the human mind to divine facts (that is to say, to the divine

---

[1] Is. lx. 9. See Jn xii. 20—1, comp. vii. 35.

[2] [1702 *b*] This cosmopolitan view of things may, in part, explain Jn's omission of many of the names given by one or more of the Synoptists, *e.g.* Matthew, Bartholomew, Lebbaeus, or Thaddaeus, and the names of the brethren of the Lord.

[1702 *c*] But on the other hand "Cephas" appears for the first time in the Fourth Gospel as the equivalent of the Synoptic "Peter," and we cannot feel sure that Synoptic names may not be latent under "Nathanael" whom our Lord calls "An Israelite indeed, in whom is no guile."

[1702 *d*] Jn and Lk. alone mention "Annas," Lk. in the phrase "Annas and Caiaphas being High Priests." John explains that he was not High Priest but the High Priest's influential father-in-law. Other names that Jn has, in common with Lk. alone, are Martha, Mary, Lazarus, Siloam. The whole group requires careful investigation, as also do the names peculiar to Jn—Aenon, Bethany beyond Jordan, Bethesda (?), Salim, Sychar, etc.

[3] [1703 *a*] The exact statement about ὁράω is that, including forms of ὄψομαι, and ὤφθην, it occurs in Jn 30 times, and in Mk-Mt.-Lk. 32 times. The Perfect, ἑώρακα, occurs as follows, Mk (0), Mt. (0), Lk. (2 or 3), Jn (19).

facts of love and self-sacrifice) analogous to that correspondence between a man's words and his thoughts which is called "sincerity" or "veracity," and to that correspondence between his words and external actualities which implies knowledge and is called "truth."

[1704] What some have called "the egotistic element" in the Fourth Gospel will be found reflected in its abundant use of "I," "my," "myself" etc. as shewn below. It must not be supposed, however, that these pronominal forms exclude the impersonal phrase "the Son of man." This is found in John almost as often as in Mark, and he employs it towards the close of his account of Christ's public teaching in a passage that may perhaps explain in part why he substituted for it, as a general rule, the first person (xii. 34) "How sayest thou '*The Son of man* must be lifted up'? *Who is this Son of man?*" This is the last utterance of the bewildered "multitude." Other causes—moral causes especially—beside the various meanings of "Son of man," caused their bewilderment. But still it may have occurred to an Evangelist writing largely for educated Greeks that this Jewish technical term—even though it was actually and habitually used by our Lord instead of the first personal pronoun, to denote ideal humanity as created in God's image—ought to be sparingly used in a Gospel intended mainly for Gentiles.

[1705] Instances will be found where John appears to be alluding to words, names, or phrases, that might (1811) cause difficulty to the readers of Mark and Matthew, as, for example, John's use of the word translated "groaning" in the Raising of Lazarus. It will also be noticed that the epithet "eternal," or "everlasting," applied sometimes by Mark and Matthew to "sin," "fire" etc., is applied by John to nothing but "life," and that John's doctrine about "fire" is confined to one brief metaphorical passage. Occasionally, attention will be called to passages where John may be alluding to doctrines like those of Epictetus. For example, the conception of the

Son as "*testifying*" or "*bearing witness*" to the Father, can be illustrated far more fully from Epictetus than from the Prophets. Negatively, too, John's avoidance of the word "*humble*," and his condemnation (in the Epistle) of "*fear*," indicate that he may have been impelled by Greek influence to discard these and other Biblical terms that conveyed to the Greeks a suggestion not of good but of evil.

[1706] Under the head of "*trouble*," however, reasons will be given for thinking that John is allusively dissenting from Epictetus, with whom "freedom from trouble" was the highest of blessings. Not improbably, many things in the Fourth Gospel imply a similar dissent. For example, John lays great stress (**1226**) upon the fact that the Son does all things "*for the sake of*" the Father or "*for the sake of*" the disciples. But Epictetus says (i. 19. 11) "Whatever lives has been so framed as to do all things *for its own sake* (αὐτοῦ ἕνεκα). For even the sun does all things *for its own sake*, and, indeed, so does Zeus Himself." Of course Epictetus could prove philosophically that this is consistent with real unselfishness. But from the point of view of a plain man with no pretensions to philosophy, this means either selfishness or solitude. And, since God cannot be selfish, it reduces Him to a solitary Being. John teaches that God was from the beginning not alone, because the Word, or the Son, was with Him: and instead of "doing all things *for His own sake*," He is revealed in the Washing of Feet as making Himself—in the person of His Son—the Servant of His creatures, doing all things "for the sake of" others.

JOHANNINE WORDS COMPARATIVELY SELDOM OR NEVER USED BY THE SYNOPTISTS[1]

English	Greek	Mk	Mt.	Lk.	Jn
[1707] Abide, remain[2]	μένω	2	3	7	40

---

[1] [1707 * s. 1885 (ii) foll.] This Vocabulary includes words characteristic of the Fourth Gospel as contrasted with the words used by the Three collectively. Occasionally—in order to group kindred words together, or to supply a reader that may be ignorant of Greek with a fairly complete alphabetical list of important Johannine terms—it will include a word used by only two of the Synoptists (*e.g.* "judge," κρίνω, not found in Mark) or sometimes only one (*e.g.* "manifest," φανερόω, not found in Matthew or Luke). But, where that is the case, such a word will be repeated later on under one of the following headings:

(1) Words peculiar to Jn and Mk (**1729—44**).
(2) ,, ,, Jn and Mt. (**1745—57**).
(3) ,, ,, Jn and Lk. (**1758—1804**).
(4) ,, ,, Jn, Mk, and Mt. (**1805—17**).
(5) ,, ,, Jn, Mk, and Lk. (**1818—35**).
(6) ,, ,, Jn, Mt., and Lk. (**1836—66**).

[2] [1707 *a*] "Abide." Mk vi. 10 (sim. Mt. x. 11 and Lk. ix. 4, x. 7) "There *abide* until ye go forth," Mk xiv. 34 (Mt. xxvi. 38) "*abide* here and watch." Jn uses the word to denote the abiding of the Word of God, or Christ, in man (v. 38, xv. 4, 5 etc.), of man in Christ (vi. 56, xv. 4, 5 etc.) or in Christ's Word (viii. 31), or in Christ's love (xv. 9, 10); also the abiding of the Father in the Son (xiv. 10), and of the Son in the love of the Father (xv. 10). It is also used, without respect to locality, to denote the permanence of the "food" that "abideth unto eternal life" (vi. 27), and of the "sin" of the proud (ix. 41). Jn, alone of the Evangelists, in recording the descent of the Holy Spirit on Jesus, says that (i. 32—3) "it *abode* on him."

[1707 *b*] The predominance of the thought of "abiding" in the writer's mind may be inferred from the fact that "abide" occurs in the First Epistle of St John almost as many (23) times as in all the non-Johannine Epistles taken together (25).

[1707 *c*] In LXX, μένω freq. = קום "stand upright," concerning an ordinance that "stands," *i.e.* holds good, *e.g.* Prov. xix. 21, "The counsel of the Lord—that shall *stand* (LXX εἰς τὸν αἰῶνα μένει)," Is. xl. 8 "The word of the Lord *standeth* (μένει) for ever," Deut. xix. 15 "at the mouth of two witnesses...shall a matter *stand* (R.V. be established)," LXX στήσεται. Mt. xviii. 16, merely alluding to Deut. xix. 15, has σταθῇ

SYNOPTIC DEVIATIONS

English	Greek	Mk	Mt.	Lk.	Jn
Abiding-place[1]	μονή	0	0	0	2
About (w. numbers etc.) (1)	ὡς	2	1 or 0	2	8
About (w. numbers etc.) (2) (**1670**)	ὡσεί	0	1	7	0
Above, up[2]	ἄνω	0	0	0	3
Above, from above[3]	ἄνωθεν	1	1	1	5
Advocate, s. Paraclete	παράκλητος	0	0	0	4
Aenon[4]	Αἰνών	0	0	0	1
Again[5]	πάλιν	28	17	3	43
Age, s. Eternal					
Already, s. Now					
Always	πάντοτε	2	2	2	7
Am, I[6]	εἰμί	4	14	16	54
[1708] Ask (the Father)[7]	ἐρωτάω	0	0	0	6

"*made to stand*," but Jn viii. 17, quoting it as "written," has "*is true.*" In the same verse of Deut. "One witness shall not *rise up* (יקום)" is rendered by Jer. Targ. "The testimony of one witness shall not *be valid,*" and LXX renders it ἐμμενεῖ. This illustrates the connexion in the Jewish mind between "*abiding*," "*standing fast*," and "*truth*."

[1] "Abiding-place." See *Paradosis*, **1393—7**.

[2] [**1707** *d*] "Above," "up," means "heaven(ward)" except in Jn ii. 7 "filled them to *the brim* (ἕως ἄνω)." The only instance alleged of ἕως ἄνω is 2 Chr. xxvi. 8 "to the top," *i.e.* to the utmost.

[3] [**1707** *e*] "Above," "from above." Ἄνωθεν in Mk xv. 38, Mt. xxvii. 51 is used of the veil of the temple "rent *from top* to bottom," in Jn xix. 23 of Christ's coat, or tunic, "woven *from the top* throughout," concerning which the soldiers say "Let us not rend it." Elsewhere Jn (iii. 3, 7, 31) uses it of the heavenly birth "from above" (comp. Jn xix. 11). In Lk. i. 3 it means "from the source, or fountainhead." For the proof that it does not mean "anew" in Jn, see **1903** foll.

[4] [**1707** *f*] "Aenon" is mentioned only in Jn iii. 23, "And John also was baptizing in Aenon near to Salim, because there was much water there." The locality of Aenon (as well as that of Salim) is disputed.

[5] [**1707** *g*] "Again" occurs in Lk., only vi. 43 (om. by many author.) where, if genuine (but ? ΠΑΛΙ for ΠΑΝ), it would mean "on the other hand"; xiii. 20 (D diff.); xxiii. 20 "But again Pilate..." (where the parall. Mk xv. 12, and Jn xix. 4 also have "again").

[6] "Am." See "I am" (**1713**).

[7] [**1708** *a*] "Ask." Jn xiv. 16 "I will *ask* the Father," and so xvi. 26, xvii. 9 (*bis*), 15, 20, always in Christ's words, and in the 1st person (**1704**).

FROM JOHANNINE VOCABULARY [1708]

English	Greek	Mk	Mt.	Lk.	Jn
Barley (adj.)[1]	κρίθινος	0	0	0	2
Bear, beget[2]	γεννάω	1	5	4	18
Because (narr.)[3]	ὅτι	4+[1]	3	9	26
Before (adv.)	(τὸ) πρότερον	0	0	0	3
Beget, s. Bear	γεννάω	1	5	4	18
Beginning (Chri.)[4]	ἀρχή	3	4	0	4
Beginning (narr.)[5]	ἀρχή	1	0	1	4
Behold (vb.)[6]	θεωρέω	7	2	7	23
Behold! See! Lo![7]	ἴδε	8	4	0	15
Bethany (beyond Jordan)[8]	Βηθανία...πέραν τοῦ Ἰορδάνου	0	0	0	1

[1] "Barley," Jn vi. 9, 13.

[2] **[1708 *b*]** "Bear," "beget." The numbers above do not include the use of γεννάω (40 times) in Mt. i. 2—16. Both there and in Lk. i. 13, 57, xxiii. 29, Jn xvi. 21, the vb is act. In Mt. i. 2—16 the act. means "beget"; elsewhere it means "bring forth" (of the mother). In the Synoptists it is never used spiritually, as it freq. is in Jn.

[3] **[1708 *c*]** "Because" occurs in Evangelistic statement (which alone is here meant by "narr."), in Mt., only in ix. 36, xi. 20 and xiv. 5. Mt. xi. 20 resembles Mk App. [xvi. 14] "reproached them *because* they believed not." The numbers are taken from Bruder (1888). See also **1712** *c*.

[4] **[1708 *d*]** "Beginning" (Chri.), occurs in Mk x. 6, Mt. xix. 4 concerning the making of male and female "from *the beginning* (ἀπ' ἀρχῆς)," to which Mt. adds, as to divorce (Mt. xix. 8) ἀπ' ἀρχῆς δὲ οὐ γέγονεν οὕτως. The other Synoptic instances are (Mk xiii. 8, Mt. xxiv. 8) "These things are *the beginning* of travails (ἀρχὴ ὠδίνων ταῦτα)" and (Mk xiii. 19, Mt. xxiv. 21) "from *the beginning* of creation (Mt. of the world)."

[1708 *e*] Jn has viii. 44 "He was a murderer from *the beginning* (ἀπ' ἀ.)," xv. 27 "because ye are with me from *the beginning* (ἀπ' ἀ.)," xvi. 4 "these things I told you not from *the beginning* (ἐξ ἀ.)." Also in reply to "Who art thou?" Jn has (viii. 25) εἶπεν αὐτοῖς [ὁ] Ἰησοῦς Τὴν ἀρχὴν ὅτι καὶ λαλῶ ὑμῖν (txt interrog., marg. affirm.) (**2154—6**).

[5] **[1708 *f*]** "Beginning" (narr.) occurs in Mk i. 1 "*The beginning* of the Gospel...," Lk. i. 2 "those who were from *the beginning* eye-witnesses...," comp. Jn i. 1 "In *the beginning* was the word...."

[6] "Behold" (vb.). Used by Jn sometimes of unintelligent wonder (**1598**).

[7] "Behold!" ἴδε. Contrast "Behold!" ἰδού (**1674**).

[8] **[1708 *g*]** "Bethany beyond Jordan" is mentioned only in Jn i. 28 "These things were done in Bethany beyond Jordan, where John was baptizing." Its locality is disputed, and there are v.r. Bethabarah, Betharabah etc. See **610—16**.

[1709] SYNOPTIC DEVIATIONS

English	Greek	Mk	Mt.	Lk.	Jn
Bethesda[1]	W.H. txt Βηθζαθά, marg. Βηθσαιδά	0	0	0	1
Break, destroy[2]	λύω	0	1	0	4
Brethren, the (*i.e.* the Church) (narr.)[3]	οἱ ἀδελφοί	0	0	0	1
But[4]	ἀλλά	43	36	36	101
[1709] Cana	Κανᾶ	0	0	0	4
Catch, seize, take[5]	πιάζω	0	0	0	8
Cephas[6]	Κηφᾶς	0	0	0	1
Choose (Chri.)[7]	ἐκλέγομαι	1	0	1	5

[1] [1708 *h*] "Bethesda" is mentioned only in Jn v. 2 "Now there is in Jerusalem by the sheep[gate] a pool which is called in Hebrew Bethesda (v.r. Bethsaida, Bethzatha), having five porches." Other various readings are Βηζαθά, Βελζεθά, Betzatha etc. Its locality is disputed, and so is the interpretation of the "sheep[gate]," the ellipsis of which is said by Westcott to be "(apparently) without parallel" (2216).

[2] [1708 *i*] "Break," "destroy," occurs in Mt. v. 19, Jn v. 18, vii. 23, x. 35 of *breaking* a "commandment," "the sabbath," "the law of Moses," "the Scripture," Jn ii. 19 "*destroy* this temple." These numbers do not include λύω="loose," "unbind."

[3] [1708 *j*] "Brethren, the," *i.e.* the Church (narr.): Jn xxi. 23 "This saying therefore went forth among (εἰς) *the brethren*." Comp. Acts i. 15, xiv. 2 etc.

[4] [1708 *k*] "But," ἀλλά, mostly follows a negative: and Jn's habit of stating things negatively and positively with a "but" appears early in his Gospel, i. 8 οὐκ...ἀλλ' ἵνα, i. 13 οὐκ ἐξ αἱμάτων...ἀλλ' ἐκ θεοῦ (2055).

[5] "Catch." See 1721 *j* and 1723 *b—c*.

[6] [1709 *a*] "Cephas," in Jn, only i. 42 "thou shalt be called Cephas which is interpreted *Petros*," i.e. a stone. Comp. Mt. xvi. 18 "thou art *Petros*," i.e. a stone. The naming is mentioned by the Synoptists thus, Mk iii. 16 κ. ἐπέθηκεν ὄνομα τῷ Σίμωνι Πέτρον, Mt. x. 2 πρῶτος Σ. ὁ λεγόμενος Πέτρος, Lk. vi. 14 Σ. ὃν κ. ὠνόμασεν Π. See 1728 *l₂*.

[7] [1709 *b*] "Choose" (Chri.) occurs, in Mk, only in xiii. 20 "the chosen whom *he hath chosen*," where Mt. has merely "the chosen." In Lk., "choose" does not occur in the Lord's words except Lk. x. 42 "(Mary) *hath chosen* the good part." In Jn it occurs almost always in the phrase "I (Christ) have chosen," and in two instances with an allusion to Judas Iscariot in the context (vi. 70 "*Have not I chosen* you the twelve, and one of you is a devil," xiii. 18 "I know whom *I have chosen*, but that the Scripture may be fulfilled, 'He that eateth my bread lifted up his heel against me'").

198

FROM JOHANNINE VOCABULARY [1710]

English	Greek	Mk	Mt.	Lk.	Jn
Circumcision[1]	περιτομή	0	0	0	2
Clay[2]	πηλός	0	0	0	5
Comforter, s. Paraclete	παράκλητος	0	0	0	4
Cry (appl. to Christ)[3]	κράζω	0	1	0	3
Cry aloud[3]	κραυγάζω	0	1	0	6
Cut off[4] (1671 c)	ἀποκόπτω	2	0	0	2
[1710] Darkness (1)[5]	σκοτία	0	2	1	8
Darkness (2)[5]	σκότος	1	6	4	1
Death (lit.)[6]	θάνατος	6	6	6	6
Death (metaph.)[6]	θάνατος	0	1	1	2

[1] [1709 c] "Circumcision." The verb περιτέμνω occurs in Jn (1), Lk. (2). In Lk. (i. 59, ii. 21) the verb is used with reference to the circumcision of the child Jesus; in Jn (vii. 22—3) the verb and the noun are used to shew that, if circumcision is allowed on the sabbath, Christ's act of healing must be allowable.

[2] "Clay." Jn ix. 6—15, of "making clay" in the healing of the man born blind.

[3] "Cry," "cry aloud," κράζω and κραυγάζω, see 1752 a—f.

[4] [1709 d] "Cut off." Ἀποκόπτω—a word freq. connected with mutilation—is used by Jn (xviii. 10, 26), to describe the cutting off of the ear of Malchus where all the Synoptists have ἀφαιρέω. Comp. Gal. v. 12. See also 1734 b.

[5] [1710 a] "Darkness." Moreover, in the Epistle, Jn uses (5) σκοτία and (1) σκότος, which is also in Jn iii. 19 "they loved rather *the darkness* (τὸ σκότος) *than the light* (ἢ τὸ φῶς)," where perhaps the neuter form is preferred as supplying a more complete antithesis of sound illustrating the antithesis of sense.

[1710 b] Σκοτία and σκότος are always metaphorical in the Synoptists except as to the darkness during the crucifixion (Mk xv. 33, Mt. xxvii. 45, Lk. xxiii. 44). In Jn, σκοτία is metaph. except in vi. 17, xx. 1, where however it probably has a metaphorical suggestion, as "night" has in Jn xiii. 30 "He [Judas Iscariot] went out straightway. Now it was *night*."

[6] [1710 c] "Death." The six instances of "death" (lit.) in Mk and Mt. are all in *verbatim* agreement. Lk. (ix. 27) "shall surely not taste *death*" agrees with only one of them (Mk ix. 1, Mt. xvi. 28) uttered before the Transfiguration. The only Synoptic metaph. instances are in Mt. iv. 16, Lk. i. 79, not parall., but both quoting Is. ix. 2 "the shadow of *death*."

[1710 d] Jn has θ. (lit.) (xi. 4, 13) about Lazarus, (xii. 33, xviii. 32) about the Crucifixion ("by what *death* he was to die"), and (xxi. 19) about

[1710] SYNOPTIC DEVIATIONS

English	Greek	Mk	Mt.	Lk.	Jn
Denarii (plur.) (apart from parables)¹ (**1671** c)	δηνάρια	2	0	0	2
Didymus²	Δίδυμος	0	0	0	3
Die³	ἀποθνήσκω	8	5	10	28
Disobey	ἀπειθέω	0	0	0	1
Draw (water, wine etc.)	ἀντλέω	0	0	0	4
Draw⁴, drag	ἑλκύω	0	0	0	5
Eat⁵	τρώγω	0	1	0	5
Ephraim⁶	Ἐφραίμ	0	0	0	1

Peter's martyrdom. In v. 24, viii. 51 Jesus uses θ. metaphorically, but in viii. 52, whereas Jesus had said "He shall not *behold death*," spiritually, the Jews misquote it as "he shall not *taste of death*," and take it literally.

¹ [**1710** e] "Denarii." Mk vi. 37 "Are we to buy bread for two hundred *denarii*?" xiv. 5 "sold for above three hundred *denarii*," Jn vi. 7 "bread of [the price of] two hundred *denarii*," xii. 5 "sold for three hundred *denarii*." I hope to discuss these passages in a future treatise.

² "Didymus," applied (Jn xi. 16, xx. 24, xxi. 2) to Thomas, whom Jn mentions 7 times, and each Synoptist once.

³ [**1710** f] "Die," ἀποθνήσκω, is freq. in Jn in connexion with Lazarus, and with Christ's "dying for the people" or "dying" on the Cross. It is metaphorical in vi. 50 μὴ ἀποθάνῃ, xi. 26 οὐ μὴ ἀποθάνῃ, but perh. nowhere else. Τελευτάω, "die," occurs in Mk (2), Mt. (4), Lk. (1), Jn (1).

⁴ [**1710** g] "Draw." Metaph. in Jn vi. 44 "Except the Father *draw* him," xii. 32 "I will *draw* all men unto myself," lit. in xviii. 10 (a sword), xxi. 6, 11 (a net). Epictetus says that man (i. 2. 4) "is *drawn* (ἑλκόμενον) to nothing so much as to the (**1700**) Good Logos," and (ii. 20. 15) "nature" is "the strongest of all things in man, *drawing* him to her will (βούλημα) despite his reluctance and bewailings." He uses the Johannine word ἑλκύω to mean "drag" (iii. 22. 3) or to describe the seduction of vain imagination (ii. 18. 23). Acts (xvi. 19, xxi. 30) uses the two words to mean "dragging" a person violently away. Jn uses ἑλκύω in both meanings.

⁵ [**1710** h] "Eat," τρώγω. From the numerous instances of this word in Steph. it would seem to be used in ordinary Greek exclusively to mean eating vegetables, fruit, sweetmeats etc., never flesh. In Mt. xxiv. 38, where it perhaps means "eating sweetmeats or delicacies," the parall. Lk. xvii. 27 has ἐσθίω. Jn has (vi. 54—8) "He that *eateth* my flesh (*bis*)," "he that *eateth* me," "he that *eateth* this bread." Jn xiii. 18 uses it in quoting Ps. xli. 9 "He that *eateth* my bread," where the LXX (which never uses τρώγω) has ἐσθίων. See also "eat" ἐσθίω (**1680**).

"Ephraim." Jn xi. 54 "a city called *Ephraim*."

200

FROM JOHANNINE VOCABULARY [1711]

English	Greek	Mk	Mt.	Lk.	Jn
Eternal, everlasting[1]	αἰώνιος	3	6	4	17
[1711] Father (divine)[2]	πατήρ	4	44	16	120

[1] [1710 i] "Eternal," αἰώνιος, in Jn is always used of "life," never of "punishment," "fire" etc. In the Synoptists, it is used with ζωή (8), πῦρ (2), κόλασις (1), ἁμάρτημα (1), σκηναί (1). Lk., like Jn, always uses it of good, never of evil.

[2] [1711 a] "Father" (divine). Mk viii. 38 "When he shall come in the glory of his *Father*," xi. 25 "that your *Father* who is in the heavens may forgive you," xiii. 32 "...not even the angels of heaven, nor yet the Son, but only the *Father*," xiv. 36 "Abba, *Father*....." Apart from doctrine about the Last Day (where the Father is mentioned in connexion with the Son expressed or implied) *Mk nowhere mentions God as the Father of men exc. in the warning about forgiveness* (xi. 25) parall. to Mt. vi. 14—15 but to nothing in Lk. But the single passage in Mk, containing an apparent reference to the Lord's Prayer, confirms the belief (based on Mt.-Lk.) that a large part of Christ's doctrine must have referred to "the Father" by name.

[1711 b] Epictetus says (i. 3. 1 foll.) "If one were thrilled as he should be with the thought that we [men] have all been uniquely (προηγουμένως) brought into being (γεγόναμεν) by God, and that God is the Father of both men and gods, I think we should be far from all ignoble and servile notions about ourselves": and again (*ib.*), "If Caesar were to adopt you as a son, there would be no enduring your arrogance. If you know that you are son of Zeus, will you not *be lifted up* (ἐπαρθήσῃ) by that? But as it is, we do no such thing." We turn aside, he says, from the divine sonship, which we have in virtue of "the purpose and the Logos" within us, and we prefer our kinship (which we have in virtue of our body) with the brute beasts. A man calls himself Athenian or Corinthian, (i. 9. 4—6) "Why should he not also call himself 'Cosmian'?" (as being citizen of the Cosmos) "Why not son of God?"

[1711 c] John would agree with a great deal of this, but not (not, at least, without a *caveat*) that a man should be "lifted up" by the thought of being "son of God." His Prologue, indeed, distinguishes those "begotten of God" from those begotten of "blood" or of "the will of flesh," and describes the former class as receiving "*authority* to become children of God"—a phrase that recalls the "adoption by Caesar" above mentioned. But it is nothing to be "lifted up" about, if "to be lifted up" means "to be proud." John, it is true, represents the Son of God as being "lifted up (ὑψοῦσθαι)," but it is the "lifting up" on the Cross. He also has "authority," but it is "authority to lay down life that he may take it again." The silence of Mk and the teaching of Epictetus may have influenced John in the development of the Christian doctrine of the divine Fatherhood.

SYNOPTIC DEVIATIONS

English	Greek	Mk	Mt.	Lk.	Jn
Father (human)[1]	πατήρ	14	19	37	12
Feast[2]	ἑορτή	2	2	3	17
Fire (of coals)[3]	ἀνθρακιά	0	0	0.	2
Fish[4]	ὀψάριον	0	0	0	5

[1] [1711 d] "Father" (human). Jn viii. 44 also uses πατήρ thrice concerning the devil as the father of liars etc., thus making 15 instances where it is not applied to God. (As to insertion in this list, see **1670—1**.)

[2] [1711 e] "Feast." Mk xiv. 2, Mt. xxvi. 5 Μὴ ἐν τῇ ἑορτῇ, Mk xv. 6, Mt. xxvii. 15 κατὰ δὲ ἑορτὴν εἰώθει.... Lk. (besides ii. 41, 42) has xxii. 1 ἤγγιζεν δὲ ἡ ἑορτὴ τῶν ἀζύμων. Jn mentions several feasts for which Jesus goes up to Jerusalem.

[3] [1711 f] "Fire (of coals)." Ἀνθρακιά in Jn xviii. 18 is the "fire of coals" in the High Priest's hall, Mk xiv. 54 φῶς, Lk. xxii. 55—6 πῦρ... φῶς, Mt. xxvi. 58 om. (**180—5**). Luke's astonishing phrase πῦρ περιάπτω is unlike any use of περιάπτω in Steph. except Phalar. *Epist.* v. p. 24 (L. S. 28) ἐνεβιβάσαμεν αὐτὸν κ. περιήψαμεν, "we put him in and kindled [a fire] round [him? round the man enclosed in the bull]" where Steph. adds "recte, ut videtur, Lennep. πῦρ ἥψαμεν."

[1711 g] Ephrem (p. 237) says "Near the coal fire he denied, near the coal fire he confessed," which suggests that some may have regarded the fire in Peter's Denial as a symbol of a "fiery trial " of temptation, and later on, of purification (xxi. 9) "they see a *fire of coals* laid ready...and a loaf." The phrase "cake baken *on the coals*" occurs in O.T. only in the story of Elijah's being strengthened (1 K. xix. 6) for the journey to Horeb in which may be seen a parallelism to the Eucharistic "breakfast" in Jn whereby the Apostles are strengthened to preach the Gospel to the world. The Heb. word used for "coal" in 1 K. xix. 6 occurs nowhere else (Gesen. 954 a) in O.T. except in Is. vi. 6, where the Prophet Isaiah is purified by a "coal" from the altar for his prophetic task. Ephrem's tradition, "he *confessed* near a coal fire," is curiously like Philo's tradition that the ἄνθραξ, i.e. "*coal*," or "*carbuncle*," represents Judah as being (i. 60) "a *confessing* (ἐξομολογητικός) disposition," which "is inflamed in the eucharist of (*i.e.* thanksgiving to) God (πεπύρωται ἐν εὐχαριστίᾳ θεοῦ)." Not improbably John had in view traditions of this kind.

[1711 h] It may be worth noting that (1) Aquila has ψῆφος *i.e.* stone, or pebble, for "coal" in Is. vi. 6, (2) LXX freq. has ἄνθραξ, "coal," to represent a precious stone (Gen. ii. 12, Ex. xxviii. 18, xxxvi. 18, Ezek. x. 9 etc.), (3) Rev. ii. 17 combines "manna" with "white *stone* (ψῆφον λευκήν)" as a gift to "him that overcometh"—an expression that has perplexed commentators and perhaps remains to be explained (**2409 a**).

[4] [1712 a] "Fish." Jn uses ἰχθύς to mean "fish" (xxi. 6, 8, 11), apparently restricting ὀψάριον to mean "fish" *for eating* (**1736 e**).

FROM JOHANNINE VOCABULARY [1712]

English	Greek	Mk	Mt.	Lk.	Jn
Flesh[1]	σάρξ	4	5	2	13
For (conj.) (narr.)[2]	γάρ	c. 33	12	11	c. 30
For ever[3]	εἰς τὸν αἰῶνα / εἰς τοὺς αἰῶνας	2	1	2	12
Free (adj.)[4]	ἐλεύθερος	0	1	0	2
Free (vb.)	ἐλευθερόω	0	0	0	2
Freely, openly[5]	(ἐν) παῤῥησίᾳ	1	0	0	9

[1] [1712 b] "Flesh." Of Jn's 13 instances, 7 are from vi. 51—63 "my flesh" etc.

[2] [1712 c] "For" (narr. here meaning (1672*) Evangelistic statement). This is more characteristic of Mk than of Jn; but it is inserted for comparison with "because" (narr.) (1708). In Jn the question is complicated by the great difference of opinion among commentators as to passages that are and that are not, Evangelistic comment (2066).

[3] [1712 d] "For ever." In Mk iii. 29, xi. 14 (parall. Mt. xxi. 19) "for ever" is connected with a negative and with condemnation ("hath not forgiveness *for ever*," "let none eat fruit from thee *for ever*"); in Lk. i. 33, 55 with an affirmative and with promise ("shall reign...*for ever*," "to Abraham and his seed *for ever*"). In Jn iv. 14 "shall not thirst *for ever*," vi. 51 "shall live *for ever*," and sim. vi. 58, viii. 51, 52, x. 28, xi. 26, xiv. 16, it is connected, positively or negatively, with promise, like αἰώνιος (1710 *i*) in Jn. See also 1672 *a*. On Jn viii. 35, see 2263 *e*.

[4] [1712 e] "Free" (adj.). Mt. xvii. 26 "Then are the sons *free*," *i.e.* free from paying tribute. This occurs in a difficult context describing the finding of the stater in the fish's mouth. Origen (*ad loc.*) says, "They are free who abide in the truth (Huet μείναντες τῇ ἀληθείᾳ ?ins. ἐν, or leg. ἐμμείναντες) of the Word of God and thereby know the truth that they may be also freed by (ἀπ'? leg. ὑπ') it." Origen had in mind Jn viii. 32—6 "If ye abide in my word...ye shall know the truth and the *truth* shall *make you free*....Everyone that committeth sin is the bondservant [of sin]. And the bondservant abideth not in the house for ever; the son abideth for ever. If therefore the Son shall make you free ye shall be *free* indeed." The connexion between a Gospel of *sonship* and a Gospel of *freedom* is manifest: and it is recognised abundantly in the Pauline Epistles. But the Triple Tradition says practically nothing about "*freedom*," and very little, directly, about "*sonship*," though Matthew and Luke frequently imply it in doctrine about the Father in Heaven. It remained for the Fourth Gospel to give prominence to the spiritual doctrine latent in the tradition peculiar to Matthew, "*The sons are free*."

[5] [1712 f] "Freely, openly." Mk viii. 32 "He was speaking the word *openly* (παῤῥησίᾳ)." Jn uses it twice in Christ's words: xviii. 20 "I have spoken *openly* to the world," xvi. 25 (R.V.) "I shall tell you *plainly* of the Father." See 1744 (xi) *a* and 1917 (i).

[1713] SYNOPTIC DEVIATIONS

English	Greek	Mk	Mt.	Lk.	Jn
Gabbatha	Γαββαθά	0	0	0	1
Gird[1]	διαζώννυμι, ζώννυμι	0	0	0	5
Glorify[2]	δοξάζω	1	4	9	21
Glory[3]	δόξα	3	7	13	18
[1713] Go (metaph.)[4]	ὑπάγω	1	1	0	c. 18
Greeks[5]	Ἕλληνες	0	0	0	3

[1] [1712 g] "Gird," in Jn, is always literal, of the Lord or Peter xiii. 4, 5, xxi. 7, 18 (bis). Περιζώννυμι (not in Mk-Mt.) occurs thrice in Lk. xii. 35, 37, xvii. 8, alw. metaphor or parable.

[2] [1712 h] "Glorify," in the Synoptists, is mostly applied to *men "glorifying* God" because of miracles. In Jn, it is used concerning the glorifying of the Father by the Son, and the glorifying of the Son by the Father, but most freq. of the Son's being "*glorified*," with reference to the Crucifixion and its sequel. Comp. Heb. ii. 9. Only once is it used in Jn concerning a *man* glorifying God (xxi. 19) " signifying by what death he (*i.e.* Peter) should *glorify* God."

[3] [1712 i] "Glory." Mk viii. 38 "when he shall come *in the glory of his Father*," parall. Mt. xvi. 27 sim., but parall. Lk. ix. 26 "*in his glory and that of* the Father"; Mk x. 37 "that we may sit *in thy glory*," parall. Mt. xx. 21 "that these may sit...*in thy kingdom*" (Lk. om.); Mk xiii. 26 "the Son of man coming in (Mt. on the) clouds (Lk. cloud) *with power and great glory*" (parall. Mt. xxiv. 30, Lk. xxi. 27).

[1712 j] These three passages speak of the "glory" of the Son as future. Jn i. 14, ii. 11 speak of it as manifested by the Son in the past (" we beheld his *glory*," "manifested his *glory*" at Cana): xi. 40 (comp. xi. 4) "thou shalt see *the glory of God*" means apparently "thou shalt see God's glory manifested in the raising of Lazarus"; xii. 41 says that Isaiah "saw his [*i.e.* Christ's] *glory*": xvii. 5, 22, 24 speak of "glory" (apparently that of the divine unity, implying the devotion of the Son and the love of the Father) as possessed by the Son "before the world was," and as already "given" to the disciples by the Son; at the same time the Son prays "that they may be beholding my *glory*, which thou hast given to me, because thou lovedst me from the foundation of the world."

[4] [1713 a] "Go" (metaph.). Mk xiv. 21, Mt. xxvi. 24 "the Son of man goeth (ὑπάγει)," where parall. Lk. xxii. 22 has πορεύεται. On the difference between the two verbs, see 1652—64.

[5] [1713 b] "Greeks." Jn vii. 35 "Will he go to the Dispersion of (2046) the *Greeks*, and teach the *Greeks*?" In this specimen of Johannine irony the Jews unconsciously predict what seems to them absurd. The same thing is predicted in action subsequently (Jn xii. 20) "Now there were certain *Greeks* of them that came up...." Mk vii. 26 alone has the fem. Ἑλληνίς where the parall. Mt. xv. 22 omits it.

FROM JOHANNINE VOCABULARY [1713]

English	Greek	Mk	Mt.	Lk.	Jn
Greek, in[1]	Ἑλληνιστί	0	0	0	1
Grief, sorrow[2]	λύπη	0	0	1	4
Groan, murmur[3]	ἐμβριμάομαι	2	1	0	2
Hate[4]	μισέω	1	5	7	12
Hebrew, in[5]	Ἑβραϊστί	0	0	0	5
I (nom.) (**1704**)	ἐγώ (incl. κἀγώ)	16	37	25	155
I-am (1st pers.)	εἰμί	4	14	16	54
I am [he] (Chri.)[6]	ἐγώ εἰμι	2	1	1 (?)	9
Interpret (**1728** l_2)	ἑρμηνεύω	0	0	0	2

[1] [**1713** c] "In Greek." Jn xix. 20 "It was written in Hebrew and in Roman [*i.e.* in Latin] and *in Greek*."

[2] [**1713** d] "Grief," "sorrow." Jn xvi. 6, 20—22 describes Jesus as *mentioning* on the last night the "sorrow" of the disciples that is described by Luke as *occurring* on the last night (Lk. xxii. 45) "He found them sleeping for *sorrow*."

[3] [**1713** e] "Groan," "murmur." Ἐμβριμάομαι in Jn xi. 33, 38 is prob. used, in part, allusively to explain the difficulty caused by its use in Mk i. 43, Mt. ix. 30, where it might seem to some to represent Jesus as "roaring against" those whom He healed. See **1811** a—c.

[4] [**1713** f] "Hate." Mk xiii. 13 "Ye shall be *hated* by all for my name's sake," parall. to Mt. xxiv. 9 (and x. 22), Lk xxi. 17. Lk. xiv. 26 makes "*hating* one's own *life*" a condition for discipleship, an expression not found in Mk or Mt. Jn adopts it, with a qualification (xii. 25) "He that *hateth his life in this world*" (**1450**).

[5] [**1713** g] "In Hebrew," in Jn, thrice of names, v. 2 (?) "Bethzatha," xix. 13 "Gabbatha," xix. 17 "Golgotha": also xix. 20 "written *in Hebrew*, in Roman, in Greek," and xx. 16 "She saith to him *in Hebrew*, Rabboni."

[6] [**1713** h] "I (emph.) am [he]" (Chri.). Mt.'s single instance is in the Walking on the Waters (Mt. xiv. 27) where it is also inserted by Mk (vi. 50) and Jn (vi. 20). (Lk. omits the whole narrative.)

[**1713** i] Mk's second instance is in the Trial, in answer to the question "Art thou the Christ?" where Mk xiv. 62 has "*I am*" (but Mt. xxvi. 64 "Thou saidst it," Lk. xxii. 70 "Ye say that *I am* (ὅτι ἐγώ εἰμι)" not included above as not being the utterance of Christ in His own person).

[**1713** j] Lk. places a form of the phrase, with αὐτός, after the Resurrection, xxiv. 39 "See my hands and my feet that it is I myself (ὅτι ἐγώ εἰμι αὐτός)."

[**1713** k] In Jn, besides the utterance in the Walking on the Waters (vi. 20), the phrase is used, with no predicate expressed, in viii. 24

[1714] SYNOPTIC DEVIATIONS

English	Greek	Mk	Mt.	Lk.	Jn
Is	ἐστι	c. 75	c. 120	c. 100	c. 170
Israelite[1]	Ἰσραηλείτης	0	0	0	1
Jesus	Ἰησοῦς	c. 82	c. 150	c. 87	c. 237
Jew, a[2]	Ἰουδαῖος	0	0	0	3
Jews (plur.)[3]	Ἰουδαῖοι	6	5	5	68
[1714] John (Peter's father)[4]	Ἰωάνης	0	0	0	4
"Jordan, beyond"[5]	πέραν τοῦ Ἰορδάνου	2	3	0	3
"Judas, not Iscariot"[6]	Ἰούδας, οὐχ ὁ Ἰσκαριώτης	0	0	0	1

"Except ye believe that *I am* [*he*]" where R.V. marg. gives "I am" absolutely, and so in viii. 28. The meaning in these and other instances needs detailed comment (**2220** foll.). The command Deut. xxxii. 39 ἴδετε ἴδετε ὅτι ἐγώ εἰμι "See, see, that I AM," is interpreted by Philo (i. 258) as a command to "behold the existence (ὕπαρξιν) of God."

[1] "Israelite," Jn i. 47 "an *Israelite* indeed in whom is no guile." See **1702** *a*.

[2] [**1713** *l*] "Jew, a," occurs in Jn iii. 25 "questioning…with *a Jew*" (txt. perh. corrupt), sarcastically in iv. 9 "How is it that thou being *a Jew* askest drink of me?" and contemptuously in xviii. 35 "Am I *a Jew*?"

[3] [**1713** *m*] "Jews" (plur.). This includes "king of *the Jews*," Mk (5), Mt. (4), Lk. (3), Jn (6). Apart from this title, the Synoptists use the word only as follows, Mk vii. 3 "The Pharisees and all *the Jews*," Mt. xxviii. 15 "This saying was spread abroad among *the Jews*," Lk. vii. 3 "He [*i.e.* the centurion] sent unto him [*i.e.* Jesus] elders of *the Jews*," xxiii. 51 "Arimathaea, a city of *the Jews*." On Jn's use of "Jews," mostly in a bad sense, see **1702**. On Jn iv. 22 see **1647—8**: xviii. 36 (Chri.) may mean "So far from my being 'king of *the Jews*' in your sense, my servants would contend against '*the Jews*,'" repeating Pilate's phrase.

[4] [**1714** *a*] "John" (Peter's father). Jn i. 42. "Thou art Simon, the son of *John*: thou shalt be called Cephas"; xxi. (thrice) 15, 16, 17 "Simon [son] of *John*, lovest thou me?"

[5] [**1714** *b*] "Beyond Jordan" occurs in Mt. iv. 15 quoting Is. viii. 23 and apparently meaning "west of the Jordan." It was an ambiguous term. Lk. never uses it. The Synoptists and Jn apparently use it always (except in Mt. iv. 15) to mean "east of the Jordan." See **1813** *b*.

[6] [**1714** *c*] "Judas, not Iscariot" is unique in Jn xiv. 22. But the name Judas, apart from genealogies and not applied to Iscariot, occurs in Mk vi. 3 "the brother of James and of Joses and of *Judas*," Mt. xiii. 55 "his brothers James…and *Judas*," Lk. vi. 16 "*Judas* of James" (in the list of the Twelve). This last is parall. to Mk iii. 18 "*Thaddaeus*,"

FROM JOHANNINE VOCABULARY [1714]

English	Greek	Mk	Mt.	Lk.	Jn
Judge (vb.)[1]	κρίνω	o	6	6	19

Mt. x. 3 "*Thaddaeus*" (Tisch. "*Lebbaeus*"). If this "Judas" was variously characterized in early times, Jn's characterization would have the advantage of not committing the writer to one tradition against another.

[1] [1714 d] "Judge, to." This verb will be repeated in the Jn-Mt.-Lk. Vocab. (1859 a): but it is too characteristic of the Fourth Gospel not to be given here although it does not belong to the Synoptic Tradition—which, strangely enough, contains nothing about "judging." Even the Double Tradition contains no precept about judging justly; and the negative precept in it (Mt. vii. 1, Lk. vi. 37) "*Judge* not that ye may not (Lk. and ye shall not) *be judged*" might be taken as prohibiting all judgment, even judging righteously.

[1714 e] Mt. v. 25 "(R.V.) Agree with (ἴσθι εὐνοῶν) thine adversary," where the parall. Lk. xii. 58 has δὸς ἐργασίαν ἀπηλλάχθαι [ἀπ'] αὐτοῦ, can hardly be intended to command "agreement" with unjust, extortionate, or oppressive claims, without any regard to circumstances. Moreover, Steph. and Thayer give no instance of εὐνοεῖν, "agree with." Its regular meaning is "be well disposed to," "have good will to": and it is possible to entertain this feeling even for the unjust, and even while one is defending one's just claims against the unjust. Is "the adversary" Satan, or an avenging angel, or a personification of the prayer of the injured person? It is hard to say. Luke puts before the difficult passage the words (xii. 57) "But why, even of yourselves, *judge* ye not that which is righteous?" That is intelligible and fair. But it does not explain how we are justified in "agreeing with" an "adversary" under all circumstances. Moreover Matthew omits this fair and intelligible precept. The whole is very obscure.

[1714 f] John accumulates passages to shew that the divine judgment consists (in one sense) in *not* judging (viii. 15 "I judge *no* man") but in *making the guilty judge themselves* through the conviction of the Logos within their hearts, so that the Son really does "*judge*," in that sense (viii. 16 "And yet, *if I judge*, my judgment is true"). The Son came, "not to judge" but to "save," and to bring "light." Yet the rejection of the light causes "judgment," by the laws of spiritual Nature, to fall on those who reject it. At the same time John records an appeal to the Jews (resembling Lk. xii. 57 above quoted) for "justice" in the Gentile sense of the term, conformity with the moral, as distinct from the Mosaic Law (Jn vii. 24 "Judge not according to appearance, but *judge righteous judgment*"). See also 1859 a.

[1714 g] The Epistle to the Romans is profuse in condemnations of "*judging*" (Rom. ii. 1—27, xiv. 3—22) and the First Epistle to the

English	Greek	Mk	Mt.	Lk.	Jn
Keep, watch[1]	τηρέω	1	6	0	18
[1715] Know (1)[2]	οἶδα	22	25	24	85
Know (2)[2]	γινώσκω	13	20	28	56
Last day, in the[3]	(ἐν) τῇ ἐσχάτῃ ἡμέρᾳ	0	0	0	7
"Law, your"[4]	τὸν νόμον ὑμῶν	0	0	0	3
Lay down one's life[5]	τίθημι ψυχήν	0	0	0	8

Corinthians says (iv. 5) "*Judge* nothing before the time," apparently looking forward to the Day of Judgment. But the Apostle himself goes on to say of a certain offender (*ib.* v. 3) "I have already *judged* him that hath thus wrought this thing." In proportion as the expectation of an immediate Day of final Judgment diminished, it would be necessary to bring out the spiritual meaning of Christ's doctrine about *not* "judging," and to shew that the old Greek and Hebrew rules about "judging justly" were to be fulfilled, not supplanted, by the New Law of love.

[1] [1714 *h*] "Keep." Τηρέω, "*keep*" (metaphorically) a commandment etc., occurs in Mt. xix. 17, xxiii. 3, and in Jn viii. 51, 52, 55, xiv. 15 etc. In Mk vii. 9, ἵνα τὴν παράδοσιν ὑμῶν τηρήσητε (but D, SS etc. have στήσητε) is parall. to Mt. xv. 3 διὰ τὴν π. ὑμῶν. See **1816**.

[2] "Know." On the distinction between οἶδα "know" and γινώσκω "come to know," "recognise" see **1621—9**.

[3] [1715 *a*] "Last day." Jn does not use ἔσχατος except in this phrase; LXX has "last of the days." For Synoptic ἔσχατος see **1685**.

[4] [1715 *b*] "Law, your." Jn viii. 17 "In *your law* it is written...." x. 34 "Is it not written in *your law*...?" No other instance is given by Westcott, and probably none could be given, of any prophet or teacher, Hebrew or Jewish, speaking of the Law of Moses to his countrymen as "*your* law." Theoretically it could be justified as meaning "the Law that you yourselves recognise as given to you and as binding on you." But, if our Lord used the phrase thus, why is it not found in any of the Synoptists? The natural conclusion is that the Fourth Gospel anticipates the phraseology of a later date when Christians had separated themselves from the Law so that they spoke of it to Jews as "*yours*." In Pilate, of course, this is natural, and it implies contempt (Jn xviii. 31) "Judge him according to *your law*."

[1715 *c*] A similar anachronism is to be found in Christ's words to the Disciples, (Jn xv. 25) "That the word might be fulfilled which is written in *their law*, 'They hated me without a cause.'"

[5] [1715 *d*] "Lay down one's life." Jn x. 11, 15, 17, 18 (*bis*), xiii. 37, 38, xv. 13. The phrase is used 7 times by our Lord, including one instance where he says (xiii. 38) τὴν ψ. σου ὑπὲρ ἐμοῦ θήσεις; in answer to Peter's protest (xiii. 37) τὴν ψ. μου ὑπὲρ σοῦ θήσω (**1336**).

FROM JOHANNINE VOCABULARY [1716]

English	Greek	Mk	Mt.	Lk.	Jn
Lazarus[1]	Λάζαρος	0	0	4	11
Life (spiritual)	ζωή	4	7	4	36
Life (physical)[2]	ζωή	0	0	1	0
Life eternal	ζωὴ αἰώνιος	2	3	3	17
Light[3]	φῶς	1	7	7	22
[1716] Linen cloth[4]	ὀθόνιον	0	0	[1]	4
Little, a (adv.)[5]	μικρόν	2	2	0	9
Live, cause to, quicken[6]	ζωοποιέω	0	0	0	3

[1] [1715 e] "Lazarus," in Lk., is the name of the beggar in the story of Dives and Lazarus; in Jn it is the name of the brother of Martha and Mary (1702 d).

[2] [1715 f] "Life (physical)." Lk. xvi. 25 "Thou receivedst to the full thy good things during thy *life* (ἐν τῇ ζωῇ σου)." Βίος in Mk xii. 44 (Lk. xxi. 4) means the widow's "*living*," and sim. in Lk. xv. 12, 30, comp. Lk. viii. 14 ("the pleasures of *life* (τ. βίου)"). Mt. and Jn nowhere use βίος.

[3] [1715 g] "Light." Mk xiv. 54 "Warming himself near the *light* [of the fire]," and sim. Lk. xxii. 56 "seated near the *light*," see **180—5**. Where Mt. v. 14—16 has "ye are the *light*," and "let your *light* shine," there intervenes a precept (v. 15) about the "*lamp*," λύχνος, and the parall. Mk (iv. 21) mentions only "*lamp*." Mk never uses "light" metaphorically. Lk. xvi. 8 in the Parable of the Unjust Steward, peculiar to himself, speaks of "*sons of light*," and so do Jn xii. 36 and 1 Thess. v. 5. Comp. Eph. v. 8 "Walk as children of *light*." On "light of the world," see **1748**.

[4] [1716 a] "Linen cloth." Ὀθόνιον occurs in Lk. xxiv. 12 in a doubly bracketed passage parall. to Jn xx. 5. It means "linen bandage." Mk xv. 46, Mt. xxvii. 59, Lk. xxiii. 53, in their parall. to Jn xix. 40 have "*linen* (σινδόνα)"; but Mt.-Lk. (**520—1**) deviate in the context from Mk, and prob. Jn is emphasizing Mk's tradition by insisting that the body of our Lord, when buried, was not only "swathed in linen" but "bound fast with linen bandages."

[5] [1716 b] "Little, a" (adv.). In Mk-Mt., only in the narrative of Gethsemane, Mk xiv. 35, Mt. xxvi. 39 προελθὼν μικρόν, and in Peter's Denial, Mk xiv. 70, Mt. xxvi. 73 μετὰ μικρόν. In Jn, μικρόν is always prophetic, xiii. 33, xiv. 19, xvi. 16—19, and means "a little while." Jn also has vii. 33, xii. 35 μικρὸν χρόνον, a non-synoptic phrase. Mk i. 19, Lk. v. 3 have ὀλίγον (adv.) "a little space," Mk vi. 31 (adv.) "a little time."

[6] "Live, cause to." Jn v. 21 (*bis*), vi. 63.

SYNOPTIC DEVIATIONS

English	Greek	Mk	Mt.	Lk.	Jn
Love (n.)[1]	ἀγάπη	0	1	1	7
Love (vb.) (1)[2]	ἀγαπάω	5	7	11	37
Love (vb.) (not "kiss") (2)[3]	φιλέω	0	4	1	13

[1] [1716 c] "Love" (n.) belongs to Jn-Mt.-Lk. Vocab. but is ins. here as being a characteristic word of the Fourth Gospel. In Mt. it occurs only in xxiv. 12 "The *love* of the many shall wax cold," an insertion, peculiar to Mt., in the discourse on the Last Days. In Lk., it occurs only in xi. 42 "Ye pass by judgment and the *love* of God," parall. to Mt. xxiii. 23 "Ye have left undone the weightier matters of the Law, judgment and mercy and faith." Perhaps Lk interpreted "the weightier matters of the Law" as referring to the first and greatest commandment, to "love God." It is noteworthy that Mk nowhere mentions "love."

[2] [1716 d] "Love" (vb.) ἀγαπάω. Of the Synoptic instances, 2 in Mk, 4 in Mt., 1 in Lk., are in quotations from O.T. All Mk's instances (except x. 21 "He (*i.e.* Jesus) loved him (*i.e.* the ruler)") are in the discussion on the command to love God and one's neighbour (xii. 30—33).

[3] [1716 e] "Love" (vb.) φιλέω. On the distinction between ἀγαπάω and φιλέω in Christ's Dialogue with Peter, see **1436—7**. The first few instances of each word in Jn are as follows :—

1. iii. 16 οὕτως γὰρ ἠγάπησεν ὁ θεὸς τὸν κόσμον.
2. iii. 19 ἠγάπησαν οἱ ἄνθρωποι μᾶλλον τὸ σκότος ἢ τὸ φῶς.
3. iii. 35 ὁ πατὴρ ἀγαπᾷ τὸν υἱὸν καὶ πάντα δέδωκεν ἐν τῇ χειρὶ αὐτοῦ.

1. v. 20 ὁ γὰρ πατὴρ φιλεῖ τὸν υἱὸν καὶ πάντα δείκνυσιν αὐτῷ ἃ αὐτὸς ποιεῖ.
2. xi. 3, 36 ἴδε, ὃν φιλεῖς ἀσθενεῖ ...ἴδε πῶς ἐφίλει αὐτόν.
3. xii. 25 ὁ φιλῶν τὴν ψυχὴν αὐτοῦ ἀπολλύει αὐτήν.

[1716 f] Φιλέω sometimes implies the love that comes from use and wont, and hence from home-life, and ἀγαπάω sometimes implies the love that looks abroad. Comp. Jn xv. 19 "If ye were from the world the world *would love* (ἐφίλει) [you as being] its own (τὸ ἴδιον)." The nouns do not exactly follow the verbs in all their shades of meaning. Φιλία occurs nowhere in N.T. except Jas iv. 4 "the *friendship* of the world." Jn can say "God is ἀγάπη," but he could not say "God is φιλία," although he says (xvi. 27) αὐτὸς γὰρ ὁ πατὴρ φιλεῖ ὑμᾶς ὅτι ὑμᾶς ἐμὲ πεφιλήκατε, "The Father *hath a fatherly love* for you because ye *have had a brotherly love* for me." As compared with ἀγαπάω, φιλέω might be used of still retaining a "friendship" or "liking" after the higher love has passed away (see **1436** and **1728** *m*).

[1716 g] Φιλέω occurs in Mk xiv. 44, Mt. xxvi. 48, Lk. xxii. 47, meaning "*kiss.*"

FROM JOHANNINE VOCABULARY [1717]

English	Greek	Mk	Mt	Lk.	Jn
Manifest (vb.) (1)[1]	ἐμφανίζω	0	1	0	2
Manifest (vb.) (2)[2]	φανερόω	1+[2]	0	0	9
[1717] Manna[3]	μάννα	0	0	0	2
Martha[4]	Μάρθα	0	0	3	9
Mary (sister of Martha)[5]	Μαριά(μ)	0	0	2	9
Messiah[6]	Μεσσίας	0	0	0	2

[1] [1716 h] "Manifest" (vb.) (1) ἐμφανίζω belongs to Jn-Mt. vocab. It occurs in Mt. xxvii. 53, of "the bodies of the dead" that arose and "*were manifested* to many," Jn xiv. 21 "I will *manifest* myself to him," xiv. 22 "What is come to pass that thou art about to *manifest* thyself to us and not to the world?" In the Pentateuch, the word occurs only in Ex. xxxiii. 13, 18 where Moses says to God (LXX) "*Manifest* thyself (ἐμφάνισον σεαυτόν) to me." The word is also used of God's self-manifestation in Wisd. i. 2, and of phantasmal apparitions in Wisd. xvii. 4. Josephus (*Ant.* i. 13. 1) uses it of God manifesting Himself to Abraham. The Gk word would naturally convey to a reader of the LXX the notion of a *visible* "manifestation," and it would naturally prepare a reader of Jn for the following question, "How can the Lord *manifest* Himself to us and not to the world?"

[2] [1716 i] "Manifest" (vb.) (2) φανερόω occurs in Mk iv. 22 "For there is nothing hidden except in order that it *may be manifested* (φανερωθῇ)," where Mt. x. 26 has ἀποκαλύπτω, Lk. viii. 17 φανερὸν γενήσεται. Mk App. [xvi. 12, 14] has "he *was manifested*" of Christ risen, a phrase also found in Jn. For the adj. φανερός, see **1686**.

[1716 j] Jn xxi. 1 (*bis*) uses "*manifested himself*," and xxi. 14 "*was manifested*," to describe Christ's self-manifestations after His resurrection, whereas 1 Cor. xv. 5—7 uses ὤφθη, i.e. "*appeared*," or "*was seen*." Jn's first use of the word is in the person of John the Baptist i. 31 "That he [*i.e.* Jesus] should be *manifested* to Israel, for this cause came I...."

[3] "Manna." Jn vi. 31, 49.

[4] [1717 a] "Martha." Jn xii. 2 "*Martha* served," comp. Lk. x. 40 "*Martha* was cumbered about much serving" (**1717 e, 1771 a**).

[5] [1717 b] "Mary" (sister of Martha). Jn xii. 3 "*Mary*...anointed the feet of Jesus," comp. Lk. x. 39 "*Mary*, who also sat at the Lord's feet" (**1771 b**).

[6] [1717 c] "Messiah." In Jn i. 41 "We have found *the Messiah*" is said by Andrew to Peter. The context adds "which is, being interpreted, Christ." The woman of Samaria says (iv. 25) "I know that *Messiah* cometh." The context again adds "which is called Christ." The word is not found elsewhere in N.T. See **1728 l_2**.

[1717] SYNOPTIC DEVIATIONS

English	Greek	Mk	Mt.	Lk.	Jn
Minister (n.)[1]	διάκονος	2	3	0	3
Minister (vb.)[2]	διακονέω	4	5	8	3

[1] [1717 d] "Minister" (n.). The n. διάκονος is used in Mk ix. 35 parall. to Mt. xxiii. 11 and in Mk x. 43 parall. to Mt. xx. 26. Both passages deal with Christ's doctrine of Service as constituting the true primacy. This is expressed in Jn xii. 26 (after the Washing of Feet) where he uses both the noun and the verb, "If any one *be ministering* (διακονῇ) to me, let him follow me, and where I am, there also shall my *minister* be. If any one *be ministering* (διακονῇ) to me, him will the Father honour." The other instances, in Jn, are in the "sign" at Cana, ii. 5 "His mother saith to the *ministers*," ii. 9 "But the *ministers* knew, they that had drawn the water."

[2] [1717 e] "Minister" (vb.). Lk. never uses the n. διάκονος, either in the Gospel or in the Acts, but Lk. xxii. 26 "let him become as *he that ministereth*" uses the vb. parall. to the n. in Mk x. 43, Mt. xx. 26 "shall be your *minister*." In the parall. to Mk ix. 35, "he shall be last of all and *minister* of all," Mt. xxiii. 11 "he shall be your *minister*," Lk. ix. 48 has "he that is least among you all, the same is great." The vb. is used once in connexion with a "supper" by Jn (xii. 2) ἡ δὲ Μάρθα διηκόνει. Lk. uses the n. διακονία (not found elsewhere in the Gospels) also about Martha in connexion with the statement that she "received (ὑπεδέξατο)" Jesus, (Lk. x. 40) ἡ δὲ Μάρθα περιεσπᾶτο περὶ πολλὴν διακονίαν.

[1717 f] Mk x. 43—4 and Mt. xx. 26—7 place "shall be *slave* of all (δοῦλος)" and "shall be your *slave*" after "shall be your *minister*," giving the impression that they are synonymous terms, and that the meaning of "shall be slave of all" is "shall be reduced, as a punishment, to the level of slave of all." Perhaps for this reason Lk. xxii. 26 substitutes "let him become" for "shall be" in order to indicate that the meaning is (Gal. v. 13) "in love *be ye slaves* to one another." And perhaps he avoids "minister," as it had come to have an ecclesiastical meaning.

[1717 g] Greeks might be repelled by Mk's apparent use of "slave" and "minister" as parall. terms. As to slaves, Epictetus says (*Fragm.* 8) "Freedom and *slavery* are, severally, names of virtue and *vice*. Both are results of will (προαιρέσεως)....No man is a *slave* as long as he keeps his will free." As for the man that cringes to fortune or to his fellow-men (iv. 1. 57) "Even though twelve rods" [the insignia of a consul] "precede him, call him a slave." A "minister" is a very different thing: "I count God's will," he says (iv. 7. 20), "better than mine. I will attach myself to Him, as His *minister* and follower," (iii. 22. 69) "The true philosopher (lit. Cynic) should give himself wholly to the *ministry* of God." See **1784—92** on Jn xv. 15 "No longer do I call you *slaves*."

212

FROM JOHANNINE VOCABULARY [1718]

English	Greek	Mk	Mt.	Lk.	Jn
Morrow, on the[1]	τῇ ἐπαύριον	1	1	0	5
[1718] Murmur, murmuring[2]	γογγύζω, -σμός	0	1	1	5
My, mine (**1704**)	ἐμός (not incl. μου)	2	5	3	37
Myself (**1704**)[3]	ἐμαυτοῦ, -όν	0	1	2	16
Nathanael (**1671** *b*)	Ναθαναήλ	0	0	0	6
Nation (sing.)[4]	ἔθνος	2	3	4	5

[1] [**1717** *h*] "Morrow, on the." Mk xi. 12 "*On the morrow* when they came forth from Bethany," Mt. xxvii. 62 "*On the morrow*, which is the day after the Preparation." In Jn, "*on the morrow*" occurs i. 29, 35, 43, in such a way as to lead the reader to perceive, but only after a careful reckoning of the days, that a week, excluding the sabbath, has elapsed. A week of "six days" is also more definitely expressed in Jn xii. 1, as closing Christ's work in the flesh.

Αὔριον—not used by Mk or Jn—occurs Mt. (3), Lk. (4), alw. in words of the Lord.

[2] [**1718** *a*] "Murmur," "murmuring." In Mt. (xx. 11 (pec.)) the "murmuring" is against the householder, who gives the denarius to all alike. It is inserted by Lk. (v. 30) in a Triple Tradition (where Mk ii. 16, Mt. ix. 11, have simply "said")—describing complaints made by the Pharisees against Jesus for eating with publicans and sinners. Elsewhere, in portions of Lk's Single Tradition (xv. 2, xix. 7) διαγογγύζω is used to describe similar complaints.

[**1718** *b*] In Jn, the first three mentions of "murmuring" (vi. 41, 43, 61) refer to the offence caused by Christ's saying that He is the bread that came down from heaven, and that His flesh and blood are to be given as the food and drink of men. In O.T., the Israelites "murmur" for the first time when they crave drink and food (Ex. xv. 24, xvi. 7—13).

[3] [**1718** *c*] "Myself." In Mt. viii. 9, Lk. vii. 7, 8 the centurion uses the word "*myself*," and it occurs nowhere else in Mt.-Lk. In Jn it occurs always in words of Christ about Himself.

[4] [**1718** *d*] "Nation" (sing.). (For plur., see **1687**.) Two of the Synoptic instances occur in the phrase "*nation* against *nation*" (Mk xiii. 8, Mt. xxiv. 7, Lk. xxi. 10). Mt. alone adds to the Parable of the Vineyard xxi. 43 "Therefore I say unto you, The kingdom of God shall be taken away from you, and shall be given to *a nation* bringing forth the fruits thereof."

[**1718** *e*] Lk. represents the elders of the Jews as saying to Jesus concerning the centurion (vii. 5) "He loveth *our nation* (i.e. the Jews)," and as saying to Pilate (xxiii. 2) "We found this man perverting *our nation*."

[**1718** *f*] The instances in Jn are in speeches of the chief priests and the Pharisees (xi. 48) "The Romans will come and take away both our

[1719] SYNOPTIC DEVIATIONS

English	Greek	Mk	Mt.	Lk.	Jn
Near (adv.)[1]	ἐγγύς	2	3	3	11
Nicodemus	Νικόδημος	0	0	0	5
Night (metaph.)[2]	νύξ	0	0	0	2
[1719] Not yet[3]	οὔπω	5	2	1	13

place and *our nation*," Caiaphas (xi. 50) "That one man should die for the people (λαοῦ), and that *the whole nation* perish not," with the comment "he prophesied that Jesus should die for *the nation*; and not for *the nation* only, but that he might also gather together into one the children of God that are scattered abroad," and Pilate (xviii. 35) "Thine own *nation* and the chief priests delivered thee unto me."

[1] [1718 g] "Near" (adv.). Jn compensates for the abundant use of the adv. by the non-use of the vb. ἐγγίζω Mk (3), Mt. (7), Lk. (18) (1687).

[2] [1718 h] "Night" (metaph.). Jn ix. 4 a "The *night* cometh when no man can work," xi. 10 "But if a man walketh in the *night* he stumbleth because the light is not in him." The second of these passages indicates internal darkness, not the "night" of temptation but the "night" of "sin." The first (ix. 4 a) must be taken with (ix. 4 b) "Whenever I am in the world I am the light of the world," and it indicates a period in which the world rejects the light, so that "no man," not even the Light, or Logos, "can work"—not, at least, for "the world."

[1718 i] Apart from actual metaphor we may note what may be called "sympathetic" emphasis laid on "night" by some Evangelists as being not only the *actual* time of an occurrence but also (apparently) as being an *appropriate* time, *because the occurrence is of the nature of a trial or temptation*. Thus in the Prediction of Peter's Denial, Mk xiv. 30 has "to-day, this *night*," Mt. xxvi. 34 "this *night*." But there Hebraic and Greek reckonings of "day" and "night" might influence the text. Or Mark might add "this night" to emphasize the accuracy of the prediction. The Walking on the Waters mentions first (Mk vi. 47, Mt. xiv. 23, Jn vi. 16) "evening," and then (Mk vi. 48, Mt. xiv. 25) "the fourth watch of the *night*," (Jn vi. 17) "it was now dark."

In Lk. xii. 20 and xvii. 34 "on this *night*" is connected with the sudden death of the rich man, and with the coming of the Day of Judgment.

[1718 j] In Jn xiii. 30 "he [Judas Iscariot] went forth: now it was *night*," it is manifest that "sympathetic" emphasis is intended, and it is probably intended also in Jn xxi. 3. Similarly "darkness" probably has a "sympathetic" meaning in Jn vi. 17, xx. 1, where the disciples are (owing to different causes) apart from their Lord. The coming of Nicodemus to Jesus (Jn iii. 2) "by *night*" and the repetition of the phrase in Jn xix. 39, are probably intended to illustrate his character.

[3] [1719 a] "Not yet" occurs in Lk only once, and concerning the past (xxiii. 53). Where Mk xiii. 7, Mt. xxiv. 6 have "The end is *not yet*,"

FROM JOHANNINE VOCABULARY [1719]

English	Greek	Mk	Mt.	Lk.	Jn
Now (*i.e.* this moment)	ἄρτι	0	7	0	12
Now (*i.e.* at the present time)[1]	νῦν	3	4	14	29

Lk. xxi. 9 has "*not straightway* (οὐκ εὐθέως)." Jn assigns the word four times to Jesus, concerning His "hour" or "season" or "ascension" (ii. 4, vii. 6, 8, xx. 17) as being "*not yet*," also Jn vii. 8 "I go *not yet* up to this feast (v.r. *not*)."

[1] [1719 *b*] "Now (νῦν)." Jn sometimes uses νῦν δέ, as in classical Gk—without ref. to past time, but with ref. to what *might have been*—for "but, [as things] now [are]," viii. 40, ix. 41, xv. 22, 24, xviii. 36 (xv. 24 may mean "but now [at last]"). Lk xix. 42 perh. means "but as things are," but more prob. "*but now [it is too late and]* it is hidden from thine eyes" (as in Lk xvi. 25 "*but now [on the other hand]*," with reference to the past time when Lazarus received evil things). See **1915** (i) foll.

[**1719** *c*] In Jn iv. 23, v. 25 "The hour is coming and [indeed] *now* is," there is a contrast between the past, when the "hour" might be called "future" or "*coming*," and the present, when the hour "*is*." Generally, in Jn, νῦν seems to imply a contrast with the past, unless it is expressly contrasted with the future as in xvi. 22 "Now on the one hand (μέν) ye have sorrow, but..." xiii. 36 "Thou canst not *now*...but thou shalt *hereafter*."

[**1719** *d*] Hence we should suppose a reference to the past in Jn ii. 8 "Draw water *now* [i.e. *now that the water-pots have been duly filled*]," iv. 18 "He whom thou *now* hast [as thy husband, *like thy five past husbands*]..." vi. 42 "We know his father and mother [*and his past life among us*]: how then doth he *now* say...?" ix. 21 "[*He was blind*] but how he *now* seeth we know not."

[**1719** *e*] There is ambiguity in xi. 22 "If thou hadst been here my brother had not died; *and now* (καὶ νῦν) [? in spite of his death] I know that whatsoever thou shalt ask of God, God will give thee." In classical Gk καὶ νῦν would naturally mean "*even* now": but it could hardly be used in this sense at the beginning of a sentence; because in that position, καί would naturally be taken as "*and*." The question is complicated by the use of καὶ νῦν in LXX, where νῦν represents more than a dozen Heb. words, see **1915** (i) foll.

[**1719** *f*] In view of Jn's usage, νῦν should probably be rendered "*now at last*," "*now in the time foreordained by the Father*," in Jn xii. 27 "*Now* is my soul troubled," xii. 31 "*Now* is the judgment of this world, *now* shall the ruler of this world be cast out," and so in xvii. 5, 7, 13.

[**1719** *g*] In Jn xi. 8 "*but now* [i.e. *recently*] (νῦν) the Jews were seeking," νῦν is used for the classical νῦν δή. But is this the meaning

215

[1720] SYNOPTIC DEVIATIONS

English	Greek	Mk	Mt.	Lk.	Jn
Officer, or minister[1]	ὑπηρέτης	2	2	2	9
Openly, freely[2]	(ἐν) παρρησίᾳ	1	0	0	9
[1720] Own[3]	ἴδιος	1	4 or 5	4	15

in Jn xxi. 10 "Bring of the fish that ye [have] caught *now* (ἐπιάσατε νῦν)"? Considering (1) the position of the word—at the end of the sentence, where it must necessarily be emphatic—(2) the superfluity of "recently" in such a context, and (3) above all, the ordinary meaning of νῦν in Jn, it seems best to translate thus, "the fish that ye have caught *at last*," i.e. after long toiling (xxi. 3) "in that night," before they heard the voice of the Saviour and obeyed His command. See **1915** (i) foll.

[1] [**1719** *h*] "Officer": used in Mt. v. 25 of the "officer" arresting a debtor and in Mk-Mt. elsewhere of the "officers" that arrested Jesus. In Lk. i. 2, iv. 20, the word means a "minister" of the Gospel or of the Synagogue. In Jn it always means "officers" of the Jews sent to arrest Jesus, except in xviii. 36 (R.V. txt) "then would my *servants* fight," on which see *Paradosis* (**1388**—**92**).

[2] "Openly." See "Freely" (**1712** *f*) and **1917** (i) foll.

[3] [**1720** *a*] "Own" (1) in "his own disciples." This phrase, not elsewhere found in N.T., is used by Mk in the sole instance in which he uses the adj. "*own*." Jn uses "*his own* (pl. masc.)," but never "*his own disciples*." After saying that Jesus "spake not without a parable," in which Mt. agrees with Mk, the latter alone continues thus, Mk iv. 34 "But privately *to his own disciples* he expounded all things." These words must be compared with

Mk iv. 10.	Mt. xiii. 10.	Lk. viii. 9.
"And when he was alone, they that were about him with the Twelve...."	"The disciples."	"His disciples."

[**1720** *b*] These facts suggest, in Mk, conflation from some Hebrew word capable of meaning "privately" and also, in various senses, "disciples." And, as a fact, the Hebrew *beth*, "house," in various contexts means (1) "at home," "privately," (2) "disciples" (as Beth Hillel)—which might be subdivided into (2 *a*) "they that were about him," (2 *b*) the inner circle of "the Twelve." Mt. and Lk. have simply (2). Mk has in one passage (iv. 10) conflated three renderings, and in another (iv. 34) two of them. In Esth. v. 10, "his *house*" is variously rendered (*a*) "his *house*," (β) "his *own* (τὰ ἴδια)." Ezr. vi. 11 "his *house*" is parall. to 1 Esdr. vi. 31 "his *own* (τῶν ἰδίων αὐτοῦ)." See also **370**.

[**1720** *c*] There may have been early controversy as to the existence of an inner circle of "*his own*" disciples within the Twelve (*e.g.* Gal. ii. 9

"the pillar" Apostles) which might induce Mt.-Lk. to omit the epithet as unedifying : but more probably the epithet did not exist in traditions (earlier than Mk) to which Mt. and Lk. have returned.

[1720 *d*] Jn uses οἱ ἴδιοι—but without μαθηταί—in a double sense, 1st of the Jews and of Christ's brethren, who did not, as a whole, receive Him, 2nd of those among them who did (exceptionally) receive Him (i. 11) "He came to [his] own [home] (τὰ ἴδια) and [*his*] own (οἱ ἴδιοι) did not receive him ; but, as many as received him, to them gave he...." (xiii. 1) "Having loved [*his*] own (τοὺς ἰδίους) that were in the world...." Whether Jn wrote with, or without, a reference to Mk's phrase "*his own disciples*," it is probable that he would deprecate any suggestion of a distinction between "disciples" that were in some peculiar sense Christ's "*own*," and others that were not.

[1720 *e*] "Own" (2) in its general use. Ἴδιος expresses, or implies, contrast—like "own" in English ("my *own* [and not another's])." The only Johannine instance where contrast might be questioned is Jn i. 41 ("He first findeth *his own* brother (τὸν ἀ. τὸν ἴδιον)") where it might be argued that Jn simply means "*his* brother," on the following grounds :

[1720 *f*] (i) Jn never uses the possessive ἑαυτοῦ, -ῶν, found in Mk vi. 4 (Tisch.), viii. 35 (but Tisch. αὐτοῦ), xi. 7 (marg.), Mt. viii. 22, xviii. 31, xxi. 8 (but Mk αὐτῶν), xxv. 1 (but Tisch. αὐτῶν), xxv. 4, 7, Lk. ii. 3, 39, iv. 24 (Tisch.), ix. 60, xi. 21, xiii. 19, 34 (ἑαυτῆς), xiv. 26 (but Tisch. αὐτοῦ), xiv. 26 (no v.r.), xiv. 27, 33, xv. 20 (but Tisch. αὐτοῦ), xvi. 4, 5, 8, xviii. 13 (but Tisch. αὐτοῦ), xix. 13, xix. 36 (but Tisch. αὐτῶν).

[1720 *g*] (ii) In the LXX, ἴδιος corresponds to αὐτοῦ in 1 Es. v. 8 ἕκαστος εἰς τὴν ἰδίαν πόλιν parall. to Ezr. ii. 1 ἀνὴρ εἰς πόλιν αὐτοῦ. It corresponds to the simple Heb. pers. suffix in Job ii. 11 "every one from *his* [*own*] place," ἰδίας, and in Dan. i. 10 "So should ye endanger *my* head" Theod. μου, but Dan. i. 10 κινδυνεύσω τῷ ἰδίῳ τραχήλῳ.

[1720 *h*] (iii) In recording the visit of the Lord to His "country," where all the Synoptists (W.H. txt (Mk vi. 1, 4, Mt. xiii. 54, Lk. iv. 24)) have simply "*his* (αὐτοῦ) country," Jn alone uses ἴδιος (Jn iv. 44 τῇ ἰδίᾳ πατρίδι). [But Mt. marg. xiii. 57 τῇ ἰδίᾳ π.]

On these three grounds it may be argued that Jn may have used ἴδιος to express the Synoptic αὐτοῦ.

[1720 *i*] Against these arguments it may be replied that there is a special reason here for supposing emphasis to be intended, namely, the repetition of the article (**1982**). When the article is repeated with ἴδιος elsewhere (v. 43, vii. 18) the meaning is "*his own* [and not another's]," *e.g.* vii. 18 "He that speaketh from himself seeketh *his own* glory." Ἴδιος with the repeated article is very rare in N.T. and appears to be always emphatic, Acts i. 25 "*his own* place," xx. 28 "*his own* blood." It is also highly characteristic of this Evangelist that he should in this indirect way suggest, instead of stating, that after Andrew had

English	Greek	Mk	Mt.	Lk.	Jn
Parable, s. Proverb	παροιμία	0	0	0	4
Paraclete[1]	παράκλητος	0	0	0	4
Philip (the apostle)[2]	Φίλιππος	1	1	1	12

"first" found "*his own*" brother, Andrew's companion (1901 *b*) did the same thing. On the whole, then, ἴδιος is probably emphatic in Jn i. 41.

[1] [1720 *j*] "Paraclete." Jn xiv. 16 "I will ask the Father and he shall give you another *Paraclete* that he may be with you for ever, [even] the Spirit of truth, whom the world cannot receive...," xiv. 26 "the *Paraclete*, the Holy Spirit, whom the Father will send in my name...," xv. 26 "the *Paraclete*...the Spirit of truth," xvi. 7 "If I go not away, the *Paraclete* will assuredly not come to you, but if I go, I will send him unto you." Comp. 1 Jn ii. 1 "We have a *Paraclete*, with the Father, Jesus Christ, a righteous [Paraclete]."

[1720 *k*] "Paraclete," *i.e.* "called in [to aid]," "advocatus," or "Advocate," was a Greek word, Hebraized as *Parklete*, in the sense of a legal advocate. But the ancient "advocate" differed from the modern in that the former did not take a reward but pleaded a friend's cause for the friend's sake. The nearest Synoptic equivalent to Christ's promise of a Paraclete is

Mk xiii. 11	Mt. x. 20	Lk. xxi. 15
"For it is not ye that speak, but the Holy Spirit."	"For it is not ye that speak, but the Spirit of your Father that speaketh in you."	"I will give you a mouth and wisdom that all your adversaries shall not be able to withstand or gainsay."

Jn's doctrine guards against a narrowing of the Synoptic tradition, especially Lk.—as though the object of the Paraclete would be merely to help the Christian to make a successful defence when brought before kings and rulers. On *Parklete*, see *Hor. Heb.* on Jn xiv. 16.

[1720 *l*] The variations in the Synoptists favour the view that Jesus used some expression like the Aramaic *Parklete*, which was variously paraphrased by the Synoptists. Against any superstitious notion that the Advocate would procure special favours from God, contrary to justice, Jn guards by saying that it is "the Spirit of *truth*," or "the *Holy* Spirit," or "Jesus Christ, a *righteous* [Paraclete]."

[2] [1720 *m*] "Philip," the only Apostle described by Jn in his first chapter as being (i. 43) "found" by Jesus Himself. The others, and Nathanael, either (i. 37—8) "followed" Jesus, or were (i. 41, 45) "found" by other disciples.

FROM JOHANNINE VOCABULARY [1721]

English	Greek	Mk	Mt.	Lk.	Jn
Pool[1]	κολυμβήθρα	0	0	0	3
[1721] Proverb, parable[2]	παροιμία	0	0	0	4

[1] [1720 n] "Pool" is used in connexion with the healing of a man described as "in infirmity" (Jn v. 2—7) and the name Bethzatha, Bethsaida, etc. varies greatly in MSS. and versions. "Pool" is also used in connexion with the healing of a man born blind, where it is called (Jn ix. 7) "the *pool* of Siloam" (1708 h).

[2] [1721 a] "Proverb," παροιμία, is rendered by R.V. (txt) "parable"—the usual rendering of παραβολή (which Jn never uses)—in Jn x. 6 "This *proverb* spake Jesus to them, but they (ἐκεῖνοι δέ) understood (ἔγνωσαν) not what things they were that he was speaking to them (τίνα ἦν ἃ ἐλάλει αὐτοῖς)." He had been saying that (x. 1—5) the "sheep" follow the "shepherd" whose "voice" they "know," but do not follow a "stranger." These facts were, and are, "*proverbial*," both as to the literal shepherd of sheep and as to the metaphorical "shepherd of the people" mentioned in the Bible and the Iliad; and they could hardly be misunderstood. But perhaps "understood not etc." means that those whom Jesus was addressing had no conception of the idea of the true shepherd. They could not misunderstand the proverb, but they could and did fail to understand the spiritual truth that it represented.

[1721 b] Jn's other instances are xvi. 25—9 "These things have I spoken unto you in *proverbs*. There cometh an hour when I shall no longer speak to you in *proverbs* but I shall bring you word plainly about the Father." To this the disciples reply "See, now [at last] (1719 f) (ἴδε νῦν) thou speakest plainly and speakest no *proverb*," contradicting their Master. But His answer to them, and the sequel, shew that they were wrong, and that His words had not been "plain" to them.

[1721 c] Why does John avoid the Synoptic word "parable" (1687) and introduce, in its place, a word unused by the Synoptists? Partly, perhaps, because the Synoptic tradition varied. Mark alone (iv. 33) says that Jesus taught by parables "*as they were able to understand.*" Matthew alone (in the parallel to Mk iv. 33—4) quotes an O.T. saying about "things hidden from the foundation of the world" (xiii. 35). Luke omits all this. Matthew (as well as Luke) omits Mark's statement that Jesus "*explained in private all things to his own disciples.*" Moreover, Mark (iv. 11—12) and Luke (viii. 10) differ considerably from Matthew (xiii. 11—13) in their descriptions of the reason for teaching in parables (Mk-Lk. "*that*...hearing *they may not* understand," Mt. "*because*...hearing they hear not neither do they understand*").

[1721 d] In any case, Jn prefers to say that Jesus taught by "*proverbs,*" i.e. by truths of general import, whereas the Paraclete was to teach truths of particular import, appealing to the experience of the

[1721] SYNOPTIC DEVIATIONS

English	Greek	Mk	Mt.	Lk.	Jn
Quicken[1]	ζωοποιέω	0	0	0	3
Raise up[2]	ἀνίστημι (active)	0	1	0	4
Receive (a person)[3]	λαμβάνω	0	0	0	11
Remain, s. Abide	μένω	2	3	7	40
Remember[4]	μνημονεύω	1	1	1	3

individual. Παροιμία does not appear to mean "dark saying" either in Jn or anywhere in Greek literature. But a proverb, or general saying, being brief, and dispensing with qualifications and modifications (which the hearer has to supply according to circumstances) is always liable to become a "dark saying" to those that will not take the trouble to think about its special meaning or application.

[1] "Quicken," see (1716) "Live, make to."

[2] [1721 e] "Raise up," in Mt., only xxii. 24 "raise up seed," quoting Deut. xxv. 5; Jn vi. 39, 40, 44, 54 "raise up [from the dead]," always foll. by "on the last day." (The numbers above do not include ἐγείρω.)

[3] [1721 f] "Receive (a person)." (The numbers above do not include δέχομαι (1689 c).) In all but two passages (Jn vi. 21, xix. 27) the receiving means spiritual reception, i.e. "receiving" doctrine, influence, or spirit. In the saying "He that *receiveth* me *receiveth* him that sent me," Jn xiii. 20 uses λαμβάνω whereas Mk ix. 37, Mt. x. 40, Lk. ix. 48 use δέχομαι. The latter word Jn never uses except in Jn iv. 45 "the Galilaeans *received* (ἐδέξαντο) him" describing our Lord's visit to His native place where He was *not* honoured. Perhaps Jn means that they merely "welcomed" or "entertained" Him, because of the signs He had wrought, but did not believe in Him. Jn uses λαμβάνω in the Prologue (i. 12) "But as many as *received* him, to them he gave authority to become children of God." The word λαμβάνω is used by Mk-Mt. (but not by Lk.) in the Eucharistic precept "*Receive* [it], This is my body," and in Jn xx. 22 "*Receive* the Holy Spirit." Lk. xxii. 17 has "Receive (λάβετε) this, i.e. the cup, and divide it among yourselves." See 1341.

[1721 g] Λαμβάνω τινά meaning "welcome" must be distinguished from λ. τινά meaning "take," e.g. (Mk ix. 36) "*taking* a child," (Lk. xx. 29) "*taking* a wife," (Jn xix. 6) "*take* him and crucify him." The instances of "welcoming" in Jn are applied to the receiving of the Logos, of Christ, of those whom He sends, of the Spirit, of the mother of Jesus when committed to the beloved disciple.

[4] [1721 h] "Remember," only in words of the Lord, Mk viii. 18 (Mt. xvi. 9) "*remember* ye not?" about the loaves, Lk. xvii. 32 "*remember* Lot's wife." Jn's instances are all in the Last Discourse, (xv. 20, xvi. 4) about "*remembering*" Christ's warnings, and xvi. 21 "she *remembereth* not the anguish."

[1721 i] Forms of μνησθῆναι occur in Mt. (3), Lk. (6), Jn (3). Jn's

FROM JOHANNINE VOCABULARY [1722]

English	Greek	Mk	Mt.	Lk.	Jn
Retain (sins) (?)[1]	κρατέω	0	0	0	2
Romans[2]	Ῥωμαῖοι	0	0	0	1
Roman, in[3]	Ῥωμαϊστί	0	0	0	1
Sake of, for the (w. persons)[4]	διά	4	4	0	9
Salim[5]	Σαλείμ	0	0	0	1
[1722] Scripture, another[6]	ἑτέρα γραφή	0	0	0	1
Scripture, the	ἡ γραφή	0	0	0	10
Scripture, this	ἡ γραφὴ αὕτη	1	0	1	0

instances all say that the disciples (ii. 17, 22, xii. 16) "remembered (ἐμνήσθησαν)" prophecies about Christ, or words of Christ, (ii. 22) "when he was raised from the dead," or (xii. 16) "when he was glorified."

[1] [1721 *j*] "Retain (sins)," only in Jn xx. 23 "whose soever sins *ye retain they are retained*, ἄν τινων κρατῆτε [sc. τὰς ἁμαρτίας] κεκράτηνται." The meaning is obscure (**2517—20**). See also **1691**.

[2] [1721 *k*] "Romans," Jn xi. 48 "The *Romans* will come and take away both our place and our nation."

[3] [1721 *l*] "In Roman," Jn xix. 20 "It was written in Hebrew, and *in Roman* [i.e. in Latin], and in Greek."

[4] [1721 *m*] "For the sake of (a person)." This excludes διὰ τοῦτο etc. On the Synoptic "sake," ἕνεκα, see **1692**. On the double meaning of διά, see **1884** *a—b*, and **2294** foll. On ὑπέρ see **2369—71**.

[5] [1721 *n*] "Salim." Only in Jn iii. 23 "Ænon near to *Salim*." Both localities are variously identified. "Ænon" may mean "fountains." "Salim" may mean "peace." Comp. Gen. xxxiii. 18 (R.V. txt) "peace," (marg.) "Shalem"; Ps. lxxvi. 2 "in Salem," LXX "peace."

[6] [1722 *a*] "Scripture, another" etc. "The Scripture" occurs in Jn at least twice without any Scriptural quotation in the context, ii. 22 (R.V.) "When therefore he was raised from the dead his disciples remembered that he spake this; and they believed *the scripture*, and the word which Jesus had said," xx. 8—9 (R.V.) "Then entered in therefore the other disciple also, which came first to the tomb, and he saw, and believed. For as yet they knew not *the scripture* that he must rise again from the dead." Westcott (*ad loc.*) and Lightfoot (Gal. iii. 22) take "the Scripture" as Ps. xvi. 10 "Thou wilt not leave my soul in Sheol," or some other single passage of Scripture in the Evangelist's mind. But against this are the following facts.

[1722 *b*] "The Scripture" (sing.) occurs in N.T., Clement of Alexandria, and Origen, in two senses, 1st, and most freq., the Scripture speaking through a single text (as we say, "The *Bible says*, 'Pride cometh before a fall'"), 2nd, the Scripture as a whole, or as a person representing God's voice, or will, or action. Before considering these usages, it will be convenient to discuss the plural.

[1722] SYNOPTIC DEVIATIONS

English	Greek	Mk	Mt.	Lk.	Jn
Scriptures, the	αἱ γραφαί	2	4	3	1

[1722 c] "The Scriptures" (pl.) is the form preferred by the Synoptists to mean all the books of Scripture, and hence, loosely, the Scripture as a whole. They never use the sing. except in Mk xii. 10 "Have ye not even read *this scripture*, 'The stone...'?" [where Mt. xxi. 42 has, loosely, "Have ye never read *in the scriptures*, 'The stone...'?" and Lk. xx. 17 "What then is *this that is written* (τί οὖν ἐστὶν τὸ γεγραμμένον τοῦτο), 'The stone...'?"] and Lk. iv. 21 "This day is fulfilled *this scripture* in your ears," *i.e.* the passage of Isaiah just read.

[1722 d] "The Scriptures" (pl.) is the form used by Mk-Mt. (*a*) with reference to the resurrection of the dead (Mk xii. 24, Mt. xxii. 29 "Ye err not knowing *the scriptures*," Lk. om.) and (*b*) with reference to the "delivering up" of the Messiah (Mk xiv. 49, Mt. xxvi. 56 "that *the scriptures* (Mt. + of the prophets) might be fulfilled," comp. Mt. xxvi. 54 "how then should the scriptures be fulfilled?" Lk. om.). The first of these passages indicates a belief on the part of Mark and Matthew that the doctrine of the general resurrection of the dead runs through the Scriptures, but Luke does not imply this. The second indicates a belief in Mark that the doctrine of Paradosis runs through the Scriptures; but Matthew limits this to "the *scriptures of the prophets*," and Luke again dissents.

[1722 e] "The Scriptures" is used twice by Luke in the Walk to Emmaus (xxiv. 27—32) "And beginning from Moses and from all the prophets he interpreted to them in all *the scriptures* the things concerning himself.... While he opened to us *the scriptures*," and, later on, xxiv. 44—5 "how that all things must needs be fulfilled which are written in the law of Moses, and the prophets, and the psalms, concerning me. Then opened he their mind that they might understand *the scriptures*." The object of this appeal to "the Scriptures" was to shew that "it behoved" the Messiah (Lk. xxiv. 26) "to suffer these things and to enter into his glory"; and, in this process, the promise to Abraham, the sacrifice of Isaac, his restoration as it were (Heb. xi. 18—19) "from the dead," the typical life of Joseph, the Story of the Brazen Serpent, and many other things "written in the Law of Moses" might play a part. Thus we can understand that St Paul may be referring to the general tenor of Scriptural types as well as texts when he says 1 Cor. xv. 3—4 "Christ died for our sins according to *the scriptures*...he hath been raised on the third day according to *the scriptures*."

[1722 f] These facts indicate room for individual difference of expression. On such a point, for example, as the Paradosis, or "delivering up," of Christ, Mark might say that it was predicted by "the scriptures," Matthew might correct this by saying "the scriptures *of the prophets*,"

Luke might prefer not to apply so broad a term as "Scriptures" to a single Messianic event. When Luke uses the plural he applies it to the whole of the divine Messianic plan for redeeming mankind. On the other hand another author might dislike the plural "Scriptures" except where the term denoted the different "writings" of the Bible and a passing from one "writing" to another or a comparison of one with another.

[1722 g] "The Scriptures," in Jn. This last remark prepares us for the fact that John, as against ten instances of "the Scripture," *uses the Synoptic term "the Scriptures" only once*, (v. 39) "Ye search *the scriptures*, for ye (*emph.*) think to have in them eternal life." The context appears to shew that the meaning is: "Ye pass from book to book, searching, and comparing, and studying this passage and that, and losing the whole in the parts, failing to recognise the testimony of *the Scripture* while poring over *the Scriptures*."

[1722 h] Returning to "the Scripture" (sing.), and considering it first outside Jn, we find that it mostly introduces a quotation: Acts i. 16—20 "*the s.* that the Holy Spirit uttered...(Ps. lxix. 25 and cix. 8)," viii. 32—5 "The passage of *the s.* that he was reading...from *this s.*," Rom. iv. 3 "What saith *the s.*...," ix. 17 "*The s.* saith to Pharaoh...." (simil. x. 11, xi. 2, Gal. iv. 30, 1 Tim. v. 18, Jas ii. 23, iv. 5 (?)—all of which have "saith" etc.), Jas ii. 8 "according to *the s.* 'Thou shalt love thy neighbour,'" 1 Pet. ii. 6 "it contains *in s.*"

[1722 i] "The Scripture" in N.T. apart from quotations. Where there is no such form as "saith," "uttered," "contains," and no quotation, "the Scripture" *is regarded as a whole and sometimes personified*. Even where there is a quotation, it is personified in Gal. iii. 8 "*The s., foreseeing...preached.*" There is no quotation in Gal. iii. 22 "*The s....shut up all things* under sin...," 2 Pet. i. 20 "every prophecy of *s....*" Gal. iii. 22 resembles Rom. xi. 32 "God *hath shut up all men*...," which indicates that "Scripture," in Gal. iii. 22, means "the will of God as expressed in Scripture." There is no single passage of Scripture that mentions this "shutting up": the Apostle is probably referring to a number of passages such as those quoted in Rom. iii. 10—18, and also to Ps. cxliii. 2 and Deut. xxvii. 26 quoted in Gal. ii. 16, iii. 10. Schöttgen (Gal. iii. 8) quotes Siphra 186 *b* for a similar personification of Scripture: "What did Scripture *have in view, in placing* the New Year and the Day of Atonement between Passover and Pentecost?"

[1722 j] "The Scripture" in Clem. Alex. and Origen. The Greek Fathers most akin to the Fourth Gospel are Clement of Alexandria and Origen. Clement uses "the Scripture saith," to introduce quotations or allusions, but also such phrases as (883) "collecting testimonies from *Scripture* (ἐκ γ.)," (890) "wresting *the Scripture* (τὴν γ.)," "believing *the Lord's Scripture* (τῇ κυριακῇ γ.)," meaning Scripture as a whole. Origen

also (Huet i. 26—7) speaks of "the Scripture" as having a body and a soul. He says that our faculties are strengthened by reading "the Scripture," that "the whole Scripture (πᾶσαν τὴν γ.)" is (Huet i. 204 D) "God's one complete and perfectly adapted instrument." Similarly he says in the *Philocalia*, chap. x. "There is not a jot or tittle written in *the Scripture* that...does not perform its work." Chrysostom says (on Rom. xvi. 5) "not even apparently small points *in the Scripture* are placed there at random or in vain." Suicer also quotes Chrys. *Homil.* xcii. *tom.* vi. "Whatsoever things *the Scripture* saith, these things are more trustworthy than the things that are seen (πιστότερα τῶν ὁρωμένων)." Clem. personifies Scripture when he says that it (882) "*sells* to strangers those who have fallen away" (comp. 506 "*saith* they are sold," and see Judg. ii. 14, iii. 8, iv. 2, x. 7, 1 S. xii. 9, Is. l. 1 which describe Jehovah as "selling Israel" because of its sins).

[1722 *k*] "The Scripture," in Jn, apart from the two passages under consideration, occurs as follows. vii. 38 "Even as *the s.* [hath] said...," obscure, perh. quotation, but perh. general tenor of Scriptural promises to them that (vii. 37) "thirst." On. vii. 42 "Did not *the s.* say that the Christ comes from the seed of David and from Bethlehem the village where David was?" Westcott himself refers the reader to Is. xi. 1, Jer. xxiii. 5, Mic. v. 2, without mentioning any one of these as specially in the Evangelist's mind. Probably the meaning is "the general tenor of the Psalms and the Prophets concerning the birth and birthplace of the Son of David," who, it was assumed, must be born in the city of David. In x. 34—5 "Is it not written...If...*the scripture* cannot be destroyed (λυθῆναι) (lit. loosed)," the reference may be to the passage just quoted ("I said ye are gods") but it is more in accordance with Johannine style to suppose Scripture as a whole to be intended (for "loosing" comp. ii. 19 and perh. 1 Jn iv. 3). After xiii. 18, xix. 24, 36 "that *the s.* might be fulfilled," there follow quotations. In xvii. 12, there is probably a reference to the previously quoted Scripture so that we must render, "that *the* [*above-quoted*, xiii. 18] *s.* might be fulfilled." In xix. 28, "Jesus,...that *the s.* might be perfectly accomplished, saith, 'I thirst,'" the words 'I thirst' are printed by W.H. as a quotation. In xix. 37, a quotation is introduced with the phrase, "And again another *s.* saith."

[1722 *l*] There remain for consideration Jn ii. 22 "they believed *the scripture*," xx. 9 "they knew not *the scripture*." As to the former, Origen, in a very full comment, suggests no one passage of Scripture that the Evangelist must have had in view. Nor does Chrysostom. Cyril (Cramer *ad loc.*) *paraphrases in the plural*, "comparing with the issue *the things that had been written* (τὰ γεγραμμένα)." Also in his brief commentary on the context of the second passage, Chrysostom mentions no definite text of Scripture. Westcott, though maintaining that one definite

FROM JOHANNINE VOCABULARY [1723]

English	Greek	Mk	Mt.	Lk.	Jn
[1723] See (1)[1]	βλέπω	15	20	14	17
See (2)[1]	θεάομαι	[2]	4	3	6
See (3)[1]	θεωρέω	7	2	7	23
See (4)[1]	ὁράω	7	13	12	30
Seize, catch, take[2]	πιάζω	0	0	0	8

passage is intended, does not profess to say with certainty what it is (Westc. Jn ii. 22 "hardly any other than Ps. xvi. 10," but on Jn xx. 9 "the reference is probably to Ps. xvi. 10"). It is extremely unlikely that Christians in the first century would have fastened their faith in the Scriptural prediction of the Messiah's resurrection on one passage (excluding, for example, Isaiah and Hosea, and limiting themselves to a single text in the Psalms). Much more probably they would have adopted Luke's view that the Saviour, after the Resurrection, "beginning from Moses and from all the prophets," revealed to the disciples (xxiv. 27, 32, 45) "all the Scriptures," *i.e.* the tenor of the Scriptures. It would be quite in harmony with Johannine style and thought to represent this by "*the Scripture.*"

[1] [1723 a] "See." On βλέπω see **1607**, on θεάομαι **1604**, on θεωρέω **1598**—**1603**, on ὁράω **1605**—**6** and **1703** a. Ἰδεῖν is the most frequent word for "seeing" in all the Gospels, but less freq. in Jn than in the rest. On Jn's use of εἶδον see **1610**.

[2] [1723 b] "Seize." In Jn xxi. 3, 10 πιάζω is used of catching fish. Elsewhere in Jn it always describes attempts of the Jews to "catch" Jesus.

The Synoptists differ among themselves in their language in

Mk xii. 13	Mt. xxii. 15	Lk. xx. 20
ἵνα αὐτὸν ἀγρεύσωσιν λόγῳ.	ὅπως αὐτὸν παγιδεύσωσιν ἐν λόγῳ.	ἵνα ἐπιλάβωνται αὐτοῦ λόγου ὥστε παραδοῦναι αὐτὸν τῇ ἀρχῇ καὶ τῇ ἐξουσίᾳ τοῦ ἡγεμόνος.

—where Lk. is at some pains to shew that the "catching" was to be more (at all events in its results) than mere "catching in word."

Mk xiv. 1	Mt. xxvi. 4	Lk. xxii. 2
πῶς αὐτὸν ἐν δόλῳ κρατήσαντες ἀποκτείνωσιν.	ἵνα...δόλῳ κρατήσωσιν καὶ ἀποκτείνωσιν.	τὸ πῶς ἀνέλωσιν αὐτόν.

[1723 c] In view, perhaps, of various and slightly conflicting traditions, Jn uses habitually one word, without adding λόγῳ or δόλῳ. Its use (in the sense of "catching" a prisoner) in writings so various as Acts xii. 4, 2 Cor. xi. 32, Rev. xix. 20, shews that it must have been freq. in Christian communities. In Cant. ii. 15 "*catch* foxes," LXX πιάσατε

[1723] SYNOPTIC DEVIATIONS

English	Greek	Mk	Mt.	Lk.	Jn
Send[1], including—	πέμπω	1	4	10	32
"He that sent (me, him)"[1]	ὁ πέμψας (με, αὐτόν)	0	0	0	26

Sym. has συλλάβετε. In Sir. xxiii. 21 πιασθήσεται, A has κολασθήσεται. [In Jer. xviii. 20 κόλασις is perh. a conflate rendering of a word meaning "pit," which suggests "snaring" or "catching."]
  For "Seize," κρατέω, see **1691** a.
  [1] **[1723** d**]** "Send" etc., πέμπω. In the canonical LXX this word occurs only 6 times (whereas ἀποστέλλω occurs about 480). It is the mark of a non-Hebraic style, occurring 4 times in Wisd. and 14 in Macc. In the Pentateuch, it occurs only where Rebecca (Gen. xxvii. 42) "*sent* and called Jacob," who is presumably in the same house with her or not far off. In the Synoptists, it is used of sending (on a short errand) messengers, soldiers, executioners, servants etc., who for the most part have to return with something accomplished or with some report. Mk's only instance, however, is Mk v. 12 "*send* us into the swine" (parall. Mt. ἀπόστειλον, Lk. ἐπιτρέψῃ ἀπελθεῖν). The Synoptists use far more frequently ἀποστέλλω, which is also used by Jn, thus :—Mk (20), Mt. (22), Lk. (25), Jn (28).

  [1723 e**]** "Send" etc. in Jn. Jn's frequent use of πέμπω arises in part from the frequency of the phrase "He that *sent*" (almost always applied to the Father) in the words of Christ, occurring more than 20 times. If this phrase were deducted, Jn would use πέμπω only about six times, *i.e.* less frequently than Luke. Except in Jn i. 22, 33 ("that we may give an answer to them that sent us," "he that sent me to baptize") πέμπω always occurs in words of Christ. Apart from the phrase "He that *sent*" are (xiii. 20) "He that receiveth whomsoever I *send*," (xiv. 26) "[The Spirit] which the Father will *send* in my name," (xv. 26) "[The Paraclete] whom I will *send* to you from the Father," (xvi. 7) "But if I go, I will *send* him [the Paraclete] unto you," (xx. 21) "Even as the Father HATH SENT (ἀπέσταλκεν) me, I also (κἀγὼ) *send* (πέμπω) you."

  [1723 f**]** Πέμπω and ἀποστέλλω. This (xx. 21) terminates the instances in Jn both of ἀποστέλλω and of πέμπω; and it cannot be doubted that Jn intends a difference of meaning by the different words. Had he wished to use the perfect of πέμπω ("hath sent," πέπομφα), no grammatical considerations need have deterred him; for there are two instances of it in the LXX alone (1 Esd. ii. 26, 2 Macc. xi. 32).

  [1723 g**]** Πέμπω is never used in the First Epistle at all, but ἀποστέλλω is used concerning the Father's sending of the Son in three solemn passages (1 Jn iv. 9, 10, 14) and six times in the Last Prayer in the Gospel, where we find (xvii. 18) "Even as thou didst SEND (ἀπέστειλας) me into the world, I also (κἀγὼ) did SEND (ἀπέστειλα) them into the

226

English	Greek	Mk	Mt.	Lk.	Jn
Servant (Chri. precepts, not parables)[1]	δοῦλος	1	3	1	6
Sheep[2]	πρόβατον	2	11	2	17 or 19
[1724] Sick[3]	ἀσθενής	1	3	1	0
Sick, be[3]	ἀσθενέω	1	3	1	8
Sickness[3]	ἀσθένεια	0	1	4	2

world." Comparing the passage in question (xx. 21) with xvii. 18 and with others where ἀποστέλλω is defined by various contexts (1 Jn iv. 9, 10, 14), we are perhaps justified in thinking that ἀποστέλλω means "sending away into the world at large," but πέμπω "sending on a special errand." The Saviour sends all the Apostles collectively into the world to preach the Gospel (ἀποστέλλει), but He sends them on special errands to Jews, Gentiles, Rome, Athens, Antioch etc. (πέμπει). If so, the distinction in Jn xx. 21 is between the mission of the incarnate Son now accomplished, and the mission of His followers now beginning: "Even as the Father HATH SENT (ἀπέσταλκε) me [into the world], I also *send* (πέμπω) you [severally to the several nations of the world]."

[1] [1723 *h*] "Servant" (Chri. precepts, not parables). Δοῦλος, "servant" or "slave," in parables, occurs in Mk xii. 2, 4, xiii. 34, and much more freq. in Mt.-Lk. But, in Synoptic precepts, it occurs only Mk x. 44 "Whosoever may desire among you to be first shall be *servant* of all," Mt. xx. 27 sim. Lk. diff. (on which see **1276—80**); Mt. x. 24—5 "nor is a *servant* above his lord...and the *servant* as his lord" (where Lk. vi. 40 differs); Lk. xvii. 10 (after a parable) "Say ye, we are unprofitable *servants*." As regards παῖς, see **805—11**, and **1862**.

[1723 *i*] It was shewn above (**1717** *d—g*) that Epictetus regards a "servant" or "slave"—if a slave in *mind* and not merely in social condition—as essentially bad, being the slave of his fears, passions etc. So Jn says (viii. 34) "Everyone that doeth sin is (W.H.) a *slave* [of sin]," and adds that (viii. 35) "the *slave* doth not abide in the house for ever," contrasting the "slave" with the "son," who "abides for ever (**2263** *e, f*)." Later on, he follows Matthew (x. 24—5) above quoted in saying (xiii. 16) (rep. xv. 20) "A *servant* is not greater than his lord," applying the word to the apostles. Later still, he says (xv. 15) "No longer do I call you *servants* because the *servant* knoweth not what his lord doeth." He adds, "But you have I called *friends*." On the connexion between this and Lk. xii. 4 "you, my *friends*," see **1784—92**. These and many other facts indicate a mental friction arising from the collision, or intermixing, of Greek and Hebrew words and notions about "service."

[2] [1723 *j*] "Sheep." Comp. Mt. x. 6, xv. 24 "the lost *sheep* of the House of Israel," with Jn x. 16 "other *sheep* that are not of this fold," where Jn suggests that the precept in Mt. x. 6 was but for a time.

[3] [1724 *a*] "Sick" etc. Jn nowhere uses the word νόσος. Mt. once

English	Greek	Mk	Mt.	Lk.	Jn
Signify[1]	σημαίνω	0	0	0	3
Simon (father of Judas Iscariot)[2]	Σίμων	0	0	0	3
Soldier[3]	στρατιώτης	1	3	2	6
Sop[4]	ψωμίον	0	0	0	4
Speak, I (Chri.)[5]	λαλέω	0	1	1	c. 30
[1725] Stand[6]	στήκω	2	0	0	2
Stand (appl. to Jesus)[7]	ἵστημι	1	2	4	5

(viii. 17) uses ἀσθένεια in a quotation from Is. liii. 4 (Heb. not LXX). In canon. LXX ἀσθένεια occurs only 5 times, once (Job xxxvii. 7) in error, and twice (Jer. vi. 21, xviii. 23) to express moral "stumbling."

[1] [1724 b] "Signify." Always in the phrase (xii. 33, xviii. 32, xxi. 19) "*signifying* by what death" he should die, or glorify God. Apart from Acts xxv. 27 ("*signify* the charges against him"), it occurs in N.T. elsewhere only in Acts xi. 28 "*signified* through the Spirit," Rev. i. 1 "*signified*...to his servant John."

[2] [1724 c] "Simon" (father of Judas Iscariot): Jn vi. 71 Ἰούδαν Σίμωνος Ἰσκαριώτου, xiii. 2 Ἰούδας Σίμωνος Ἰσκαριώτης, xiii. 26 Ἰούδᾳ Σίμωνος Ἰσκαριώτου.

[3] [1724 d] "Soldier," in Jn, all in the narrative of the Passion (xix. 2—34).

[4] [1724 e] "Sop," only in Jn xiii. 26—30, and not elsewhere in N.T.

[5] [1724 f] "I speak" (Chri.). The numbers include the first pers. sing. of any tense of λαλέω in Christ's words. See **1704**. Mt.'s single instance is xiii. 13 "Therefore speak I to them in parables," and Lk.'s is xxiv. 44 "These are my words which I spake unto you."

[6] [1725 a] "Stand," στήκω, generally means "stand fast (or, upright)" as in Rom. xiv. 4, 1 Cor. xvi. 13, Gal. v. 1. It is appropriate in Mk xi. 25 "When ye *stand steadfastly* praying," but not so obviously in Mk iii. 31 (where D has ἑστῶτες) unless it means that the mother and brethren of Jesus "took their stand" at the door with persistence. In Jn viii. 44, the meaning is "He was a murderer from the beginning and did not *stand fast* in the truth." In i. 26 μέσος ὑμῶν στήκει, "there *standeth* in the midst of you [a certain one], whom ye know not," the verb perh. has (as Origen suggests *ad loc.*) a spiritual as well as a local meaning.

[7] [1725 b] "Stand," ἵστημι, appl. to Jesus. The Synoptists associate the "standing" of Jesus (Mk x. 49, Mt. xx. 32 στάς, Lk. xviii. 40 σταθείς (**1725 d**)) with a cure of blindness. The tradition peculiar to Lk. vi. 17 "having gone down [from the mountain] he *stood* (ἔστη) with them," suggests a parallel between the Sermon on the Mount and the Law given on Mount Sinai, whence Moses descended and spoke to his brethren. Lk. v. 1 "*standing* (ἑστώς) by the Lake" (in the Call of Peter and the

Miraculous Draught) suggests parallelism to Mk i. 16 "passing (Mt. iv. 8 walking) by the sea" (in the Call of Peter), or to Jn xxi. 4 "he *stood* (ἔστη) on (εἰς) the beach" (in the Repentance of Peter and the Miraculous Draught). On Lk. xxiv. 36, "stood in the midst" (ἔστη ἐν μέσῳ) see **1793**—7.

[**1725** c] "Stand steadfastly," σταθῆναι, is applied to Jesus in Mt. xxvii. 11, Lk. xviii. 40, and is prob. not adequately rendered by R.V. "stood," which suits the form used by Mk x. 49, Mt. xx. 32 στάς. Lk. uses σταθείς because he means that Jesus "stood still," "refused to go on" in spite of His followers, who were rebuking the blind man because they did not want to have the procession interrupted. Mk xiii. 9 σταθήσεσθε does not mean "ye shall stand," but "ye shall *stand* (Jer. i. 18) *as 'pillars'* before kings for my sake," *i.e.* stand as steadfast witnesses for me (where Mt.-Lk., missing the meaning of this, have Mt. x. 18 ἀχθήσεσθε, Lk. xxi. 12 ἀπαγομένους). In the LXX, σταθῆναι, when not meaning "weighed," regularly means "established," or is, at all events, distinct from "stood," *e.g.* Ex. xl. 17, Numb. ix. 15 (R.V.) "reared up," Deut. xix. 15 (A), 2 K. xiii. 6, Eccles. ii. 9, Dan. vii. 4, 5, 1 Mac. xiv. 29. In Judg. xx. 2, ἐστάθησαν (A ἔστη) is prob. intended to represent the Heb. exactly, "presented themselves," "took their stand" (Gesen. 426).

[**1725** d] Σταθῆναι, in N.T. generally, must be distinguished from στῆναι. On Col. iv. 12 ἵνα σταθῆτε, Lightf. says "*stand fast*"—not as R.V. "stand"—"doubtless the correct reading rather than στῆτε; comp. Mt. ii. 9, xxvii. 11, where also the rec. txt substitutes the weaker word." Hence we should render Mt. ii. 9 "*stood still*," and Lk. xxi. 36 "that ye may be able to...... *stand fast*" (where D alters σταθῆναι to στήσεσθε). In Lk. xviii. 11—13, a contrast is intended between the Pharisee "*standing erect* (σταθείς)" and the Publican "*standing* (ἑστώς) afar off." Lk. xxiv. 17 is one of the very few passages correctly rendered by R.V. "*they stood still.*"

[**1725** e] "Stand as a steadfast witness" is a meaning of σταθῆναι that naturally follows from the above-mentioned Hebrew notion of a prophet as (Jer. i. 18) "an iron *pillar*"—the word "pillar" meaning "that which stands"—standing to testify for Jehovah: and such a meaning would be favoured by the saying of Deuteronomy xix. 15 "in the mouth of three witnesses shall every word *be made to stand*," LXX στήσεται, but A σταθήσεται, and alluded to in the latter form in Mt. xviii. 16. Hence, something more than the mere attitude of "standing" is implied in the precept (Acts v. 20) "*Stand and* (σταθέντες) speak in the temple to the people," where the angel means "*stand fast as witnesses* for the Lord," and this is the meaning of σταθείς applied to Peter and Paul in Acts ii. 14, xvii. 22, xxvii. 21. This, too, is probably the meaning in the tradition peculiar to Matthew (xxvii. 11) "Now Jesus *stood* [*erect*], or *stood* [*as a witness for God*], before the Governor."

[**1725** f] Jn has (besides the above-mentioned (**1725** a) i. 26 στήκει)

vii. 37 "Jesus *stood* (ἱστήκει) and cried saying, If any man thirst, let him come unto me," xx. 14 "[Mary Magdalene] beholdeth Jesus *standing* (ἑστῶτα)," xx. 19 "Jesus came and *stood in the midst* (ἔστη εἰς τὸ μέσον)," rep. in xx. 26, and xxi. 4 "Jesus *stood* on (ἔστη εἰς) the shore." On the last three instances, see 1796.

[1725 *g*] It is a commonplace with Philo that (i. 94) "None but the true God *standeth* (ἑστῶτα)," and he speaks of (i. 93) "the *standing*, wholesome, and right Logos." Comp. i. 269, 276, 425, 586, 591, 687, 688. "That which is phenomenal," he says (i. 383) "does not *stand*." Simon Magus is said to have claimed to be the Standing One (Clem. Alex. 456). Origen (Huet ii. 128—9) connects the "standing (στήκει)" in Jn i. 26 with the "standing (ἱστήκει)" in vii. 37, and speaks of the Father as preeminently "standing" : "*But there stands also His Logos ever in the act of saving* (ἔστηκε δὲ καὶ ὁ Λόγος αὐτοῦ ἀεὶ ἐν τῷ σώζειν)—whether He be flesh, or whether He be amidst of men, not apprehended, nay, not even seen (κἂν γένηται σὰρξ κἂν μέσος ᾖ ἀνθρώπων οὐ καταλαμβανόμενος ἀλλ' οὐδὲ βλεπόμενος)—but He stands also teaching, inviting all to drink......" (and then he quotes Jn vii. 37 "If any man thirst..."). No doubt Origen also has in view (as regards "stood and cried" and the invitation to "drink") Prov. viii. 2—3 "Wisdom *standeth* (ἔστηκε)... She *crieth* aloud," and Prov. ix. 5 "Eat ye of my bread and *drink* of the wine that I have mingled." Probably John had the same passage in view.

[1725 *h*] The phrases "*saw...Jesus standing*," and "I *behold...the Son of man standing*" (like that connected with Mary Magdalene "she *beheld* Jesus *standing*") are used of the Martyr Stephen in Acts vii. 55—6, with the addition, "at the right hand of God." Chrysostom (Cramer *ad loc.*) says, "Why, then, 'standing' and not 'seated'? To shew the active help (ἀντίληψιν) [extended] to (εἰς) the Martyr. For also about the Father it is said, 'Arise, O God' (ἀνάστα, ὁ θεός), and again, 'Now will I arise (ἀναστήσομαι), saith the Lord.'" But the word "Arise" thus quoted twice from the Psalms is quite different as to its Hebrew meaning from the word ἔστηκα, used of (Gen. xviii. 2) the three angels "*standing*" before Abraham, and of God (Ps. lxxxii. 1) "*standing* in the congregation of the gods," and of Wisdom (Prov. viii. 2) "*standing* in the midst of the ways" and "crying aloud." The latter means "stand as a pillar," "stand fast," "stand as a watchman or sentinel." The explanation given by Basilius (Cramer *ad loc.*) is more like that of Philo and Origen, and more consonant with the LXX use of ἔστηκα or ἔστην : "I think the standing and fixedness (τὴν μὲν στάσιν κ. τ. καθίδρυσιν) suggests the compactness of nature and its universal stability (τὸ πάγιον τῆς φύσεως κ. πάντῃ στάσιμον ὑποφαίνειν)." The Revelation (iii. 20) represents Jesus as saying, "Behold, I *stand* at the door and knock." Perhaps John wished to describe Him, after the Resurrection, as thus "standing," and Mary Magdalene as the first to respond to the call.

FROM JOHANNINE VOCABULARY [1726]

English	Greek	Mk	Mt.	Lk.	Jn
[1726] Stone (vb.)[1]	λιθάζω	0	0	0	4
"Stoop and look in"[2]	παρακύπτω	0	0	[1]	2
Sychar[3]	Συχάρ	0	0	0	1
Synagogue, put out of[4]	ἀποσυνάγωγος	0	0	0	3
Take, seize, catch[5]	πιάζω	0	0	0	8
Testify, testimony, witness[6]	μαρτυρέω	0	1	1	33
	μαρτυρία	3	0	1	14
	μαρτύριον	3	3	3	0
	μάρτυς	1	2	2	0
That, or because (2174 foll.)	ὅτι	c. 100	c. 140	c. 180	c. 270

[1] [1726 a] "Stone"(vb.). Always applied to an attempt to "stone" Jesus, Jn x. 31—3, xi. 8 (comp. viii. 59 "they therefore took up stones to cast at him"). Λιθάζω is also in [Jn viii. 5]. Λιθοβολέω occurs Mk (0), Mt. (2), Lk. (1), Jn (0).

[2] [1726 b] "Stoop and look in" (so R.V. in Gospels, but?). In Jn, only in xx. 5, 11, of the beloved disciple and Mary looking into the sepulchre; perh. also in [[Lk. xxiv. 12]]. In N.T. elsewhere, only in Jas i. 25, 1 Pet. i. 12, of a metaphorical looking into the Law of Liberty or the mysteries of Redemption. See **1798—1804**.

[3] "Sychar," Jn iv. 5, SS "Shechem," see *Enc.* "Sychar."

[4] "Synagogue, put out of," Jn ix. 22, xii. 42, xvi. 2. Not elsewhere in N.T.

[5] "Take." See notes on "seize" (1723 b—c), and on "receive" (1721 f—g).

[6] [1726 c] "Testify," "testimony" etc. The word μαρτυρία is very rare in canon. LXX. It nowhere represents a Heb. word, exc. in the phrase Ex. xx. 16, Deut. v. 20, Prov. xxv. 18 μ. ψευδῆ, in 1 S. ix. 24 (A) εἰς μαρτυρίαν (B -ον), and in Ps. xix. 7 "The *testimony* of the Lord is sure, making wise the simple."

[1726 d] Epictetus, toward the end of the first century, had probably made μαρτυρία (to denote the "testimony" that every good man is bound to give to God) a household word among many serious Greeks (i. 29. 48) "What *testimony* dost thou give to God?" (iv. 8. 32) "He testifieth a *testimony* to virtue." (Comp. i. 29. 49, iii. 22. 86.) The same writer introduces God as saying to man (i. 29. 47) "*Testify* unto me," describes (i. 29. 49) what man is to "*testify*," and inculcates (i. 29. 56) "*testifying* by action to one's words." He also freq. uses μάρτυς in this sense (iii. 26. 28) "God doth not cease to care for His ministers and *witnesses*." Reasons have been given above (**1696 e**) for Jn's avoidance of the term μάρτυς, as being, in some Christian circles, used in the technical sense of "martyr." On the Synoptic phrase εἰς μαρτύριον, see **1695 b**.

[1727] SYNOPTIC DEVIATIONS

English	Greek	Mk	Mt.	Lk.	Jn
That, *i.e.* in order that (1695 *c*)	ἵνα	c. 65	c. 40	c. 50	c. 150
Thomas[1]	Θωμᾶς	1	1	1	7
Thou (nom.) (2402)	σύ	10	18	c. 26	c. 60
Tiberias[2]	Τιβεριάς	0	0	0	3
[1727] Together[3]	ὁμοῦ	0	0	0	3
Trouble[4]	ταράσσω	1	2	2	6

[1] "Thomas." Mk iii. 18, Lk. vi. 15 Μαθθαῖον κ. Θωμᾶν, Mt. iii. 3. Θωμᾶς κ. Μαθθαῖος ὁ τελώνης.
[2] [1726 *e*] "Tiberias," in N.T. only in Jn vi. 1 "the sea of Galilee which is [the sea] of *Tiberias*," vi. 23 "There came boats from *Tiberias*," xxi. 1 "Jesus manifested himself again to the disciples at the sea of *Tiberias*." Mk-Mt. use "sea of Galilee" or "sea," Lk. "lake" or "lake of Gennesaret."
[3] [1727 *a*] "Together," Jn iv. 36, xx. 4, xxi. 2. In N.T., the only other instance is Acts ii. 1 "They were all *together* in the same place," where it appears not to be superfluous but to imply *unity of purpose*. This is also implied in Jn iv. 36 "that he that soweth may rejoice *together and* he that reapeth," where instead of ὁμοῦ καί we should have expected ὁμοίως καί. Probably it is also implied in the account of the two disciples "running *together*" to the sepulchre, Jn xx. 4 ἔτρεχον δὲ οἱ δύο ὁμοῦ (comp. the Targ. on Gen. xxii. 8 ἐπορεύθησαν ἀμφότεροι (xxii. 6 οἱ δύο) ἅμα, Onk. "*as one*," Jer. I "*in heart entirely as one*"). The last instance in Jn denotes the unity of the Seven shortly before the Feast on the One Bread, where the first places in the list are given to Peter the Denier and Thomas the Unbeliever (Jn xxi. 2) "There were *together* Simon Peter and Thomas...." In the canon. LXX, ὁμοῦ occurs nowhere except Ezr. ii. 64 AR ὁμοῦ (B om.), Job xxxiv. 29 ὁμοῦ (א ὁμοίου). It is 13 times in Wisd. and Macc.

[4] [1727 *b*] "Trouble," ταράσσω, in the Synoptists, means (pass.) "alarmed," Mk vi. 50 (parall. Mt. xiv. 26), Mt. ii. 3, Lk. i. 12, xxiv. 38. In Jn, it occurs (Chri.) in xii. 27 "Now is my soul *troubled*," and xiv. 1, 27 "Let not your heart be *troubled*." On its threefold application to Christ as "troubling himself," "troubled in soul," and "troubled in spirit" (xi. 33, xii. 27, xiii. 21) see **920**.

[1727 *c*] "Freedom from trouble," ἀταραξία, is, according to Epictetus, the gift of God to man, and *no one has a right to be* "*troubled*," (*Ench.* § 5) "Men are *troubled* (ταράσσει) not by facts but by their notions about facts. For example, death is not terrible—since else it would have appeared [so] to Socrates—but the notion about death, the notion that it is terrible —this it is that is the terror. When therefore we feel pestered (ἐμποδιζώμεθα), or *troubled*, or grieved (λυπώμεθα), let us never blame others, but only ourselves, that is to say, our own notions." No group of words

FROM JOHANNINE VOCABULARY [1727]

English	Greek	Mk	Mt.	Lk.	Jn
True (1)[1]	ἀληθής	1	1	0	14
True (2)[2]	ἀληθινός	0	0	1	9

is perhaps more frequent in Epictetus than those bearing on "*trouble*" and "freedom from *trouble*"; and it is almost certain that Jn, in describing Christ as thrice "troubled," and as on one occasion "troubling himself," is writing with allusion to this Stoic doctrine which must have been familiar to all educated Greeks at the beginning of the second century.

[1] [1727 d] "True" (1), ἀληθής, in Synoptists, only in Mk xii. 14, Mt. xxii. 16 "We know that thou art *true*," parall. Lk. xx. 21, "We know that thou sayest and teachest rightly." It is not surprising that Lk. deviates: for "true" is perh. only once applied to persons in canon. LXX (Nehem. vii. 2 "a faithful man," ἀνὴρ ἀ.): and Steph. gives very few instances, except where the poets speak of a "*truthful* accuser," a "*truthful* friend," or (*Iliad* xii. 433) "an *honest* sempstress" (lit. truthful in weighing out her work). Jn thrice applies it to persons, once, generally, vii. 18 "he that seeketh the glory of him that sent him is *true*" i.e. not tempted to falsehood by self-interest, or affectation, and twice of God, iii. 33 "God is *true*," viii. 26 "He that sent me is *true*."

[1727 e] In Jn vi. 55 "my flesh is *true* food and my blood is *true* drink," Origen (once) and other authorities have "truly," and Chrys., while reading "true," appears to give "truly" as one of two interpretations. But it may be used in the sense in which Socrates maintained (Plato 36—40) in the *Philebus*, that some pleasures are "true (ἀληθεῖς)," others "false." So in the *Phædo*, Socrates speaks of (Plato 69 B) "*true* virtue."

[2] [1727 f] "True" (2), ἀληθινός, in classical Greek, means "genuine," and could not mean "truthful" except in special contexts as when one speaks of a "*genuine* prophet, judge etc." In this sense it occurs in Lk. xvi. 11 "If ye have not been faithful in the unrighteous mammon, who will entrust to you *the genuine* [riches]?" But in LXX it is applied to God, as in Exodus (xxxiv. 6) "*abounding in truth*," ἀληθινός; and where Ezr. ix. 15 has "O Lord,...thou art *righteous* (δίκαιος)," the parall. 1 Esdr. viii. 89 has ἀληθινός. Philo ii. 599 contrasting "the *genuine* God" with "the falsely so-called god," and St Paul (1 Thess. i. 9 "Ye turned....from idols to serve a living and *genuine* God"), use the word in its classical sense: but in Rev. iii. 7—14, vi. 10, where "true," ἀληθινός, is combined with "holy" and "faithful," the meaning seems to be "truthful."

[1727 g] In Jn, an attempt is made to combine the Greek meaning of "*genuine*" with the Hebraic meaning of "*true*" (i.e. "faithful to one's word," "keeping one's promise"). A false god, or a false prophet, might speak "*truth*"—and deceive, "keeping the word of promise to the ear"—as wizards and witches do in Shakespeare. Isaiah says bitterly to Israel, trusting in false lights (l. 11) "Walk ye in the light of your fire."

[1727] SYNOPTIC DEVIATIONS

English	Greek	Mk	Mt.	Lk.	Jn
Truly[1] (s. 1696 a)	ἀληθῶς	2	3	3	7

Jn's Prologue calls the Logos (i. 9) "the light, *the genuine [light]*," and the Epistle says (1 Jn ii. 8) "A new commandment I write unto you, which thing is *true* (ἀληθές) in him and in you, because the darkness is passing away and the *light, the genuine [light]* (τὸ φῶς τὸ ἀληθινόν), now shineth." This means that the new light is not only "true" but "the only genuine light," the source of all light from the beginning of the world, now at last to be revealed not in twilight but in daylight.

[1727 *h*] In Jn, ἀληθινός is never confused with ἀληθής. It never means merely "true" in the sense of *veracious*. As in Hebrews (viii. 2) "the *true* tabernacle" is the one that "the Lord pitched and not man," and the earthly sanctuary is regarded not as being the "true one" but only (Heb. ix. 24) "typical of *the true [one]*," so in Jn, (vi. 32) "the *true* bread" and (xv. 1) "the *true* vine" mean that the ideal is now at last revealed. It has been stated above that "*genuine*," when applied to a "prophet" or a "judge," necessarily includes the additional meaning of "*truthful*," and so it does in Jn viii. 16 "My judgment is *genuine* [judgment]" *i.e.* not biassed, xix. 35 "His testimony is *genuine [testimony]*" i.e. the testimony of an eye-witness, one that has enjoyed the sight, or vision, of that to which he testifies. In vii. 28 "I have not come of myself, *but he that sent me is—*," the antithesis requires that the italicised clause should mean "but I have *a real* mission" as opposed to a false prophet, who has *no "real"* mission. Hence what has to be supplied is "*a real and true Sender.*" The "reality" (no doubt) here includes not only "*really*" *sending* but also sending with a "*real*" *message*, i.e. a *true* message. Hence ἀληθινός may here be described as *including*—but not as *meaning*—"true."

[1727 *i*] Jn iv. 37 (R.V.) "Herein is the saying *true*, One soweth, and another reapeth (ἐν γὰρ τούτῳ ὁ λόγος ἐστὶν ἀληθινὸς ὅτι, "Ἄλλος...)" is not a correct rendering. The meaning is—as Cyril, in effect, says about the context (Cramer *ad loc.*) and as Origen's comment suggests (*ad loc.* Huet ii. 233—4, 241—2)—"The cynical worldly saying about 'one sowing and another reaping' *finds its ideal and true expression* in the world of the spiritual harvest to which I have bidden you 'lift up your eyes,' in which the sower and the reaper rejoice together." This, says Cyril, "does not happen in the material world but *it does in the spiritual*." Ἀληθινός, then, (as in Hebrews) means here "really, ideally, or spiritually existent." Chrysostom, although misled by reading ὁ ἀληθής, is not much misled as to the sense: "This saying was in use among the common folk (οἱ πολλοί)...and He means that this saying *finds its truth more especially herein* (ἐνταῦθα μάλιστα τὴν ἀλήθειαν ἔχει)," and he explains "herein" as referring to the spiritual sowing of the prophets.

[1] [1727 *j*] "Truly," in Lk., only in (Chri.) "I say unto you *of a truth*

English	Greek	Mk	Mt.	Lk.	Jn
Truth[1]	ἀλήθεια	3	1	3	25

(*d.*)" Lk. ix. 27, xii. 44 (D ἀμήν), xxi. 3: never (Chri.) in Mk-Mt. but used in assertions that Peter is " truly " one of Christ's disciples or that Christ is the Son of God (Mk xiv. 70, Mt. xxvi. 73, Mk xv. 39, Mt. xiv. 33, xxvii. 54).

[1727 *k*] In Jn it is applied to assertions of believers about Christ in iv. 42 "*truly* the Saviour of the world," vi. 14, vii. 40 "*truly* the prophet." In vii. 26, " Can it be that the rulers *truly recognised* (ἀληθῶς ἔγνωσαν) that this is the Christ ?" the meaning may be " that they *really* recognised [*i.e.* knew *in their hearts* though they would not own it]" or "*can it be really true* that they recognised."

[1727 *l*] In Jn, it occurs in Christ's words as follows, i. 47 " See, [here is one that is] *truly* an Israelite," viii. 31 "[then] are ye *truly* my disciples," xvii. 8 "and they *recognised truly* (ἔγνωσαν ἀληθῶς) that I came forth from thee." In these three cases the meaning is probably "*in fact* [*and not merely in name*]," or "*in heart* [*and not merely in word*]," and perh. in i. 47 there is some play on the word " Israel," the root of which, though distinct from *Yashar*, " upright," " straightforward," is identical with the latter without vowel points. [*Yashar*=Tromm. once ἀλήθεια, five times ἀληθινός.] This is more likely than that Jn (like Lk.) should represent Jesus as using "truly" in the sense "I speak the truth."

[1] [1727 *m*] " Truth," in the Synoptists, occurs only in the phrase " in *truth*" (Mk xii. 14, 32, Mt. xxii. 16, Lk. iv. 25, xx. 21, xxii. 59 ἐπ' ἀληθείας, exc. in Mt. xxii. 16 ἐν ἀ.), and in Mk v. 33 "told him all the *truth*." As an attribute of God, or a subject of Christ's teaching, it is non-existent in the Three Gospels.

[1727 *n*] " Truth," with " grace " in Jn, occurs twice where the Prologue (i. 14—17) describes the incarnate Logos as "full of grace and *truth*," and "the Law" (*i.e.* the Law mentioned in O.T.) as " given through Moses" but "the grace and the *truth*" (i.e. perh. the grace and the truth mentioned in O.T.) as " brought into being through Jesus Christ." The O.T. constantly couples "mercy" and "truth" where we should rather speak of "kindness and truth." Jn, systematically avoiding the Greek word " mercy (ἔλεος)" (Heb. " kindness (or, mercy)") probably represents it here by "grace" *i.e.* "graciousness." We might expect that the Fourth Gospel would proceed to develop this twofold revelation of (1) "*grace*," (2) "*truth*." But the Pauline Epistles had sufficiently developed the doctrine of "*grace*." The Fourth Evangelist says that we have received from the fulness of the Logos (i. 16) " grace for grace," but after this passage he never mentions "grace" again in the Gospel or First Epistle. He concentrates himself on the doctrine of "truth."

[1727 *o*] " The truth," in Jn, cannot be discussed apart from "the

Spirit." For John regards it primarily as a correspondence between God and the Word, or the Father and the Son, in "the Spirit." This harmonizes with the philosophy of Epictetus about "the spirit" of man and its mission. Explaining how the images of things we see are conveyed through the eyes, Epictetus says (ii. 23. 3) "Did God give you eyes for nothing? Did He for nothing *infuse in them a spirit* so strong and of such a graphic power that it darts out far away and takes the impressions of the things seen? What *messenger* could be so quick and careful?" So St Paul asks (1 Cor. ii. 11) "What man knoweth *the things of the man*, save only *the spirit of the man*?" i.e. the "Spirit" that is "infused" in his senses; and he says that, similarly, *the things of God* are searched by "*the Spirit of God.*"

[1727 *p*] The Johannine phrases of connexion between "the truth" and "the Spirit" are largely explained by the facts of the last paragraph. Sometimes they are both regarded as spheres, sometimes "the Spirit" is a witness to, or a guide to, the sphere of spiritual "truth." The "genuine (ἀληθινός)" worshipper is to worship (iv. 23—4) (*bis*) "*in spirit and truth.*" Satan (viii. 44) "did not stand fast *in the truth*" and "there is *no truth in him.*" The Last Discourse thrice mentions (xiv. 17, xv. 26, xvi. 13) "*the Spirit of the truth*," and says that it will guide the disciples (xvi. 13) "*into all the truth.*" The Epistle not only repeats (1 Jn iv. 6) "*the Spirit of the truth*," but adds (v. 6) "the Spirit it is that testifieth, because *the Spirit is the truth*,"—that is to say, the Spirit, like the "swift messenger" described by Epictetus, cannot help "testifying" because its very being is that kind of eternal coming and going in the correspondence or harmony between God and His children by which man is enabled to "search the deep things of God."

[1727 *q*] "The truth," or "the Spirit of truth," being identified with the "correspondence" between the Father and the Son, might be called the Spirit of sonship, or the Spirit of Freedom as opposed to that of Slavery. Hence our Lord says (viii. 32) "The *truth* shall *make you free*" (as St Paul says, 2 Cor. iii. 17 "where *the Spirit of the Lord* is, [there] *freedom* is"). And since many religions move the mind mainly through fear, and their priests and prophets and "holy men" make gain out of false fears, stress is laid by John upon the connexion between "holiness" and truth (xvii. 17) "Make them *holy* in *thy truth.*" The Logos also says to God the Father (xvii. 17) "Thy Logos is *truth*": and since, through this Logos or Truth, one passes to life in the Father, Jesus is represented as saying (xiv. 6) "I am the *way, the truth*, and the *life.*"

[1727 *r*] This doctrine of "*truth*" the Evangelist describes as being put before both the Jewish and the Gentile world in vain. The Jews, when they hear Christ saying (viii. 32) "Ye shall know *the truth* and *the truth* shall make you free," put aside "the truth" and fasten on "free"

FROM JOHANNINE VOCABULARY   [1728]

English	Greek	Mk	Mt.	Lk.	Jn
[1728] Up, s. Above	ἄνω	0	0	0	3
Wash[1]	νίπτω	1	2	0	13
Wash[1], *i.e.* bathe	λούω	0	0	0	1
Water (Chri.)[2]	ὕδωρ	2	0	3	7
Whence?[3]	πόθεν	3	5	4	13
Where?[4]	ποῦ	3	4	7	18
Whole, healthy[5]	ὑγιής	1	1	0	6

as an insult: "We are Abraham's seed and have never been in bondage to any man"—the fact being that they had no right conception of "freedom" and hence no right conception of "truth." Again, when Jesus says to Pilate (xviii. 37) "Everyone that is of *the truth* hearkeneth to my voice," the Roman Governor, who has some smattering of Greek philosophy, taking the view attacked by Epictetus, replies, not asking what "*the* truth" may be, but questioning whether there is any such thing, "What is *truth*?" This is the last mention of the word in the fourth Gospel.

[1] [1728 *a*] "Wash," νίπτω, in Jn, refers, 5 times, to the washing of the blind man in the pool of Siloam, and 8 times to the Saviour washing the feet of the disciples. Mk vii. 3, Mt. xv. 2 refer to the Jewish washing of hands before meals. Mt. vi. 17 "*wash* thy face" is the only instance (Chri.) in the Synoptic Gospels. Jn xiii. 10 "he that is *bathed* (A.V. washed)" distinguishes the washing of the whole body from the washing of a part.

[2] [1728 *b*] "Water" (Chri.), in Mk ix. 41 "a cup of *water*," is parall. to Mt. x. 42 "a cup of cold [water] (ψυχροῦ)": Mk xiv. 13 (Lk. xxii. 10) "a man bearing a pitcher of *water*" is wholly omitted by Mt.: Lk. vii. 44 "thou gavest me no *water* for my feet" is peculiar to Lk., and so is Lk. xvi. 24 (parable) "that he may dip the tip of his finger in *water*." None of these passages are doctrinal. The Johannine instances—with the exception of ii. 7—are all doctrinal (iii. 5) "born of *water* and spirit," iv. 10—15 (the dialogue on the "living *water*"), vii. 38 "rivers of living *water*."

[3] [1728 *c*] "Whence." Πόθεν freq. occurs in discourses as to the origin of the Spirit, the Messiah, and Jesus, among the Jews and in words of the Lord Jn iii. 8, vii. 27 (*bis*), 28, viii. 14 (*bis*) ix. 29, 30, also in Pilate's question (xix. 9) "*Whence* art thou?" (2403).

[4] [1728 *d*] "Where." Ποῦ, in Jn, occurs first in i. 38 "Rabbi, *where* abidest thou?" and then freq. of the goal or abiding-place of the Lord, or of the Spirit, Jn iii. 8, vii. 35, viii. 14 (*bis*), xiii. 36, xiv. 5, xvi. 5; also in Mary Magdalene's doubt (xx. 2, 13, 15) "*where* they have laid him."

[5] [1728 *e*] "Whole," "healthy." Jn's instances of ὑγιής all refer to the man healed on the Sabbath, v. 6—15, vii. 23. In Jn v. 4, it is part of an

English	Greek	Mk	Mt.	Lk.	Jn
Wilderness (of Arabia)[1]	ἔρημος	0	0	0	3
Will[2]	θέλημα	1	6	4	11
Witness, s. testify, testimony	μαρτυρέω	0	1	1	33
	μαρτυρία	3	0	1	14
	μαρτύριον	3	3	3	0
	μάρτυς	1	2	2	0
Work (n.)[3]	ἔργον	2	6	2	27

interpolation. In Mk v. 34, ἴσθι ὑγιὴς ἀπὸ τῆς μάστιγός σου—where it is one of three Mk-clauses, of which Lk. has one, and Mt. two—it seems to be a conflation. In Mt. xii. 13, "it was restored *whole, as the other*," Mk Lk. omit "*whole as the other.*" Lk. has the vb ὑγιαίνω (3), not in Mk, Mt., or Jn.

[1] **[1728 *f*]** "Wilderness" (of Arabia), in Jn iii. 14, vi. 31, 49 referring to the brazen serpent, or the manna, "in the wilderness." [In xi. 54 Jn appears to mean "the wilderness of Judæa," and in i. 23 Jn (like the Synoptists) quotes Is. xl. 3.] On ἔρημος (adj.) see **1679**.

[2] **[1728 *g*]** "Will," in Mk, occurs only in Mk iii. 35 "Whosoever shall do the *will of God*," where parall. Mt. xii. 50 has "the *will of my Father*" and Lk. viii. 21 "the *word of God*." The contrast in Lk. xxii. 42 "Not my *will* but thine" (expressed by the vb. θέλω in the parall. Mk xiv. 36, Mt. xxvi. 39) occurs in Jn v. 30 "I seek not mine own *will* but the *will* of him that sent me," and vi. 38 "not that I may do mine own *will* but the *will* of him that sent me." The children of God are said to be begotten (Jn i. 13) "not from the *will* of the flesh nor from the *will* of man (? ἀνδρός) but from God."

[3] **[1728 *h*]** "Work" (n.). The only Synoptic precept about works of righteousness is in Mt. v. 16 "that they may see your good *works*," unless one can be said to be implied in the parable in Mk xiii. 34 "having given ...to each his *work*." Jn mentions "works" in two ways, 1st as good or bad, in men, who accordingly come to the light or flee from it (Jn iii. 19, 20, 21, vii. 7, viii. 39) and comp. viii. 41 "ye do the *works* of your father," the "father" being afterwards called "the devil": 2nd, as the "works" appointed for the Son by the Father. Evil "works" are recognised in two of the three instances of the word in the Epistle (1 Jn iii. 8) "that he may destroy the *works* of the devil," (iii. 12) "because his *works* were evil," (iii. 18) "let us not love in word...but in *work* and truth."

[1728 *i*] Epictetus says (i. 29. 56) "It is not maxims that are now wanting. The books are choke full of Stoic maxims. What then is wanting? The man to use these maxims. The man to testify in *action* (ἔργῳ) to his words (τοῖς λόγοις)." Pouring scorn on the philosopher that tests his progress by the amount of his reading, he bids him seek

English	Greek	Mk	Mt.	Lk.	Jn
Work (vb.)[1]	ἐργάζομαι	1	4	1	7
World, age[2]	αἰών	2	7	5	1
World	κόσμος	2	8	3	75
Ye (nom.) (2399)	ὑμεῖς	10	31	c. 20	68
Yet, not[3]	οὔπω	5	2	1	13

progress in *action* (i. 4. 11). Jn agrees with him in the importance that he attaches to action, but differs from him in one very important point. In Epictetus, "action" consists (i. 4. 11, ii. 14. 7) in so regulating one's desires and impulses that one may be "in harmony with what goes on (τοῖς γινομένοις)," and that nothing may happen to us against our will. In Jn, "action" consists in such deeds as a father would do to children or a brother to brothers.

[1] [1728 *j*] "Work" (vb.) ἐργάζομαι, occurs in Mk xiv. 6 (parall. Mt. xxvi. 10) "she *hath wrought* (ἠργάσατο) a good work on me," where Lk. om., and Jn differs. Lk. has xiii. 14 "there are six days in which one must *work*." Ἐργάτης, "labourer" or "doer," occurs Mk (0), Mt. (6), Lk. (4), Jn (0).

[2] [1728 *k*] "World," *i.e.* the creation of the world. Jn ix. 32 "*From the [creation of the] world* (ἐκ τοῦ αἰῶνος) it was never heard...." The numbers above do not include the phrase εἰς τὸν αἰῶνα (or εἰς τοὺς αἰῶνας), on which see "For ever" (1712 *d*).

[3] [1728 *l*] "Not yet," in Lk., only in xxiii. 53 "*not yet* laid." In Mk iv. 40, viii. 17, 21, Mt. xvi. 9 "Have ye *not yet* faith, understanding etc." In Mk xiii. 7, Mt. xxiv. 6 "But *not yet* is the end." In Mk xi. 2 "had *not yet* sat." In Jn, "not yet" occurs in connexion with "my hour, or season," ii. 4, vii. 6, and with "his hour" vii. 30, viii. 20. Comp. xx. 17 "*Not yet* have I ascended...."

[1728 *l*₂] Ἑρμηνεύω, in N.T., is connected with Jn i. 42 Κηφᾶς, ix. 7 Σιλωάμ, Heb. vii. 2 Μελχισεδέκ. Μεθερμηνεύω is in Mk v. 41, xv. 22, 34, Mt. i. 23, Jn i. 38, 41. The Synoptists always translate the Aramaic "Cephas" and "Messias" into Gk.; Jn transliterates the Aramaic and adds the Gk. interpretation.

ADDITIONAL NOTE ON ἀγαπᾶν AND φιλεῖν

[1728 m] The variations in the use of ἀγαπᾶν and φιλεῖν may be illustrated by Xen. *Mem.* II. vii. 9, 12, where Socrates tells Aristarchus that, because he gives his fourteen dependent female relations nothing to do, he (at present) does not "*like* (φιλεῖν)" them nor they him; but, if he will give them some occupation, then, says Socrates, "You will *like* (φιλεῖν) them, seeing they are profitable to you, and they will *love* (ἀγαπᾶν) you when they see that you take pleasure in them." The narrative goes on to say that Aristarchus took this advice, and "They began to *like* (φιλεῖν) him as their protector and he began to *love* (ἀγαπᾶν) them as being profitable to him"— a curious reversal of terms that may be explained as humorous (if Aristarchus was a little too fond of money) but hardly as unintentional. L.S. (ἀγαπᾶν) quotes this passage as shewing that ἀγαπᾶν "strictly differs from φιλεῖν as implying regard or affection rather than passion": but no passion is contemplated here either in ἀ. or in φ. Steph. (ἀγαπᾶν) also quotes Dio 44, p. 175, ἐφιλήσατε αὐτὸν ὡς πατέρα καὶ ἠγαπήσατε ὡς εὐεργέτην, "you *were fond of* him as a father and *loved* him as a benefactor."

[1728 n] The following passage from Plato's *Lysis* suggests that ἀγαπᾶν sometimes implies "being drawn towards," and φιλεῖν "drawing towards oneself," (215 B) "'And he that needs (δεόμενος) nothing would consequently be drawn towards nothing (οὐδέ τι ἀγαπῴη ἄν)?' 'He would not.' 'And that which he was not *drawn towards*, he consequently would not *draw towards himself* (ὃ δὲ μὴ ἀγαπῴη, οὐδ' ἂν φιλοῖ)?'" The element of choice (but sometimes also sexual love) in φιλεῖν comes out also in passages where some man or woman is said to be loved or favoured above another (Steph. *Iliad* vii. 204, ix. 450 etc.). In Aelian *Var. Hist.* ix. 1 πάνυ σφόδρα

ἀγαπήσας αὐτοὺς καὶ ὑπ' αὐτῶν φιληθεὶς ἐν τῷ μέρει, the phrase ἐν τῷ μέρει, "for their part," is probably to be explained as Xen. *Anab.* vii. 6. 36 ἐν τῷ μέρει καὶ παρὰ τὸ μέρος, "*in the discharge of duty* and beyond duty." Hence the meaning probably is "being loved by them *in their turn*," almost equivalent to "*as in duty bound*"; and it perhaps implies a slight contrast to the "exceeding affection (σφόδρα ἀγαπήσας)" on the other side.

[1728 *o*] These facts are important as shewing that a distinction between ἀγαπᾶν and φιλεῖν was recognised in Greek literature—as also the distinction in Latin between "amo" and "diligo" (Wetst. on Jn xi. 3)—from Plato downwards. But John would also be influenced by the LXX, where φιλεῖν more often (14) represents the Hebrew "kiss" than the Hebrew "like" or "be fond of" (10), and in the latter sense is applied to "liking" food or drink in Gen. xxvii. 4, 9, 14, Prov. xxi. 17, Hos. iii. 1. It also describes Jacob's favouring Joseph in Gen. xxxvii. 4, and is used of "lovers," in a bad sense, in Jer. xxii. 22, Lam. i. 2. The dislike of the LXX to apply this comparatively low-class word to the Wisdom of God comes out clearly in Prov. viii. 17 "I *love* (ἀγαπάω) them that love (φιλοῦντας) me," where the same Heb. verb that is rendered φιλεῖν when applied to men is rendered ἀγαπᾶν when applied to the Wisdom of God—assuredly not for variety or euphony, but for seemliness

[1728 *p*] John, who says that God is ἀγάπη, and that the fundamental command of Christ is ἀγαπᾶν, could not but use ἀγαπᾶν to signify the highest kind of love. The lower word, φιλεῖν, John uses as follows. (1) Twice (xi. 3, 36) it is put into the mouths of the sisters of Lazarus and the Jews, as the word used by *them* about Christ's special love, where the Evangelist himself prefers to say (xi. 5) ἠγάπα. (2) Once (xx. 2) it is used by the Evangelist to describe the beloved disciple himself when he had temporarily fallen into unbelief and was for the moment not worthy of the higher love.

(3) In our Lord's lips it is used thrice, in special contexts (v. 20, xvi. 27 *bis*) metaphorically about "taking into the circle of one's friends and household[1]." (4) Twice (xii. 25, xv. 19) the Lord uses it to describe the sensual and selfish love of one's life or the love of the world for its favourites: (5) He also uses it once, and for the last time (xxi. 17) concerning the lower love, to cause the repentant Peter to be (*ib.*) "grieved," that he may rise from the lower love to the higher. (6) In the context, it is used four times (xxi. 15, 16, 17 *bis*) in the same sense by Peter and the Evangelist. These are all the instances of the Johannine use of the word.

---

[1] [1728 *q*] See **1784—92**. Comp. Rev. iii. 19 "as many as I *place among my friends* (φιλῶ) I reprove and chasten." In Tit. iii. 15 ἄσπασαι τ. φιλοῦντας ἡμᾶς ἐν πίστει, the meaning is doubtful. Not much can be inferred from 1 Cor. xvi. 22 εἴ τις οὐ φιλεῖ τ. Κύριον, as οὐ φιλῶ is freq. in Gk. literature in a sense nearly equivalent to ἐχθαίρω. The fourth and last instance of φ. in N.T., outside the Gospels, is Rev. xxii. 15 πᾶς φιλῶν κ. ποιῶν ψεῦδος. The rarity of φ. in the Epistles, and the fact that the Synoptists scarcely use it except of the "kissing" by Judas, make Jn's use of it all the more remarkable, and confirm the view that he has a purpose in employing the word and in distinguishing it from ἀγαπᾶν on which see **1744** (i)—(xi).

BOOK III
JOHANNINE AND SYNOPTIC AGREEMENTS

CHAPTER I

WORDS PECULIAR TO JOHN AND MARK

§ 1. *Antecedent probability*

[**1729**] Mark is the most concrete of the Evangelists, John the most abstract. Mark deals mostly with "mighty works," especially works of healing (and these, largely, of an exorcistic character); John describes only seven "signs," and no exorcisms. In Mark, Christ's sayings are brief, and the Evangelistic comments turn largely on local and contemporary affairs (the death of John the Baptist, Herodias, Herodians, washings of the Pharisees, Corban, etc.): John —whether in reporting Christ's words or in commenting on them—deals in discourses and long dialogues and cosmopolitan or celestial things. Hence we should not expect to find much affinity between the vocabulary of these two Evangelists.

[**1730**] There is another reason for supposing, antecedently, that John would have few or no words or phrases peculiar to himself and Mark. Mark (**318**), at all events in large part, contains traditions that have been borrowed by Matthew and Luke. If therefore John also borrowed from Mark, he might of necessity, in many cases, agree with Matthew and Luke where the three borrowed identically. And indeed we may well ask, Why should John ever borrow from Mark anything that Matthew and Luke agreed in rejecting—whether as being erroneous, or obscure, or too detailed—unless, in each case, he had some special motive for so doing?

§ 2. *The fact*

[**1731**] The fact is, however, that John has several striking agreements with Mark alone, where Matthew and Luke abandon Mark (besides others with Mark and Matthew together where Luke alone abandons Mark). By way of explaining this antecedently improbable fact, some have suggested that these agreements—which, for brevity, we may call "John-Mark agreements"—are of late date, added to Mark after the publication of Matthew and Luke, and borrowed by John from a larger edition of Mark, which is the one we now use. But these John-Mark agreements do not bear the stamp of late addition. They do not remove difficulties, or soften abruptness. On the contrary, they often create abruptness or difficulty. Moreover Matthew, as well as John, sometimes follows Mark where Luke abandons Mark, as in the Walking on the Waters, and the Anointing of Christ by a woman; and this is a serious blow to the hypothesis that all the agreements of John with Mark where Luke deviates from Mark are late additions. These facts tend to shew, not only that John borrowed from an early edition of Mark—or from early traditions contained in Mark—but that he also sometimes borrowed, perhaps by preference, such passages as might cause difficulty to an educated Evangelist like Luke.

[**1732**] What John's special purpose may have been in borrowing these traditions from Mark—whether to clear up obscurity, or to substitute a spiritual for a materialistic interpretation, or to do both these things—cannot be fully discussed except as part of a detailed examination of the relation between the Fourth Gospel and the Three. For the present, we have to bear in mind, 1st, that the John-Mark agreements in the following list are probably not late but early traditions, and 2nd, that previous investigations[1] favour the view that they must be connected with Luke's deviations from Mark. There are not enough of them to make an alphabetical arrangement in English necessary, especially as some derive their interest not from their English meaning, but from their being unusual and perhaps low-class Greek;—such as the word κράβαττος, for "*bed*," in the Lord's command "Take up thy *bed* and walk"; the word "*pistic*" which is given by R.V. margin (txt "spikenard") in the account of the Anointing of the Lord; and a word meaning literally "blows with the palm of the hand," or "slappings," in the account of the Passion.

§ 3. *Parallels and Quasi-parallels*

[1733] Of the three words κράβαττος, πιστική, and ῥάπισμα, the last two are marked † to denote that they are not only peculiar to Mark and John but also parallel; that is to say, they are used in the description of the same detail of the same event. But the first, κράβαττος, is marked ?† to denote, by the query, that the contexts differ. In Mark, the command "take up thy *bed*" is uttered to a paralytic, in John, to an "impotent" man lying near a pool. The same query is applied to the word "beggar," προσαίτης, and to "spit," πτύω, to denote not parallelism, but quasi-parallelism, as is explained in the foot-notes. On the other hand no query is attached to "two hundred" or "three hundred" because the traditions about "buying bread for two hundred denarii" or "selling ointment for three hundred denarii"— although assigned by John to Philip and to Judas Iscariot severally, and not thus assigned by Mark nor stated by the latter in exact agreement with John—undeniably refer to the

---

[1] See 1282—8, 1309, 1311, 1344, 1373.

same detail in the same narrative. True parallelism also will be found in the references to the crown "of thorns" under the adjective ἀκάνθινος, and "embalming," ἐνταφιασμός, both of which however are, in effect, to be found in Matthew as well as in Mark. The description of Peter as "warming himself" at the fire in the High Priest's hall is, perhaps, the only other point of interesting agreement between the two Evangelists. As to the words not marked †, such as "thunder" βροντή, "porter" θυρωρός, "catch" (or "apprehend") καταλαμβάνω etc., they mostly occur in altogether different contexts and will be found of very little importance as bearing on the relation between the Fourth Gospel and the Three.

JOHN-MARK AGREEMENTS[1]

	Mk	Jn		Mk	Jn
[1734] † ἀκάνθινος[2]	1	1	ἀποκόπτω[3]	2	2
βροντή	1	1	† γίνομαι (in connexion w. Ἰωάνης)[4]	1	1
† διακόσιοι[5]	1	2	† ἐνταφιασμός[6]	1	1

[1] [1734 a_1] An asterisk attached to a word denotes that Mk and Jn use it in different senses : † denotes that the word not only has the same meaning in Mk and Jn but also occurs in parallel passages : ? † indicates quasi-parallelism, on which see 1733. Words not annotated occur in the same sense but in quite different contexts.

[2] [1734 a] ʼΑκάνθινος, "of thorns," (Mt. xxvii. 29, Jn xix. 2 πλέξαντες στ. ἐξ ἀκανθῶν) is in Mk xv. 17 πλέξαντες ἀκάνθινον στ., Jn xix. 5 φορῶν τ. ἀκάνθινον στ., concerning the "crown of thorns," all reference to which is omitted by Lk. This word, in effect, belongs to the list of words used by Mk Mt. and Jn in common (1805—6).

[3] [1734 b] Ἀποκόπτω, "cut off," Mk ix. 43 (Mt. xviii. 8 ἐκκόπτω), ix. 45. Jn xviii. 10, 26 uses the word about Malchus, prob. with a double meaning, Malchus being taken as the representative of the High Priest. Comp. Deut. xxiii. 1 (2), Gal. v. 12, and (for the notion of retribution) Deut. xxv. 12, 2 S. iv. 12 Aq., Judg. i. 6, 7.

[4] [1734 c] Γίνομαι in connexion with Ἰωάνης. Ἐγένετο Ἰωάνης occurs in Mk i. 4, and in Jn i. 6 ἐγένετο ἄνθρωπος......ὄνομα αὐτῷ Ἰωάνης. Ἦν, not ἐγένετο, is the more usual word to introduce a new character in N.T. (Lk. ii. 25, 36, Jn iii. 1, xi. 1, 2). Lk. uses ἐγένετο to introduce the father of John the Baptist (Lk. i. 6) "Zachariah." The first book of Samuel opens with the words "*and there was a man*," and Job with "*a man there was*." The LXX has 1 S. i. 1 ἦν (A ἐγένετο), Job i. 1 ἦν : add Judg. xiii. 2 ἦν (A ἐγένετο), xvii. 1 ἐγένετο (A ἐγενήθη), 1 S. ix. 1 LXX om. vb. but A ἦν. Jn i. 6 contrasts ἐγένετο, applied to "a man," with ἦν, applied to "the Word" (1937).

[5] [1734 d] Διακόσιοι, "two hundred." Mk vi. 37, Jn vi. 7 "bread for 200 denarii" (1710 e, 1733). Comp. Jn xxi. 8 "about 200 cubits away."

[6] [1734 e] Ἐνταφιασμός, "embalming," is in Mk xiv. 8 (Mt. xxvi. 12 ἐνταφιάσαι), Jn xii. 7. Practically this word belongs to the Mk-Mt.-Jn list. Jn xix. 40 ἐνταφιάζειν refers to Nicodemus and Joseph.

249

[1735] WORDS PECULIAR

	Mk	Jn		Mk	Jn
[1735] ἕως (w. indic. pres.)[1]	1	3	?+ ἤθελον (without rel. or οὐ)[2]	2	3
+ θερμαίνομαι[3]	2	3	θυρωρός	1	3
Ἱεροσολυμεῖται	1	1	καταλαμβάνω[4]	1	2

[1] [1735 a] ἕως with indic. pres., "while," in Mk, only in Mk vi. 45 ἕως αὐτὸς ἀπολύει, where parall. Mt. xiv. 22 ἕως οὗ ἀπολύσῃ. Jn ix. 4 ἕως (marg. ὡς) ἡμέρα ἐστίν "*while* it is yet day," xxi. 22 (lit.) "If I desire him to remain *while I am coming* (ἕως ἔρχομαι)," rep. in xxi. 23. Comp. 1 Tim. iv. 13 "*While I am coming* (ἕως ἔρχομαι) give heed to the reading." See **1638**, also **2089, 2201**.

[2] [1735 b] Ἤθελον without relative or οὐ. The importance of this agreement arises from the fact that Mark and John use the rare form ἤθελον in the Walking on the Waters, but in different contexts, the former "*He* desired to *pass by* them," the latter " *They* desired, therefore, to *receive* him":—Mk vi. 48 ἤθελεν παρελθεῖν αὐτούς, Jn vi. 21 ἤθελον οὖν λαβεῖν αὐτόν. Negations and relative constructions (such as Mt. xxvii. 15, Jn vi. 11, xxi. 18) being excluded, ἤθελον occurs elsewhere only in Mk vi. 19 "...*desired*...and could not," and Jn vii. 44, xvi. 19 : also in Acts x. 10, xiv. 13, xix. 33 *always about desire of which the fulfilment is prevented* (in Jn xvi. 19 by fear). The 1st pers. is so used in Gal. iv. 20 (comp. *Test. Abr.* § 5 ἤθελα). In LXX, it occurs in Esth. i. 11 (A ἠθέλησεν), Dan. vii. 19 ἤθελον ἐξακριβάσασθαι, Theod. ἐζήτουν ἀκριβῶς, viii. 4 ἐποίει ὡς ἤθελε, Theod. ἐποίησεν κατὰ τὸ θέλημα αὐτοῦ, also 1 Macc. iv. 27 (with οἷα), 2 Macc. iv. 16, xv. 38.

[1735 c] The difficulty of supposing that Jesus entertained an *unfulfilled desire* might well cause corrections of the text in Mk vi. 48. D reads ἠθέλησεν, which—when compared with Deut. ii. 30 "Sihon *desired not that we should go across through him* (i.e. through his land)," οὐκ ἠθέλησε παρελθεῖν ἡμᾶς—suggests an interpretation, "Jesus *willed that they should go across*," or, (comp. Jn vi. 21) that they should be "*immediately on the land to which they were going.*" But others may have read ἤθελον παρελθεῖν αὐτόν taking it to mean "*they desired that he should come to* [*them*]." John may have paraphrased this as "they desired to receive him."

[3] [1735 d] Θερμαίνομαι, "warm oneself," Mk xiv. 54, 67, Jn xviii. 18, 25, always of Peter "warming himself," at the High Priest's fire. Jn xviii. 18 also mentions the servants and officers "warming themselves." See "Fire of Coals" (1711 *f*—*h*).

[4] [1735 e] Καταλαμβάνω means "catch," or "take" in Mk ix. 18 and in Jn xii. 35, "lest the darkness *catch, surprise*, or *overtake* you." In Jn i. 5, R.V. txt has "the light shineth in the darkness and the darkness *apprehended* (κατέλαβεν) it not," but the margin has "overcame." It never means "overcome" except so far as that may be implied in "catching," or

TO JOHN AND MARK [1736]

	Mk	Jn		Mk	Jn
[1736] ?† κράβαττος¹	5	4	μισθωτός²	1	2

"*taking.*" It seems to mean "*take*" in the sense of "*apprehend* (mentally)" (compare our vernacular "Do you *take* me?") in Micah vi. 6 (LXX) expressing "Whereby may I *attain to*, or *apprehend*, the Lord?" This meaning of intellectual apprehension is very common in Greek philosophic writers and in Philo, *e.g.* (i. 579, ii. 654) "Real Being is not *apprehended* by any man," "One must needs begin by becoming a God before one can have strength to *apprehend* God." Simon Magus (Hippol. vi. 18) maintained that the First Principle of things was an "*inapprehensible* silence."

[1735 *f*] St Paul plays on καταλαμβάνω and λαμβάνω in a manner best expressed perhaps by "take," thus (Phil. iii. 12) "Not that I have already *taken* (ἔλαβον) [the prize]......but I press on, if perchance I might *overtake* (or, *take as my prize*, καταλάβω) that for which I have been *taken over* (or, *taken as his captive*, κατελήμφθην) by Christ." Perhaps Jn wishes—by using a word habitually employed in two distinct meanings— to suggest that the mere intellectual apprehension of light would be distinct from moral "reception" (Jn i. 11 παραλαμβάνω) and would, if it were possible, result in an imprisonment, "taking captive," of the light. If so, we are not called on to decide whether he means (1) "did not *take captive*," or (2) "did not *apprehend*"; for in that case he means both.

[1735 *g*] Origen says (Huet ii. 74 B) "*In two ways* (διχῶς) the darkness hath 'not apprehended' the light." But his interpretations of the darkness has *persecuted* the light but not *taken* it *captive*, or *suppressed* it; (2) the darkness, in *following after* the light and coming too close to it, has not *overtaken* it, but has fallen into the snare (so to speak) set for it by the light, and has perished by absorption in the light. Chrysostom takes much the same view, but adds that the light "is unsubduable (ἀκαταγώνιστον), not being willing to *dwell in the souls that do not desire to be enlightened* (οὐκ ἐμφιλοχωροῦν ταῖς μὴ φωτισθῆναι βουλομέναις ψυχαῖς)"—which rather suggests *intellectual* "apprehending."

[1735 *h*] In the interpolated Jn [viii. 3—4], καταλαμβάνω (*bis*) means "catch."

¹ [1736 *a*] Κράβαττος, "pallet," a word condemned by Phrynichus, is repeatedly used in Mk ii. 4—12, Jn v. 8—11, about the healing of a man to whom Jesus says, "Arise, take up thy *pallet*." But in several important circumstances the narratives differ. The word is therefore marked ?†. Elsewhere in N.T. the word is used only in Mk vi. 55, Acts v. 15 and ix. 33 [of cures, in both cases in Acts, wrought by Peter].

² [1736 *b*] Μισθωτός, in Mk i. 20 of Zebedee's "hired servants," Jn x. 12, 13 "hireling," as opposed to the Good Shepherd.

[1737]   WORDS PECULIAR

	Mk	Jn		Mk	Jn
† νάρδος[1]	1	1	* πηγή[2]	1	3
† πιστικός[3]	1	1	πλοιάριον[4]	1	3
[1737] ?† προσαίτης[5]	1	1	?‡ πτύω[6]	2	1

[1] Νάρδος, "spikenard," Mk xiv. 3, Jn xii. 3, see below (1736 *d*).
?†Παρρησία, Mk (1), Jn (9), see 1252—4, 1432—5, 1744 xi. *a*, 1917 (i) foll.
[2] [1736 *c*] Πηγή. The asterisk denotes that the meanings are entirely different. Mk v. 29 uses πηγή about "the woman with the issue." In Jn iv. 6—14 it is used of Jacob's well and once in metaphor.
[3] [1736 *d*] Πιστικός, of doubtful meaning, occurs in Mk xiv. 3, Jn xii. 3 "*pistic* nard." This adjective is nowhere else known to be applied to things, but it is applied to a "faithful" wife by Artemidorus (A.D. c. 150) ii. 32, πιστικὴ καὶ οἰκουρός, elsewhere ii. 66, iii. 54 πιστὴ καὶ οἰκουρός. Wetstein (Mk xiv. 3) gives abundant instances of σπικάτον as the name of an ointment (from "spica"). Codex D om. the clause, but *d* has "pistici," *k* "piscicae," vulg. "spicati," *a* "optimi." Wetstein quotes passages indicating that this ointment (σπικάτον) was in use among women of luxury. Possibly an early Galilæan tradition, finding in the original some form of σπικάτον, played upon it by saying "not σπικάτον but πιστικόν." Jerome (Swete on Mk xiv. 3) played thus on the word, "ideo vos vocati estis 'pistici,'...." There is no evidence to shew that it was a tradesmen's term meaning "genuine."
[4] [1736 *e*] Πλοιάριον "little boat," and ὠτάριον (1738 *b*) lit. "little ear," are two diminutives peculiar to Jn and Mk. Jn has also ὀνάριον "ass," ὀψάριον "fish," and παιδάριον "youth." Variations in the MSS., and Jn's apparent liking for diminutives, lessen the weight of any inference from his use of them in common with Mk [In Lk. v. 2, W.H. have txt πλοῖα, marg. πλοιάρια]. According to W.H., Jn gives the name (vi. 24) πλοιάρια to vessels previously called (vi. 23) πλοῖα. He seems to do this in xxi. 3—8, perhaps wishing to suggest in xxi. 8 that the boat, being small, was readily brought ashore (but? "in the little boat").
[5] [1737 *a*] Προσαίτης "beggar," Mk x. 46 the blind Bartimaeus, Jn ix. 8 a man born blind. Since the narratives are not parallel except in the coincidence of "blindness" the word is marked ?†. It should be added that the parall. Lk. xviii. 35 has ἐπαιτῶν. But the parall. Mt. xx. 30 (which mentions two blind men) omits all mention of "begging." Προσαίτης is used by Lucian (iii. 264, *Navig.* 24) to mean "a common beggar," or "beggar of the lowest class," "The millionaires of the present day, in comparison with me, are [such as Homer's] Irus and [*common*] *beggars* ("Ιροι καὶ προσαῖται)." Steph. quotes Plut. *Hellen. Probl.* p. 294 A "taking rags and wallet and becoming *a* [*common*] *beggar*."
[6] [1737 *b*] Πτύω, "spit," is marked ? ‡ (not ? †) to indicate that only one of the two instances in Mk is in a quasi-parallel with Jn. Mk vii. 33

252

		Mk	Jn		Mk	Jn
	πωρόω[1]	2	1	'Ραββουνεί[2]	1	1
	† ῥάπισμα[3]	1	2	στήκω[4]	2	2
[1738]	† τριακόσιοι[5]	1	1	φανερόω[6]	1	9
	φανερῶς[7]	1	1	χιλίαρχος[8]	1	1
	† ὠτάριον[9]	1	1			

refers to the healing of a man deaf and dumb, to which there is nothing even remotely similar in Jn. Mk viii. 23 refers to the healing of a blind man, and so does Jn ix. 6. The two passages, therefore, agree in describing Jesus as healing blindness by "spitting," but they differ in other respects.

[1] [1737 c] Πωρόω, "harden" is in Mk vi. 52 "But their heart was *hardened*," viii. 17 "Have ye your heart *hardened*?" of disciples; Jn xii. 40 only in a free quotation (Is. vi. 10) "He *hardened* their heart," of the Jews, ἐπώρωσεν, on the meaning of which see **2449** a.

[2] [1737 d] 'Ραββουνεί, uttered by (Mk x. 51) Bartimaeus, (Jn xx. 16) Mary Magdalene. The former occurs in a prayer "that I may receive my sight," the latter in an exclamation after Mary's eyes have been opened to see the risen Saviour.

[3] [1737 e] 'Ράπισμα, lit. "slapping," in Mk xiv. 65, Jn xviii. 22, xix. 3, refers to blows given to Jesus, comp. Is. l. 6 (LXX) εἰς ῥαπίσματα. The parall. Mt. xxvi. 67 has the vb. ῥαπίζω. The n. ῥάπισμα was condemned (**492—3**) by Phrynichus, and Lk. uses neither ῥάπισμα nor ῥαπίζω: but the former might commend itself to Mk and Jn owing to its Messianic associations in Isaiah. The parall. Lk. xxii. 63 has δέροντες.

[4] Στήκω, "stand fast," Mk iii. 31, xi. 25, Jn i. 26, viii. 44. See **1725** a.

[5] Τριακόσιοι, "three hundred," Mk xiv. 5, Jn xii. 5, "sold for *three hundred* denarii (**1710** e, **1733**)."

[6] [1738 a] Φανερόω, "manifest" (vb.), is in Mk iv. 22 along with ἔλθῃ εἰς φανερόν: the parall. Mt. x. 26, and Lk. xii. 2, have ἀποκαλυφθήσεται along with γνωσθήσεται, and the parall. Lk. viii. 17 has φανερὸν γενήσεται along with γνωσθῇ καὶ εἰς φανερὸν ἔλθῃ. In Jn xxi. 1 (*bis*), 14, it is thrice used of Christ's "manifesting himself" or "being manifested" after the Resurrection, and so, too, in Mk App. [xvi. 12, 14].

[7] Φανερῶς, "openly." Mk i. 45, Jn vii. 10 both refer to Christ's not going "openly" or "publicly" to a city or to a festival at Jerusalem: but the circumstances are quite different.

[8] Χιλίαρχος, "captain of thousand," is in Mk vi. 21 "his great men and *chiliarchs*," Jn xviii. 12 "the cohort therefore and the *chiliarch*."

[9] [1738 b] 'Ωτάριον, "ear" (lit. "little ear") is in Mk xiv. 47 (Mt. xxvi. 51 ὠτίον, Lk. xxii. 50 οὖς) and Jn xviii. 10. Note that Jn xviii. 26 (in parenthetic explanation) has ὠτίον (**1736** e) and so has Lk. xxii. 51.

§ 4. *Jn xii.* 9 "*the common people,*" lit. "*the great multitude*"

[1739] To the preceding list we may perhaps add the phrase used by John alone (xii. 9, 12) ὁ ὄχλος πολύς, contrary to Greek syntax. Mark xii. 37 has ὁ πολὺς ὄχλος, in accordance with Greek syntax. Matthew and Luke nowhere use πολὺς ὄχλος with ὁ. "Ὁ πολὺς ὄχλος" has a meaning of its own, quite distinct from πολὺς ὄχλος. Concerning the former, "the great multitude," Philo says (ii. 4) "they welcome vice": and this and kindred phrases mean (Lobeck, *Phryn.* p. 390) "the riff-raff." In Mk xii. 37 "the common people were hearing him gladly," Syr., Diatess., and SS have "*all the multitude,*" the Latin MSS. have "multa turba," D has καὶ πολὺς ὄχλος καὶ....*i.e.* "and [there was] a great multitude and...." All these readings avoid the suggestion of "a foolish vulgar mob" which Mark's true text might convey. See full quotations in Stephen's *Thesaurus* and Field. The parall. Mt.-Lk. omit the whole clause. Even where Mk (xi. 18) says "all the *multitude* (ὄχλος) were astonished at his teaching"—a phrase that need not suggest contempt—Lk. (xix. 48) has "all the *people* (λαός) hung on his lips."

[1740] Jn has xii. 9 (BאL) ἔγνω οὖν ὁ ὄχλος πολὺς ἐκ τῶν Ἰουδαίων, xii. 12 (BL) ὁ ὄχλος πολὺς ὁ ἐλθὼν εἰς τὴν ἑορτήν... (but א ὄχλος πολὺς ἐλθ.), and the question arises why he thus (if these MSS. are correct) breaks the rules of Greek syntax. It is intelligible that such a phrase as πνεῦμα ἅγιον, "Holy Spirit," should be (very rarely) treated as a compound noun, and have the article irregularly prefixed (1 Cor. vi. 19 W. H. marg.). But it is quite unintelligible that in ὁ πολὺς ὄχλος—a recognised form of speech, meaning "the riff-raff"— a writer should interchange the noun and the adjective, breaking one of the strictest canons of Greek, unless he intended to convey some different meaning. Perhaps John wished to meet the charge brought by enemies of the Church against Mark's tradition, not by suppressing the words (which Matthew and Luke, if they knew them, have done) but by adopting them with a modification intended to express that the phrase did not have the bad signification that was ordinarily attached to it. B is sometimes untrustworthy as to the letter O when near C (**1961**) as here, and the explanation of B's reading, if correct, is very obscure. Possibly some editions of Mark contained a marginal correction ὄχλος πολύς for πολὺς ὄχλος. The former, finding its way into the text without omitting ὁ, may have been adopted by John, meaning, in xii. 9, "*the great multitude* of the citizens," and, in xii. 12, "*the great multitude* of the pilgrims." He will not say ὁ πολὺς ὄχλος, for that would mean "the riff-raff." He says ὁ ὄχλος πολύς, "*the multitude in great numbers.*"

§ 5. *Inferences*

[**1741**] No less than four of the words marked † above[1] belong to the Anointing of Christ by a Woman—a narrative given by all the Evangelists but Luke, and one that has caused difficulty to commentators from early times because of its points of agreement and disagreement with Luke's narrative of the Anointing by a Woman that was a Sinner. Another refers to "the crown of thorns," mentioned, with slight difference, by Matthew, but wholly omitted by Luke. Another describes the humiliating blows inflicted on Christ; and here, too, Matthew uses an almost identical word, but Luke an entirely different one[2]. These facts confirm the view that John's intervention is in some way connected with Luke's deviation or omission; and they suggest that in a few

---

[1] Ἐνταφιασμός (Mt. ἐνταφιάζω), νάρδος, πιστικός, τριακόσιοι.

[2] Ἀκάνθινος and ῥάπισμα, Mt. ἀκανθῶν and ἐράπισαν, Lk. om. and δέροντες.

such special cases John (contrary to his usual custom) adopted the actual words of Mark in order to explain them in a new sense.

[1742] Two words, severally marked ? † and ? ‡, "beggar" and "spit," belong to John's Healing (in Jerusalem) of "a man born blind." In Mark, the former word ("beggar," προσαίτης) belongs to the Healing (near Jericho) of the blind "Bartimaeus"—which is supposed to be related by all the Synoptists[1]; but the latter word ("spit," πτύω (**1737** *b*)) belongs to the Healing of a blind man near "Bethsaida," a story peculiar to Mark. It must be added that a narrative peculiar to Matthew[2] describes the healing of two blind men at a place unnamed, containing many features in common with the Healing of Bartimaeus. The impression left by all these narratives is, that there was early difficulty in distinguishing the cures of the blind wrought by Jesus; that Matthew and Luke omitted Mark's detail about the use of "spittle" in performing some of these cures; and that John reverted to the old tradition. These facts once more confirm the view that John intervened on account of the omission of primary facts by secondary Evangelists: but in this case the burden of omission is thrown, not on Luke alone but on Matthew as well. The same conclusion is suggested by Mark's and John's traditions concerning two hundred and three hundred denarii[3].

[1743] Comparing this Vocabulary with the following ones in this Book the reader will find that the proportion of words marked † is very large. And the fact that, in some of these instances, Matthew is nearly identical with Mark so that

---

[1] The three narratives probably refer to the same event. But Mt.-Lk. omit "Bartimaeus," and Mt. represents two blind men as being healed.

[2] Mt. ix. 27—30.

[3] [1742 *a*] The former is omitted by Matthew, as well as by Luke, in the Feeding of the Five Thousand. The latter, in the Anointing of Christ by a Woman, is modified by Matthew, who substitutes "*much*" (xxvi. 9 "it could have been sold for *much*") for the definite sum mentioned by Mark and John.

John is *practically in agreement with Matthew as well as Mark*, ought to make the inquirer defer any final judgment that he might be disposed to base upon the present list till he has seen the list of words peculiar to John, Mark, and Matthew, which, *if Mark is earlier than Matthew and if Mark is largely followed by Matthew*, may shew that John follows Mark even more than appears from the facts given above.

[**1744**] Meantime, regard being had to the fact admitted by all critics, that John wrote long after Mark, and to the probability (assumed as a certainty by some) that Mark had an authoritative position at the end of the first century, a good case is already made out for the contention that John intervenes in favour of Mark where the later Evangelists deviate from him. This contention does not assume that, in these instances, Mark and John are historically right. The former may have led the latter to an erroneous intervention. But the point is, not that Mark is in such cases right, but that Mark is supported by John. It will subsequently be considered whether John also intervenes in favour of Matthew and of Luke, singly, or in favour of Matthew and Luke, jointly, where the two agree. But that will not affect the present question, which is, whether John occasionally intervenes in favour of Mark.

ADDITIONAL NOTE ('Αγαπάω in Jn-Mk narr.)

[**1744** (i)] ἈΑγαπάω, in strict narrative (**1672***), does not occur in Matthew and Luke, but occurs once in Mark in the story of the man with "great possessions," of whom Mark says (x. 21) "Jesus looked on him and *loved him* (ὁ δὲ 'Ι. ἐμβλέψας αὐτῷ ἠγάπησεν αὐτόν)." But the end was that "he went away sorrowing," after being commanded to sell whatever he had and to "give to the poor." The character and conduct of the man are discussed by Clement of Alexandria, Origen, Ephrem, and Chrysostom, and we learn from them that there was difference of opinion. But none of these writers deal effectually[1] with the difficulty—difficulty to some early Christians though perhaps only a pathetic fact to us—that this unique mention of Christ in the Synoptic Gospels as "loving" some one, ends in what seems worse than nothing— "he went away sorrowing." The difficulty is so great that we cannot be surprised at the omission of the clause ("looked on him and loved him") by Matthew and Luke.

[1744 (ii)] One way of removing or minimising the difficulty in Mark would be to take "loved" as meaning "treated kindly, or gently"; and one of the best English scholars of the last century says, " Perhaps we might translate 'caressed him,'[2]" quoting a passage from Plutarch in support of this rendering. He might also have alleged Clement of Alexandria (940) "Accordingly Jesus does not convict him as one that had failed to fulfil all the words of the Law; on the contrary He *loves and greets him with unusual courtesy* (ἀγαπᾷ καὶ ὑπερασπάζεται)." Moreover codex *b* renders the Greek by "osculatus est eum." Ephrem and Epiphanius both have "*rejoiced*[3]." These facts suffice to shew that, in the much discussed precept about selling all one's goods and giving to the poor[4], this particular phrase, "Jesus looked on him and

---

[1] Tertullian is briefer than any of these, and most severe, *De Monogam.* 14 "Discessit et ille dives, qui non ceperat substantiae dividendae egenis praeceptum, et dimissus est sententiae suae a Domino. Nec ideo duritia imputabitur Christo de arbitrii cuiuscumque liberi vitio." This can hardly be called "effectual."

[2] Field, *Ot. Norv.* ad loc.

[3] [**1744** (ii) *a*] Ephrem p. 168 "Sed cum observator legis monstrasset se legem diligenter servasse, tunc legislator de eo gavisus est et exultavit," Epiphan. 690 B εἶτά φησι, Ταῦτα πάντα ἐποίησα ἐκ νεότητός μου. κ. ἀκούσας ἐχάρη. This he repeats expressly, διὰ γὰρ τοῦ εἰπεῖν ὅτι ἐχάρη, "by saying that he 'rejoiced.'"

[4] [**1744** (ii) *b*] Besides the authorities above quoted, Justin and Irenaeus and many other early writers have quoted freely the different

loved him," would be likely to attract special attention because of its apparently ineffectual result.

[**1744** (iii)] Before referring to John's use of ἀγαπάω in narrative, some notice will be necessary of its use in Greek literature as bearing on Field's suggested translation of Mark, "Jesus *caressed* him." Ἀγαπάω seems, from the *Odyssey* onwards, to have meant a "going forth to meet," a "demonstration of affection[1]." It does not occur in Æschylus or Sophocles. But Euripides has it twice, and ἀγαπάζω once——always meaning "pay the last obsequies" to the dead[2]. Xenophon and Plutarch use it in the sense of "fondling" the young[3]. But in very many cases it means simply "love," without allusion to external action, differing perhaps, sometimes, from φιλέω in that ἀγαπάω less frequently refers to "favour" and sexual love. The LXX uses ἀγαπάω very frequently in every sense of the word "love," but hardly ever in the sense above mentioned—"*manifesting love in action*[4]." The aorist ἠγάπησα occurs for the first time in the

versions of this story, and passages of Irenaeus (i. 3. 5 quoting as Syr. Burk., and i. 20. 2) shew that it was much quoted by early heretics.

[1] [**1744** (iii) *a*] It does not occur in the *Iliad*. But ἀγαπάζω, which occurs once (xxiv. 464) ἀγαπαζέμεν ἄντην, means "make the first approaches to." Ἀγαπάω occurs (L. S.) twice in the *Odyssey*, xxiii. 214 "Be not angry that I did not *embrace* thee thus (ὧδ' ἀγάπησα) at the first," (referring to 207—8 where Penelope kisses and embraces Ulysses), xxi. 289 "Dost thou not *hug* [*thy good fortune*]?" i.e. "art thou not *well pleased*"—a freq. meaning in later Gk. esp. with negative. Ἀγαπάζω, -ομαι, in *Odyssey* freq. means "embrace."

[2] [**1744** (iii) *b*] Eurip. *Hel.* 937 πρόσω σφ' ἀπόντα δακρύοις ἂν ἠγάπων, *Suppl.* 764 φαίης ἂν εἰ παρῆσθ' ὅτ' ἠγάπα νεκρούς. The reply is "Did he himself wash the wounds of the unhappy men?" Comp. *Phoen.* 1327 νέκυν τοι παιδὸς ἀγαπάζων ἐμοῦ.

[3] [**1744** (iii) *c*] Plut. (153) *Vit. Pericl.* 1 κυνῶν τέκνα...ἐν τοῖς κόλποις περιφέροντας κ. ἀγαπῶντας. Also Steph. quotes (? ref.) "Xen. *Cyrop*. vii. 5. 18 p. 447" μονονοὺκ ἐν ταῖς ἀγκάλαις περιφέρομεν αὐτοὺς ἀγαπῶντες.

[4] [**1744** (iii) *d*] In Ps. xciv. 19 "thy comforts *delight* (lit. *fondle*) my soul," ἠγάπησαν, Aא[2] ηὔφραναν, Is. v. 7 "the plant of his *fondling* (ἠγαπημένον)." By error the LXX has Ps. cxix. 166 ἠγάπησα, confusing the word with the Heb. for ἐποίησα, which Aq. and Sym. have.

Temptation of Abraham ("thine only son, whom thou *lovest* (ἠγάπησας)" and frequently thus to represent the Hebrew past where it approximates to the English present: but in the next instance ("and he *loved* her") and in many others it represents the English past[1]. In the LXX, then, the context must in each case be called in to determine the meaning.

[1744 (iv)] In the Pauline Epistles, the active verb, when not used of human love, is almost always in the aorist, referring to the love of Christ in *act*, as redeeming mankind, Rom. viii. 37 "we are more than conquerors through him that *loved* (ἀγαπήσαντος) us[2]," Gal. ii. 20 "the Son of God, who *loved* me and gave himself for me," Eph. v. 2 "as Christ also *loved* you and gave himself up for you (marg. us)," v. 25 "even as Christ also *loved* the church and gave himself up for it." So in Rev. iii. 9 "Behold I will make them to come and worship before thy feet and to know that I *loved thee*," it is the Son, not the Father, that is speaking, and "I *loved thee*" implies "I *delivered and made thee victorious*[3]."

---

[1] [1744 (iii) *e*] Gen. xxii. 2, xxiv. 67. The imperf., which is very rare, occurs in Gen. xxxvii. 3 ἠγάπα παρά, 1 S. i. 5 ἠγάπα ὑπὲρ ταύτην (but *ὑ. τ.* is a LXX addition) where "love" implies favouritism. Comp. Gen. xxv. 28 ἠγάπησε δὲ Ἰσαὰκ τὸν Ἠσαύ...Ῥεβέκκα δὲ ἠγάπα τὸν Ἰακώβ (where the Heb. tenses differ) and 1 S. xviii. 28 πᾶς Ἰσρ. ἠγάπα αὐτόν, where LXX differs from Heb. and perh. takes the meaning to be "loved him [David] more than Saul."

[2] [1744 (iv) *a*] In view of the preceding (Rom. viii. 35) "love of Christ," and the prevalent Pauline use of aor. of ἀγαπάω, this must refer to the Son, not to the Father. Comp. Phil. iv. 13 "I have strength [for] all things in him that makes me powerful" *i.e.* "Christ" (comp. 1 Tim. i. 12). But it does refer to the love of the Father in Eph. ii. 4—5 "God...for the great love wherewith he *loved* us...quickened us together with Christ," and to the love of the Father and the Son in 2 Thess. ii. 16 "now our Lord Jesus Christ himself, and God our Father, who loved (ὁ ἀγαπήσας) us..." where, though ἀγαπήσας agrees grammatically with θεὸς κ. πατήρ, it is intended to include the redeeming love of the Son.

[3] [1744 (iv) *b*] Ign. *Magn.* 6 ἐπεὶ οὖν ἐν τοῖς προγεγραμμένοις προσώποις τὸ πᾶν πλῆθος ἐθεώρησα ἐν πίστει κ. ἠγάπησα seems to mean "Since

[**1744** (v)] Coming to Johannine usage, and bearing in mind this double use of the verb to express the emotion and the act, we should first note an insistence on the latter aspect in 1 Jn iii. 18, "Little children, *let us not love in word nor with the tongue, but in work and truth.*" The whole of the Epistle insists on the active nature of God's love and of man's love so far as it imitates the divine original.

[**1744** (vi)] Then, in the narrative portions of the Gospel, we find the following: iii. 16 "For God so *loved* (ἠγάπησεν) the world that he gave the only begotten Son...[1]," xi. 5 "Now Jesus *was wont to love* (ἠγάπα) Martha and her sister and Lazarus[2]," xiii. 1 "Now before the feast of the Passover, Jesus, knowing that his hour had come that he should pass out of this world to the Father, *having loved* (ἀγαπήσας) his own that were in the world—*to the end he loved them* (εἰς τέλος ἠγάπησεν αὐτούς)," xiii. 23 "There was lying at table one of his disciples, in the bosom of Jesus, *whom Jesus was wont to love* (ὃν ἠγάπα [ὁ] Ἰ.)," xix. 26 "Jesus therefore having seen his [lit. the] mother, and the disciple standing by, *whom he was wont to love* (ὃν ἠγάπα)," xxi. 7 "So that disciple whom Jesus *was wont to love* saith to Peter, It is the Lord (λέγει οὖν ὁ μ. ἐκεῖνος ὃν ἠγάπα ὁ Ἰ. τῷ Πέτρῳ, Ὁ κύριός ἐστιν)." After this, comes the dialogue between our Lord and Peter, ("*lovest* (ἀγαπᾷς) thou me more than these?" "lovest thou me?")— not a part of narrative, but not without bearing on the use of

---

then I beheld in faith and *embraced* [in the spirit] the whole multitude [of the Magnesian Church] in the above-mentioned persons [of their deputation]," *Polyc.* 2 ἐγὼ κ. τὰ δεσμά μου ἃ ἠγάπησας "I and my bonds, which thou didst *lovingly welcome*," perh. personified as in Phil. i. 14 "trusting in my *bonds*"—the "bonds" being, in each case, a sign or messenger from God, revealing His power to strengthen His martyrs.

[1] Probably an utterance of the Evangelist (not of Christ, **1497**).

[2] [**1744** (vi) *a*] "*Wont,*" perh. better "*always used*" (s. Skeat), is an attempt to render the imperfect. Other statements about man's love are iii. 19 "men *loved* the darkness rather than the light," xii. 43 "for they [*i.e.* the rulers] *loved* the glory of men rather than the glory of God."

the word in narrative—and finally xxi. 20 "Peter, having turned, noteth *the disciple that Jesus was wont to love*, following (βλέπει τὸν μ. ὃν ἠγάπα ὁ 'Ι. ἀκολουθοῦντα)."

[**1744**(vii)] Reviewing these passages, we find that the first mention of the Son's being "wont to love" introduces the greatest of all His "signs," the victory over death at the grave of Lazarus. As to the next, it will hereafter (**2319** foll.) be shewn that "*loved them to the end* (εἰς τέλος ἠγάπησεν αὐτούς)" means, not only "loved them *to the end*," but also "loved them *to the supreme and victorious consummation of love.*" It refers to the Washing of Feet as well as to the Sacrifice on the Cross. In the former, the Lord is regarded (**1283**) as wiping off upon Himself the impurities of the disciples, so that all of them that will accept His love accept at the same time His purification—all but Judas, who will not accept it.

[**1744** (viii)] In the same scene that brings before us one disciple *spiritually refusing this act of love*[1], there is introduced about another disciple, "in the bosom of Jesus," the novel phrase "*whom Jesus was wont to love.*" At first, this adjective clause is not inseparable from "disciple." It is not "*the* disciple *that* Jesus was wont to love," but "*one of the disciples*"; and there is added "whom Jesus was wont to love." So stated, it might apply to several disciples, of whom this disciple was one. But it recurs as "*the* disciple standing by, *whom* Jesus was wont to love[2]," and lastly as "*the* disciple

---

[1] [**1744** (viii) *a*] Peter refuses it (for the moment) in word and outwardly ("Lord, thou shalt never wash my feet") but accepts it in spirit. Judas accepts it outwardly but rejects it spiritually.

[2] [**1744** (viii) *b*] The intervention of "standing by," and the consequent possibility of pause, afford a loop-hole for regarding the relative here as not essential to the antecedent. It might just possibly mean "the disciple [about whom I have so often spoken] standing by, one of whom Jesus was very fond." But there is no such loop-hole in the next instance. The usage of the LXX (**1744** (iii) *e*) would facilitate the use of ἠγάπα to mean "was specially fond," "loved above others."

that Jesus was wont to love," and in this last instance preeminence is unmistakeable.

[**1744** (ix)] Whether intentional or not, there is certainly a striking contrast between the incipient disciple in Mark, who proved to be no disciple—although he called Jesus "Good teacher" and although Jesus "*loved him*"—and "*the disciple that Jesus loved*" in the Fourth Gospel. The former "went away sorrowing." To the latter the Lord, when on the point of death, entrusts His own mother. To him, alone, on the shore of Tiberias, it is given to say, "It is the Lord," when Peter and the rest had not yet discerned Him. He, too, though not "following" the Lord in the path assigned to Peter (the path of the Cross) is nevertheless seen "following" in another way; and the last recorded utterance of the Saviour includes a mysterious saying suggestive of the prolonged abidance of this disciple upon earth: "*If I will that he tarry till I come*, what is that to thee?"

[**1744** (x)] This typical aspect of "the disciple that Jesus loved" is quite compatible with the literal aspect in which he is regarded as literally lying on the bosom of Jesus. Origen assuredly accepted the latter, but he accepted the former also. "The Word of God on earth," he says, "since He is become man, we see as a being of man's nature...but, *if we have lain on the breast of the Word made flesh*, and if we have been able to follow Him when He goeth up to the High Mountain, we shall say, 'We saw[1] his glory.'" And again, "We must therefore dare to call the Gospels the prime of the Scriptures, and the Gospel according to John the prime of the Gospels. Of this Gospel none can receive the meaning except he have fallen back (Jn xiii. 25 ἀναπεσών) on the breast of Jesus, and except he have received Mary from Jesus so that she becomes (lit. becoming) his own mother also. And this

---

[1] [1744 (x) *a*] Orig. *Philocal.* 19. The reference is to the Transfiguration. He quotes Jn i. 14 ἐθεασάμεθα as εἴδομεν, "we saw."

other future 'John' must also become such a one that (so to speak) the 'John' is pointed out by Jesus as being 'Jesus.' For, if there is no other son of Mary (according to those who entertain wholesome opinions about her) except Jesus, and [if] Jesus says to His mother, 'Behold, thy son,' and not, 'Behold, this, too, [is] thy Son'—this is all the same as if He has said 'Behold, this is Jesus, whom thou didst bear.' For indeed every one that is initiated (Gal. ii. 20) liveth no longer [of himself] but Christ liveth in him: and, since Christ liveth in him, it is said concerning him to Mary, 'Behold, thy Son, the Christ!¹'"

[**1744** (xi)] It may be taken as certain that John has *some* meaning and purpose (beyond mere graphic or euphonic variation) in his various descriptions of the beloved disciple; and it is highly probable that Origen has helped us to elucidate a part of his purpose, in bringing before us this unnamed and mysterious character as a permanent witness —"tarrying" till the Lord's "coming"—to the all-conquering love of Christ. And having regard to the early and wide discussions about the parallel phrase in Mark, we may regard it as by no means improbable that the Fourth Evangelist is tacitly contrasting this "disciple that Jesus loved" with the ineffectual approacher to discipleship, of whom Mark records that he called Jesus "teacher," and that Jesus "looked on him and loved him," and yet that, in the end, "he went away sorrowing².''

---

¹ Orig. Huet ii. 6.

² [**1744** (xi) *a*] As to ? † παρρησία, omitted by error in **1736** but placed in note there, it will be shewn that John may be writing with allusion to Mk viii. 32 π. τὸν λόγον ἐλάλει (omitted by Mt.-Lk.) or even in parallelism to Mk as given by SS and *k*. See **1917** (i) foll.

CHAPTER II

WORDS PECULIAR TO JOHN AND MATTHEW

§ 1. *Parallelisms very few*

[**1745**] In this list, though larger than that of words peculiar to John and Mark, only one word will be found marked †, and that with a query, namely, βῆμα, "judgment seat," concerning which John says that Pilate "sat down on *a judgment seat*," just before he said to the Jews, "Behold your king." Matthew has "While he was sitting on *the judgment seat*, his [*i.e.* Pilate's] wife sent unto him…" Then follows the mention of her dream, of which John makes no mention. The word occurs frequently in the Acts to mean the "platform," or "tribunal," of a judge, so that it might well be used by the two Evangelists independently. The absence of the article, however, in John ("*a* judgment seat") may indicate that he is calling attention to a fact that might pass unnoticed by readers of Matthew[1].

[**1746**] The reader will notice the large number of asterisks denoting that Matthew and John use the same word in

---

[1] [1745 *a*] Comp. Joseph. *Bell.* ii. 14. 8, where Florus erects "*a* tribunal" and then crucifies a number of Jews in front of it. Pilate may have first "sat on *the* tribunal" in the Praetorium (as Matthew says) and may have then had *a special "tribunal"* set up in Gabbatha for the purpose of final decision. Such a course would be all the more natural as the Chief Priests (Jn xviii. 28) would not come into the Praetorium to hear his decision. The Article is inserted before βῆμα when used in N.T. absolutely elsewhere, Acts xii. 21, xviii. 12, 16, 17, xxv. 6, 10, 17.

different senses, as where the former uses δωρεάν to mean "with a liberal hand," but the latter to mean "without a cause." So βρῶσις in Matthew means "rust," but in John "food"; and τιμή means in Matthew "price," but in John "honour[1]." For the most part the words in this list tell us nothing of interest. For example, λαμπάς, *i.e.* "torch" or "lamp," is connected by Matthew with the Virgins that go out to meet the Bridegroom and by John with the soldiers that arrest Jesus: σμύρνα, "frankincense," in Matthew refers to the offering of the Magi to the infant Jesus, in John to the act of Joseph of Arimathaea and Nicodemus placing the Lord's body in the tomb.

[1747] It will be found suggested in one of the foot-notes (1752 *a—f*) that, when John applies to Jesus the word κραυγάζω, "cry aloud,"—used by some authors to mean "scream" or "cry in terror"—he may be possibly alluding to a tradition peculiar to Matthew, who quotes a saying of Isaiah "He shall not *cry aloud*," and who uses κραυγάζω in his peculiar rendering of the prophecy. But this is a conjecture that would need support from many other Johannine passages of allusive tendency. There is greater probability in the hypothesis that John's version of the naming of Peter, "Thou *shalt be called Cephas, which is by interpretation Petros* [i.e. *Stone*]," was written with allusion to the tradition peculiar to Matthew "Thou *art Petros* [i.e. Stone]." But this hypothesis is not based on anything in the list given below, because it does not rest on any word peculiar to John and Matthew.

§ 2. *"Light of the world," "my brethren"*

[1748] Taking the list as a whole we find no *one* word, by itself, as to which John can be said with confidence to be alluding to Matthew. But the *two* words making the phrase φῶς κόσμου, "*light of the world*," stand on a different footing.

---

[1] In the Jn-Mk list only one word (πηγή) was thus marked.

TO JOHN AND MATTHEW [1749]

In Matthew, our Lord says "*Ye are* the light of the world"; in John, "*I am* the light of the world." It has been maintained in an earlier part of this series (**435**) that Matthew is in error, and that John, when emphasizing the doctrine that Christ *is* the Light of the world and that other people *have* the light, was not writing without some allusion to this corruption, peculiar to Matthew, namely that Jesus said to the disciples, "*Ye are* the light of the world." This appears extremely probable[1].

[**1749**] Another combination of two words peculiar to Matthew and John is the phrase "*my brethren*" in Christ's words after the Resurrection[2]. Matthew says that the women, when the risen Saviour met them, "*took hold of his feet*," and that He said "Go back, bear word to *my brethren* that they go away into Galilee[3]." In John, the Lord says to Mary Magdalene "*Touch me not*, for I have not yet ascended to the Father: but go to *my brethren* and say to them, I am

---

[1] [**1748** *a*] Mt. v. 14 "Ye are (ὑμεῖς ἐστέ) *the light of the world.*" It has been shewn (**435**) that this might be an error, either through Gk or through Heb. corruption, for "*ye have* the light of the world." Both Jewish and Christian doctrine would teach that the saints are (Phil. ii. 15) "lights," or (Jn v. 35) "lamps," but not "*the light*" : and no authority has been alleged for the view that even the collective body of the saints could receive this name. No other Synoptist supports Mt. in his version, and Jn may not improbably be writing allusively to it, and with the purpose of tacitly correcting it, in the following passages: (i. 8) "He [*i.e.* John] was *not* the light," (viii. 12, ix. 5) "*I am the light of the world,*" (xii. 35) "Walk (R.V.) while *ye have the light*," xii. 36 (R.V.) "While *ye have the light* believe on the light that ye may become sons of light." That a body of men should believe themselves to be a collection of "lights" reflecting the Light of the World, differs radically from the doctrine that the same men should believe themselves to be "*the* Light of the World" : and Jn appears to be protesting against the latter belief.

[2] [**1749** *a*] This is to be distinguished from Mk iii. 33—4, Mt. xii. 48—9, Lk. viii. 21 "my mother and my brethren," where our Lord gives a spiritual interpretation to "my brethren." The only other instance (Chri.) of "my brethren" is Mt. xxv. 40 (in parable).

[3] Mt. xxviii. 10.

ascending unto my Father and your Father and my God and your God[1]." The tradition of Matthew uses the past "took hold," which John perhaps read as the imperfect "began (or, wished) to take hold"—the action being checked by the words of Jesus, "Do not touch me[2]." Luke omits all mention of this manifestation of Christ to women. Mark's Gospel breaks off just before it. The Mark-Appendix, which takes up the narrative, simply says that the Saviour "appeared (ἐφάνη)[3] first to Mary Magdalene." There is a very strong probability indeed that John here, writing with allusion to the narrative peculiar to Matthew, wishes (1) to retain the beautiful tradition "Go tell *my brethren*" as part of the first utterance of the ascending Saviour, (2) to indicate that the women did *not* "take hold" of His feet[4].

---

[1] Jn xx. 17.

[2] [1749 *b*] Even Thomas is not represented in Jn as actually "touching" or "taking hold of" the risen Saviour. The Apostle is described as being invited to "reach" his "hand." But apparently he believes without this evidence (Jn xx. 29 "Because thou hast *seen* thou hast believed!").

[3] [1749 *c*] Ἐφάνη is here used for the more common ὤφθη. It is also used in Mt. i. 20, ii. 13, 19, but with κατ' ὄναρ, "in a dream." In Lk. ix. 8 Ἠλίας ἐφάνη it is without κατ' ὄναρ. It is also applied to the shining of a star (Mt. ii. 7) or to a character bright as a star (Phil. ii. 15).

[4] [1749 *d*] "*My* brethren" might be interpreted literally by Gentile readers ignorant of Christian vocabulary. In Mt., ℵ* reads "the brethren." The Johannine context, "my Father and your Father," makes it clear that the brotherhood is spiritual. In Acts i. 14, "his brethren" means James and Jude etc. because preceded by "his mother."

TO JOHN AND MATTHEW [1752]

JOHN-MATTHEW AGREEMENTS[1]

		Mt.	Jn		Mt.	Jn
[1750]	αἰγιαλός	2	1	ἁρπάζω	2	4
	ἄρτι	7	12	?† βῆμα[2]	1	1
	* βρῶσις[3]	2	4	διψάω[4]	5	6
[1751]	* δωρεάν (adv.)[5]	2	1	ἐλεύθερος[6]	1	2
	ἐμφανίζω[7]	1	2	ἐνταφιάζω[8]	1	1
	* ἐξετάζω[9]	2	1	κατάγνυμι[10]	1	3
[1752]	κραυγάζω[11]	1	6	λάθρᾳ	2	1

[1] [1750 a_1] An asterisk attached to a word denotes that Mt. and Jn use it in different senses : † denotes that the word not only has the same meaning in Mt. and Jn but also occurs in parallel passages.

[2] Βῆμα, "judgment seat," Mt. xxvii. 19 "*the* j.," Jn xix. 13 "*a* j." See **1745**.

[3] [1750 *a*] Βρῶσις, in Mt. "rust," in Jn "food."

[4] [1750 *b*] Διψάω, "I thirst," in Mt. xxv. 35, 37, 42, 44 means physical thirst, in Mt. v. 6 "hunger and *thirst after righteousness*" (where Lk. vi. 21 has merely "hunger now"). In Jn, the woman of Samaria interprets Christ's "shall never thirst" literally ("that I may not *thirst*"). Apart from this dialogue, the word is never used literally in the Fourth Gospel, unless it be in xix. 28 where it is printed by W.H. as a quotation. If it is, the most likely source is Ps. xlii. 2 "My soul is *athirst*" (not as W.H., Ps. lxix. 21). In that case the meaning would be spiritual as well as literal.

[5] [1751 *a*] Δωρεάν (adv.), in Mt. x. 8 (*bis*) "freely," in Jn xv. 25 (quoting Ps. xxxv. 19) "without a cause," "gratuitously."

[6] [1751 *b*] Ἐλεύθερος, in Mt. xvii. 26 "the sons are *free*," Jn viii. 33—6 "ye shall become *free*...the Son shall free (ἐλευθερώσῃ) you...ye shall be *free*." Ἐκχέω, Mt. ix. 17 "spill" (Jn ii. 15 "pour out" money) may be regarded as = Lk. v. 37 ἐκχύννομαι, and is therefore omitted above.

[7] Ἐμφανίζω, "manifest" vb., see **1716** *h*.

[8] [1751 *c*] Ἐνταφιάζω, "embalm," Mt. xxvi. 12. The parall. Mk xiv. 8 has ἐνταφιασμόν. Jn has the n. parallel to Mk (**1734** *e*), and the vb. xix. 40 "as it is the custom to embalm" not parall. to Mk or Mt.

[9] Ἐξετάζω, in Mt. ii. 8, x. 11, "ascertain"; in Jn xxi. 12, "question."

[10] Κατάγνυμι, in Mt. xii. 20 (loosely quoting Is. xlii. 3) "a bruised reed he shall not *break*"; in Jn xix. 31—3 of "breaking" limbs.

[11] [1752 *a*] Κραυγάζω, "cry aloud," is used eight times in N.T. Seven of these are (*a*) Jn xii. 13, of the multitude shouting "Hosanna!" (*b*) Jn xviii. 40, xix. 6, 12, 15, Acts xxii. 23, of the multitude clamouring for some

one's death, (c) Jn xi. 43. "He *cried aloud* (ἐκραύγασεν), Lazarus! [Come] out, hither!"

[1752 b] The remaining instance is (d) Mt. xii. 19 "He shall not strive (ἐρίσει) nor *cry aloud* (οὐδὲ κραυγάσει), nor shall one hear in the streets his voice," quoting Is. xlii. 2 "He shall not *cry*, nor *lift up*, nor cause to be heard his voice in the street." LXX renders "lift up" (as though it were "lift (the burden of sin)," *i.e.* "forgive") by ἀνήσει, "forgive"—as in Is. i. 14, ii. 9 (and freq.)—having οὐ κεκράξεται (A κράξεται) οὐδὲ ἀνήσει. Mt. quotes Isaiah's context in full as illustrating Christ's avoidance of publicity in His acts of healing (Mt. xii. 16 "He rebuked them that they should not make him manifest"). Perhaps Mt. takes "cry" as "cry, or summon, to arms," a meaning of the Niph. (Gesen. 858 b): but Kimchi and Ibn Ezr. (*ad loc.*) explain it as denoting the loud harsh tone used by a judge in order to impress his hearers with a sense of authority. Sym. substitutes "shall be deceived (ἐξαπατηθήσεται)" for "lift"—an error arising from Hebrew confusion.

[1752 c] These facts indicate that there were early difficulties in interpreting the Isaiah passage, and that there would be, toward the end of the 1st century, different views about applying to the Messiah either κράζω (LXX) or κραυγάζω (Mt.). Κραυγάζω, in O.T., is used only in Ezr. iii. 13 of a multitude crying aloud with mingled feelings; and Atticists, when not applying it to clamouring crowds, would probably use it (as Plat. *Rep.* x. 607 B (in poet. quot.)) of a "yelping" hound, or (Demosth. *Con.* p. 1258, 26) of a drunkard "yelling." Phrynichus says that κραυγασμός (for κεκραγμός) is illiterate. Epictetus applies κραυγάζω (apart from the discordant cry of a raven (iii. 1. 37)) to shouting in the theatre, crying to Caesar for help, and to a bad-tempered master bawling at his slaves (iii. 4. 4, 22. 55, 26. 22)—in all cases implying want of self-control.

[1752 d] For these reasons many Evangelists would shrink from applying κράζω, and still more κραυγάζω, to Christ. But Matthew extends his quotation of Isaiah so that it might be read thus, "He shall *not cry aloud...until he bring forth judgment to victory.*" This might mean that the "*crying aloud*" *did not take place till Christ's death when He overcame death upon the Cross*: and Matthew, though he does not use κραυγάζω in connexion with the last cry, uses there the kindred word (xxvii. 50) κράξας, alone among the Evangelists.

[1752 e] Others might take the view that both κράζω and κραυγάζω were forbidden by the words of Isaiah to be applied to the Messiah: and neither of these words is applied to Him by Mark or Luke. On the Cross, Jesus is described by Mark as βοῶν φωνῇ μεγάλῃ or ἀφεὶς φωνὴν μεγάλην, by Luke as φωνήσας φωνῇ μεγάλῃ, but not as "*crying*" or "*crying aloud.*"

[1752 f] John takes a different course. He represents Jesus as "*crying* (κράζω)" in solemn announcements of doctrine (vii. 28, 37, xii. 44) thrice,

TO JOHN AND MATTHEW [1754]

		Mt.	Jn		Mt.	Jn
	λαλιά	1	2	λαμπάς	5	1
	λόγχη[1]	[[1]]	1	* μεθύω[2]	1	1
[1753]	μεστός[3]	1	3	νύσσω[4]	[[1]]	1
	οὐ μόνον[5]	1	4	* περισσός[6]	1	1
	πλευρά[7]	[[1]]	4	πολύτιμος[8]	1	1
[1754]	πρωία[9]	1	1	qu. Σιών[10]	1	1
	* σκληρός[11]	1	1	σμύρνα[12]	1	1
	συμφέρω	4	3	* σφραγίζω[13]	1	2

but not on the Cross, where the simple words "saith" or "said" are used (xix. 26—30 λέγει, εἶπεν). But he applies "cry aloud (κραυγάζω)" to the single occasion (xi. 43) of the raising of Lazarus. Then, too, Jesus "wept" and "troubled himself." Perhaps the Evangelist felt that the Messiah, who could neither "weep" nor "cry aloud" for His own sake, might be rightly described as "crying aloud" for the sake of Lazarus, His "friend," whom He "loved."

[1] Λόγχη, "spear." See 1756.

[2] Μεθύω (-ομαι), "to be satisfied with wine," or "intoxicated." In Jn ii. 10 "when they have drunk freely (pass.)," not so strong as in Mt. xxiv. 49 (act.) (parall. Lk. xii. 45 μεθύσκεσθαι).

[3] Μεστός, "full," in Jn always literal, in Mt. xxiii. 28 metaphorical.

[4] Νύσσω, "pierce." See 1756.

[5] Οὐ μόνον, "not only," in Mt., only in xx. 21 "Not only the [work, or, miracle] of the fig-tree shall ye do."

[6] Περισσός, "superabundant," Mt. v. 37, 47. In Jn x. 10 "that they may have life (ζωήν) and have it superabundantly (περισσόν)" the adj. is used adverbially, a usage of which instances are given in pl. περισσά, and also in sing. compar. περισσότερον (by L. S. and Steph.), but no instance of περισσόν.

[7] Πλευρά, "side." See 1756.

[8] Πολύτιμος, "precious," Mt. xiii. 46 "one precious pearl," Jn xii. 3 "of nard pistic (1736 d) precious."

[9] Πρωία, "early," ὥρα being understood. In Mt. xxvii. 1, Jn xxi. 4, πρωίας δὲ (Jn + ἤδη) γενομένης (Jn γινομένης) occurs to introduce (in Mt.) the morning of the crucifixion and (in Jn) the manifestation of the risen Saviour to the seven disciples.

[10] [1754 a] Σιών, "Sion," quoted by Mt. xxi. 5 and Jn xii. 15 from Zech. ix. 9, see 1456 a and 1757.

[11] Σκληρός, "hard," Mt. xxv. 24 "a hard man," Jn vi. 60 "the saying is hard."

[12] Σμύρνα, "frankincense," Mt. ii. 11, the gift of the Magi to Christ in the cradle ; Jn xix. 39, the gift of Nicodemus to Christ in the tomb.

[13] Σφραγίζω, "seal," Mt. xxvii. 66 "sealing" the stone of Christ's sepulchre, Jn iii. 33, vi. 27 metaph. = "attesting."

	Mt.	Jn		Mt.	Jn
[1755] * τιμή[1]	2	1	* τρώγω[2]	1	5
ὑπάντησις[3]	2	1	φορέω[4]	1	1

§ 3. *Inferences*

[1756] Two inferences may be drawn from the facts given above. One relates to the three words with [[1]] opposite to them, λόγχη, νύσσω, and πλευρά, "spear," "pierce," "side." They all come from one passage, found in some of the best Greek MSS. of Matthew, and given by R.V. in marg. thus, "And another (ἄλλος δέ) took a *spear* and *pierced* his *side* and there came out water and blood[5]." These resemble the words of John, " But one (ἀλλ' εἷς) of the soldiers with a *spear pierced* his *side* and there came out straightway blood and water[6]." Matthew places the piercing before the death, and gives no explanation of it; John places it after the death, and explains that the soldiers had received orders to kill those who were on the crosses. If the passage was originally a part of Matthew and was omitted by the Syriac and Latin versions because of its inconsistency with John, we should then have to suppose that John (on the hypothesis that he knew Matthew's Gospel) was here intervening to place the piercing in its right order, as having occurred *after*, not before,

---

[1] Τιμή, in Mt. xxvii. 6, 9, "price"; in Jn iv. 44 "honour."

[2] [1755 a] Τρώγω, "eat," in Mt. xxiv. 38, "eating [gluttonously]"; in Jn alw. in good sense (exc. xiii. 18 (quot. Ps. xli. 9, but LXX ἐσθίων)) of spiritual "eating."

[3] Ὑπάντησις, "meeting," Mt. viii. 34 (exorcism), xxv. 1 (parable) ἐξέρχεσθαι εἰς ὑ.: Jn xii. 13 has the same phrase in the Riding into Jerusalem.

[4] Φορέω, "wear," in Mt. xi. 8 "they that *wear* soft clothing" (parall. Lk. "in glorious raiment and luxury"), Jn xix. 5 "*wearing* the crown of thorns."

[5] Mt. xxvii. 49.   [6] Jn xix. 34.

Christ's death. But had he done this, he would not—so far as we can judge from the list given above—have used Matthew's exact words. Regarded as an intervention of John, the phenomena would be unique. Regarded as a careless and misplaced interpolation from Johannine tradition (in which perhaps the Johannine ΑΜΕΙC was taken as ΑΜΟC) the insertion in Matthew is fairly explicable.

[1757] The second inference is of a more general character. It is derived from the fact that we find only one word marked ?†, but many words marked *; that is to say, when John happens to use a somewhat rare word peculiar to Matthew, he frequently uses it in a different sense from Matthew's, and almost always in an entirely different context[1]. The word Σιών is marked *qu.* That is because it is quoted both by John and by Matthew from Zechariah; and it has been shewn above (1456 *a*) that John actually ventures to differ from both the prophet and the Evangelist by omitting the word "meek," which is an integral part of the prophecy. In this list, then, there are (practically) none of the agreements that we found in the John-Mark list. Consequently, when we come, later on, to a number of passages where John agrees with traditions reported identically by Mark and Matthew (but not by Luke), it is a reasonable inference that *John's real agreement is with Mark.* John's agreement with Matthew is most reasonably explained by the fact that he and Matthew are borrowing from identical passages of Mark.

---

[1] [1757 *a*] It is fair to add that Mt. and Jn agree in applying the word λύω to metaphorical "loosing." But they never do it in parallel contexts, even where it might be expected (2517—20).

CHAPTER III

WORDS PECULIAR TO JOHN AND LUKE

§ 1. *Antecedent probability*

[1758] Luke is recognised by all as having not only written in his own style but also compiled traditions in various styles, the differences between which are clearly perceptible. This may be seen in the Pauline, Petrine, and other portions of the Acts. It is also manifest in his Gospel, which contains (1) a short Preface in Attic style, (2) a History of Christ's Birth and Childhood in Hebraic style, (3) a History of Christ's acts and short sayings in which he agrees largely with Mark, (4) a Collection of Christ's longer sayings (including the Lord's Prayer, the Beatitudes and their context, etc.) in which he closely agrees with Matthew, (5) a Collection of parables in common with Matthew, (6) a Collection of parables and other traditions peculiar to himself, in which a variety of styles is manifest, (7) an Account of the Passion, differing in style and matter from those of Mark and Matthew, (8) an Account of the Resurrection quite different in subject-matter from that in Matthew, and differing in style from Luke's own History of the Birth and Childhood.

[1759] A compilation of this kind, even though revised by the compiler, and in parts perhaps rewritten by him, would naturally have a wider vocabulary than a book written in one style. Hence we may naturally expect Luke to include a large number of words that would be independently employed by any educated evangelists at the end of the first century, though not used by Mark or Matthew. We should therefore expect to find the "John-Luke" more numerous than the "John-Matthew" and very much more numerous than the "John-Mark" agreements, but—in view of the instances where John supports Mark against Luke's silence or deviation—to find also that the number of words marked †, as being parallelisms between John and Luke, is very small.

§ 2. *The fact*

[**1760**] The fact harmonizes with this expectation. The list of verbal agreements is very long, and would be longer still if we placed in it some words that belong rather to grammar than to vocabulary[1] and will be mentioned later on. But even when the word is rare, there is hardly ever any strict parallelism in the context. "Napkin," for example, in Luke's parable, wraps up a talent, but in John it is used for entombments[2]. "Breast," in Luke, occurs twice to describe "beating on the breast"; but in John it refers to the disciple lying on the breast of Jesus[3].

[**1761**] Such parallelisms as there are will be found to be confined either to Luke's Single Tradition, or to the Double Tradition of Matthew and Luke. As to this, it was pointed out above (**1450**) that John supports Luke against Matthew in retaining the apparently harsh precept about "hating one's own life[4]." Another instance will be given from the Double Tradition (**1784—92**), where Christ's appellation of the disciples as "my friends," which occurs in Luke's version (but

---

[1] [**1760** *a*] For example, μετά is common to all the Gospels, but μετὰ ταῦτα is peculiar to Jn-Lk. Νῦν (Chri.) is almost peculiar to Jn-Lk. Πρός after verbs of "speaking" (exc. in the phrase "to one another") is prob. peculiar to Jn-Lk. See **2394** *b*, **1915** (vi) *d*, and **2366** *b*.

[2] Lk. xix. 20, Jn xi. 44, xx. 7 σουδάριον.

[3] Lk. xviii. 13, xxiii. 48, Jn xiii. 25, xxi. 20 στῆθος.

[4] This, however, not being a word but a phrase, does not appear in the list below.

not in Matthew's), is repeated by John. Luke's Single Tradition describes the Saviour as coming after the Resurrection and "standing in the midst" of the disciples: a similar phrase is used by John. These are about all the parallelisms, strictly so called, that can be found between John and Luke.

§ 3. *Quasi-parallels*

[1762] Other instances, however, occur where John and Luke use the same words, and these rare words, in describing events that are apparently not identical though similar. For example, the word ἐκμάσσω, "wipe," is used by both writers in describing the Anointing of Jesus by a woman. Luke says, "*with the hair* of her head she *began to wipe* [his feet]," and again, "*with her hair* she *wiped*" them. John speaks of Mary the sister of Martha as "the one that *wiped* his feet with her hair," and afterwards describes the act, "*she wiped with her hair* his feet." But Luke, in the Anointing, calls the woman "a sinner," and speaks of Mary the sister of Martha elsewhere, without any suggestion of identity. Commentators are divided, and have been from very early times, in their attempts to explain John's agreement with Mark and Matthew in their general account of the Anointing, but with Luke in this detail. For the present[1] it must suffice to say that the phrase in the two Gospels, although apparently not referring to the same event, appears nevertheless allusive in the later (John) to the narrative contained in the earlier (Luke).

[1763] "Disembark," ἀποβαίνω, occurs in Luke's version of the Calling of Peter on the lake of Gennesaret[2]. In this, it is said that Jesus "saw two boats standing by the lake but the fishermen had *disembarked* from them"; Peter, one of the fishermen, had "toiled all night" and "taken nothing"; but,

---

[1] The point will be fully discussed in *The Fourfold Gospel* (see Preface above, p. ix).   [2] Lk. v. 2 foll.

at Christ's command, they let down their nets and take such a multitude of fishes that "the nets were breaking." According to John[1], Jesus, after the Resurrection, "stood on the beach" and called to the disciples who "in that night had caught nothing." At His command they cast the net on the right side of the ship[2] and take one hundred and fifty-three great fishes, yet "the net was not rent." It is after catching this draught that, according to John, "they *disembarked* on the land." Ἀποβαίνω, though frequently thus used in classical Greek, nowhere else has this meaning in the Greek Testament Old or New[3]. Hence this single verbal coincidence would suffice to claim attention: but when it is combined with the similarities in the context, the total effect suggests that John is writing allusively to Luke's tradition, or, at all events, that the two traditions are in some way related.

---

[1] Jn xxi. 4—9.

[2] **[1763 *a*]** There is nothing in Lk. parall. to Jn xxi. 6 "cast your net on the *right* side of the ship." But in Ps. lxxxix. 12 "the *right* (lit. the south)" is rendered "*sea*" in LXX by Hebrew confusion. Comp. Lk. v. 4 "put out into the *deep* and let down your nets for a draught."

[3] **[1763 *b*]** In LXX, it is freq. and means "turn out," "prove to be," and it means this in Lk. xxi. 13, Phil. i. 19. "Disembark"=ἐξέρχομαι in Mk vi. 34, Mt. xiv. 14. These facts make the Jn-Lk. agreement somewhat more remarkable.

JOHN-LUKE AGREEMENTS[1]

	Lk.	Jn		Lk.	Jn
[1764] * ἀγωνίζομαι[2]	1	1	ἀδικία[3]	4	1
ἀληθινός[4]	1	9	Ἄννας[5]	1	2
ἀντιλέγω[6]	1	1	?† ἀποβαίνω[7]	2	1
[1765] ἀπόκρισις	2	2	ἀριθμός[8]	1	1
ἀριστάω	1	2	ἄρχοντες[9] (Jews)	4	3

---

[1] [1764 a₁] An asterisk denotes that the same word is used in different senses by Jn and Lk. e.g. ἀγωνίζομαι, Jn "fight," Lk. "strive (to)." No words are marked †, because there is no certain instance of parallelism. ?† denotes a quasi-parallel context. Ὀθόνιον and παρακύπτω occur in a passage enclosed by W.H. in double brackets, which will be discussed later on (1798—1804).

[2] Ἀγωνίζομαι, in Lk. xiii. 24 "*Strive* to enter" (parall. Mt. vii. 13 "enter"), Jn xviii. 36 "My officers would *strive*," i.e. *fight*.

[3] [1764 a] Ἀδικία, "unrighteousness," which in Lk. xiii. 27 is parall. to Mt. vii. 23 ἀνομία, occurs, in Jn, only in vii. 18, "this man is true and there is no *unrighteousness* in him": but it is also in 1 Jn i. 9, v. 17. For the most part Jn uses "darkness," or "lie," to express "unrighteousness."

[4] Ἀληθινός, "true," i.e. genuine, Lk. xvi. 11, see 1727 *f—i*.

[5] [1764 b] Ἄννας, Lk. iii. 2 "In the high-priesthood of *Annas* and Caiaphas." That of Annas ended (*Enc.* "Annas") A.D. 15. That of Caiaphas lasted A.D. 18—36. Jn xviii. 13—24 explains that Annas was the father-in-law of Caiaphas, and leads us to infer that he at all events occasionally exercised the civil authority of the high-priesthood, since Christ's captors (xviii. 13) "led him to *Annas first*."

[6] Ἀντιλέγω, Lk. ii. 34 "a sign *spoken against*," Jn xix. 12 "*speaketh against* Caesar."

[7] Ἀποβαίνω, "disembark," see 1763.

[8] Ἀριθμός, "number," Lk. xxii. 3 "of the *number* of the Twelve," Jn vi. 10 "in *number* about five thousand."

[9] [1765 a] Ἄρχοντες (of the Jews), mentioned in the sing. by Mt. ix. 18 "a [certain] *ruler*" where parall. Mk v. 22, Lk. viii. 41 indicate that he was a "*ruler* of the synagogue." But, in the pl., Lk. xxiii. 13, 35, xxiv. 20 refer to members of the Sanhedrin (there is nothing to indicate the meaning in Lk. xiv. 1). In Jn vii. 26, 48, xii. 42 it probably means members of the Sanhedrin, and Jn iii. 1 "Nicodemus...a *ruler* of the Jews" is subsequently represented as taking part in the deliberations of the Sanhedrin (vii. 51).

TO JOHN AND LUKE [1769]

		Lk.	Jn		Lk.	Jn
	* βαθύς[1]	1	1	βάπτω[2]	1	2
[1766]	βουλεύομαι	1	2	βοῦς	3	2
	βραχίων[3]	1	1	βραχύ	1	1
	γείτων	3	1	γνωρίζω	2	2
[1767]	γνωστός[4]	2	2	* γράμμα[5]	2	2
	διαδίδωμι	2	1	ἔθος	3	1
	εἶδος[6]	2	1	εἰσάγω	3	1
[1768] ?†	ἐκμάσσω[7]	2	3	ἐμπίμπλημι[8]	2	1
	ἐνθάδε	1	2	ἐνιαυτός[9]	1	3
	ἐντεῦθεν	2	5	ἐνώπιον[10]	22	1
[1769]	ἐξηγέομαι[11]	1	1	ἔπειτα	1	1

---

[1] Βαθύς, "deep," Lk. xxiv. 1 '*early* (lit. *deep*) dawn," Jn iv. 11 "the well is *deep*."

[2] Βάπτω, "dip," Lk. xvi. 24 "that he should *dip*...and cool my tongue," Jn xiii. 26 (*bis*) of Jesus "*dipping*" the sop.

[3] Βραχίων, "arm," Lk. i. 51 "He hath shewed strength with his *arm*," (quot. Ps. lxxxix. 10, or xcviii. 1), Jn xii. 38 (quoting Is. liii. 1), "To whom hath the *arm* of the Lord been revealed?"

[4] Γνωστός, "acquaintance," Lk. ii. 44, xxiii. 49 of the "*acquaintance*" of Christ's parents, and of Christ, Jn xviii. 15, 16 of the beloved disciple as being an "*acquaintance* of the high priest."

[5] Γράμμα, in Lk. xvi. 6, 7 "Take thy *bond*," Jn v. 47 "his [*i.e.* Moses's] *writings*," vii. 15 "How knoweth this man *letters*?"

[6] Εἶδος, "appearance," Lk. iii. 22 "in bodily *appearance*," ix. 29 "The *appearance* of his face became different," Jn v. 37 "Ye have neither seen his [*i.e.* God's] *appearance*."

[7] [1768 a] Ἐκμάσσω θριξίν, "wipe with hair," occurs in Lk. vii. 38, 44 and Jn xi. 2, xii. 3, concerning the "wiping" of Christ's feet with the hair of a woman described by Lk. as "a sinner," but by Jn as Mary the sister of Lazarus (1762). Jn (xiii. 5) also uses the word concerning the "wiping" of the feet of the disciples by Christ.

[8] Ἐμπίμπλημι, "fill." Lk. i. 53 "The hungry he hath *filled* with good things," vi. 25 "Woe unto you, O ye that are *filled* now," Jn vi. 12 "But when they [*i.e.* the 5000] were *filled*."

[9] Ἐνιαυτός, "year," Lk. iv. 19 (Is. lxi. 2) "the acceptable *year* of the Lord," Jn xi. 49, 51, xviii. 13 "the high priest in that *year*," i.e. Caiaphas.

[10] [1768 b] Ἐνώπιον, "before the face of," "in the sight of," in Jn, only in xx. 30 "many other signs, therefore, did Jesus *in the sight of* the disciples," comp. Lk. xxiv. 43 "and he did eat *in their sight* (ἐ. αὐτῶν)." Jn is probably referring to manifestations, like that in Lk. xxiv. 43, of the risen Saviour, "in the sight of" the disciples alone.

[11] Ἐξηγέομαι, "relate," "describe." Lk. xxiv. 35 "they *described* that

[1770] WORDS PECULIAR

	Lk.	Jn		Lk.	Jn
* ἐπίκειμαι[1]	2	2	ἱματισμός[2]	2	1
κῆπος	1	4	κόλπος[3]	3	2
[1770] κυκλόω[4]	1	1	κύριος, ὁ[5] (Jesus) (narr.)	c. 14	5
λαγχάνω[6]	1	1	* Λάζαρος[7]	4	11
Λευείτης[8]	1	1	* λογίζομαι[9]	1	1
[1771] λύπη[10]	1	4	Μάρθα[11]	3	9
Μαριά(μ)[12]	2	9	* μηνύω[13]	1	1

which had occurred to them in the way," *i.e.* the appearance of the risen Saviour, Jn i. 18 "the only begotten hath *described* him," *i.e.* God, whom "no man hath seen."

[1] Ἐπίκειμαι in Lk. v. 1, xxiii. 23, means "to be pressing upon, or importunate," in Jn xi. 38, xxi. 9 "lying on the top of."

[2] Ἱματισμός, "clothing," Lk. vii. 25, ix. 29; Jn xix. 24 (quoting Ps. xxii. 18 "on my vesture they cast lots").

[3] Κόλπος, "bosom," Lk. vi. 38 "good measure...into your *bosom*," xvi. 22, 23 of Abraham's "*bosom*," Jn i. 18 "the *bosom* of the Father," xiii. 23 "in the *bosom* of Jesus."

[4] Κυκλόω, "surround," Lk. xxi. 20 "Jerusalem *surrounded* by armies," Jn x. 24 "the Jews therefore *surrounded* him," *i.e.* Jesus.

[5] Κύριος, ὁ, "the Lord," meaning Jesus (not in vocative), see **1779—81**.

[6] Λαγχάνω, "draw lots for," "obtain by lot," Lk. i. 9, Jn xix. 24.

[7] Λάζαρος, Lk. xvi. 20—5, Lazarus the beggar; Jn xi. 1—43, xii. 1—17, the Lazarus that was raised from the dead.

[8] Λευείτης, "Levite," Lk. x. 32 in the parable of the Good Samaritan, Jn i. 19 "priests and Levites."

[9] Λογίζομαι, "reckon," "consider," in Lk. xxii. 37 (quoting Is. liii. 12) "he was *reckoned*," in Jn xi. 50 "nor do ye *consider*."

[10] Λύπη, "sorrow," Lk. xxii. 45 "He found them sleeping for *sorrow*," Jn xvi. 6, 20—22 in words of Christ, concerning the "*sorrow*" of the disciples at the thought of being parted from their Master.

[11] **[1771 a]** Μάρθα, in Lk., only in x. 38, 40, 41; in Jn xi. 1—39 (the raising of Lazarus) and xii. 2 "Martha was *serving* (διηκόνει)," which corresponds to the noun "service" in Lk. x. 40 "M. was distracted about much *service* (διακονίαν)."

[12] **[1771 b]** Μαριά(μ), in Lk., only in x. 39, 42; in Jn xi. 1—45 (the raising of Lazarus) and xii. 3 "Mary...anointed the feet of Jesus." Lk. x. 39 describes her as "sitting at the feet of the Lord," and Jn xi. 20 as "sitting in the house."

[13] Μηνύω, in Lk. xx. 37 "Moses *indicated* in the passage about the bush," in Jn xi. 57 "if any man knew...he was to *give information*."

		Lk.	Jn		Lk.	Jn
	* μονογενής[1]	3	4	νικάω[2]	1	1
[1772]	ὀθόνιον[3]	[[1]]	4	ὀκτώ	2	1
	παρακύπτω[4]	[[1]]	2	περιτέμνω	2	1
	πλήρης (of Christ)[5]	1	1	πράσσω[6]	6	2
[1773]	προτρέχω	1	1	Σαμαρία	1	3
	* Σιλωάμ[7]	1	2	σουδάριον	1	2
	στῆθος	2	2	συγγενής	3 or 4	1
[1774]	συντίθεμαι[8]	1	1	σωτήρ[9]	2	1

[1] Μονογενής. Lk. vii. 12, viii. 42, ix. 38 of "an only child"; Jn i. 14, 18, iii. 16, 18 "the only begotten" Son of God.

[2] [1771 c] Νικάω, "conquer," Lk. xi. 22 "But when the man that is stronger than he shall come against him and *conquer* him," Jn xvi. 33 "Be of good cheer, I have *conquered* the world." In the rest of N.T. νικάω occurs only in Rom. iii. 4 (quotation), xii. 21 (*bis*), 1 Jn (6), Rev. (14 or 15).

[3] Ὀθόνιον, "linen bandage," perh. in Lk. xxiv. 12, see **1798, 1804**.

[4] Παρακύπτω, "stoop (?) and look into," like ὀθόνιον in last note, occurs perh. in Lk. xxiv. 12, see **1798—1804**.

[5] [1772 a] Πλήρης "full," applied to Christ in Lk. iv. 1 "*full* of the Holy Spirit," Jn i. 14 (of the Logos) "*full* of grace and truth." Both passages occur at the outset, where the two Evangelists are describing Christ's entrance into public life. Both might naturally be written with some reference to contemporary discussions about the manner in which (Col. ii. 9) "the fulness of the Godhead dwelt" in Jesus "bodily." Luke, who uses the expression "bodily" in connexion with the "dove," might interpret the "fulness" as referring to the Holy Spirit descending at baptism. John might see the "fulness" in the human, yet divine, "graciousness and truth," *i.e.* probably "kindness and truth," manifested in the incarnate Logos and imparted by Him to men. Acts xi. 24 "full of the Holy Spirit" is applied to Barnabas (comp. Acts vi. 3, vii. 55). If Christ's disciples were commonly described as "full of the Holy Spirit," John may well have considered that the "fulness" of Christ, at the outset of the Gospel, needed a different description.

[6] [1772 b] Πράσσω, in Lk., (iii. 13. xix. 23) "*exact*," elsewhere (xxii. 23, xxiii. 15, 41 *bis*) "*do* [*evil*]." In Jn iii. 20, ὁ φαῦλα πράσσων opp. to iii. 21 ὁ δὲ ποιῶν τὴν ἀλήθειαν: in Jn v. 29 οἱ τὰ ἀγαθὰ ποιήσαντες precedes οἱ τὰ φαῦλα πράξαντες. Comp. Rom. vii. 19 οὐ γὰρ ὃ θέλω ποιῶ ἀγαθόν, ἀλλὰ ὃ οὐ θέλω κακὸν τοῦτο πράσσω.

[7] Σιλωάμ, "Siloam," Lk. xiii. 4 "tower," Jn ix. 7 "pool."

[8] Συντίθεμαι, "agree," Lk. xxii. 5 "they *agreed* to give him [Judas Iscariot] money," Jn ix. 22 "The Jews had *agreed*" to cast out of the synagogue any one that professed belief in Christ.

[9] [1774 a] Σωτήρ, "Saviour," Jn iv. 42 "This is indeed *the Saviour of*

[1775] WORDS PECULIAR

	Lk.	Jn		Lk.	Jn
σωτηρία¹	4	1	ταχέως	2	1
τελειόω²	2	5	ὑμέτερος	1	3
[1775] ὑπομιμνήσκω	1	1	?† φίλος (not appl. to Christ)³	14	6

the world." This remarkable utterance is assigned to Samaritans. "Saviour of the world," in N.T., occurs elsewhere only in 1 Jn iv. 14 "The Father hath sent his Son [to be the] *Saviour of the world.*" Lk. has i. 47 "My spirit hath rejoiced in God my *Saviour,*" and ii. 11 "There was born for you to-day a *Saviour.*"

¹ [1774 b] Σωτηρία, "salvation." On Jn iv. 22 "*Salvation* is from the Jews," see **1647**. In Lk., it occurs in his Introduction i. 69—77, and in the story of Zacchaeus, Lk. xix. 9 "to-day hath *salvation* come to this house."

² [1774 c] Τελειόω, "accomplish," or "perfect," occurs in Lk. ii. 43 "when they had *accomplished* the days," Lk. xiii. 32 "on the third day I am to be *perfected* (τελειοῦμαι)." In Jn iv. 34, v. 36, xvii. 4, it is used of the Son "perfecting" the work appointed by the Father. In xvii. 23 "that they all may be *perfected* into one," it describes the unity of the Church. The last instance is xix. 28 "that the Scripture may be *accomplished.*"

³ [1775 a] Φίλος, "friend," occurs once in Mt. xi. 19, applied to Christ (parall. to Lk. vii. 34) "*friend* of publicans and sinners." Apart from this, it occurs, in Lk., in the Discourse of Christ where, after the appointment of the Twelve, Jesus prepares them for persecution. Mt. x. 24, 28 omits 'friends," thus : "The disciple is not above the teacher...And ∧ be not afraid of them that kill the body." Lk. separates these precepts, having (vi. 40) "The disciple is not above the teacher," and, much later (xii. 4) "*But I say unto you,* [*being*] *my friends,* be not afraid of them that kill the body." John, in the Last Discourse, has a division similar to that of Luke, first (Jn xiii. 16) " The bondservant is not greater than his lord, nor yet an apostle greater than he that sent him," and then (Jn xv. 14, 15, 20) "Ye are my *friends,* if ye continue doing that which I command you. No longer do I call you bondservants...but I have called you *friends....* The bondservant is not greater than his lord : if they persecuted me, they will also persecute you."

[1775 b] This then is one of the few passages where Jn follows a tradition found in Lk. alone, or rather in Lk.'s version of the Double Tradition. But, whereas Lk. wraps up a great deal in the appositional phrase "you, [being] my friends," Jn shews both *why* the disciples are henceforth to be called friends and *what* they must be prepared for, as the consequence of the title. On this tradition, and its origin, see **1784—92**.

	Lk.	Jn		Lk.	Jn.
φρέαρ	1	2	φωτίζω[1]	1	1
χάρις[2]	8	4	ὡς (when)[3]	15 or 16	15

§ 4. "*Son of Joseph*"

[1776] In addition to the single words above mentioned there are several phrases of great importance peculiar to Luke and John[4]. Foremost among these, in Johannine order, comes (1) "Son of Joseph" applied to Christ. There are also (2) the above-mentioned application of "the Lord" to Jesus in narrative; (3) "sons of light" used in both Gospels by Christ; (4) "my friends" applied by Jesus to the disciples; (5) "Jesus...*stood in the midst*," describing Christ's manifestation after the Resurrection; (6) the combination of the rare words "glancing into" and "linen bandages" in a description of what was seen by a disciple in Christ's sepulchre after He

---

[1] Φωτίζω, "enlighten," in Lk. xi. 36 in a simile, of a "*lamp*"; Jn i. 9, in a metaphor, of "*the true light*."

[2] [1775 c] Χάρις, "grace," Lk. i. 30 "thou hast found *grace* with God," at the Annunciation, ii. 40, 52 of the "grace" of God on Jesus as a child and as a youth, iv. 22 of the words of "grace" from His mouth, vi. 32, 33, 34 "What *thank* have ye?" xvii. 9 "Does he give *thanks*?" In Jn, it occurs of (i. 14—17) "*grace* and truth" (as distinct from "Law") coming to man through the incarnate Logos.

[3] [1775 d] Ὡς, "when," occurs (15) in Jn with aorist (incl. ἦν)—a frequent meaning in LXX. Except in xix. 33 (where ὡς occurs in parenth.) Jn always has δέ, or οὖν, before, or after, ὡς "when." With imperf. (xx. 11 ἔκλαιεν) it means "*while*" ("*while* she was weeping"). On Jn xii. 35—6 (*bis*) see **2201**.

[1775 e] The number given above (15 or 16) in Lk. excludes xxiv. 32 (*bis*) (R.V.) "*while*" (with imperf.), xii. 58 "*while* thou art going," xx. 37 "*when* (or, *since*) he calleth." In Lk., ὡς never precedes οὖν, and it never precedes δέ except in Lk. v. 4, vii. 12. Mk-Mt. prefer ὅτε (*e.g.* in Mk xi. 1, Mt. xxi. 1, contrasted with Lk. xix. 29 ὡς).

[4] There is also the tradition about "hating one's own life" which has been discussed above (**1450**) as a specimen of Jn's allusiveness. It occurs in Lk.'s version of the Double Tradition. On βαστάζω σταυρόν, see **1792 b**.

had risen—a passage certainly genuine in John, but bracketed by W. H. in Luke. Each of these requires separate discussion, and they will now be taken in their order.

[1777] Mark and Matthew say that when Jesus visited "his own country," people in the synagogue said "Is not this the carpenter," or, "the son of the carpenter?[1]" Luke, relating a visit to "Nazareth where he had been brought up," makes the people in the synagogue say, "Is not this [*the*] *son of Joseph*?[2]" John gives no such utterance in his account of our Lord's visit to Galilee where He quotes the proverb about "a prophet in his own country[3]": but in his account of Christ's Eucharistic teaching in the synagogue at Capernaum[4] he makes the Jews say "Is not this Jesus *the son of Joseph* whose father and mother we (emph.) know?[5]" Mark and Matthew agree with John in mentioning or implying "mother" (Mk "the son of Mary," Mt. "is not his mother called Mary?") and both add a mention of brothers and sisters: but the names of the brothers vary.

[1778] At the outset of the Gospel, John represents Philip as saying to Nathanael, "We have found him of whom Moses in the Law wrote, and the Prophets [wrote], Jesus [*the*] *son of Joseph*, [Jesus] of Nazareth[6]." Nathanael raises no objection except on the ground of "Nazareth," and almost immediately afterwards confesses Jesus to be "the Son of God" and "King of Israel." Thus John's narrative brings Nathanael's belief in "the son of Joseph" as being also "the Son of God," into contrast with the unbelief of the Jews in "the son of Joseph" because they "know" His "father and mother." Luke certainly does *not* believe Jesus to have been "son of Joseph" any more than he believes him to have been

---

[1] Mk vi. 3, Mt. xiii. 55.
[2] Lk. iv. 22 οὐχὶ υἱός ἐστιν ’I. οὗτος;
[3] Jn iv. 43—4.   [4] Jn vi. 59.
[5] Jn vi. 42 οὐχὶ οὗτός ἐστιν ’I. ὁ υἱὸς ’I.;
[6] Jn i. 45 Ἰησοῦν υἱὸν τοῦ Ἰωσὴφ τὸν ἀπὸ N.

born at Nazareth. It is the Jews, according to Luke, that are in error. The Jews call Nazareth (Lk. iv. 23) "thy *country*," Luke calls it (Lk. iv. 16) "Nazareth *where he was brought up*": and similarly Luke intends us to believe that the Jews were deceived about Christ's being "the son of Joseph" and that Jesus did not undeceive them. John seems to differ from Luke on both points. But in any case the great error of the Jews, according to John, would seem to have consisted in their imagination that the Son of God could not be incarnate in a man whose "father and mother" they "knew." We cannot, however, say that John is here alluding to Luke's particular phrase, "son of Joseph," for it must have been the subject of many controversies before the end of the first century, and John may be alluding to these as a whole, differing from Luke's view of the controversy, but not referring specially to Luke's language.

§ 5. "*The Lord*" *meaning* "*Jesus*"

[1779] In Evangelistic narrative—strictly so called, *i.e.* excluding speech of any kind as well as the speech of Christ—"the Lord" means "Jesus" about fourteen times in Luke[1] and five times in John: and there is a great difference between the two in usage as well as in frequency. In Luke, for example, this title introduces the raising of the widow's son at Nain ("and when *the Lord* saw her he had compassion on her") and the sending of the Seventy ("Now after these things *the Lord* appointed seventy others") and Christ's

---

[1] [1779 a] Lk. vii. 13, 19, x. 1, 39, 41, xi. 39, xii. 42, xiii. 15, xvii. 5, 6, xviii. 6, xix. 8, xxii. 61 (*bis*), comp. xxiv. 3 τὸ σῶμα [[τοῦ Κυρίου Ἰησοῦ]]. Some Latin MSS., as well as ℵAD, have it (SS "our Lord") in Lk. xxii. 31. In xii. 42, xvii. 5 (if compared with Mt. xviii. 21), xxii. 61, there is mention of Peter in the context or in parallel Mt. In Lk. xxii. 31, if genuine, it precedes an utterance of our Lord to Peter.

definition of the faithful steward (in reply to a question of Peter's) "And *the Lord* said, Who then is the faithful and wise steward...?" Luke also describes John the Baptist as sending disciples "to *the Lord*"; Mary, the sister of Martha, as "sitting at *the Lord's* feet," and "*the Lord*" as gently rebuking Martha. In all these cases, the phrase containing "the Lord" is an integral part of the narrative.

[1780] But this is not so clearly the case in John *e.g.* iv. 1 "When, therefore, *the Lord* knew...he left Judæa," where the sentence might be regarded not exactly as narrative, but rather as comment intended to explain the situation and to prepare the way for what was done. Still less can the phrase be called "integral" in vi. 23 "Howbeit there came boats from Tiberias nigh unto the place where they ate the bread after *the Lord* had given thanks"—which R.V. prints as a parenthesis, being indeed a parenthetic explanation of the situation. So, too, in xi. 2 (R.V.) "It was that Mary which anointed *the Lord* with ointment," the sentence is not a part of the narrative of the raising of Lazarus (which immediately follows) but a parenthetic definition of this particular Mary —since there were others of that name. There remain xx. 20 "rejoiced at seeing *the Lord*" and xxi. 12 "knowing that it was *the Lord*." Both of these may perhaps be explained with reference to a previous mention of "the Lord" in speech. In the former case, Mary had on that same day come to the disciples saying "I have seen *the Lord*" and bringing a message to them. Then when He appeared to them they rejoiced that they too had "seen *the Lord*." In the latter case, the beloved disciple had just said to Peter (xxi. 7) "It is *the Lord*," and the narrative proceeds, "Simon Peter, having heard the words[1] 'It is *the Lord*.'" Afterwards, when the disciples were convinced that this was true, the Evangelist

---

[1] Jn xxi. 7 ὅτι is prob. equival. to inverted commas, or "the words (**2189—90**).

not unnaturally records their conviction by a repetition of the same phrase ("it is *the Lord*"). Or perhaps the meaning may be "knowing [and saying to themselves] 'It is *the Lord.*'"

[1781] The fact above noted (1779 *a*) that some of the passages in Luke mentioning "the Lord" are connected with Peter, deserves to be studied along with the fact that *the fragment of the Gospel of Peter speaks of Christ as "the Lord,"* and by no other term, and this, before the Resurrection. In that fragment, He is not called "Jesus," even by enemies: they cannot, of course, call Him Lord, but they use the personal pronoun or leave a pronoun to be supplied[1]. Also, in a passage where Luke has "The Apostles said to *the Lord*, 'Increase our faith,'" the preceding verse in Luke about "forgiving seven times" is parallel to a passage in Matthew in which Peter asks how many times one must forgive a brother[2]. Most of the passages in Luke are peculiar to his Gospel: and they give the impression of having been taken from some book (perhaps containing the teaching or preaching of Peter) in which Jesus was habitually called "*the Lord.*" There is no ground for thinking that in this point John alludes to Luke or imitates his usage.

§ 6. "*Sons of light*"

[1782] Luke has, in the Parable of the Unjust Steward, (xvi. 8) "The sons of this world are, for their own generation, more prudent than the *sons of the light.*" John has (xii. 36) "Believe in the light that ye may become *sons of light.*" In Luke, "the sons of this world" would naturally take, as its

---

[1] [1781 *a*] *Evang. Pet.* § 1 "Herod the king commands *the Lord* to be taken (παρ[αλημ]φθῆναι)...§ 2 Joseph the friend of Pilate and of *the Lord*...asked the body of *the Lord*...Pilate sending to Herod asked for *his* body...Herod said, Brother Pilate, even if no one had asked for *him* we should have buried *him*..."

[2] Lk. xvii. 5 "increase our faith," preceded by xvii. 4 "if seven times a day he sin," which is parall. to Mt. xviii. 21 foll. containing Peter's question "until seven times?"

antithesis, "the sons of the world to come," of which Wetstein and Schöttgen give abundant instances while giving none of "the sons of light." But the occurrence of "*sons of light*" and "*children of light*" in two of the Epistles[1] shews that such expressions must have been in early use among Christians. The Book of Enoch contains several kindred phrases, indicating that "light" will not only "appear to the righteous" but will pass upon them: "The light of the Lord of spirits is seen on the face of the holy and righteous and elect"; it also classes "the holy ones who are in heaven" with "the elect who dwell in the garden of life and every spirit of light"; and it speaks of "the spirits of the good who belong to *the generation of light*[2]."

[1783] Matthew and Luke record Christ's doctrine that "the light of the body is the eye," but they say nothing about "the light of the soul": and some readers might infer that each man's "light" belongs to himself, instead of being the Light of the World accepted by each through the eye of the soul. Mark does not mention the word "light" except as that of the fire at which Peter warms himself. On the subject of spiritual light he has nothing except a sentence or two about a "lamp." Yet the three Synoptists say just enough to shew that our Lord must have said a great deal more about the "light" that "the Lord of spirits" imparts to men. There were many reasons why He might prefer the Enoch metaphor of "light" to the metaphor subsequently adopted by the Talmudists, "The sons of the world that is to come." The latter might be restricted to the future and to those who should hereafter have risen from the dead. The former might be applied, as St Paul applies it, to living Thessalonians and Ephesians, with the practical precept,

---

[1] 1 Thess. v. 5 "Ye are *sons of light* and sons of day," Eph. v. 8 "But now are ye light in the Lord, walk as *children of light*."

[2] Enoch (ed. Charles) xxxviii. 2—4, lxi. 12, cviii. 11. These extracts are of different dates but all (*ib.* p. 33) "before the beginning of the Christian era."

"Walk as children of light." There is not the slightest reason to think that John, in using the phrase "sons of light," is referring to Luke's single use of it.

§ 7. *"My friends"*

[1784] Where Luke represents our Lord as saying to the disciples "my friends," the parallel Matthew contains two prominent thoughts. The first is, that the disciple is not greater than his master, so that the former ought to be prepared to share the persecutions endured by the latter. The second is, that the disciples must not be afraid of any earthly enemy, for he has no power beyond the grave. Luke and John separate the two[1], as follows:

Mt. x. 24—8	Lk. vi. 40	Jn xiii. 16—17
"A disciple is not above his teacher nor a bond-servant above his lord...if they called the Master of the House Beelzebul, how much more them of his household (οἰκιακούς)! Fear them not therefore...What I say to you in the darkness, say (εἴπατε) in the light...And be not afraid of (ἀπό) them that kill the body..."	"A disciple is not above his teacher, but everyone [when] perfected shall be as his teacher..." xii. 3—4 "...Wherefore, what things ye said (εἴπατε) in the darkness shall be heard in the light...*But I say unto you* [*being*] *my friends*, Be not afraid of them (accus.) that kill the body...."	"A bond-servant is not greater than his lord nor one sent (lit. apostle) greater than he that sent him. If ye know these things, blessed are ye if ye be doing them." xv. 14—15, 20 "*Ye are my friends* if ye be doing that which I command you. No longer do I call you bond-servants...but I have called you *friends*... Remember the word that I said to you, The bond-servant is not greater than his lord. If they persecuted me they will also persecute you."

---
[1] Moreover, in Lk. and Jn, the *first* thought has nothing to do with

[1785] Here Matthew uses first "bond-servant," and then "them of his household," to express the relation of the disciples to their Teacher. Luke, giving the words as two distinct utterances made at different times, makes no reference to "bond-servants" nor to "them of his household," but in the second he inserts, "*I say unto you [being] my friends.*" John agrees with Luke in mentioning "*friends*" in the second utterance; but he disagrees from Luke, and agrees with Matthew, in retaining the word "*bond-servant.*" He represents Jesus as saying to the disciples, in effect, "I called you once *bond-servants*, and indeed it is true that, if their lord be persecuted, the *bond-servants* must expect persecution: but now I call you *my friends*...."

[1786] In order to explain Matthew's omission of "I say unto you, my *friends* (dat.)," recourse may be had to the analogy of the Sermon on the Mount, where he frequently omits introductory clauses inserted by Luke stating the persons to whom, and the circumstances in which, the utterances were severally made, because he prefers to treat the whole as one continuous discourse. Moreover the Greek dative of "friends," following "to you," might easily be taken as vocative, and consequently as not very important. Indeed, if "my friends" occurred in the Aramaic original, it may have very well been actually vocative, but may have been interpreted by Luke as *implying* a reason for not fearing: "I say unto you, *my friends*,"—i.e. "since you are my friends," or "[being] my friends (φίλοις),"—"do not be afraid." This makes excellent sense, but translators might be excused for not rendering a vocative thus, and some, not seeing its force, might omit the noun.

[1787] This explanation however fails to take into account that Matthew here uses a word ("them of his household")

---

persecution; the inference, in Jn, from "not greater than his lord," is (Jn xiii. 16—17) that the disciple must serve his brethren as the Lord served them.

that might be taken as meaning "*relations*" or "*friends and relations*,"—a word, too, that is actually taken by him in this sense (quoting Micah) a little later on: "I came to set a man at variance against his father...and a man's foes [shall be] *they of his own household*[1]." In Micah, the Hebrew is "men of his house"; in Matthew, the Syriac has "sons of his house." Either of these terms might well be rendered "*friends*" in Greek. Suppose, then, that a Greek Evangelist attempted to explain to Greeks the words in Matthew, "A disciple is not above his teacher, nor a *bond-servant* above his lord...if they called the Master of the House Beelzebul, *how much more the men of his house! Fear them not therefore*...": might he not think it necessary to bring out the meaning of this ambiguous term "men of his house"? This he might do by calling attention to the fact that Jesus had previously used the term "*bond-servants*," and that this new term meant something different: "The Lord had before called them *bond-servants* but now He called them *friends*, saying, Fear them not..."?

[1788] According to this view John is intervening in the Double Tradition in order to bring out the full meaning of a doctrine that he conceived to be partially and imperfectly expressed by Matthew and Luke; and, while adopting Luke's phrase "my *friends*," he throws the essence of Matthew's version into the first person as the teaching of Christ, "I before called you bond-servants, but now I call you friends." A Greek would naturally take "bond-servant" as antithetical to "friend[2]." John perhaps regards "bond-servant," not as

---

[1] [1787 a] Mt. x. 36 quoting Mic. vii. 6 "The son dishonoureth the father...a man's enemies are *the men of his own house* (LXX οἱ ἐν τῷ οἴκῳ αὐτοῦ)." In the LXX of Esther, "*friends* (φίλοι)" is loosely used to denote the inner circle of the counsellors of the King or of Haman, Esth. i. 3, ii. 18, vi. 9 "princes," i. 13 the "wise men that knew the times," vi. 13 "wise men."

[2] [1788 a] This antithesis would be familiar to those whom Epictetus taught to say (iv. 3. 9) "I am *free* and a *friend of God*" (comp. iii. 22.

antithetical, but rather as inferior, and preparatory, to "friend." But that will be considered later on[1].

[1789] It is possible, and indeed probable, that our Lord repeated more than once His doctrine of encouragement under persecution: and a juxtaposition of "*servant*" and "*friend*" occurs in the passage in which Isaiah, after describing the making of an idol by "the carpenter" and "the goldsmith," encourages his countrymen in the name of Jehovah to refuse to conform to idolatry: "But thou, Israel my *servant*, Jacob whom I have chosen, the seed of Abraham (R.V.) my *friend*; thou whom I have taken hold of from the ends of the earth...*fear thou not*, for I am with thee[2]." This suggests a possibility that the doctrine of "*friendship*" with God, and of a distinction between His "*friends*" and His "*servants*," may have formed a larger part of the higher Jewish teaching, and also of Christ's Gospel, than is generally supposed.

---

95 and 24. 60). Not improbably, John had Epictetus in view in another use of the word "friend." Pilate, servilely truckling to the Jews, is intimidated by their cry (Jn xix. 12) "If thou let this man go, thou art not a *friend of Caesar*." Epictetus frequently satirises the man that is proud to call himself "a friend of Caesar" (a title resembling our "Right Honourable" applied to Privy Councillors): (iv. 1. 8—14) "I am of senatorial rank," says one, "and I am a *friend of Caesar*, and I have served as consul, and I have crowds of slaves...Who can put constraint on me, save Caesar, who is Lord of all?" To which the philosopher replies that, if this poor rich man can have *constraint put upon him* by Caesar, he is, by his own confession, a slave, his only distinction from common slaves being that he is—"a slave in a large house." Just so, he says, the servile Nicopolitans "have a way of shouting '*By Caesar's fortune, we are free*'!"

[1] Jesus says (Jn xv. 15) "*No longer do I call you* bond-servants," which suggests that the "bond-service" was recognised by Him as a rudimentary stage, and not condemned by Him as essentially bad.

[2] [1789 a] Is. xli. 8 "Israel, my *servant*," LXX παῖς μου, but the other translators δοῦλέ μου, "Abraham, my *friend*" (Ibn Ezra, "my *lover*"), LXX ὃν ἠγάπησα, Aq. ἀγαπητοῦ μου, Sym. τοῦ φίλου μου. Comp. 2 Chr. xx. 7 "the seed of Abraham thy *friend*," LXX σπέρματι Ἀ. τῷ ἠγαπημένῳ σου, *i.e.* "thy beloved seed of Abraham," al. τῷ φίλῳ, al. τοῦ φίλου.

[1790] Take, for example, the following parallel between the Fourth Gospel and Philo in which the essence of free service is defined:

Jn xv. 15

"The *bond-servant* knoweth not what his lord doeth: but I have called you *friends*: for all things that I heard from my Father I have made known unto you."

Philo i. 401

"For wisdom is God's *friend* (φίλον...θεῷ) rather than *bond-servant* (δοῦλον): wherefore also [the sacred writer] says clearly about Abraham 'Shall I hide [it] from Abraham my *friend*?'[1]"

Philo's reference is to the passage in Genesis where God reveals His purpose of destroying Sodom. The Hebrew omits "friend," having simply, "Shall I hide from Abraham that which I do?"; but the LXX has "from Abraham my *servant*" (παιδός, not "bond-servant"), and the Jerusalem Targum has "from Abraham *my friend*[2]." Without stopping to investigate the origin of the variations in quoting from, or translating, Genesis, we may take it to be almost a matter of demonstration that the implied Johannine definition of a free servant, or friend, of a "lord," as one that "knoweth what his lord doeth" is connected with the thought of Abraham "the *friend* of God," which pervades Jewish literature, and which has left its mark upon the most Jewish of our Canonical Epistles[3].

---

[1] [1790 a] Gen. xviii. 17, Philo has Μὴ ἐπικαλύψω ἐγὼ ἀπὸ Ἀβραὰμ τοῦ φίλου μου; where LXX has Μὴ κρύψω ἐγὼ ἀπὸ Ἀ. τοῦ παιδός μου ἃ ἐγὼ ποιῶ;

[2] The Targum has, for "friend," רחם, which closely resembles the last three letters of the preceding word "Abraham" (רהם).

[3] [1790 b] Jas ii. 23 "he was called *the friend of God*." From the Jews the name passed to the Arabians with such effect as to supplant the old name, "Hebron," of Abraham's burying place, known in modern times as El Khalil, "The Friend." It would be interesting to ascertain whether Epictetus was to any extent indebted to Jewish thought, or to Jewish expression (through Philo or other writers) for such sayings as that quoted above (1788 a) "I am *free* and a *friend of God*, that I may willingly obey Him."

[**1791**] These circumstances, no doubt, weaken the evidence for the view that John in his doctrine about the "friends" of Christ is alluding to the Double Tradition. For they seem to shew that Jewish doctrine about "the *friends* of God" and Christian doctrine about "the *friends* of Christ" may have been ampler than we supposed; and John may have been describing one part of this ample province while Matthew and Luke may have been describing another. Moreover, if the reader looks at the context of the passage in Isaiah he will see that *there is no antithesis between Israel the "servant" and Abraham the "lover" of God.* On the contrary, it is implied that *because* Israel is the true seed of Abraham the "*lover,*" *therefore* he is the "*servant.*" The honourable title of "servant" is given to the Messiah in the following words, "Behold my *servant* whom I uphold, my chosen in whom my soul delighteth[1]." Jews might say "The distinction between 'servant' and 'freeman' is not a true one with respect to God. We are all His servants. But some of us are His free and willing servants, others His slavish and unwilling servants. We recognise the difference; but whereas the Greeks can express this in two nouns, $\pi\alpha\hat{\imath}\varsigma$ and $\delta o\hat{\upsilon}\lambda o\varsigma$, we cannot, or at all events seldom do, in our Scripture."

[**1792**] This is perfectly true, and it confirms our hesitation in finding a real antithesis in the passage quoted from Matthew above ("A disciple is not above his teacher, *nor a bond-servant above his lord...*"). "*Bond-servant*" may have been used by Matthew here as we have found it used (**1789** *a*) by most of the translators in Isaiah where the LXX has "*servant,*" to mean "a devoted servant" of God. The two clauses, then, in Matthew, are more probably parallel than antithetical, and John would be wrong in finding an antithesis in them. But did he find one? If he had done so, and if he had used $\delta o\hat{\upsilon}\lambda o\varsigma$ in the sense of "servile," or "slavish," would

---

[1] Is. xlii. 1.

he have introduced our Lord as saying to the disciples, in effect, (Jn xv. 15) "*No longer do I call you 'slavish' or 'servile'*"? Much more probably John found among educated Greeks a misappreciation of the Jewish use of "bond-servant," which had led Luke to omit it in an important passage of the Double Tradition. And where Luke omitted, there—as is frequent in matters of importance—John intervened[1].

---

[1] [1792 a] The conclusion that Jn is here alluding to Mt. x. 24—5 in the Double Tradition is confirmed by the fact that elsewhere he seems to allude to passages not indeed in Mt.'s context but in Lk.'s parallels to Mt.'s context. Mt. x. 36—7 says "*A man's enemies* (ἐχθροί) [*shall be*] *they of his household*...he that loveth father or mother above me is not worthy of me." The italicized words might be paraphrased "*A man's haters must be his relations*," or, "*A man must hate his relations*." Lk. xiv. 26 says "If a man cometh unto me and *hateth not his own father and mother*... yea, and his *own life*...he cannot be my disciple," and we have seen above (**1450**) that John alludes to "*hating one's own life*."

[1792 b] The next verse in Mt. is, "Whosoever taketh (λαμβάνει) not his cross." The parall. Lk. has "*supporteth* (βαστάζει) *his own* (ἑαυτοῦ) cross." This last phrase occurs nowhere else in the Synoptists, who have in their Triple Tradition (Mk viii. 34, Mt. xvi. 24, Lk. ix. 23) "Let him *take up* (ἀράτω) his cross." In the narrative of the Crucifixion, no Synoptist uses the word "support," but the three—though not in exact agreement—describe Simon the Cyrenian as bearing the cross altogether or in part. Jn on the other hand expressly says that Jesus went forth (xix. 17) "*supporting* (βαστάζων) the cross *for himself* (ἑαυτῷ)." It is easy to conceive that such traditions as "whosoever would follow the Lord Jesus must take, or bear, *his* cross" may have been confused with "bear *His* cross," and such confusions may have led Luke to substitute "support *his own* cross" (like St Paul's "each man must bear *his own* burden"). Others may have objected to this emphasis. John may have thought that so emphatic a phrase was best reserved for our Saviour Himself—especially in view of heretical legends that Simon not only bore the cross but also suffered crucifixion in Christ's place. See **928** (i)—(x).

[1792 c] John's apparent interventions in the traditions about (1) "my friends," (2) "bond-servants," (3) "hating one's own life," all of which occur in a few verses of Matthew or in Luke's parallels, make it probable that he was also familiar with the phrase (4) "support one's own cross": and the cumulative evidence increases the probability that he intervenes in the first three passages.

§ 8. "*Standing in* (ἐν *or* εἰς) *the midst*" *applied to Jesus*

[1793] "In the midst" occurs in Mark and Matthew concerning the little child, whom Jesus "*made stand* (ἔστησεν) *in the midst of* them [*i.e.* the disciples]" as His representative[1], and in Mark and Luke concerning a man called by Jesus to stand "in the midst" of the synagogue, before being healed[2]. Matthew has it in Christ's promise to be with "two or three" of His disciples, "There am I *in the midst of* them," a tradition peculiar to himself, which is repeated at the close of his Gospel in a different form, "Behold I am *with* you[3]." The *Aboth* says, "When ten sit and are occupied in words of the Law the Shekinah is *among them*, for it is said, (Ps. lxxxii. 1) *God standeth in* the congregation of the mighty. And whence [is the same proved concerning] even five? Because it is said, He judgeth *in the midst* (LXX ἐν μέσῳ) of gods[4]." Thus, although Matthew does not mention "*standing in the midst*," we see that his doctrine about Christ's abiding presence might naturally be expressed thus in Jewish Tradition.

[1794] The Epistle to the Hebrews says, "He that is sanctifying and they that are being sanctified are all from

---

[1] [1793 a] Mk ix. 36, Mt. xviii. 2 ἔστησεν αὐτὸ ἐν μέσῳ αὐτῶν. The parall. Lk. ix. 47 has ἔστησεν αὐτὸ παρ' ἑαυτῷ. The action might remind a Jew of Deut. xviii. 15, "The Lord thy God will cause to stand up for thee a prophet *from the midst of thee*, of thy brethren, like unto me." Samuel anointed David (1 S. xvi. 13) "*in the midst of* his brethren." The Spirit of the Lord came on a prophet (2 Chr. xx. 15) "*in the midst of* the congregation." As the tree of life is (Gen. xx. 9) "*in the midst of* the garden," and (Ex. viii. 22) "the Lord *in the midst of* the earth," so an impartial judge must be (metaphorically) Ps. lxxxii. 1 "*in the midst of*" (R.V. among) those whom he judges, and a prophet (Is. vi. 5) "*in the midst of*" those to whom, or against whom, he testifies. (Ps. xxii. 22) "I will declare thy name unto my brethren, *in the midst of* the congregation will I praise thee."

[2] Mk iii. 3 ἔγειρε (Lk. vi. 8 + καὶ στῆθι) εἰς τὸ μέσον (Mt. om.).

[3] Mt. xviii. 20, xxviii. 20.

[4] *Aboth* iii. 9.

one. For this cause he is not ashamed to call them 'brethren,' saying, I will announce thy name to my brethren: *in the midst of the congregation will I sing hymns to* (ὑμνήσω) thee[1]." This is from the 22nd Psalm beginning "My God, my God, why hast thou forsaken me?" Justin Martyr, after quoting (*Tryph.* 98) Ps. xxii. 1—23 (including the words "*in the midst of the congregation will I sing hymns to thee*") says that Jesus "*Stood in the midst* (ἐν μέσῳ) of His brethren the Apostles...and (?) spending the time (διάγων)[2] with them, *sang hymns to* God," where the context ("who repented... after He rose from the dead") indicates that he does not refer to the "hymn" sung at the Eucharist[3], but to Luke's tradition that Christ "*stood in the midst* (ἐν μέσῳ)[4]" of the disciples after the Resurrection. In the Apocalypse, "the Lamb" is seen "standing *in the midst* of the elders," *i.e.* in the midst of the Church, or "walking *in the midst* of the seven candlesticks," *i.e.* in the midst of the Seven Churches; and the Oxyrhynchian Logia represent Jesus as saying "*I stood in the midst* of the world and I appeared to them in the flesh[5]."

[1795] Two Evangelists alone, Luke and John, apply the phrase "stood in the midst" to Jesus in their narratives.

---

[1] Heb. ii. 12, quoting Ps. xxii. 22.

[2] [1794 a] *Tryph.* 106. Διάγω also means "*nourish.*" Comp. Acts i. 4 "*being assembled together* with them," marg. "*eating* with them" (συναλιζόμενος) where Field rejects both renderings. If Justin refers to the period after the Resurrection, could he be reading, instead of συναλιζόμενος, συναλαλαζόμενος? Ἀλαλάζω is freq. in LXX, and sometimes = "sing in triumph," "shout in triumph." The act. and mid. fut. are interchanged in v. r. It might be supposed to represent the Heb. "Hallel."

[3] Mk xiv. 26, Mt. xxvi. 30 ὑμνήσαντες ἐξῆλθον, not in Lk.

[4] Lk. xxiv. 36. The *Acts of John*, however, says that before Jesus went forth to Gethsemane, He said (§ 11) "Let us sing a hymn to the Father" and "*placing Himself in the midst* (ἐν μέσῳ δὲ αὐτὸς γενόμενος)" bade them say Amen to His utterances.

[5] Rev. v. 6, ii. 1, comp. i. 13, vii. 17. The passage in the Logia, however, continues, "and I found all men eating and drinking...," so that it does not refer to the appearance of Christ after the Resurrection. It seems to describe the Incarnation.

Luke uses it only once concerning a manifestation of Christ after the Resurrection, to which, as we have seen (**1794**), Justin Martyr appears to refer. At the moment when the disciples were hearing the tidings "He hath appeared to Simon," suddenly "He himself stood *in the midst* of them." To convince them of His identity He said, "Have ye aught to eat ($\beta\rho\omega\sigma\iota\mu\text{ον}$)?" and ate some fish in their presence[1].

[**1796**] The Fourth Gospel begins with a kindred expression uttered by the Baptist, "There standeth fast ($\sigma\tau\eta\kappa\epsilon\iota$) *midst* ($\mu\epsilon\sigma\text{ος}$) of you one whom ye know not[2]," words probably (as suggested above (**1725** *a*)) intended to have a mystical allusion to the pre-existing and all-supporting Logos. The next application of the adjective to Jesus is in the crucifixion where John says that they crucified "Jesus *in the midst* ($\mu\epsilon\sigma\text{ον}$)[3]." Then, after the Resurrection, he says that Jesus "came and *stood in* (lit. to) *the midst*[4]," and gave the disciples the Holy Spirit and the power of remitting and retaining sins. On the next occasion, in order to convince Thomas, "cometh Jesus and *stood in* (lit. to) *the midst*[5]." But on neither of these occasions does He eat with the disciples nor they with Him: and for some reason or other, John uses the peculiar phrase "*to the midst*" and not Luke's phrase "*in the midst of them.*" On the third manifestation Jesus "stands," but not "in (lit. to) the midst": He "*stood* on (lit. to) the beach" of the Lake of Tiberias. There He asks a question rendered by R.V. in terms similar to those of the question recorded by Luke, "Have ye aught to eat ($\pi\rho\text{οσ}\phi\acute{α}\gamma\iota\text{ον}$)?[6]" But this rendering

---

[1] Lk. xxiv. 36—43. [2] Jn i. 26.

[3] Jn xix. 18. The Synoptists mention one malefactor on the "right" and another on the "left," and do not use $\mu\epsilon\sigma\text{ος}$. Jn does not here make these distinctions of "right" and "left."

[4] Jn xx. 19 $\tilde{\eta}\lambda\theta\epsilon\nu$ ὁ Ἰησοῦς καὶ ἔστη εἰς τὸ μέσον.

[5] Jn xx. 26.

[6] [**1796** *a*] Jn xxi. 5 (R.V.). Field "Have ye *taken* any *fish*?" Field shews that ἔχετε; regularly means "Have you [had] any [sport]?" "Have

is probably not quite accurate. And, instead of eating in their presence, He "comes" to them and gives them the food that He has provided.

[1797] If Luke's Gospel was authoritative, or even in wide circulation, at the time when John wrote, it is difficult to doubt that the latter wrote here with allusion to the former. And John's omission of all mention of (1) Christ's eating, and his parallel statement that (2) Christ gave food to the disciples, indicate that he believed the former tradition to have arisen out of a misunderstanding of the latter.

§ 9. *"Stooping (?) and looking in"*

[1798] We come now to the two words distinguished by bracketed numbers. The passage where they occur in Luke is enclosed by W.H. in double brackets, thus:

Lk. xxiv. 12—13

"[[But Peter having risen up ran to the tomb and, *having stooped (?) and looked* (παρακύψας), *seeth* (βλέπει) the linen *cloths* (ὀθόνια) alone (μόνα): and he departed to his home (πρὸς αὑτόν) wondering at that which had come to pass.]] And behold, two of them were going on that same day etc."

Jn xx. 3—11

"There went out therefore Peter and the other disciple and they began to come to the tomb. But the two were running together. And the other disciple ran first, more quickly than Peter, and came first to the tomb and, *having stooped (?) and looked* (παρακύψας), he *seeth* (βλέπει) lying [there] (κείμενα) *the linen cloths* (ὀθόνια). Howbeit he entered not in. There cometh therefore Simon Peter also, following him, and he entered into the tomb: and he beholdeth (θεωρεῖ) *the linen cloths* lying and the napkin (which had

---

you [caught] anything?" Steph. shews that προσφάγιον is a low-class word meaning something "eaten in addition [to bread]" and hence, more particularly, ὀψάριον, "fish." R.V. seems to have taken it as "[fit] for" (πρός) "eating" (φαγεῖν). The question arises whether Luke (xxiv. 41 "*Have* ye *aught to eat* (ἔχετέ τι βρώσιμον) here?") has made the same mistake. If so, ἔχετε interrog. ought to appear in the list of John-Luke agreements, marked with an asterisk.

Lk. xxiv. 12—13	Jn xx. 3—11
[Here follows the story of the journey to Emmaus.]	been upon his head) not lying with the linen cloths, but apart, rolled up into one place. Then therefore entered in the other disciple also, he that came first to the tomb: and he saw and believed.... The disciples therefore departed again to their own homes. But Mary was standing at the tomb outside weeping. While, therefore, she was weeping, she *stooped* (?) [*and looked*] into the tomb and beholdeth two angels...."

§ 10. *What does παρακύπτω mean?*

[1799] Παρακύπτω is translated above with a query "stooped and looked," nearly as R.V. But that is probably incorrect. In Greek of every kind and period, the word is applied to those who *take a rapid—but not necessarily careless— glance at anything* (1) out of a window, open door, hole of a cave, etc., or (2) in at a window, door, or other aperture. This is its meaning in Demosthenes, Aristophanes, Theocritus, and Lucian[1]. Hence Achilles Tatius applies it to youth, which just "*peeps up*" *and vanishes*[2]. Hence Demosthenes uses it of those who "*give just one glance*" to the affairs of Athens and then *go about their own business*: and Dio Cassius says "one cannot just *peep* at playing with empire and *then go back into one's hole*[3]." "When the weather won't let us sail," says Epictetus, "we sit on thorns, perpetually *glancing out*—which way is the wind[4]?" In LXX it means "*glancing out*, or, *in*"

---

[1] [1799 a] See Steph. In Lucian's Index it is always used with μόνον, μηδέ, or μικρόν (if we read προκύψας τῷ θριγκῷ (for παρακύψας) in *Dial. Mer.* 12, Vol. iii. p. 313) "just glancing," "not even a glance."

[2] Steph. qu. Achill. Tat. ii. 35 παρακύψαν μόνον οἴχεται. It is used of coy glances (Steph.) in Aristoph. *Pac.* 983, *Thesm.* 797—9, Theocr. iii. 17.

[3] Steph. Demosth. 46, 27, Dio Cass. 52, 10. [4] Epict. i. 1. 16 καθήμεθα σπώμενοι κ. παρακύπτομεν συνεχῶς τίς ἄνεμος πνεῖ;

(1804 c). In the description of Sisera's mother, who is perhaps *continuously* looking out of the window, Codex A substitutes διέκυπτεν for B's παρέκυψεν[1]. Philo uses παρακύπτω metaphorically, to note the absurdity of supposing that the "ignorant" can even "*glance into*, or, *catch a glimpse of*," the counsels of "an imperial soul[2]."

[1800] The Epistle of St James, at first sight, appears to use παρακύπτω, instead of ἐγκύπτω, to mean, "looking continuously upon," "peering intently into." But the writer is distinguishing those who perceive their own faces in a mirror, and go away and forget, from the man that first *glances at*, or, *catches a glimpse of*, the perfect law and then *abides* by it, being captivated by its beauty: "But he that hath *caught a glimpse of* the perfect law of liberty and hath abode by it, not letting himself become a forgetful hearer but a doer of work—he will be blessed in his doing[3]." The Epistle of St Peter speaks of "angels" as desiring to "*catch a glimpse of*" the developments of the mysteries of the prophesied redemption of mankind[4]. The context here suggests that the

---

[1] Judg. v. 28. Note the imperf., A also adds κ. κατεμάνθανεν.

[2] [1799 b] Philo ii. 554 ποῦ γὰρ τοῖς ἰδιώταις πρὸ μικροῦ θέμις εἰς ἡγεμονικῆς ψυχῆς παρακῦψαι βουλεύματα; Here πρὸ μικροῦ seems to mean that they cannot glance into them even "a little while before [their fulfilment]." This is the meaning assigned to πρὸ μικροῦ in Steph. (πρό) and in L.S. referring to Poll. i. 72.

[1799 c] Philo frequently uses other forms of κύπτω, mostly in metaphor, to describe the soul of man looking out, or up, or beyond, the bars of material nature into the spiritual world *e.g.* διακύπτω, ὑπερκύπτω, less freq. ἀνακύπτω and ἐκκύπτω (Philo i. 16, 471, 478 (lit.), 488, 570; ii. 17 (lit.), 44 (lit.), 62, 85, 195, 299, 540 (lit.), 546, 665). Steph. quotes προκύπτω of the mind (Sext. Emp. p. 441) "peering through the avenues of the senses as it were through chinks."

[3] [1800 a] Jas i. 25 ὁ δὲ παρακύψας εἰς νόμον τέλειον τὸν τῆς ἐλευθερίας καὶ παραμείνας. Perh. the context implies a contrast. Those who "*take careful note* (κατανοέω)" of their faces in the glass cannot, somehow, remember them for a moment. Some, "*catching a mere glimpse*" of the Perfect Law, abide, and cannot forget it. These are blessed.

[4] [1800 b] 1 Pet. i. 12 εἰς ἃ ἐπιθυμοῦσιν ἄγγελοι παρακύψαι. Hort

"angels" are good, but the difficulty of deciding whether they are good or bad is illustrated by the usage in the Acts of Thomas where the verb is used in consecutive chapters to describe first, a spectator "*glancing* (or, *peeping*) *into*" the several torture pits of hell, and then the attempts of the tortured souls to "*peep out of*" the cave in which they are imprisoned[1]. Παρακύπτω does not appear in any case to mean "stoop down and look at," "pore over," or "examine minutely[2]."

[1801] The Gospel of Peter says that the women, finding the sepulchre of Christ opened, "approached and *glanced in* there and saw there a young man sitting in the midst of the grave[3]." This may perhaps correspond to Luke's description of the women as "bending their faces to the earth" when they see "two men," after entering the tomb[4]; but it is also used

---

assumes that the angels "look down from heaven" as in Enoch ix. 1 παρέκυψαν ἐπὶ τὴν γῆν, but this is not certain, see 659. Hort says (*ad loc.*) "When used figuratively, it (*i.e.* π.) commonly implies a rapid and cursory glance, never the contrary. Here, however, nothing more seems to be meant than looking down out of heaven." In Enoch, the word means that the angels, hearing the cry of the oppressed come up to heaven, "glanced on the earth" and saw bloodshed everywhere. *Imprisoned* "angels" (Jude 6) might wish παρακύπτειν "peep *out*" (not "*in*") as below.

[1] [1800 c] Act. Thom. § 52—4 "He caused me to *peep into* (π. εἰς) each pit...and *peeping in* I saw mud and worms—*peeping into* which I saw souls...But many souls were *trying to peep out from it* (ἐκεῖθεν παρέκυπτον) wishing for a breath of air, but their keepers would not let them *peep out* (παρακύπτειν)."

[2] [1800 d] This meaning is reserved for ἐγκύπτω, Clem. R. 40 ἐγκεκυφότες εἰς τὰ βάθη τῆς θείας γνώσεως, 45 εἰς τὰς γραφάς, 53 εἰς τὰ λόγια τοῦ θεοῦ, Polyc. *Phil.* 3 (poring over (εἰς) the Epistles of St Paul), Clem. Hom. iii. 9 (dat.) Scriptures.

[3] [1801 a] Evang. Petr. 13 προσελθοῦσαι παρέκυψαν ἐκεῖ.

[4] [1801 b] Lk. xxiv. 3 εἰσελθοῦσαι indicates that the women had entered the tomb. Evang. Petr. speaks of them as "having approached (προσελθοῦσαι)." Could Lk. have understood παρακύπτω as "stooping down"? It would be less improb. that he should have read it as προκύπτω (see 1799 a).

by John to describe Mary as "*catching a glimpse* (lit.) *into* (εἰς) the tomb" and beholding "two angels." Finally, to come to the John-Luke passages under consideration, Luke describes Peter, near the tomb, as "*glancing in*," and "seeing the linen cloths alone" and "going to his home." John assigns the "*glancing in*," not to Peter, but to another disciple, who outran Peter. This disciple (John says) subsequently entered the tomb and "saw and believed"; Peter also entered and saw, but is not said to have "believed."

[1802] Although the two disciples have the same evidence before them, the Fourth Gospel here restricts the mention of "belief" to "the other disciple" ("*he believed*") implying that Peter did *not* "believe." It is not surprising that some authorities substitute "*they believed*[1]." But perhaps the earliest tradition taught that Peter believed in consequence of Christ's appearing to him ("He appeared to Cephas; then to the Twelve[2]")—whereas others had previously believed because they had "seen a vision of angels[3]" or had been enabled to "catch a glimpse of" the mystery of the Resurrection, and, as St James says, to "abide" in the possession of that truth. It will be observed that the bracketed passage in Luke, though it gives such prominence to Peter as to mention no companions[4], nevertheless does not say that Peter believed, but merely that he "went away to his home wondering."

---

[1] SS, Chrys., and a comment in Cramer *ad loc.* Codex ℵ, prob. by homoioteleuton, omits xx. 5 *b* and 6, so that it makes no mention of Peter's entering the tomb, and then alters "they knew" to "he knew" for consistency.

[2] 1 Cor. xv. 5.   [3] Lk. xxiv. 23.

[4] [1802 *a*] Contrast this with Lk. xxiv. 24 "*Some of those with us* went to the tomb." "*Those with him*" (and still more easily "*those with us*") might be confused in Hebrew with "*Simon.*" And this may explain Ign. *Smyrn.* § 3 "When He came to *those with Peter* (i.e. the Eleven) (τοὺς περὶ Πέτρον)." Hence we may explain conflations, and interchanges, of "those with him," "disciples," "the Eleven," "those with Peter," "Peter" etc. Mary, or the women, bring tidings of the Resurrection (Mk App. (1) xvi. 10) "to *those that had been with him*

[1803] The inconsistency in Luke, who in the bracketed passage mentions Peter alone, but, later on, "some of those with us," as going to the tomb, is an additional reason for supposing that the former passage is genuine, and that Luke copied it *verbatim* from early tradition, not altering the words although he knew that "Peter," in such traditions, often meant more than one disciple, and although he himself implies more than one later on. The bracketed words are omitted, it is true, by D, by several Latin MSS., and by other authorities: but almost all of these MSS. *place John before Luke in their pages*, and, after writing John's elaborate account, the scribes of these MSS. might naturally shrink from inserting Luke's account using the same rare words but in a narrative so curt and (as it would seem to them) so one-sided[1]. Moreover, in answer to those who maintain that the passage is interpolated in Luke from John, it may be urged that it is incredible that anyone but a heretic or a rejecter of the Fourth Gospel could interpolate such a truncated and falsified version of John's consistent narrative, without even taking the trouble to reconcile it with Luke's later statement ("some of those with us").

[1804] The most probable conclusion is, that the words in Luke are not an interpolation but an isolated tradition inserted by him in his Gospel, as he found it, without attempt to explain its exact meaning or to reconcile it with other traditions, and that John writes with allusion not only to Luke, but also to other traditions in which the rare word

---

(i.e. *with Jesus*)," (Mk App. (II)) "*to those with Peter*," (Lk. xxiv. 9) "to the Eleven and the rest." Perh. there is conflation in Mk xvi. 7 "to *his disciples* and *Peter*" (compared with the parall. Mt. xxviii. 7 "to *his disciples*") and in Lk. ix. 32 "But Peter and *those with him*." Note also Mk iv. 10 "*those with him* [Jesus] (οἱ περὶ αὐτόν) *with* (σύν) *the twelve*," parall. Mt. xiii. 10 "the *disciples*," Lk. viii. 9 "his *disciples*." Comp. the chapter on "Nos qui cum eo fuimus" in *Sons of Francis* by A. Macdonell (p. 27 foll.).

[1] The Diatessaron also omits the words.

under consideration was connected with "angels" and with the mystery of the Resurrection of Christ. Luke mentions "two disciples," immediately after this visit to the tomb, as having this mystery revealed to them, when their hearts had been opened to discern the Scriptures. John says that the two disciples that visit the tomb "knew not yet the Scriptures"; yet one of them was enabled to "catch a glimpse" of facts that led him to "see and believe," even before Peter had believed. Mary Magdalene attained yet more. She remained by the tomb weeping, and she "caught a glimpse (lit.) into [the spiritual revelation of] the tomb (παρέκυψεν εἰς τὸ μνημεῖον)," where she beheld, not "*linen cloths alone*," but "*angels*," preparing the way for a full revelation of the risen Saviour. John is perhaps alluding to Luke in his detail of the "*linen cloths*" lying "*apart*" from the head covering, which seems to be an interpretation of Luke's "*linen cloths alone (μόνα).*" But the question before us is whether John is writing allusively to Luke in respect of the words παρακύπτω and ὀθόνια. To this the preceding investigations give an affirmative answer. And, as in the instances of Ἄννας, ἐκμάσσω, ἀποβαίνω, ἔστη εἰς μέσον, so as regards παρακύπτω and ὀθόνια, John appears to be not only allusive, but also corrective[1].

---

[1] **[1804 *a*]** W.H. also enclose in double brackets (*a*) Lk. xxiv. 36 καὶ λέγει αὐτοῖς, Εἰρήνη ὑμῖν, (*b*) xxiv. 40 καὶ τοῦτο εἰπὼν ἔδειξεν αὐτοῖς τὰς χεῖρας καὶ τοὺς πόδας. Comp. (1) Jn xx. 19 καὶ λέγει αὐτοῖς, Εἰρήνη ὑμῖν, καὶ τοῦτο εἰπὼν ἔδειξεν καὶ τὰς χεῖρας καὶ τὴν πλευρὰν αὐτοῖς. In Lk., D and the best Lat. MSS. om. both *a* and *b*. SS om. *b*. Lk. never uses the historic present λέγει (freq. in Mk and Jn) of Jesus. If therefore (*a*) is genuine, it was prob. inserted by Lk. from some ancient tradition, which Lk. preferred not to revise or alter (**1803**). The Latin MSS. may have omitted it because Lk.'s text goes on to say that the disciples "were afraid," and such fear would more naturally precede, than follow, the words "Peace be unto you." As to (*b*), it could not have been interpolated from Jn without the violent alteration of πλευράν to πόδας, which seems improbable. But it may have been a genuine insertion of Lk.—perh.

added by him in a late edition of which there were only a few copies—omitted by the Latin MSS. because Jn's account seemed preferable.

[1804 b] It is probable that Jn wrote with a view to these traditions of Lk. and especially to Lk.'s tradition that our Lord said "*Handle me* (ψηλαφήσατέ με)" to the Eleven. According to Jn there was no mention of "handling" to the assembled disciples, until Thomas had refused to believe without the evidence of touch, for which he was rebuked in a second manifestation. The word "handle" occurs in 1 Jn i. 1 "and our hands *handled*," probably attesting the genuine Incarnation against heretics of Gnostic tendencies, who asserted that Christ had not come in the flesh. It does not appear to refer, as the word does in Lk., to any actual "handling" of the Lord's body after the Resurrection. St Paul uses it in a bold metaphor in the Acts xvii. 27 "to seek God, if haply they might *handle him* (or, *feel him with their hands*) and [thus] find him."

[1804 c] Παρακύπτω, in LXX—apart from Judg. v. 28, where (**1799**) A reads διέκυπτεν, and from 1 K. vi. 4 θυρίδας παρακυπτομένας Theod. διακυπτομένας—means "looking through a window," Gen. xxvi. 8 of Abimelech seeing Isaac with Rebecca, 1 Chr. xv. 29 of Michal seeing David dancing, Prov. vii. 6 of the "strange woman," whom the LXX erroneously regards as looking at the young man passing in the street, Cant. ii. 9 of a lover in the street looking through the windows of the house of his beloved. In Sir. xxi. 23 it is used of a fool prying through an open door (paradoxically used in a good sense in Sir. xiv. 23). The Heb. word regularly rendered παρακύπτω, *is never thus rendered when applied to God looking out of heaven*, e.g. Ps. xiv. 2, liii. 2 (comp. lxxxv. 12), Lam. iii. 50 διακύπτω, Ps. cii. 19 ἐκκύπτω etc.

[1804 d] The Syriac of παρακύπτω in Jn xx. 5, 11 and Lk. xxiv. 12 is simply "look" (without "stoop"). The Latin versions have (Jn xx. 5) *a*(?) "proscultans," *b* and *ff* "se inclinasset et prospexisset," *d* and *e* "prospiciens," *f* "se inclinasset"; (Jn xx. 11) *a* "...dspexit" (?[a]dspexit), *b* and *f* "inclinavit se et prospexit," *d* and *e* "prospexit," *f* "inclinavit se et prospexit." Lk. xxiv. 12 is om. by *a*, *b*, *d* (with D) and *e*; *f* has "procumbens." In Jn xx. 11, Chrys. throws no light, but Cramer has (from Euseb. of Cæs.) ἔτι δὲ καὶ ἀπὸ πολλοῦ λόγου παρέκυπτεν, where the imperf. as in Judg. v. 28 (A) perh. denotes (**1799**) continuousness.

CHAPTER IV

WORDS PECULIAR TO JOHN, MARK, AND MATTHEW

§ 1. *Introductory remarks*

[1805] Antecedently we might expect that the number of Johannine words peculiar to Mark and Matthew would be smaller than the number peculiar to Mark alone. Mark's style is occasionally uncouth, and, where Matthew corrects it, John cannot be identical with both. Take, for example, the narrative of the crown of thorns:

Mk xv. 17 (lit.)	Mt. xxvii. 28—9 (lit.)	Jn xix. 2 (lit.)
"And they put on (ἐνδιδύσκουσιν) him purple (πορφύραν) and place round (περιτιθέασιν) him having woven a thorn[y] (ἀκάνθινον) crown."	"And having put off from him [his own clothes]¹ (ἐκδύσαντες αὐτόν) a scarlet cloak (χλαμύδα κοκκίνην)¹ they placed round (περιέθηκαν) him and having woven a crown from thorns (ἐξ ἀκανθῶν) they placed [it] on (ἐπέθηκαν)² his head."	"...having woven a crown from thorns (ἐξ ἀκανθῶν)³ they placed it on (ἐπέθηκαν) his head (dat.) and a purple garment they clothed him withal (ἱμάτιον πορφυροῦν περιέβαλον αὐτόν)."

---

[1] V. r. "having put *on him*" and "purple garment and scarlet cloak."
[2] W.H. ἐπέθηκαν ἐπί, B περιέθηκαν ἐπί, lit. "placed it round on."
[3] [1805 a] This passage well illustrates the danger of arguing from mere statistics apart from circumstances. In the Jn-Mk list, ἀκάνθινος

[1806] WORDS PECULIAR

[1806] Here, there seems to have been a very early confusion between ΕΝΔΥΩ "put on," and ΕΚΔΥΩ "put off," and between "*placing* a purple garment *round*" the body and "*placing* a crown of thorns *round*" the head. Mark uses "place *round*" concerning the crown. Matthew uses "place *on*" concerning the crown, and, to make the distinction quite clear, adds "*the head.*" John also, like Matthew, has "placed it *on his head.*" Like Matthew, too, he has the phrase "having woven *from thorns*," where Mark has "*thorny.*" It is very probable that John accepted these corrections of Mark from Matthew[1]: but in any case the result is that the *three* writers do not agree together in the exact use of the verb of crowning ("put on" or "put round") or as regards the construction of the crown (Mk "thorny," Mt.-Jn "from thorns").

[1807] Bearing these facts in mind we may well regard the number of words peculiar to the three Evangelists as large, and the proportion of words marked † in the appended list as surprisingly large. Endeavouring to classify them, we find that one is a proper name, "Golgotha[2]"; and another is a technical term, "Hosanna[3]." The parallel Luke in both passages gives the substance of Mark-Matthew but omits "Golgotha" and "Hosanna." Perhaps some confusion between "skull" and "place of skull" induced Luke to omit

---

appeared, because of Jn xix. 5 "wearing the *thorny* crown." The *adjective* occurs nowhere but in Mk xv. 17, Jn xix. 5. But the *noun*, and the whole phrase, "*having woven a crown from thorns,*" occur both in Mt. and in Jn. The Jn-Mt. list, however, could not include "thorn," as the word (occurring in the Parable of the Sower in Mk-Mt.-Lk.) is not peculiar to Jn and Mt.

[1] [1806 *a*] As regards Jn xix. 2 "clothed (περιέβαλον)," it happens that Lk. xxiii. 11 (περιβαλὼν ἐσθῆτα λαμπράν) has this very word to denote Herod's clothing Christ with gorgeous raiment in mockery. Jn may have had this in mind. Περιβάλλω, however, is a more appropriate word than περιτίθημι to express clothing except as applied to a scarf or short cloak placed round the neck. Steph. quotes Herodian iii. 7. 12 τὴν χλαμύδα περιέθεσαν.

[2] Γολγοθά, see **1810**, note 4.   [3] Ὡσαννά, see **1816** *b*.

the former: and some doubt about the fitness of such a term as " Hosanna " in a Gospel for educated Greeks unacquainted with Hebrew may have induced him to omit the latter.

[1808] Apart from the Passion, the only words of importance are "money-changer[1]" in the Purification of the Temple, and "sell[2]" in the Anointing of Christ by a woman. A third, "evening[3]"—unimportant unless evidence should shew that the word may point to original symbolism—is found in the Walking on the Waters. In all these cases a reason for John's intervention may be found in Luke's omission. The latter omits, in his account of the Purification, the detail about the "money-changers"; and he altogether omits the narrative of the Walking on the Waters, and substitutes for Mark's narrative of the Anointing another of an entirely different tendency.

[1809] In the Passion, the words marked † are "cohort[4]," "crown [of thorns][5]", "plait[6]," "praetorium[7]," "put round," and "sponge[8]." In every case, Luke has omitted not only each word but also the whole narrative containing the word. In Luke, there is no "crown of thorns." The mocking of the "cohort" is either omitted, or replaced by an entirely different story concerning the soldiers of Herod Antipas, whose "palace" he perhaps identifies with the Synoptic "praetorium." The incident of the "sponge" full of vinegar —explained by John (1813 c) in connexion with "hyssop," perhaps originally the hyssop-bunch used on the Passover night—Luke wholly omits. This is not the place to consider whether John is right in all his interventions: the object now is merely to demonstrate that John's agreements with Mark and Matthew coincide almost in each case with omissions or deviations of Luke.

---

[1] Κολλυβιστής, see 1812 b.
[2] Πιπράσκω, see 1814 a.
[3] Ὀψία, see 1813 a.
[4] Σπεῖρα, see 1815 c.
[5] Στέφανος, see 1805—6.
[6] Πλέκω, see 1814 b.
[7] Πραιτώριον, see 1814 c.
[8] Περιτίθημι and σπόγγος, see 1813 c.

JOHN-MARK-MATTHEW AGREEMENTS[1]

		Mk	Mt.	Jn		Mk	Mt.	Jn
[1810]	ἀληθής (1727 d)	1	1	14	ἀναχωρέω[2]	1	10	1
	ἀπώλεια[3]	1	2	1	ἀρχή (Chri.) (1708)	3	4	4
	† Γολγοθά[4]	1	1	1	γυμνός[5]	2	4	1
	δεῦτε[6]	3	6	2	διάκονος[7]	2	3	3
[1811]	δόλος[8]	2	1	1	ἐμβριμάομαι[9]	2	1	2

[1] [1810 a_1] No word has an asterisk attached to it in this list because no word is used by Jn in a different sense from that which it has in Mk-Mt. : † denotes that the word not only has the same meaning in Jn and Mk-Mt. but also occurs in parallel passages : ?† indicates quasi-parallelism, on which see **1817**; the only word thus marked is σπεῖρα, "cohort." The list does not include parts of speech used in a special sense, e.g. διά with accus. of person, "for the sake of" (1721 m).

[2] Ἀναχωρέω, "retire," Mk iii. 7 (Mt. xii. 15), Jn vi. 15.

[3] [1810 a] Ἀπώλεια, in Mt. vii. 13, Jn xvii. 12, means "(spiritual) destruction," and Jn xvii. 12 calls Judas Iscariot "the son of *destruction*." In the parall. to Mk xiv. 4, Mt. xxvi. 8 "Why this *destruction* or *waste*?" Jn xii. 4 mentions "*Judas Iscariot*." The Original may have contained some mention of "*destruction*," variously interpreted as (Mk-Mt.) "*waste*," (Jn) "[son of] *destruction*."

[4] Γολγοθά, i.e. "skull." Mk xv. 22, Mt. xxvii. 33, Jn xix. 17. The parall. Lk. xxiii. 33 simply gives "skull," and not the Heb. equivalent.

[5] [1810 b] Γυμνός, "naked," in Mt. only in a Parable xxv. 36 "*naked* and ye clothed me" (rep. xxv. 38—44). In Mk xiv. 51—2 (twice) it refers to a young man deprived of his "linen garment"; in Jn xxi. 7, to Peter, "naked," but "girding himself" before entering his Master's presence.

[6] [1810 c] Δεῦτε, "*hither*," in (a) Mk vi. 31 "[Come] *hither* ye by yourselves into a desert place and rest (or, refresh yourselves) a little," (b) Mt. xi. 28, "[Come] *hither* unto me all that are weary...and I will give you rest (or, refreshment)," and (c) Jn xxi. 12 "[Come] *hither*, break your fast," occurs in words of Christ inviting the disciples to "take refreshment" (ἀνάπαυσιν, -ομαι), or to "break their fast": (a) is in the Triple Tradition without parall. in Mt.-Lk., (b) is in Mt.'s Single Tradition, immediately after a passage of the Double Tradition (Mt. xi. 27, Lk. x. 22 "All things were delivered to me by my Father..."), (c) in Jn, refers to the period after the Resurrection.

[7] Διάκονος, "minister." In the parall. to Mk x. 43 διάκονος, Lk. xxii. 26 has διακονῶν, so that, practically, this word is common to the Four Gospels (1717 d—g) in Christ's Doctrine of Service.

[8] Δόλος, "guile," Mk vii. 22, xiv. 1 (Mt. xxvi. 4), Jn i. 47.

[9] [1811 a] Ἐμβριμᾶσθαι is in Mk xiv. 5 (R.V.) "*murmured against*

	Mk	Mt.	Jn		Mk	Mt.	Jn
ἐπαύριον (1717 h)	1	1	5	θάλασσα (τῆς Γ.)[1]	2	2	1

(dat.) her." It describes persecutors (Euseb. v. 1. 60) "*roaring*" and gnashing their teeth, madmen (Steph. iii. 825 A) μανιώδεις καὶ ἐμβριμούμενοι. Lucian i. 484 couples ἐνεβριμήσατο ἡ Βριμώ with "Cerberus barking." The vb. and der. nouns describe God's anger in Ps. vii. 12 (Aq.), Is. xvii. 13 (Sym.), Ezek. xxi. 31 (Theod.) etc. Comp. Dan. xi. 30 (LXX).

[1811 b] In Mk i. 43, Mt. ix. 30 it is applied to Jesus (R.V. txt) "*strictly* (marg. *sternly*) *charging*" those whom He has healed. But Gk. usage seems to demand some such rendering as "roar"—used of Jehovah (R.V.) in Jer. xxv. 30 (*bis*), Hos. xi. 10 (*bis*), Joel iii. 16, Amos i. 2.

Jn applies it to Jesus twice (xi. 33—8), describing how, when He saw Mary and the Jews weeping for Lazarus, (1) ἐνεβριμήσατο τῷ πνεύματι καὶ ἐτάραξεν ἑαυτὸν καὶ......Ἰησοῦς οὖν πάλιν (2) ἐμβριμώμενος ἐν ἑαυτῷ ἔρχεται εἰς τὸ μνημεῖον. According to the analogy of the dative in the three Synoptic instances, the dat. τῷ πνεύματι should be the object of the verb; and this is not inconsistent with a parallelism between τῷ πνεύματι and ἐν ἑαυτῷ, for if anyone "roars against" his own spirit, he may be said to be doing it "in himself," *i.e.* not against another. But the meaning is uncertain and perhaps intended by the Evangelist to be so, except so far as it contains an allusion to, and perhaps a protest against, the tradition of Mk and Mt. (discarded by Lk.) that Jesus "*roared against*" those whom He healed—traditions perhaps based on a statement that He "cried out against" unclean spirits or diseases, not against the diseased.

[1811 c] As regards the positive Johannine meaning, if "spirit" is the object of "*roared against*," some might suppose that the Logos is regarded as rebuking Himself and forcing Himself to weep and to be troubled in sympathy with the friends of Lazarus, although He knows that Lazarus is not really dead. But we have to compare τῷ πνεύματι here with the only other Johannine use of it (Jn xiii. 21) "he was troubled *in the* (i.e. his) *spirit*." This suggests that John does not follow the grammatical construction of the Synoptists in the use of this rare verb, but that he uses it absolutely, without expressing an object, first, "roaring *in his spirit*," and then "roaring again *in himself*." If so, the Evangelist leaves it to us to imagine what the Messiah is "*roaring against*." Presumably, it is against all the evil that makes men slaves instead of being the free children of God. One aspect of this is death, through fear of which men were (Heb. ii. 15) "all their lifetime subject to bondage." See also (1727 b) "trouble."

[1] [1811 d] Θάλασσα τῆς Γ., "*Sea of Galilee*," is used by Jn (vi. 1) followed by "*Tiberias*," so as to explain its meaning. Lk. substitutes "*lake*" whenever that sea is mentioned or implied. Jn calls it merely (xxi. 1) "Tiberias" when he connects it with the manifestation of the risen Saviour.

		Mk	Mt.	Jn		Mk	Mt.	Jn
	θαρσέω[1]	2	3	1	θλίψις[2]	3	4	2
[1812]	ἴδε[3]	9	4	15	† κολλυβιστής[4]	1	1	1
	λυπέομαι	2	6	2	μανθάνω	1	3	2
	μεθερμηνεύω	3	1	2	μικρόν (1716 b)	2	2	9
[1813]	νίπτω (1728 a)	1	2	13	νοέω[5]	3	4	1
	† ὀψία[6]	5	6	2	παράγω[7]	3	3	1
	πέραν (τοῦ Ἰορδ.)[8]	2	3	3	† περιτίθημι[9]	3	3	1

[1] [1811 e] Θαρσέω, "be of good cheer," in Jn, only xvi. 33 "*Be of good cheer*, I have overcome the world." In Mk vi. 50, Mt. xiv. 27 "*Be of good cheer* (θαρσεῖτε), it is I, be not afraid," Jn (vi. 20) omits θαρσεῖτε. Θαυμαστός, "wonderful," should have been inserted here, occurring in Mk xii. 11, Mt. xxi. 42 (quoting Ps. cxvii. 23) and in Jn ix. 30.

[2] [1811 f] Θλίψις, "tribulation," is used by Jn only in xvi. 21, 33 "remembereth no more the *anguish*," "In the world ye have *tribulation*." In Mk iv. 17, Mt. xiii. 21 "*tribulation* or persecution," Lk. viii. 13 has "trial" or "temptation" (πειρασμός).

[3] [1812 a] Ἴδε, "see!" is never used by Mk and Mt. in parallel passages, nor by Jn in any parall. either to Mk or to Mt.

[4] [1812 b] Κολλυβιστής, "moneychanger," occurs in the Purification of the Temple in Mk xi. 15, Mt. xxi. 12, Jn ii. 15. But Jn places the Purification at the beginning, Mk-Mt. towards the end, of Christ's preaching.

[5] Νοέω, "perceive," in Jn, only in quotation Jn xii. 40 (Is. vi. 10).

[6] [1813 a] Ὀψία, "evening," occurs in Jn (1) in the Walking on the Waters, Mk vi. 47, Mt. xiv. 23—4, Jn vi. 16, (2) in the first Manifestation of the risen Saviour to the assembled disciples, Jn xx. 19. Luke has a parallel to the latter, but not to the former. In Mk-Mt.'s version of the Walking on the Waters, the disciples fear because they think Him "*a phantasm*" (SS "devil"); in Lk.'s version of the Manifestation they fear because they think He is "*a spirit*," D "*phantasm*," Ign. *Smyrn.* 3 "*bodiless demon*." Jn has no mention of "a spirit" or "phantasm" in either narrative.

[7] Παράγει, "pass by," occurs in Mt. xx. 30, Jn ix. 1, in the Healing of the Blind, concerning Jesus "passing by," but in quite different circumstances.

[8] [1813 b] Πέραν τοῦ Ἰορδάνου, "beyond Jordan." Lk. prob. om. the term as ambiguous, see 1 K. iv. 24 R.V. "*on this side* (marg. *beyond*) *the river*," LXX πέραν τοῦ π. Ezr. iv. 16, 17, 20 "*beyond the river*" is parall. to 1 Esdr. ii. 24, 25, 27 "in Celosyria (or Syria) and Phenice."

[9] [1813 c] Περιτίθημι, "put round," is in Mk xv. 36, Mt. xxvii. 48, Jn xix. 29 about the offering of the vinegar by means of a "sponge." Perhaps Mk-Mt. took a "hyssop-bunch," of which the "sponge" may have been composed, as a stalk of hyssop. See *The Fourfold Gospel*.

	Mk	Mt	Jn		Mk	Mt	Jn
[1814] † πιπράσκω¹	1	3	1	† πλέκω²	1	1	1
πλήρωμα	3	1	1	πολλάκις	2	2	1
πορνεία	1	3	1	† πραιτώριον³	1	1	4
[1815] ‡ πρωί⁴	5+[1]	2+[1]	2	'Ραββεί	3	4	8
?† σπεῖρα⁵	1	1	2	† σπόγγος			
				(1813 c)	1	1	1

¹ [1814 a] Πιπράσκω, "sell," is in Mk xiv. 5, Mt. xxvi. 9, Jn xii. 5, about the perfume that "could have been *sold*" for (Mk-Jn) "300 denarii," (Mt.) "much."

² [1814 b] Πλέκω, "plait," is in Mk xv. 17, Mt. xxvii. 29, Jn xix. 2 concerning the crown of thorns.

³ [1814 c] Πραιτώριον, "praetorium," or "palace," occurs in Mk xv. 16, Mt. xxvii. 27 as the place to which the soldiers take Jesus, *after* Pilate had pronounced sentence, where they clothe Him with purple and crown Him with thorns, just before the Crucifixion. Jn xviii. 28 mentions it as the place to which the soldiers take Jesus from Caiaphas to Pilate for trial, and from which Pilate brings Jesus out clothed in purple and wearing the crown of thorns *before* pronouncing sentence. It is implied that Jesus is led back to it, as Pilate (xix. 9) "entered into the praetorium *again*" and there speaks to Jesus. Luke never mentions the "praetorium," nor the "crown of thorns," but represents *Herod* as having clothed Jesus in "bright raiment." The Acts mentions the word once in Acts xxiii. 35 "Having bidden him to be kept in *Herod's Praetorium*." It is possible that Luke took the "Praetorium" in Jerusalem mentioned by Mk-Mt. as being *Herod's* "*palace*." This might induce John to emphasize the meaning of the word so as to correct Luke's error. On the misunderstanding that seems to have led Luke to introduce Herod in the narrative, see 56, 502—3.

⁴ [1815 a] Πρωί "early" (marked ‡ because it may refer to the same event in Mk-Jn, but certainly does not in Mt.-Jn), in Mk xvi. 2 "very *early*," and in Jn xx. 1 "*early*, it being still dark," is used about the visit of the women (Jn mentions Mary Magdalene alone) to Christ's tomb. Mk App. xvi. 9 "having risen *early*" is used about Christ's manifestation to Mary Magdalene.

[1815 b] In describing the trial, Mk xv. 1 describes the Sanhedrin as assembling "*straightway early*" i.e. immediately on dawn, while Jn xviii. 28 uses "*early*," perhaps meaning a somewhat later hour, to describe the leading of Jesus from Caiaphas to Pilate.

⁵ [1815 c] Σπεῖρα, "cohort," is not mentioned by Mk xv. 16, Mt. xxvii. 27 till after Pilate's sentence when "the whole *cohort*" is "called together" to mock the condemned. Jn mentions it earlier as having been (xviii. 3) "taken" by Judas to arrest Jesus, and as (xviii. 12) "seizing"

[1816] WORDS PECULIAR

	Mk	Mt.	Jn		Mk	Mt.	Jn
† στέφανος (1805—6)	1	1	2	? συνσταυρόω[1]	1	1	1
[1816] τέρας	1	1	1	σχίσμα[2]	1	1	3
ὑγιής (1728 e)	1	1	6	τηρέω (1714 h)	1	6	18
				ὑπάγω (metaph.)[3]	1	1	c. 18
χειμών	1	1+[1]	1	χωρέω	1	3	3
χωρίον	1	1	1	† ὡσαννά[4]	2	3	1

§ 2. *Absence of Quasi-parallels*

[1817] Comparing this list with previous ones we find the number of quasi-parallels (*i.e.* words marked ? † because though the word is the same the context is altered in such a way as to imply disagreement) very small indeed, only one (σπεῖρα) being thus marked. There are more quasi-parallels in the John-Mark list and in the John-Luke list. The reason for their absence here is, perhaps, that this list represents the cases where John agrees with *not Mark alone but Mark supported by Matthew*. The combined evidence of Mark and Matthew might seem to John too weighty to reject in the details of such narratives as the Purification of the Temple

---

Him; and, when he comes to describe the mocking, he simply mentions "the soldiers."

It has been suggested (1365) that John may have been led to infer that Judas "received *a cohort*" from a confusion of the tradition that he "received *a sign*"—"sign" and "cohort" (in the form σημαια) being similar Greek words. But Mt. xxvii. 27 συνήγαγον ἐπ' αὐτὸν ὅλην τὴν σπεῖραν, "they gathered together *against him* the whole of the cohort" is an ambiguous expression. It might very well have been understood as meaning "They gathered together the whole of the cohort *to take* Jesus," and perhaps John understood it thus.

[1] Συνσταυρόω, see 1817 *c*.
[2] [1815 *d*] Σχίσμα, "rent," "schism," in Mk ii. 21 (Mt. ix. 16) "a worse rent," lit., but in parable. In Jn vii. 43, ix. 16, x. 19, it describes a "schism" among the Jews, some favouring, some rejecting, Christ.
[3] [1816 *a*] Ὑπάγω (metaph.) "depart," "go home," Mk xiv. 21, Mt. xxvi. 24, "the Son of man *departeth* (Lk. xxii. 22 πορεύεται)." On ὑπάγω and πορεύομαι, see 1652—64.
[4] [1816 *b*] Ὡσαννά, "Hosanna," Mk xi. 9—10, Mt. xxi. 9 (rep. xxi. 15), Jn xii. 13, is parall. to Lk. xix. 38 "in heaven peace and glory (1807)."

and the Passion. And in points that might be called matters of taste, *e.g.* the question whether "Hosanna" should be retained or paraphrased in Greek Gospels, the usage of Mark when confirmed by Matthew might decide John to adopt the Jewish term in preference to the paraphrase in Luke. There are no words marked * as being used in a different sense by John from the sense in Mark and Matthew[1].

---

[1] **[1817 *a*]** Χωρέω, "find room for," "hold," is the nearest approach to such a word, for it also means "go" in Mt. xv. 17 but not perhaps in Jn except in viii. 37 (R.V. txt) "*hath* not *free course* in you." Prob. however Field is right in upholding A.V. (R.V. marg.) "*hath* no *place* in you." He compares Alciphr. *Epist.* iii. 7 where a doctor "wonders where and how food finds a place in a glutton's stomach."

[1817 *b*] For the Jn-Mk-Mt. use of "sea" in "sea of Galilee," and of "beyond" in "beyond Jordan," see θάλασσα (**1811** *d*) and πέραν (**1813** *b*).

[1817 *c*] Συνσταυρόω, "crucify together with," might perhaps have been marked ?† or even †. It occurs in Mk xv. 32, Mt. xxvii. 44 shortly before Christ's death, but in Jn xix. 32 shortly after it. In Mk Mt. it means "crucified *with*" *Jesus*, but Jn applies it to the second malefactor "crucified *with*" *the first malefactor.* See **1678**.

CHAPTER V

WORDS PECULIAR TO JOHN, MARK, AND LUKE

§ 1. *Introductory remarks*

[1818] Antecedently, if we knew nothing about the Three Gospels except that Matthew and Luke borrowed from Mark, and nothing about the Fourth except that it was written at a time when the Three had become authoritative, we might expect the number of Johannine words peculiar to Mark and Luke, and also those marked † as being in parallel passages, to be as large as the same numbers in the John-Mark-Matthew list.

[1819] But Luke follows Mark most closely in narratives of a thaumaturgic character and especially in exorcisms; and these are just the subjects that John avoids or passes lightly over. Moreover, Luke, even where following Mark closely, alters low-class Greek words such as κράβαττος, which John retains. And generally, since we find John not only supporting Mark when Luke deviates from him, but also taking different views from Luke, we ought to be prepared to find the number of John-Mark-Luke agreements small, and the number of parallelisms very small indeed.

§ 2. *"Latchet," "spices," "rouse up"*

[1820] And this is the case. Only one word, ἱμάς, "latchet," is marked † without query, occurring in the Baptist's description of the coming Deliverer, the "latchet" of whose shoe he declares himself unworthy to loose. Matthew, instead of "loosing the shoe-latchet," has "bear the shoes," perhaps blending together the performance of two menial services as explained in the foot-note (**1833** *d*). This deviation of Matthew from Mark, while Luke and John adhere to the word "latchet," accounts for the one Johannine word in the following list, parallel and peculiar to Mark and Luke.

[**1821**] The word "spices," ἀρώματα, marked ?†, is of interest, although not exactly parallel. In Mark and Luke it refers to "*spices*" prepared by the women for the body of Christ. But Matthew, though closely agreeing with Mark in the context, makes no mention of "spices," nor of any preparations for embalming on their part. John uses the word concerning the "*spices*" actually used by Joseph and Nicodemus in the burial of Christ: and, as he speaks of these, and makes no mention of "spices" in his account of the visit of the women to the tomb, we are led to infer that he agreed with Matthew that the women came simply "to behold the tomb." John appears to be tacitly correcting what seemed to him wrong in Mark and Luke by inserting what seemed to him right (**1832** *b*).

[**1822**] The word διεγείρω, "rouse up," though not marked †, derives interest from its extreme rarity (as indicated in the foot-note (**1832** *c*)) and from the possibility that it may point to some explanation of Luke's omission of the story of Christ walking on the water, which John inserts. On the other hand John omits the story of Christ falling asleep in the boat and awaking and rebuking the storm, which Luke inserts. And this rare word διεγείρω is used by Mark and Luke in the one narrative to describe *Jesus*, but by John in the other to describe the *sea*, as being "roused up."

§ 3. *Mark, Luke, and John, on "rejection"*

[**1823**] The word ἀθετέω, "reject" or "set at naught," is nowhere parallel in Mark and Luke, but it occurs in Luke and John, as will be seen below, in the phrases "he that *rejecteth you*," and "he that *rejecteth me*," with words of warning as to the consequences of rejection.

[1824] Mark uses it in a saying of the Lord that the Pharisees "*reject the word of God*" *in order that they may keep their own tradition*; that is to say, they allow a man to break the commandment about honouring one's father, under the shelter of the word "Corban." Matthew, too, has this. But, besides other deviations, Matthew uses "*transgress*" instead of "*reject*[1]."

[1825] The difference between Luke and John is worth looking into, and Luke should also be compared with the parallel Matthew:

Mt. x. 40—1	Lk. x. 16	Jn xii. 44—8
"He that receiveth you receiveth me, and he that receiveth me receiveth him that sent me. He that receiveth a prophet in the name of a prophet...."	"He that heareth you heareth me, and he that *rejecteth you rejecteth me*. But he that *rejecteth me rejecteth him that sent me*."	"He that believeth on me believeth not on me but on him that sent me... And if any man hear my words and observe them not, I (emph.) judge him not...He *that rejecteth me* and taketh not my words (ῥήματα) [into his heart] hath him that judgeth him. The word that I spake—that [word] shall judge him in the last day."

[1826] It will be noted that Matthew, omitting all mention of "*rejecting*," confines himself to the doctrine of "*receiving*."

---

[1] [1824 a] Mk vii. 9 ἀθετεῖτε, Mt. xv. 3 παραβαίνετε. The same thing is expressed by Mk vii. 13, Mt. xv. 3 ἀκυροῦν. Lk. omits all this.

His tradition may be rearranged, to shew its parallelism with the Triple Tradition and with the tradition of John on "*receiving*," thus:

Mk ix. 37	Mt. x. 40	Lk. ix. 48	Jn xiii. 20
"Whosoever shall receive (δέξηται) [one] of such little children in my name receiveth me, and whosoever is receiving (δέχηται) me is receiving not me but him that sent me."	"He that receiveth you receiveth me, and he that receiveth me receiveth him that sent me."	"Whosoever shall receive this little child in my name receiveth me, and whosoever shall receive me receiveth him that sent me."	"He that receiveth whomsoever I shall send receiveth me, and he that receiveth me receiveth him that sent me[1]."

[1827] Reviewing the evidence, we note, first, that the earliest of the Four Gospels (Mark) uses the word "*reject*" to signify the rejection, *not of man's word but of God's word*, namely, the command to honour parents. The next in date, Matthew (using the word "transgress" for "reject"), substantially agrees with Mark. These two Evangelists say, in effect, that the Pharisees *rejected the Word of God in order to keep the words of men*, and that Christ condemned this.

[1828] Luke omits the whole of this. But the distinction between *rejecting the words of individuals* and *rejecting the laws of natural religion*, or *the Word of God*, is a very important one. If the Third Evangelist failed to bring this out, it was all the more necessary for the Fourth to do so[2].

---

[1] Jn xiii. 20, as also Jn xii. 44—8, uses λαμβάνω "take [into one's heart]" instead of the Synoptic δέχομαι "receive": but, for brevity and parallelism, λαμβάνω in Jn xiii. 20 is rendered "receive" above.

[2] [1828 *a*] The distinction may be illustrated by what is probably one of the earliest of the Pauline Epistles, where the Apostle, after forbidding fornication, says (1 Thess. iv. 8) "He that *rejecteth* [this doctrine] (ὁ ἀθετῶν) *rejecteth* not man, but God, who is [ever] giving (διδόντα) his holy Spirit upon (εἰς) us."

[1829] There is also another reason why the Fourth Gospel should intervene. The earliest of the Gospels does not say " He that receiveth *you* receiveth me," but " He that receiveth *one of such little ones*." There is a great difference between the two. Mark's version struck at the root of apostolic or clerical arrogance. Luke's version in the Triple Tradition ("Whosoever shall receive *this little child*") gave no clear precept as to the future; and his version in the Double Tradition (" He that heareth *you*") was limited to the Seventy, who are mentioned in the preceding verses. Matthew's version (" He that receiveth *you*") is limited to the Twelve. Christians, therefore, with only the Three Gospels in their hands, might still require some further answer to the question " Whom are we to receive as coming from Christ?"

[1830] The full consideration of John's implied answer to this question, and of all the passages bearing on the Doctrine of Receiving, must be deferred[1]. Meantime, even a glance at the parallels suggests that John is writing with allusion to Luke's version of the Double Tradition, accepting his tradition verbally, so far as regards the use of the verb " reject," but surrounding it with such a context as to free it from all risk of being abused. Instead of Luke's ambiguous " heareth me" (which might mean hearing without doing), John (xii. 44—8) substitutes " believeth on me," connecting a subsequent mention of " hearing" with "*not* observing." Then, in case any domineering elders or bishops might judge those who " rejected " *them*, as rejecting Christ, he represents Christ Himself as deprecating such " judgment" ("*I* (emph.) judge him not"). John seems to have in mind a tradition similar to that of St Paul " Judge nothing before the time." The true judge is not to be this or that teacher or collection of teachers, but " the word that I spake"; and the time of judging will be " the last day." John, like Mark, seems to

---

[1] They will be discussed in *The Fourfold Gospel*.

represent Christ as appealing, against conventional judgments, to the first principles and fundamental decrees of humanity, the laws of spiritual Nature, those words, or laws, which "shall never pass away."

[1831] Our conclusion with reference to the Johannine use of ἀθετέω, and the Johannine phrase "*he that rejecteth me*," is that John is almost certainly writing with allusion to Luke's tradition "*he that rejecteth you* etc." It is also by no means improbable that, in the phrase " He that rejecteth me and taketh not my *words* [into his heart]," he is alluding to the tradition of Mark about Christ's condemnation of the Pharisees, "Ye reject *the Word of God*," taking it in its broadest sense, not limiting it to the commandment "Honour thy father and thy mother," but taking it as the uttered thoughts of the Father in Heaven, expressed from the beginning through the Logos, and, recently, by the "words (ῥήματα)" of the Logos incarnate upon earth.

JOHN-MARK-LUKE AGREEMENTS[1]

	Mk	Lk.	Jn		Mk	Lk.	Jn
[1832] ἀθετέω[2]	2	5 (rep.)	1	ἀπορέω[3]	1	1	1
?† ἄρωμα[4]	1	2	1	ἀτιμάζω[5]	1	1	1
γαζοφυλάκιον				γεμίζω	2	1	3
(2333)	3	1	1	διεγείρω[6]	1	2	1
[1833] ἐκλέγομαι[7]	1	4	5	* ἐλαύνω[8]	1	1	1
ἐξάγω	1	1	1	* ἐπιθυμία[9]	1	1	1

[1] [1832 a_1] An asterisk denotes that the same word is used in different senses by Jn-Mk and Lk., *e.g.* ἐλαύνω Mk vi. 48, Jn vi. 19 "row," but Lk. viii. 29 "driven [by an evil spirit]" : † denotes a parallelism, ?† a quasi-parallelism. For other signs, see the foot-notes.

[2] [1832 *a*] Ἀθετέω, "reject," see **1823—31**. It is used with accus. of pers., only in Mk vi. 26, Lk. x. 16, Jn xii. 48, 1 Thess. iv. 8. In Mk vi. 26 it perh. means "break faith with her," as in Jerem. xii. 6, Lam. i. 2 (א) ἠθέτησαν αὐτήν.

[3] Ἀπορέω, Mk vi. 20 (act.), Lk. xxiv. 4 and Jn xiii. 22 (mid.).

[4] [1832 *b*] Ἀρώματα, "spices," in Mk xvi. 1, Lk. xxiii. 56, xxiv. 1, refers to "spices" prepared by the women for the body of Jesus and brought to the tomb on the morning of the Resurrection; in Jn xix. 40 it refers to "spices" used by Joseph and Nicodemus in entombing the body. Mt. xxviii. 1 (parall. to Mk xvi. 1) mentions no "spices," and says that the women came simply "to *behold* the grave."

[5] Ἀτιμάζω is in the Parable of the Vineyard, Mk xii. 4, Lk. xx. 11 "*treated disgracefully*," in Jn viii. 49 "But ye *dishonour* me."

[6] [1832 *c*] Διεγείρω, "quite rouse," or "rouse up," is used of Jesus in the Stilling of the Storm Mk iv. 39, Lk. viii. 24 (*bis*) "*They roused him up…He was roused up* and rebuked the wind" : Jn has in the Walking on the Waters, (vi. 18) "The sea—by reason of a great wind blowing—was *roused up.*" Outside 2 Pet. (i. 13, iii. 1) the word does not occur elsewhere in N.T., and it does not occur at all in canon. LXX.

[7] [1833 *a*] Ἐκλέγομαι, in Lk., occurs only once in Christ's words, Lk. x. 42 "Mary *hath chosen* the good part." Lk.'s other instances are vi. 13 "*having chosen* twelve," ix. 35 "my *chosen* son," xiv. 7 "they *chose* the first seats." See **1709 *b*.**

[8] [1833 *b*] Ἐλαύνω in Mk vi. 48, Jn vi. 19, is used of the disciples "rowing" in the Walking on the Waters (Mt. xiv. 24 has "by the waves)." Lk. viii. 29 has the word in a different sense, "He was *driven* by the devil."

[9] [1833 *c*] Ἐπιθυμία in Mk iv. 19, Jn viii. 44, means "lusts"; Lk. xxii. 15 is different, "*with desire* have I desired to eat this passover."

TO JOHN, MARK, AND LUKE [1834]

	Mk	Lk.	Jn		Mk	Lk.	Jn
† ἱμάς[1]	1	1	1	καθαρισμός[2]	1	2	2
[1834]?† κατάκειμαι[3]	4	3	2	μαρτυρία			
				(**1726** *c—d*)	3	1	14
ὄντως	1	2	1	πεντήκοντα	1	3	1
?‡ πλῆθος[4]	2	8	2	πρόφασις[5]	1	1	1
(τὸ) τρίτον				ὕδωρ (Chri.)[6]	2	3	7
(**1695** *e*)	1	1	3				

[1] [1833 *d*] Ἱμάς, "latchet," in Mk i. 7, Lk. iii. 16, Jn i. 27 about "*loosing*" the "*latchet* of the shoe," where Mt. iii. 11 has "*carry* (βαστάσαι) the shoes." (1) "*Loosing* the shoe" and (2) "*carrying* bathing utensils to the bath" were recognised duties of a slave to his master. Possibly Mt. has confused and combined parts of the two. In any case, Jn follows Mk (and Lk.) as against Mt.

[2] [1833 *e*] Καθαρισμός, "purification," occurs in the Cure of a Leper, Mk i. 44, Lk. v. 14 "Shew thyself to the priest and offer *concerning thy purification*," where Mt. viii. 4 has "Shew thyself to the priest and offer *the gift*." The other instances are Lk. ii. 22, Jn ii. 6, iii. 25. Jn nowhere mentions lepers or anything connected with them.

[3] [1834 *a*] Κατάκειμαι, "lie [sick]," is used by Mk i. 30, where the parall. Mt. viii. 14 has βεβλημένην, "*prostrated* [*with sickness*]," and the parall. Lk. iv. 38 συνεχομένη. In the Healing of the Paralytic, Mk ii. 4 describes the letting down of "the pallet where the paralytic *lay*" (Mt. ix. 2 has, again, "*prostrated*"). Lk., at the end of the story, says (Lk. v. 25) "He took up that on which he *lay* [*sick*]." Jn, in the quasi-parallel Healing of the man with an "infirmity," uses κ. twice (Jn v. 3—6) κατέκειτο πλῆθος τῶν ἀσθενούντων...τοῦτον ἰδὼν ὁ Ἰησοῦς κατακείμενον.

[1834 *b*] Κατάκειμαι is used also in Mk ii. 15, xiv. 3, Lk. v. 29, vii. 37 and 1 Cor. viii. 10 of "lying [at table]"; and for this reason Mt. may have preferred another word. As regards Mk, Lk., and Jn, the facts prove nothing except that they did not object to using the word (though ambiguous) in the sense of "lie [sick]."

[4] [1834 *c*] Πλῆθος, "multitude," occurs in Mk iii. 7, 8 πολὺ πλῆθος, and πλῆθος πολύ, of the multitudes coming to Jesus, Jn v. 3 πλῆθος of the sick. Πλῆθος ἰχθύων πολύ is in Lk. v. 6, and ἀπὸ τοῦ πλήθους τῶν ἰχθύων in Jn xxi. 6, describing a miraculous draught of fishes (Lk. long before, Jn soon after, the Resurrection).

[5] [1834 *d*] Πρόφασις, "pretext," is in Mk xii. 40, Lk. xx. 47 προφάσει μακρὰ προσευχόμενοι, Jn xv. 22 πρόφασιν οὐκ ἔχουσιν.

[6] [1834 *e*] Ὕδωρ, "water" (in Christ's words), occurs in Mk xiv. 13, Lk. xxii. 10 "There shall meet you a man bearing a pitcher of *water*." Mt. xxvi. 18 omits the whole sentence. See **1728 *b***.

§ 4. *"The Holy One of God"*

[1835] To these words may be added the phrase ὁ ἅγιος τοῦ θεοῦ, "the Holy One of God," applied to our Lord by a demoniac in Mark and Luke[1], and used by John in Peter's Confession, "We...know that thou art *the Holy One of God*[2]."

---

[1] Mk i. 24, Lk. iv. 34, "Hast thou come to destroy us? I know thee who thou art, *the Holy One of God*."

[2] [1835 a] Jn vi. 69. Aaron is called (Ps. cvi. 16) "*the Holy One* of God," apparently with reference to Numb. xvi. 5—7 "The man whom the Lord shall choose, he shall be *holy*." Comp. Jn x. 36 "Whom the Father *made holy* (ἡγίασεν) and sent into the world." Peter's confession (in Jn vi. 69) seems to imply in the first part a Prophet ("thou hast the words of eternal life") and in the second part the ideal Priest ("the Holy One of God").

[1835 b] It is interesting to contrast the two stories—perfectly compatible with each other and perhaps even complementary—in which Peter is represented by Luke as saying at first (v. 8) "Depart from me, for I am a sinful man, O Lord!" while, later on, John (vi. 67) represents Jesus as saying to the Disciples "Do ye also desire to depart?" and Peter replies, in effect, refusing to depart ("Lord, to whom shall we go?").

CHAPTER VI

WORDS MOSTLY PECULIAR TO JOHN, MATTHEW, AND LUKE

§ 1. *Verbal agreements numerous, but parallelisms non-existent*

[**1836**] The list of words peculiar to John, Matthew, and Luke, is longer than any of the last five lists. This is not surprising, since these three Gospels deal largely or mainly with the words of the Lord, whereas Mark deals mainly with the acts. Acts may with advantage be variously reported, and we learn much about them from a variety of reporters describing various aspects of the same thing. Words are best reported just as they are uttered. We cannot therefore be surprised that the three long Gospels that attempt to record Christ's words contain such words as "hallow" (or "sanctify"), the verb "sin," the noun "love," and such words as "light" and "darkness" in a metaphorical sense etc. What is remarkable is, that in the whole of the long Vocabulary given below *we shall not find a single word* (**1866** (i) foll.) *of which we can confidently say that it is used in the same context in parallel passages of John, Matthew, and Luke, apart from Mark*.

[**1837**] Yet the list will not be without use in more ways than one. In the first place, it will shew the limited scope of Mark, by exhibiting the words that he never uses—except perhaps in a quotation or some quite subordinate fashion[1]—and it will indicate how much needed to be supplied by subsequent Evangelists in order to elucidate Christ's doctrine. In the next place, by giving us a bird's-eye view of the common vocabulary of the three "doctrinal Gospels," as we may call them—and by shewing that, whereas the two Synoptists (Matthew and Luke) agree almost *verbatim* for sentences and even for short sections, the Fourth, even while using the same vocabulary, rarely or never uses it in the same context—it may lead us to appreciate, by contrast, the significance of John's frequent parallelism with Mark, with whose vocabulary he has so little in common.

[1838] Large parts of the Double Tradition, beautiful though they are, have no direct bearing on Christ's unique nature, mission, and doctrine. The exhortations, for example, not to be anxious about the morrow, might have proceeded from Hillel, or John the Baptist, or Epictetus[2]. Not much is to be learned from a comparison of the vocabulary of these passages with the vocabulary of the Fourth Gospel. The Sermon on the Mount is full of concrete terms such as "lilies," "spin," "barn," "oven," not used by John, nor entitled to a place below, and omitted because their insertion would teach the reader nothing except what he knows already, that the author of the Fourth Gospel does not deal largely in such particularities. But the insertion of a few important abstract or doctrinal terms used by Matthew and Luke but not by John may throw light on differences of doctrine or differences in expressing it. Some of these—though not strictly entitled

---

[1] [1837 *a*] *E.g.* the word "peace" is nowhere in Mk except in Mk v. 34 "Go in peace," and "Abraham" nowhere except in a quotation about (Ex. iii. 6, quoted in Mk xii. 26) "The God of A. and of Isaac and of Jacob."

[2] Comp. Epict. iii. 22. 69 "the philosopher must be devoted with his whole being and without distraction to the service of God," and (iii. 26. 28) "God doth not fail to care for them that serve Him."

to a place in this Vocabulary—are given below in Greek, and are inserted here in English alphabetical order with their Greek equivalents:—

Alms ἐλεημοσύνη, angry (to be) ὀργίζεσθαι, babes νήπιοι, beseech δέομαι, brother (thy) (metaph.) ἀδελφός σου, enemy ἐχθρός, gather συλλέγω, humble (adj. and vb.) ταπεινός, -όω, justify δικαιόω, mercy ἔλεος, prudent φρόνιμος, understanding (adj.) συνετός, wisdom (Chri.) σοφία, wise σοφός.

§ 2. *"Lay the head to rest"*

[1839] It was shewn above (1451—8), that this phrase is not known to exist in Greek literature (including the LXX) outside the Gospels, and an attempt was made to prove that it is used by John in the sense in which all admit it to have been used by Matthew and Luke ("lay the head to rest"). Only, whereas the two earlier Evangelists employ it literally, the fourth Evangelist applied it spiritually to our Lord's finding rest for His head on the bosom of the Father. So it was maintained above. But now, if it appears that this is the only phrase peculiar to John, Matthew, and Luke, and that the contexts are not parallel, the reader may naturally say, "Unique exceptions are always to be suspected. The abstinence of the Fourth Gospel from the phrases of the Double Tradition of Matthew and Luke is so complete that it does not seem antecedently probable that this single phrase was borrowed. We admit that κλίνω κεφαλήν cannot be rendered otherwise than 'lay the head to rest.' But that meaning may have been much more common in the first century than we suppose. John may have used the phrase thus without any allusion to Matthew and Luke. And this is all the more probable because there is no connexion or affinity of thought between the contexts in the Double Tradition and John."

[1840] This objection may be partly answered by shewing that there is an affinity of thought—though latent—between the two contexts. The former, the Double Tradition, speaks of "following." According to Matthew (and Luke is very similar) a "scribe" said to Jesus "Teacher, I will follow thee whithersoever thou art departing." To this He replied, "The foxes have holes and the birds of the heaven nests but the Son of man hath not where to lay his head[1]." This appears to mean (somewhat as Chrysostom suggests) "You expect to follow me to a palace and to share in the conquests of the Messiah, but I have not even a home of my own." But does this exhaust the meaning? Does it even express the meaning— if we are to take the words in their mere literal sense— without exaggeration? Literally speaking, were there not many places where the Son of man could "lay his head"?

[1841] Origen's allusion to the words, although fancifully expressed, seems to touch the spiritual truth at the bottom of them when he says that Jesus could not "lay his head" in Jerusalem but only in Bethany as being "the House of Obedience[2]." That is to say, the Lord found rest and repose in obeying and doing the will of the Father. This harmonizes with the words, "My meat is to do the will of him that sent me." The "scribe," if Chrysostom's view is correct, supposed that a literal "following" was to end in a "laying of the head to rest" in a literal palace. Jesus replies that, in that sense, He has "no place to lay his head" on earth. That final rest could only come when the labour on earth was accomplished

---

[1] [1840 a] Mt. viii. 19—20. Lk. ix. 57—8 substitutes "*going in the way*" for "*scribe.*" Perhaps there was some early confusion between (Mt.) "a guide in the way [of the Law]," i.e. *one causing to go*, and (Lk.) "*going.*"

[2] Origen (on Mt. xxi. 27) Huet i. 446 C, where see the context. He seems to mean that Jerusalem was a House of Disobedience because the disobedient resided in it, and Bethany a House of Obedience, partly because of his interpretation of the name, partly because of the obedience of the disciples residing there.

and the labourer rested in the bosom of the Father. According to this view, our Lord, in His reply to the scribe, does not mean to insist on the fact that He had no fixed abode of His own, and, still less, to suggest that there were not many friends and devoted disciples ready to give Him hospitality. His real meaning was that, in the scribe's sense of the term, the Son of man had no " resting-place."

[1842] It was, of course, inevitable that the Apostles and Missionaries of the first century would often be able to say, with St Paul, in a literal sense, "We both hunger and thirst and are naked and are buffeted and have *no certain dwelling place*[1]." But by the end of that century there would inevitably be some, of vagrant disposition, to whom the absence of a "certain dwelling place" would not be unwelcome provided that it did not bring with it "hunger and thirst": and accordingly we find the Teaching of the Apostles forbidding believers to entertain any missionary, or, as it says, "apostle," for more than two days[2]. Long before that precept was written, it would probably be necessary to warn some converts against supposing that they were "following" Christ by merely making themselves homeless "apostles." The Synoptists, it is true, emphasize Christ's saying that "*following*" must go with "*taking up the cross*": but, even there, Luke thinks it desirable to warn his readers that they must "*take up the cross daily*[3]."

[1843] John brings out the true meaning of "following" in a dialogue between our Lord and Peter, who does not indeed (like the "scribe") proclaim that he *will* "follow," but asks "Why cannot I follow thee now? I will lay down

---

[1] 1 Cor. iv. 11 ἀστατοῦμεν.
[2] *Didach.* xi. 3—5.
[3] Mk viii. 34, Mt. xvi. 24, Lk. ix. 23, "If any one desireth to come (Mk Mt. ἐλθεῖν, Lk. ἔρχεσθαι i.e. *come daily*, **2496** *c*) after me, let him deny himself and take up his cross (Lk. +*daily*, καθ' ἡμέραν) and follow me."

my life for thee[1]." Jesus had, at an earlier period, told the Jews that they could not follow Him, and He has just declared that it applies to the disciples also for the present[2]. It is this that elicits Peter's vehement question. No direct answer is given to it[3]. But the Washing of Feet taken with its sequel constitutes an indirect answer, namely, that "following" the Son means serving the Son, and serving the Son means serving the brethren with the love with which He loved and served them[4]. This doctrine is carried on to the last page of the Gospel. Peter is warned that, in his own case, "following" will lead him to the cross. But he "turns and sees" the other disciple also "following"—the one that used to lie on the breast of Jesus. Then he learns that this disciple may perhaps "tarry" till the Lord comes, so that it is possible to "follow" Him in many ways.

[1844] If it is admitted that the Fourth Gospel contains a great deal that bears on the right and the wrong kind of "following," then it will hardly be denied that this particular tradition about the "scribe," who did not know what "following" meant, would probably attract the Evangelist's attention. It would be so likely to be misunderstood by opposite parties. The enemies of Christ might take it as a mere pathetic self-deploration, "I have no home, no resting-place!" False apostles might allege it as an excuse for

---

[1] Jn xiii. 37. This was exactly true. The Apostle *did* "lay down his life" thus, and Christ does not deny it in His reply. Lk. (xxii. 33) represents Peter as saying "I am *ready* to go both to prison and to death." This was not exactly true. The Apostle was *not* "ready."

[2] Jn xiii. 33 "Even as I said to the Jews, 'Where I go ye cannot come,' [so] I say to you also now."

[3] The answer is Jn xiii. 38 "*Thou wilt lay down thy life for me!* Verily, verily, I say unto thee, The cock shall surely not crow till thou hast thrice denied me." The italicised words are half exclamation, half interrogation (**2236** foll.). Later on (xxi. 18—19), the Lord commands and predicts that the Apostle *will* "follow" Him on the way to the Cross.

[4] Jn xiii. 34, xv. 12.

vagrancy. It might close the minds of literalists and simple people against the conception of the true rest and the true resting-place. An old tradition quoted by Clement of Alexandria and found in recently discovered Logia represents Christ as saying "He that *reigns* shall *rest*[1]." Justin Martyr twice quotes a tradition associating the "*reign*" with the "*cross*[2]." The Epistle to the Romans speaks of "suffering with [Christ] that we may be glorified with" Him[3]. The Second Epistle to Timothy mentions together "enduring" [with Christ] and "*reigning* with" Him, apparently as part of a "faithful saying[4]." All these traditions, outside the Gospels, shew how natural it would be to regard Jesus as beginning on the Cross His "rest" as well as His "reign."

[1845] The Double Tradition and the Fourth Gospel, if both are regarded as referring to the "resting" of Christ, harmonize with these early traditions—which they may have helped to originate—as well as with each other. But if in the Johannine passage we substitute "bowing the head in submission," instead of "laying the head to rest," we disconnect it from these external traditions amid which it finds a natural place, and connect it with such doctrine as that of the Epistle to the Hebrews, "He learned obedience through the things that he suffered[5]"—which is not the aspect presented by the Fourth Gospel. There is no Gospel that so consistently as the Fourth associates crucifixion with "reigning" by describing it as "glorifying" and "lifting up."

[1846] These considerations may suffice to answer the objection that "there is no connexion or affinity of thought" between the contexts of the phrase under discussion in John and the Double Tradition. For the rest, it has been pointed

---

[1] Clem. 453 and 704.
[2] *Apol.* § 41 and *Tryph.* § 73, erroneously quoting Ps. xcvi. (see context).
[3] Rom. viii. 17. [4] 2 Tim. ii. 12.
[5] Heb. v. 8.

out that John does intervene more than once in important doctrines of the Double Tradition—such as the relation between the "friends" and the "servants" of Christ (**1784—92**), the meaning of "hating one's own life" and the circumstances in which such "hate" is justified (**1450**), and also as regards the doctrine of "rejection" added by Luke in the Double Tradition where Matthew confines himself to the doctrine of "receiving" (**1823—31**). The difference was that in these cases Matthew and Luke did not agree in the use of the particular words repeated by John, whereas here Matthew and Luke do thus agree. Matthew for example (**1784**) had "bond-servant," Luke had "friends," and John repeated both terms. Here John repeats a couple of words in which the two agree. Such a repetition, though unique, is, under the circumstances, not very surprising.

§ 3. *John-Matthew-Luke Agreements (in English).*

[1847] From what has been said, it will be inferred that comparatively little information of a critical kind will be derived from the Vocabulary given below. Its main results will be to shew what a large province of doctrine Mark left untouched; how many *words* Matthew, Luke, and John have in common; how often Matthew and Luke agree *verbatim*; and how absolutely John refrains from using their *phrases* or expressing their thoughts *in the same way*. These facts, however, are of some interest in themselves, and they can be made clear to readers unacquainted with Greek. For their sakes, the words will be given first in English alphabetical order[1] and with the sign (ii)—signifying "Double"—attached to those words that occur in parallel passages of

---

[1] This list will not include particles, such as γε, given below in the Greek list alone.

the Matthew-Luke Double Tradition. The Greek equivalent will be added so that the reader may pass from this list to the Greek list and its foot-notes, which follow later on.

[1848] (ii) Mk Abraham[1] Ἀβραάμ, (ii) age (or stature) ἡλικία, another (s. other), asleep (to fall) κοιμάομαι, ass ὄνος.

(?) Bear (a child) τίκτω, (ii) behold θεάομαι, Bethlehem Βηθλεέμ, (ii) blessed μακάριος, blow (or breathe) πνέω, (ii) bondage (to be in) δουλεύω, bone ὀστέον, (ii) "boy" παῖς, (ii) bride νύμφη, burn καίω.

Caiaphas Καιάφας, (ii) clean καθαρός, (ii) come ἥκω, (ii) confess[2] ὁμολογέω, (ii) cubit πῆχυς.

(ii) Darkness (metaph.) σκοτία, σκότος, (ii) dash (s. stumble), (ii) devil διάβολος.

Ear ὠτίον, (ii) exalt (or lift up) ὑψόω.

(ii) Faithful πιστός, finish τελέω, flock ποίμνη, (ii) food τροφή, foundation καταβολή, (ii) friend φίλος, furlong στάδιος.

(ii) Guide (vb.) ὁδηγέω.

[1849] (ii) Hallow ἁγιάζω, hide κρύπτω, hope (vb.) ἐλπίζω. Inquire πυνθάνομαι.

Joseph (husband of Mary) Ἰωσήφ, (ii) judge (vb.) κρίνω, (ii) judgment κρίσις.

(ii) Law νόμος, (ii) lay (one's head) κλίνω κεφαλήν, (ii) lie (i.e. be placed) κεῖμαι, lift up ἐπαίρω, (ii) lift up (or exalt) ὑψόω, (ii) light (metaph.) φῶς, (ii) like (adj.) ὅμοιος, (ii) lot μέρος, love (n.) ἀγάπη.

(ii) Mourn θρηνέω, (ii) mouth στόμα, murmur γογγύζω, (ii) myself ἐμαυτόν.

---

[1] [1848 a] Occasionally, a word, e.g. "Abraham," that occurs in Mark as part of a quotation, or in some manner quite unimportant as compared with its use in the Double Tradition, is included in this list. Such a word is denoted by "Mk." The words "alms," "angry," and a few others, non-existent in Jn, but characteristic of the Double Tradition, have already been given in English above (1838) in a separate group, and are not repeated here, but in the Greek vocabulary they will be included with the rest.

[2] Not used in N.T. of confessing *sins* (except in 1 Jn i. 9).

Nazoraean (for Nazarene) Ναζωραῖος.
(ii) Mk open (vb.) ἀνοίγω, (ii) other (another) ἕτερος, owe (Jn ought) ὀφείλω.
Pass μεταβαίνω, (ii) Mk peace εἰρήνη, (ii) persecute διώκω, present (I am) πάρειμι.

[1850] (ii) Reap θερίζω, rejoice greatly ἀγαλλιάω, reprove ἐλέγχω, remember μιμνήσκομαι, (ii) reveal ἀποκαλύπτω, righteousness δικαιοσύνη, ruler (Jewish) (sing.) ἄρχων.

Samaritan Σαμαρείτης, (ii) sanctify ἁγιάζω, (ii) scatter σκορπίζω, (ii) serve (s. bondage), shut κλείω, sickness ἀσθένεια, (ii) sin (vb.) ἁμαρτάνω, sit καθέζομαι, sleep (n.) ὕπνος, (ii) Solomon Σολομών, strange[r] ἀλλότριος, suffice ἀρκέω, (ii) stumble προσκόπτω.

Tend (as a shepherd) ποιμαίνω, testify μαρτυρέω, (ii) thief κλέπτης, (ii) toil (vb.) κοπιάω, turn round (to speak) στρέφω.

Wedding (feast) γάμος, witness, bear (s. testify), (ii) wolf λύκος, (ii) worthy ἄξιος, wrap (?) ἐντυλίσσω (**1866** (i)).

TO JOHN, MATTHEW, AND LUKE [1851]

WORDS MOSTLY PECULIAR TO JOHN, MATTHEW, AND LUKE[1]

	Mt.	Lk.	Jn		Mt.	Lk.	Jn
[1851] (ii) Ἀβραάμ[2] (Mk)	7	15	11	ἀγαλλιάω[3]	1	2	2
ἀγάπη[4]	1	1	7	(ii) ἁγιάζω[5]	3	1	4
(ii) ἀδελφός σου[6]				(ii) ᾅδης[7]	2	2	0
(metaph.)	7	4	0	ἀλλότριος[8]	2	1	2

[1] **[1851 a_1]** Words marked (ii) occur at least once in *parallel passages* of the Double Tradition of Matthew and Luke, *e.g.* ἁγιάζω, Mt. vi. 9, Lk. xi. 2, "*Hallowed* be thy name." These are often given in Gk to shew *verbatim* agreement or the nature of disagreement.

The words distinguished by "Mk" occur in Mk, but only in quotations of O.T. or in such other special circumstances that it did not seem good to omit the word from a list attempting to give a general view of the Jn-Mt.-Lk. vocabulary.

A few words non-existent in Jn have been inserted in special cases (*e.g.* ἐχθρός, σοφία) where they seemed likely to throw light on the relation of Jn to Mt.-Lk. (**1838**).

"Pec." means that the context is peculiar to the single Evangelist Mt. or Lk.

[2] **[1851 *a*]** Ἀβραάμ is included because its single occurrence in Mk (xii. 26) is a quotation (parall. to Mt. xxii. 32, Lk. xx. 37). Six of the instances in Lk. are in the story of Lazarus. The instances in Jn are all in viii. 33—58. The parall. instances in Double Tradition are Mt. iii. 9, Lk. iii. 8 πατέρα ἔχομεν τὸν Ἀ...ἐγεῖραι τέκνα τῷ Ἀ., and Mt. viii. 11 (sim. Lk. xiii. 28) ἀνακλιθήσονται μετὰ Ἀ. κ. Ἰσαὰκ κ. Ἰακώβ.

[3] **[1851 *b*]** Ἀγαλλιάω, Mt. v. 12 χαίρετε κ. ἀγαλλιᾶσθε, Lk. i. 47 ἠγαλλίασεν τὸ πνεῦμά μου ἐπὶ τῷ θεῷ, x. 21 ἐν αὐτῇ τῇ ὥρᾳ ἠγαλλιάσατο τῷ πνεύματι τῷ ἁγίῳ, Jn v. 35 ὑμεῖς δὲ ἠθελήσατε ἀγαλλιαθῆναι πρὸς ὥραν ἐν τ. φωτὶ αὐτοῦ, viii. 56 Ἀβραὰμ...ἠγαλλιάσατο ἵνα ἴδῃ...

[4] **[1851 *c*]** Ἀγάπη, Mt. xxiv. 12 ψυγήσεται ἡ ἀγάπη τ. πολλῶν. In Lk. xi. 42 παρέρχεσθε τ. κρίσιν καὶ τ. ἀγάπην τ. θεοῦ, the parall. Mt. xxiii. 23 has ἀφήκατε τ. βαρύτερα τ. νόμου, τ. κρίσιν καὶ τ. ἔλεος καὶ τ. πίστιν.

[5] Ἁγιάζω, Mt. vi. 9, Lk. xi. 2 ἁγιασθήτω τὸ ὄνομά σου.

[6] **[1851 *d*]** Ἀδελφός σου, "thy brother," (metaph.) occurs in Mt. vii. 3, 4, 5, Lk. vi. 41, 42 (*bis*) about "the mote in *thy brother's* eye," and in Mt. xviii. 15 (*bis*), Lk. xvii. 3 "if *thy brother* sin against thee." It occurs also in Mt. v. 23—4 (*bis*) "be reconciled to *thy brother*."

[7] Ἅδης, Mt. xi. 23, Lk. x. 15 ἕως (Lk. +τοῦ) ᾅδου καταβήσῃ.

[8] Ἀλλότριος, Lk. xvi. 12 ἐν τῷ ἀλλοτρίῳ (neut.): in Mt.-Jn it is masc.

A. V.

	Mt.	Lk.	Jn		Mt.	Lk.	Jn
[1852] (ii) ἁμαρτάνω¹	3	4	3	(ii) ἀνοίγω²(Mk)	11	7	11
(ii) ἄξιος³	9	8	1	(ii) ἀποκαλύπτω⁴	4	5	1
ἀρκέω⁵	1	1	2	ἄρχων⁶(Jewish) (sing.)	2	2 or 3	1
[1853] ἀσθένεια⁷	1	4	2	Βηθλεέμ⁸	5	2	1
γάμος⁹	8	2	2	γε¹⁰	4	8	1

¹ [1852 a] 'Αμαρτάνω, Mt. xviii. 15, 21 "if thy brother *sin*," "how many times shall my brother *sin* against me," sim. parall. Lk. xvii. 3—4. Jn has v. 14 "*Sin* no more," ix. 2—3 "Who *did sin*, this man or his parents...? Neither *did* this man *sin* nor his parents." It also occurs in Jn [viii. 11].

² [1852 b] 'Ανοίγω. Included in this list (though it occurs once in Mk (vii. 35) ἠνοίγησαν αὐτοῦ αἱ ἀκοαί) because it is in the parall. Mt. vii. 7—8, Lk. xi. 9—10 "knock and it shall be *opened*." In Jn it is always used of the opening of the eyes of the man born blind, except in i. 51 "the heaven *opened*," x. 3 "to him the porter *openeth*." In Jn i. 51 it may be used (646 a) to mean "permanently opened" in contrast to the momentary "opening," or (Mk i. 10) "rending," manifested to the Baptist. If so, the Johannine allusion would be to the Triple Tradition.

³ "Αξιος occurs in the parall. Mt. iii. 8, Lk. iii. 8 ἀ. τῆς μετανοίας, and Mt. x. 10, Lk. x. 7 ἀ. γὰρ ὁ ἐργάτης, also in Jn i. 27 οὗ οὐκ εἰμὶ ἄξιος (Mk-Mt.-Lk. ἱκανός) ἵνα λύσω αὐτοῦ τὸν ἱμάντα τοῦ ὑποδήματος.

⁴ 'Αποκαλύπτω, Mt. x. 26, Lk. xii. 2 "there is nothing covered that shall not be *revealed*," and Mt. xi. 25—7 (*bis*), Lk. x. 21—2 (*bis*) καὶ ἀπεκάλυψας αὐτὰ νηπίοις...ᾧ ἐὰν (Lk. ἂν) βούληται ὁ υἱὸς ἀποκαλύψαι. In Jn only xii. 38 quoting Is. liii. 1 "To whom hath the arm of the Lord been *revealed*?"

⁵ 'Αρκέω, Mt. xxv. 9 (pec.), Lk. iii. 14 (pec.), Jn vi. 7, xiv. 8.

⁶ [1852 c] "Αρχων sing. meaning "ruler of the Jews," "of a synagogue" etc., occurs in Mt. ix. 18 (rep. ix. 23) ἄρχων, Lk. viii. 41 ἄρχων τῆς συναγωγῆς, but Mk v. 22 has εἷς τῶν ἀρχισυναγώγων, so that practically Mk, too, has ἄρχων. It occurs in Jn iii. 1 Νικόδημος...ἄρχων τῶν Ἰουδαίων. In Triple Tradition, Lk. xviii. 18 τις...ἄρχων (Mk x. 17, Mt. xix. 16 εἷς) and in Double Tradition Lk. xii. 58 ὑπάγεις...ἐπ' ἄρχοντα (Mt. v. 25 diff.) prob. mean a Jewish "ruler." On ἄρχοντες (Jewish) pl. see 1765 a.

⁷ 'Ασθένεια, in Mt., only in viii. 17 αὐτὸς τ. ἀσθενείας ἡμῶν ἔλαβεν, quoting Is. liii. 4 (Heb.).

⁸ Βηθλεέμ, in Jn, only in vii. 42 "Hath not the Scripture said that the Christ cometh...from *Bethlehem*...?" The question is urged as an objection against those who said "This is the Christ."

⁹ Γάμος, in Jn ii. 1—2 (sing.) of the marriage in Cana. It is pl. in Mt. and Lk. exc. Mt. xxii. 8, 11, 12.

¹⁰ [1853 a] Γε, in Jn, only in iv. 2 καίτοιγε (Bruder p. 146 καίτοι γε)

TO JOHN, MATTHEW, AND LUKE

	Mt.	Lk.	Jn		Mt.	Lk.	Jn
γογγύζω[1]	1	1	4	(ii) δέομαι[2]	1	8	0
[1854] (ii) διάβολος[3]	6	5	3	δικαιοσύνη[4]	7	1	2
(ii) δικαιόω[5]	2	5	0	(ii) διώκω[6]	6	3	2
(ii) δουλεύω[7]	2	3	1	(ii) εἰρήνη[8] (Mk)	4	13+[[1]]	6
[1855] ἐλέγχω[9]	1	1	3	ἐλεημοσύνη	3	2	0

a compound unique in N.T. But καίτοι is in Acts xiv. 17, Heb. iv. 3. Γε occurs in the Triple Tradition in Mt. ix. 17, Lk. v. 36, 37 εἰ δὲ μήγε (parall. Mk ii. 21 εἰ δὲ μή); also in Lk.'s version (x. 6) of Double Tradition (parall. Mt. x. 13 ἐὰν δὲ μή); and in Mt. pec. and Lk. pec.

[1] Γογγύζω, Mt. xx. 11 (of the labourers in a parable), Lk. v. 30 (of "the Pharisees and their scribes").

[2] Δέομαι, non-occurrent in Jn (**1667**) but in Mt. ix. 38, Lk. x. 2 δεήθητε οὖν τοῦ κυρίου τοῦ θερισμοῦ.

[3] [**1854** a] Διάβολος, Mt. iv. 1—11, (sim.) Lk. iv. 2—13 (of the Temptation); also in Mt.'s Single Tradition xiii. 39, xxv. 41; and in the explanation of the parable of the Sower Lk. viii. 12 ὁ διάβολος (parall. Mk iv. 15 ὁ Σατανᾶς, Mt. xiii. 19 ὁ πονηρός). Jn vi. 70 "One of you is a *devil*," viii. 44 "Ye are of your father *the devil*," xiii. 2 "*The devil* having now put it into the heart of Judas."

[4] [**1854** b] Δικαιοσύνη, Lk. i. 75, Jn xvi. 8—10 (on "conviction"). In parall. to Mt. v. 6 "hunger...after *righteousness*," Lk. vi. 21 has "hunger *now*." (See **1691** e.)

[5] Δικαιόω, Mt. xi. 19 ἐδικαιώθη ἡ σοφία ἀπὸ τῶν ἔργων αὐτῆς, parall. Lk. vii. 35 ἐδικαιώθη ἡ σοφία ἀπὸ πάντων τῶν τέκνων αὐτῆς.

[6] [**1854** c] Διώκω. Mt. xxiii. 34 ἐξ αὐτῶν ἀποκτενεῖτε καὶ σταυρώσετε... καὶ διώξετε ἀπὸ πόλεως εἰς πόλιν, parall. Lk. xi. 49 ἐξ αὐτῶν ἀποκτενοῦσιν καὶ διώξουσιν. Jn v. 16 διὰ τοῦτο ἐδίωκον οἱ Ἰουδαῖοι τὸν Ἰησοῦν, xv. 20 εἰ ἐμὲ ἐδίωξαν καὶ ὑμᾶς διώξουσιν.

[7] [**1854** d] Δουλεύω, Mt. vi. 24 (*bis*), Lk. xvi. 13 (*bis*) οὐδεὶς (Lk. +οἰκέτης) δύναται δυσὶ κυρίοις δουλεύειν...οὐ δύνασθε θεῷ δουλεύειν καὶ μαμωνᾷ. Jn viii. 33 οὐδενὶ δεδουλεύκαμεν πώποτε (which would be, literally, a violation of the precept Deut. xiii. 4 αὐτῷ δουλεύσετε (AF, om. by LXX in error), 1 S. vii. 3 δουλεύσατε αὐτῷ μόνῳ, but the Jews mean οὐδενὶ ἀνθρώπῳ).

[8] [**1854** e] Εἰρήνη, incl. because its single occurrence in Mark is the unimportant phrase (Mk v. 34) "Go in *peace*," whereas it occurs in Mt.-Lk. in the important tradition Mt. x. 34 (sim. Lk. xii. 51) "Think not that I came to send *peace* on the earth." Jn xx. 19, 21, 26 describes Jesus as thrice saying "*Peace* [be] unto you." W.H. insert the clause in double brackets in Lk. xxiv. 36.

[9] Ἐλέγχω, Mt. xviii. 15 "*shew him* [i.e. thy brother] *his fault*," Lk. iii. 19 "[Herod Antipas] *being reproved* by him [*i.e.* John the Baptist]".

[1856] WORDS MOSTLY PECULIAR

	Mt.	Lk.	Jn		Mt.	Lk.	Jn
ἔλεος	3	6	0	ἐλπίζω[1]	1	3	1
(ii) ἐμαυτόν[2]	1	2	16	? ἐντυλίσσω (see			
ἐπαίρω[3]	1	6	4	1866 (i) foll.)	1	1	1
[1856] (ii) ἕτερος[4]	9	c. 34	1	(ii) ἐχθρός[5] (Mk)	7	8	0
(ii) ἥκω[6]	4	4	4	(ii) ἡλικία[7]	1	3	2
(ii) θεάομαι[8]	4	3	6	(ii) θερίζω[9]	3	3	4
[1857] (ii) θρηνέω[10]	1	2	1	Ἰωσήφ[11] (Mary's husband)	7	5	2

[1] ἐλπίζω, Mt. xii. 21 quoting Is. xlii. 4 "And in his name shall the Gentiles *hope*," Jn v. 45 "Moses on whom ye *have set your hope* (ἠλπίκατε)." See 2474.

[2] Ἐμαυτόν, Mt. viii. 9 "having under *myself* soldiers," parall. to Lk. vii. 7—8 (*bis*), uttered by the centurion whose servant is healed. In Jn it is always uttered by Christ.

[3] Ἐπαίρω, in Mt., only xvii. 8 ἐπάραντες δὲ τοὺς ὀφθαλμοὺς αὐτῶν.

[4] [1856 a] Ἕτερος, Mt. xi. 3, Lk. vii. 19 ἢ ἕτερον προσδοκῶμεν (foll. by Lk. ἢ ἄλλον (marg. ἕτερον) προσδοκῶμεν, which, if ἄλλον is genuine, indicates that the disciples of the Baptist softened his message into "Are we to expect another of the same kind?" but the txt is doubtful), Mt. xii. 45, Lk. xi. 26 ἕτερα πνεύματα πονηρότερα. It occurs, in Jn, only in xix. 37 καὶ πάλιν ἑτέρα γραφὴ λέγει, also in Mk App. [xvi. 12].

[5] Ἐχθρός, Mt. v. 44 (Lk. vi. 27, 35) ἀγαπᾶτε τοὺς ἐχθροὺς ὑμῶν. It occurs in Mk xii. 36 as a quotation (Ps. cx. 1) parall. to Mt. xxii. 44, Lk. xx. 43.

[6] Ἥκω, Mt. viii. 11, Lk. xiii. 29 ἥξουσιν, Mt. xxiv. 50, Lk. xii. 46 ἥξει ὁ κύριος τ. δούλου.... It is applied by Christ to Himself in Jn viii. 42 ἐγὼ γὰρ ἐκ τ. θεοῦ ἐξῆλθον καὶ ἥκω, comp. 1 Jn v. 20 ὁ υἱὸς τ. θεοῦ ἥκει, Heb. x. 7, 9 ἥκω (from Ps. xl. 7), Heb. x. 37 ὁ ἐρχόμενος ἥξει (from Hab. ii. 3).

[7] Ἡλικία, Mt. vi. 27, Lk. xii. 25 "add one cubit unto his *stature*." Jn ix. 21, 23 "He is of *age* (ἡλικίαν ἔχει)."

[8] Θεάομαι, Mt. xi. 7, Lk. vii. 24 τί ἐξήλθατε εἰς τὴν ἔρημον θεάσασθαι; It occurs in Mk App. [xvi. 11, 14].

[9] Θερίζω, Mt. vi. 26, Lk. xii. 24 οὐ σπείρουσιν οὐδὲ θερίζουσιν, Mt. xxv. 24—6 (Lk. xix. 21—2) θερίζων ὅπου (Lk. ὃ) οὐκ ἔσπειρας...θερίζων ὅπου (Lk. θερίζω ὃ) οὐκ ἔσπειρα. Jn iv. 36—8 (3 times) ὁ θερίζων, (once) θερίζειν.

[10] Θρηνέω, Mt. xi. 17, Lk. vii. 32 ἐθρηνήσαμεν καὶ οὐκ ἐκόψασθε (Lk. ἐκλαύσατε). In Jn xvi. 20 κλαύσετε καὶ θρηνήσετε ὑμεῖς.

[11] [1857 a] Ἰωσήφ (Mary's husband), in Mt.-Lk., occurs only before Christ begins to preach, exc. Lk. iv. 22 οὐχὶ υἱός ἐστιν Ἰ. οὗτος; which resembles Jn vi. 42 οὐχὶ οὗτός ἐστιν Ἰησοῦς ὁ υἱὸς Ἰ.; See 1776—8.

TO JOHN, MATTHEW, AND LUKE [1858]

	Mt.	Lk.	Jn		Mt.	Lk.	Jn
(iii) κἀγώ[1]	9	5	30	(ii) καθαρός[2]	3	1	4
καθέζομαι[3]	1	1	3	Καιάφας[4]	2	1	5
[1858] καίω[5]	1	1	2	καταβολή[6]	2	1	1
(ii) κατοικέω[7]	4	2	0	(ii) κεῖμαι[8]	3	5	7
κλείω[9]	3	2	2	(ii) κλέπτης[10]	3	2	4
?† (ii) κλίνω[11]	1	4	1	κοιμάομαι[12]	2	1	2

[1] [1857 b] Κἀγώ, marked (iii) because it occurs in Mt. and Lk. (unlike the words marked (ii)) in the Triple Tradition, where Mk xi. 29 has ἐπερωτήσω ὑμᾶς ἕνα λόγον, but Mt. xxi. 24, Lk. xx. 3 have ἐρωτήσω ὑμᾶς κἀγὼ λόγον ἕνα (Lk. om. ἕνα) (**456** (iii)). It does not occur in both versions of any parallel passages of the Double Tradition of Mt.-Lk.

[2] [1857 c] Καθαρός, Mt. xxiii. 26 ἵνα γένηται κ. τὸ ἐκτὸς αὐτοῦ καθαρόν, parall. to Lk. xi. 41 ἰδοὺ πάντα καθαρὰ ὑμῖν ἐστίν. Lk. omits Mt. v. 8 μακάριοι οἱ καθαροὶ τῇ καρδίᾳ. In Mt. xxvii. 59 σινδόνι καθαρᾷ, the epithet is om. by parall. Mk xv. 46, Lk. xxiii. 53. All Jn's instances are in the Last Discourse, xiii. 10 (bis), 11, xv. 3.

[3] Καθέζομαι, applied to the child Jesus in Lk. ii. 46, and used by Jesus concerning Himself in Mt. xxvi. 55. Mk uses only κάθημαι, καθίζω.

[4] Καιάφας, in Lk., only iii. 2 ἐπὶ ἀρχιερέως Ἄννα κ. Καιάφα (**1764** b).

[5] Καίω, in Mt., only v. 15 οὐδὲ καίουσιν λύχνον: in Lk., only xii. 35 ἔστωσαν ὑμῶν...οἱ λύχνοι καιόμενοι: Jn v. 35 calls the Baptist ὁ λύχνος ὁ καιόμενος. It means "burn" in Jn xv. 6 εἰς τὸ πῦρ βάλλουσιν κ. καίεται.

[6] Καταβολή, in Jn, only xvii. 24, ἠγάπησάς με πρὸ καταβολῆς κόσμου.

[7] Κατοικέω, Mt. xii. 45, Lk. xi. 26, εἰσελθόντα κατοικεῖ ἐκεῖ.

[8] Κεῖμαι, Mt. iii. 10, Lk. iii. 9 ἡ ἀξίνη πρὸς τ. ῥίζαν τ. δένδρων κεῖται. There is some similarity between Jn xx. 12 ὅπου ἔκειτο τὸ σῶμα τ. Ἰησοῦ, and Mt. xxviii. 6 τ. τόπον ὅπου ἔκειτο (Mk xvi. 6 ὁ τόπος ὅπου ἔθηκαν αὐτόν).

[9] Κλείω, in Jn, only xx. 19, 26 τ. θυρῶν κεκλεισμένων.

[10] Κλέπτης, Mt. vi. 19—20 (sim. Lk. xii. 33) "where *thieves* break through": also Mt. xxiv. 43 (Lk. xii. 39) "if he had known in what watch (Lk. hour) the *thief* cometh." In Jn x. 1—10 "the *thief* and the robber" are contrasted with the Good Shepherd: in Jn xii. 6 Judas Iscariot is said to have been "a *thief*."

[11] [1858 a] Κλίνω, marked ?† because it is probably quasi-parallel. It occurs in Mt. viii. 20, Lk. ix. 58 οὐκ ἔχει ποῦ τ. κεφαλὴν κλίνῃ, Jn. xix. 30 κλίνας τ. κεφαλὴν παρέδωκεν τ. πνεῦμα. Prob. both mean "leaning the head" in the sense of "finding rest," and Jn prefers this expression to ἐκοιμήθη "fell asleep (in death)" (**1839—46**). Elsewhere in N.T. it occurs only in Lk. ix. 12, xxiv. 5, 29, Heb. xi. 34.

[12] Κοιμάομαι, Mt. xxvii. 52 "the saints that *had fallen asleep*," xxviii. 13 "while we were *sleeping*," Lk. xxii. 45 "*sleeping* for sorrow," Jn xi. 11—12 "Lazarus...is *fallen asleep*...if he is *fallen asleep he will recover*."

	Mt.	Lk.	Jn		Mt.	Lk.	Jn
[1859] (ii) κοπιάω[1]	2	2	3	(ii) κρίνω[2]	6	6	19
(ii) κρίσις[3]	12	4	11	κρύπτω[4]	7	3	3
(ii) λιθοβολέω[5]	2	1	0	(ii) λύκος[6]	2	1	2
(ii) μακάριος[7]	13	15	2	μαρτυρέω[8]	1	1	33

[1] Κοπιάω, Mt. vi. 28, Lk. xii. 27 "they *toil* not, neither do they spin."

[2] **[1859 a]** Κρίνω, Mt. vii. 1, Lk. vi. 37 "*Judge* not that ye be not(Lk. "and ye shall not be ") *judged*," Mt. xix. 28 (parall. to Lk. xxii. 30, but with important differences in context) "*judging* the twelve tribes of Israel." Jn contains no prohibition against "judging," but a prohibition against judging wrongly and a command to judge righteously (vii. 24) "*Judge* not according to appearance but *judge* righteous judgment," and Jn adds (viii. 15) "Ye *judge* after the flesh, I *judge* no man, and yet if I be *judging* my judgment is true."

[3] **[1859 b]** Κρίσις occurs in Mt. xi. 22, Lk. x. 14 Τύρῳ καὶ Σιδῶνι ἀνεκτότερον ἔσται ἐν ἡμέρᾳ κρίσεως (Lk. ἐν τ. κρίσει). But Mt. xi. 24 γῇ Σοδόμων ἀνεκτότερον ἔσται ἐν ἡμέρᾳ κρίσεως ἢ σοί, and Mt. x. 15 ἀνεκτ. ἔσται γῇ Σ. καὶ Γ. ἐν ἡμέρᾳ κρίσεως ἢ τῇ πόλει ἐκείνῃ, may both be taken as parall. to Lk. x. 12 Σοδόμοις ἐν τῇ ἡμ. ἐκείνῃ ἀνεκτ. ἔσται ἢ τῇ πόλει ἐκείνῃ. Other parallels are Mt. xii. 41—2, Lk. xi. 31—2 ἐν τῇ κρίσει (*bis*) (and Mt. xxiii. 23 τ. κρίσιν καὶ τ. ἔλεος καὶ τ. πίστιν, Lk. xi. 42 τ. κρίσιν καὶ τ. ἀγάπην τ. θεοῦ). The Gospel of Jn seems to define ἡ κρίσις in iii. 19 as a "loving of the darkness rather than light": it never mentions ἡμέρα κρίσεως but has v. 29 εἰς ἀνάστασιν κρίσεως and xii. 31 νῦν κρίσις ἐστὶν τ. κόσμου τούτου. The Epistle has (1 Jn iv. 17) ἐν τῇ ἡμέρᾳ τῆς κρίσεως.

[4] **[1859 c]** Κρύπτω. There is no parallelism in any of the instances. Ἐκρύβη occurs in Lk. xix. 42 νῦν δὲ ἐκρύβη ἀπὸ ὀφθαλμῶν σου (referring to "the things that belong to peace" which are "hidden" from Jerusalem) and Jn viii. 59, xii. 36 ἐκρύβη, of Jesus "hidden" from the Jews.

[1859 d] The doctrine "There is nothing *hidden* that shall not be revealed," is expressed by Mk iv. 22, Lk. viii. 17, κρυπτόν and ἀπόκρυφον, Mt. x. 26 κεκαλυμμένον and κρυπτόν, Lk. xii. 2 συγκεκαλυμμένον and κρυπτόν.

[5] Λιθοβολέω, Mt. xxiii. 37, Lk. xiii. 34 λιθοβολοῦσα τ. ἀπεσταλμένους.

[6] Λύκος, Mt. x. 16, Lk. x. 3 ἀποστέλλω ὑμᾶς...ἐν μέσῳ λύκων.

[7] **[1859 e]** Μακάριος, Mt. v. 3—11 (sim. Lk. vi. 20—22) "*Blessed* are the poor...," and Mt. xi. 6, Lk. vii. 23 "*Blessed* is he that shall not be made to stumble in me," Mt. xiii. 16 (sim. Lk. x. 23) "*Blessed* are your eyes...": Mt. xxiv. 46, Lk. xii. 43 "*Blessed* is that servant...." Jn. xiii. 17 "If ye know these things, *blessed* are ye if ye be doing them," xx. 29 "*Blessed* are they that have not seen and yet have believed." The former of Jn's instances resembles Lk. xi. 28 (pec.) "*Blessed* are they that hear the word of God and keep it."

[8] Μαρτυρέω, Mt. xxiii. 31 ὥστε μαρτυρεῖτε ἑαυτοῖς, Lk. iv. 22 πάντες ἐμαρτύρουν αὐτῷ.

	Mt.	Lk.	Jn		Mt.	Lk.	Jn
[1860] (ii) μέρος (= "lot," "destiny")[1]	1	1	1	μεταβαίνω[2]	6	1	3
(ii)* μεταξύ[3]	2	2	1	μιμνήσκομαι[4]	3	6	3
Ναζωραῖος[5]	2	1	3	(ii) νήπιοι[6]	2	1	0
(ii) νόμος[7]	8	9	14	(ii)* νύμφη[8]	1	2	1
[1861] (ii) ὁδηγέω[9]	1	1	1	(ii) ὅμοιος[10]	9	9	2
(ii) ὁμολογέω[11]	4	2	4	ὄνος[12]	3	1	1
(ii) ὀργίζομαι[13]	3	2	0	ὀστέον[14]	1	1	1
(ii) οὐχί (2231 a)	9	17	6	ὀφείλω[15]	6	5	2

[1] Μέρος, Mt. xxiv. 51, Lk. xii. 46 τ. μέρος αὐτοῦ μετὰ τ. ὑποκριτῶν θήσει, Jn xiii. 8 οὐκ ἔχεις μέρος μετ' ἐμοῦ. It also means "part," "district."

[2] Μεταβαίνω, alw. literal in Mt., and in Lk. x. 7 and Jn vii. 3; spiritual in Jn v. 24, and in Jn xiii. 1 ἵνα μεταβῇ ἐκ τ. κόσμου.

[3] Μεταξύ, marked * (1734 a_1), means, in Mt. xxiii. 35 (sim. Lk. xi. 51) "*between* the sanctuary and the altar," in Jn iv. 31 "in the *meanwhile*."

[4] Μιμνήσκομαι, in Jn ii. 17, 22, xii. 16 alw. of disciples "remembering" the correspondence between Scripture and words or deeds of Christ.

[5] Ναζωραῖος, Mt. ii. 23, xxvi. 71, Lk. xviii. 37, Jn xviii. 5, 7, xix. 19.

[6] Νήπιοι, Mt. xi. 25, Lk. x. 21 ἀπεκάλυψας αὐτὰ νηπίοις, also Mt. xxi. 16 (pec.) (quoting Ps. viii. 2) ἐκ στόματος νηπίων καὶ θηλαζόντων.

[7] Νόμος, Mt. v. 18 (sim. Lk. xvi. 17) μία κερέα...ἀπὸ τοῦ νόμου, Mk. xi. 13 (sim. Lk. xvi. 16) οἱ προφῆται κ. ὁ νόμος ἕως Ἰωάνου. See also in Triple Tradition Mt. xxii. 36, Lk. x. 26.

[8] Νύμφη, Mt. x. 35 (sim. Lk. xii. 53 (*bis*)) "*daughter-in-law* against her mother-in-law," Jn iii. 29 "He that hath the *bride*."

[9] Ὁδηγέω, Mt. xv. 14 (sim. Lk. vi. 39) "But if the blind *guide* the blind," Jn xvi. 13 "The Spirit of truth *shall guide* you."

[10] Ὅμοιος, Mt. xi. 16, Lk. vii. 32 "*Like* children sitting in the market-places," and freq. in Mt. Lk. parables. Jn viii. 55 "*like* unto you, a liar," ix. 9 "he is *like* him."

[11] [1861 a] Ὁμολογέω, Mt. x. 32 (*bis*) (sim. Lk. xii. 8 (*bis*)) "whoever shall *confess* me...." Jn ix. 22, xii. 42 says that the Jews had agreed to excommunicate a "*confessor*" of Christ and that hence some believers feared to "*confess*." Jn never uses ἐξομολογοῦμαι, which in Mk i. 5, Mt. iii. 6 means "*confess* (*sins*)," but he uses ὁμολογέω thus in 1 Jn i. 9.

[12] [1861 b] Ὄνος, Mt. xxi. 2—7 has ὄνος καὶ πῶλος, Mk xi. 2—7, Lk. xix. 30—35 have πῶλος alone, Jn xii. 14 has ὀνάριον alone (though xii. 15 quotes πῶλον ὄνου) in the Entry into Jerusalem. Lk. xiii. 15 has ὄνος in the discussion about "loosing" one's ass on the Sabbath.

[13] Ὀργίζομαι, Mt. xxii. 7, sim. Lk. xiv. 21 (the Parable of the Feast that was declined). Not parallel elsewhere.

[14] Ὀστέον, Mt. xxiii. 27, Lk. xxiv. 39, Jn xix. 36.

[15] Ὀφείλω, in Lk. xvii. 10, Jn xiii. 14, xix. 7 "ought," elsewhere "owe."

[1862] WORDS MOSTLY PECULIAR

	Mt.	Lk.	Jn		Mt.	Lk.	Jn
[1862] (ii) παῖς[1]	8	9	1	παραχρῆμα[2]	2	10	0
πάρειμι[3]	1	1	2	(ii) πῆχυς[4]	1	1	1
(ii)* πιστός[5]	5	6	1	πνέω[6]	2	1	2

[1] [1862 a] Παῖς occurs in Mt. viii. 8, Lk. vii. 7 εἰπὲ λόγῳ καὶ ἰαθήσεται (Lk. ἰαθήτω) ὁ παῖς μου. Comp. Jn iv. 51 " His bond-servants (δοῦλοι) came to meet him saying that his *son* (lit. *boy*) (παῖς) was alive," where the context relates how Jesus from a distance (being apparently in or near Cana) healed the *son* of a person in the royal retinue (βασιλικός) "whose *son* (υἱός) was sick at Capernaum." By repeatedly mentioning "*son* (υἱός)" the narrative makes it clear that παῖς, in Jn, must here mean "*son*" and not "*servant*."

[1862 b] The Double Tradition of Mt.-Lk. (Mt. viii. 5—13, Lk. vii. 1—10) describes Jesus as having "entered into Capernaum" when He receives a request to heal (Mt. viii. 6) a "*boy* (παῖς)," or (Lk. vii. 2) "*bond-servant* (δοῦλος)," of a centurion. Mt. describes the man as making his request in person, Lk. as making it through others; both use the phrase (Mt. viii. 8, Lk. vii. 7) ὁ παῖς μου. Most commentators take Mt. and Lk. as referring to the same event, and, if so, must regard "*boy*" in Mt. as meaning "*bond-servant*."

[1862 c] Irenæus (ii. 22. 3) "(Jn) *Filium* (Mt.-Lk.) *centurionis* absens verbo curavit, *Vade*, (Jn) *filius tuus vivit*"—whether quoting wrongly through lapse of memory, or combining details from narratives that he supposed to relate the same event—demonstrates the ease with which the two stories about the centurion might be confused with the Johannine story, and the ambiguity that might attach to "*boy*" in the earliest of the three. It is probable, though by no means certain, that Jn wrote with a view to this ambiguity.

[1862 d] Mt. xvii. 18 ἐθεραπεύθη ὁ παῖς, parall. to Lk. ix. 42 ἰάσατο τὸν παῖδα, is in the Triple Tradition, where Mk ix. 24 has παιδίου, previously called by all (Mk ix. 17, Mt. xvii. 14, Lk. ix. 38) υἱός.

[2] Παραχρῆμα, see 1693 e.

[3] Πάρειμι, Mt. xxvi. 50, Lk. xiii. 1, Jn vii. 6, xi. 28.

[4] Πῆχυς, Mt. vi. 27, Lk. xii. 25, ἐπὶ τ. ἡλικίαν...πῆχυν, Jn xxi. 8 ὡς ἀπὸ πηχῶν διακοσίων.

[5] [1862 e] Πιστός, in Mt.-Lk. "faithful," Mt. xxiv. 45 (Lk. xii. 42) τίς ἄρα ἐστὶν ὁ πιστὸς δοῦλος (Lk. οἰκονόμος) καὶ (Lk. ὁ) φρόνιμος; Mt. xxv. 21, 23 (twice) εὖ δοῦλε ἀγαθὲ καὶ πιστέ, ἐπὶ ὀλίγα ἦς πιστός, Lk. xix. 17 εὖγε, ἀγαθὲ δοῦλε, ὅτι ἐν ἐλαχίστῳ πιστὸς ἐγένου, Jn xx. 27 (to Thomas) " Be not unbelieving (ἄπιστος) but *believing* (πιστός)."

[6] Πνέω, Mt. vii. 25, 27, Lk. xii. 55, Jn vi. 18, is in the description of a tempest; in Jn iii. 8 it is connected with regeneration, τὸ πνεῦμα ὅπου θέλει πνεῖ.

TO JOHN, MATTHEW, AND LUKE [1864]

		Mt.	Lk.	Jn		Mt.	Lk.	Jn
	ποιμαίνω[1]	1	1	1	ποίμνη[2]	1	1	1
[1863]	πρὸ τοῦ (w. inf.)	1	2	3	(ii) προσκόπτω[3]	2	1	2
	πυνθάνομαι[4]	1	2	1	Σαμαρείτης[5]	1	3	3+[1]
	(ii) σκορπίζω[6]	1	1	2	(ii) σκοτία[7]	2	1	8
[1864]	(ii) σκότος(metaph.)[8]	5	3	1	(ii) Σολομών[9]	5	3	1
	(ii) σοφία (Chri.)[10]	2	4	0	(ii) σοφός[11]	2	1	0
	στάδιος[12]	1	1	2	(ii) στόμα[13]	11	9	1
	στρέφω[14]	6	7	4	συλλέγω[15]	7	1	0

[1] Ποιμαίνω, Mt. ii. 6 (quoting Mic. v. 1), Lk. xvii. 7 (pec.) "Which of you shall have a bond-servant ploughing or *sheep-tending* (ποιμαίνοντα)," Jn xxi. 16 "*tend* my young sheep."

[2] Ποίμνη, Mt. xxvi. 31 (quoting Zech. xiii. 7 wrongly), Lk. ii. 8, Jn x. 16 "they shall become one *flock*, one shepherd."

[3] Προσκόπτω, Mt. iv. 6 (Lk. iv. 11) "Lest thou *dash* thy foot" (Ps. xci. 12), Mt. vii. 27 "*smote upon* that house," Jn xi. 9, 10 "*stumble*."

[4] Πυνθάνομαι, Mt. ii. 4 ἐπυνθάνετο...ποῦ ὁ Χρ. γεννᾶται, Jn iv. 52 ἐπύθετο οὖν τ. ὥραν παρ' αὐτῶν.

[5] Σαμαρείτης, Mt. x. 5 εἰς πόλιν Σ. μὴ εἰσέλθητε. W.H. bracket Jn iv. 9.

[6] Σκορπίζω, Mt. xii. 30, Lk. xi. 23 "He that gathereth not with me *scattereth*," Jn x. 12 "the wolf *scattereth* them," xvi. 32 "....that ye shall be *scattered*."

[7] [1863 a] Σκοτία, Mt. x. 27 ὃ λέγω ὑμῖν ἐν τ. σκοτίᾳ, εἴπατε (imper.), parall. Lk. xii. 3 ἀνθ' ὧν ὅσα ἐν τ. σκοτίᾳ εἴπατε (indic.); also in Mt. iv. 16 (giving a version of Is. ix. 1) ὁ λαὸς ὁ καθήμενος ἐν σκοτίᾳ.

[8] [1864 a] Σκότος (metaph.), Mt. vi. 23 εἰ οὖν τὸ φῶς τὸ ἐν σοὶ σκότος ἐστὶν τὸ σκότος πόσον, parall. Lk. xi. 35 μὴ τὸ φῶς τὸ ἐν σοὶ σκότος ἐστίν. Mk has σκότος once (xv. 33) but in a literal sense. See **1710 a**.

[9] Σολομών, Mt. vi. 29, Lk. xii. 27 οὐδὲ Σ., Mt. xii. 42, Lk. xi. 31 τ. σοφίαν Σ....πλεῖον Σ., Jn x. 23 ἐν τῇ στοᾷ τοῦ Σ.

[10] Σοφία, Mt. xi. 19, Lk. vii. 35 ἐδικαιώθη ἡ σοφία, Mt. xii. 42, Lk. xi. 31 ἀκοῦσαι τ. σοφίαν Σολομῶνος. Σοφία also occurs (outside Christ's words) in Mk vi. 2 (sim. Mt. xiii. 54) τίς ἡ σοφία....

[11] Σοφός, Mt. xi. 25 (Lk. x. 21) ὅτι ἔκρυψας (Lk. ἀπέκρυψας) ταῦτα ἀπὸ σοφῶν καὶ συνετῶν.

[12] Στάδιος, Mt. xiv. 24 (txt.), Lk. xxiv. 13, Jn vi. 19, xi. 18.

[13] Στόμα, Mt. xii. 34, Lk. vi. 45 "out of the abundance of the heart the *mouth* speaketh," Jn xix. 29 "[they] brought it to his *mouth*."

[14] [1864 b] Στραφείς is applied to Jesus, "turning round," before speaking, in Mt. ix. 22, xvi. 23; Lk. vii. 9, 44, ix. 55, x. 23, xiv. 25, xxii. 61, xxiii. 28. Lk. uses the word in no other sense. Jn uses it thus once (i. 38) to introduce the first words uttered by Jesus, addressed to His first two converts, Andrew and another.

[15] Συλλέγω, Mt. vii. 16 μήτι συλλέγουσιν ἀπὸ ἀκανθῶν σταφυλάς, Lk. vi.

[1865] WORDS MOSTLY PECULIAR

	Mt.	Lk.	Jn		Mt.	Lk.	Jn
[1865] (ii) συνετός[1]	1	1	0	(ii) ταπεινός, -όω[2]	4	6	0
τε	3	9	3	τελέω[3]	7	4	2
(?) τίκτω[4]	4	5	1	(ii) τροφή[5]	4	1	1
(ii) ὑπάρχοντα[6]	3	8	0	ὕπνος[7]	1	1	1
[1866] (iii) ὕστερον[8]	7	1	1	(ii) ὑψόω[9]	3	6	5

44 οὐ γὰρ ἐξ ἀκανθῶν συλλέγουσιν σῦκα. Mt. xiii. 28—48 uses συλλέγω of gathering the tares that are to be burned; Jn xv. 6 uses συνάγω of gathering withered branches for the same purpose.

[1] Συνετός, Mt. xi. 25, Lk. x. 21 ἀπὸ σοφῶν καὶ συνετῶν (see note on σοφός).

[2] [1865 a] Ταπεινόω is in Mt. xxiii. 12 (sim. Lk. xiv. 11) (bis) "Whosoever shall *humble* himself shall be exalted...," rep. in Lk. xviii. 14. Ταπεινός is only in Mt. xi. 29 (pec.), Lk. i. 52 (pec.). Mt. xviii. 4 "*humble* himself as this little child" seems to be an explanation of Mk x. 15 "receiving the kingdom of God as a little child," Mt. xviii. 3 "turn and become as little children."

Epictetus regularly uses ταπεινός (-όω) in the sense of "servile": (iv. 4. 1) "The desire of wealth makes men *servile* and subject to others," (i. 3. 1) "One who believes that God is his Father ought to have no *servile* thoughts about himself" etc.

[3] [1865 b] Τελέω, Mt. five times (vii. 28, xi. 1, xiii. 53, xix. 1, xxvi. 1) in such phrases as ὅτε ἐτέλεσεν ὁ Ἰ. τοὺς λόγους τούτους, introducing a new section of narrative. Jn xix. 28—30 εἰδὼς ὁ Ἰ. ὅτι ἤδη πάντα τετέλεσται.... εἶπεν Τετέλεσται.

[4] Τίκτω, Mt. i. 21 τέξεται δὲ υἱόν (uttered to Joseph) may be regarded by some as parall. to Lk. i. 31 τέξῃ υἱόν (uttered to Mary): in Jn, only xvi. 21 ἡ γυνὴ ὅταν τίκτῃ λύπην ἔχει.

[5] Τροφή, Mt. vi. 25 οὐχὶ ἡ ψυχὴ πλεῖόν ἐστιν τ. τροφῆς; parall. Lk. xii. 23 ἡ γὰρ ψ. πλεῖόν ἐστιν τ. τροφῆς: Jn iv. 8 ἵνα τροφὰς ἀγοράσωσιν.

[6] Ὑπάρχοντα, Mt. xxiv. 47, Lk. xii. 44 ἐπὶ πᾶσιν τοῖς ὑ....καταστήσει αὐτόν.

[7] Ὕπνος, Mt. i. 24, Lk. ix. 32, Jn xi. 13.

[8] Ὕστερον, Mt. xxii. 27 ὕστερον δὲ πάντων ἀπέθανεν ἡ γυνή, Lk. xx. 32 ὕστερον κ. ἡ γυνὴ ἀπέθανεν. The word is marked (iii) because the passage in which Mt. and Lk. agree is in the Triple Tradition, where Mk xii. 22 has ἔσχατον πάντων: in Jn, only in Jn xiii. 36 ἀκολουθήσεις δὲ ὕστερον.

[9] [1866 a] Ὑψόω, Mt. xi. 23, Lk. x. 15 (to Capernaum) "Shalt thou be *exalted* to heaven?" also Mt. xxiii. 12 (bis) (parallel to Lk. xiv. 11 (bis)), and xviii. 14 (bis)) "Whosoever shall *exalt* himself...." In Jn, always (iii. 14 (bis), viii. 28, xii. 32, 34) concerning the "lifting up" of the Son of man (illustrated once by the "lifting up" of the brazen serpent).

TO JOHN, MATTHEW, AND LUKE   [1866]

	Mt.	Lk.	Jn		Mt.	Lk.	Jn
(ii) φίλος[1]	1	15	6	(ii) φρόνιμος[2]	7	2	0
(ii) φῶς (metaph.)[3]	6	4	23	(ii) ὥσπερ[4]	10	2	2
ὠτίον[5]	1	1	1				

[1] [1866 *b*] Φίλος, Mt. xi. 19, Lk. vii. 34 "a *friend* of publicans and sinners." On Christ's phrase "my friends," see **1784—92**. Φιλέω occurs Mk (1), Mt. (5), Lk. (2), Jn (13), but not always with the same meaning. It means "kiss" in Mk xiv. 44, Mt. xxvi. 48, Lk. xxii. 47. In Lk. xx. 46 "*loving* salutations" is parall. to Mt. xxiii. 6—7 "But they *love*....and salutations." Since it never means "love (persons)" in Lk., and since it occurs once in Mk (meaning "kiss") it is not placed above. Φιλέω means "love (persons)" in Mt. x. 37 (*bis*) and always in Jn exc. xii. 25 "he that *loveth* his life." See **1716** *e—g* and **1728** *m—p*.

[2] Φρόνιμος, Mt. xxiv. 45, Lk. xii. 42 τίς ἄρα ἐστὶν ὁ πιστὸς δοῦλος κ. φρόνιμος.

[3] Φῶς, Mt. vi. 23, Lk. xi. 35 τὸ φῶς τὸ ἐν σοί, Mt. x. 27 ὃ λέγω ὑμῖν ἐν τ. σκοτίᾳ εἴπατε (imper.) ἐν τ. φωτί, but parall. Lk. xii. 3 ὅσα ἐν τ. σκοτίᾳ εἴπατε (indic.) ἐν τ. φωτὶ ἀκουσθήσεται. In Jn xii. 36 ἵνα υἱοὶ φωτὸς γένησθε is parall. in form, though not in context, to Lk. xvi. 8 φρονιμώτεροι ὑπὲρ τ. υἱοὺς τ. φωτός. On Jn-Mt. "light of the world," see **1748**.

[4] Ὥσπερ, Mt. xxiv. 27, Lk. xvii. 24 ὥσπερ γὰρ ἡ ἀστραπή.... In Lk. and Jn, alw. foll. by γάρ exc. Lk. xviii. 11 ὥσπερ (v.r. ὡς) οἱ λοιποί.

[5] [1866 *c*] Ὠτίον is used by Mt. xxvi. 51 in the wounding of the High Priest's servant (Lk. οὖς, Mk and Jn ὠτάριον) but by Lk. xxii. 51 (pec.) in the healing, and by Jn xviii. 26 in a reference to the wounding.

ADDITIONAL NOTE (ἐντυλίσσω)

[1866 (i)] Ἐντυλίσσω occurs in Matthew's and Luke's versions of the Triple Tradition describing Christ's burial thus:

Mk xv. 46	Mt. xxvii. 59	Lk. xxiii. 53
καὶ ἀγοράσας σινδόνα καθελὼν αὐτὸν ἐνείλησεν τῇ σινδόνι.	καὶ λαβὼν τὸ σῶμα ὁ Ἰωσὴφ ἐνετύλιξεν αὐτὸ [ἐν] σινδόνι καθαρᾷ.	καὶ καθελὼν ἐνετύλιξεν αὐτὸ σινδόνι. Jn xix. 40 ἔδησαν.

In Mark, R.V. has "*wound him*" (A.V. "*wrapped him*"); in Matthew and Luke, R.V. has "*wrapped it.*" It has been explained elsewhere (520—1) that Mark might deliberately use ἐνειλεῖν, "*bind fast*," in order to shew the reality of the death, and of the burial, and the impossibility of a hasty removal of the body apart from the burial clothes, a point urged by Chrysostom[1]. But Matthew and Luke may have objected to the word (especially when applied, as by Mark, not to "body" but to "him") as being unseemly, because it is used of fettering prisoners, swathing children hand and foot, holding people fast in a net, entangling them in evil or in debt, and generally in a bad sense[2].

[1866 (ii)] Ἐντυλίσσω, apparently a much rarer word than ἐνειλέω, is free from the objection of being used in a bad or hostile sense; for it is used of wrapping oneself up in a cloak or a rug, and, so far as can be

---

[1] [1866 (i) a] Chrys. (on Jn, Migne p. 465) "John says that he was buried with a great amount of myrrh, which glues as it were the linen cloths to the body like the soldering of lead (ἡ μολύβδου οὐχ ἧττον συγκολλᾷ τῷ σώματι τὰ ὀθόνια)."

[2] [1866 (i) b] Steph. quotes Synes. *Ep.* 105 p. 248 B ἐνειλούμενον τοῖς πρὸς τὰ γεώδη μεθέλκουσιν, Plut. *Mor.* p. 830 E ὁ ἅπαξ ἐνειληθεὶς (aeri alieno) μένει χρεώστης. Artemid. i. 13 connects it with helplessness or inactivity, ἀργὰ γὰρ τὰ βρέφη καὶ ἐνειλούμενα τὰς χεῖρας, *ib.* 54 τ. δεξιὰν ἐνειλημένην ἔχειν διὰ τὸ ἀργὴν εἶναι.... Plutarch *Caes.* 66 says that Caesar ὥσπερ θηρίον ἐνειλεῖτο ταῖς πάντων χερσίν. Steph. adds Artox. c. 11 Κῦρον τοῖς πολεμίοις ἐνειλούμενον, Quintus 14, 294 Κῆρες...πολέεσσί μ' ἐνειλήσαντο κακοῖσι, and Hesych. explains ἐνείληται as ἐζημίωται. These passages and others quoted by Steph. suggest that Polyc. *Philipp.* § 1 τοὺς ἐνειλημένους τοῖς ἁγιοπρεπέσιν δεσμοῖς ἅτινά ἐστιν διαδήματα draws a contrast between the physical fettering of martyrs and their spiritual adornment, because, though they are "*fast bound*" in them, they do not regard themselves as (Ps. cvii. 10) "*fast bound* in misery and iron," but as wearing "diadems" of the elect. At the same time Polycarp emphasizes the necessity of helping those who are thus unable to help themselves.

judged from the Thesaurus, never implies constraint[1]. But no instance is alleged of its meaning "wrap up a covering," "roll up a napkin" except in John xx. 7 "[Simon] beholdeth the linen cloths lying, and the napkin, which had been on his head, not lying with the linen cloths, but apart, *rolled up* (ἐντετυλιγμένον) (lit.) into one place."

[1866 (iii)] Ἐντυλίσσω as used by John and meaning "*roll up*" is not similar in meaning to *ἐ.* as used by Matthew-Luke meaning "*wrap.*" Nor are the two words in parallel contexts. Yet, having regard to the extreme rarity of the word in Greek literature of every age and to the fact that it does not occur anywhere in O.T. or N.T. except here, it is difficult to avoid the inference that John uses it with reference to the diverging traditions of the Synoptists—Mark using "*bind fast,*" Matthew and Luke "*wrap.*" John (xix. 40), avoiding the word ἐνειλέω, substitutes a word that means the same thing, ἔδησαν, "*bound,*" and he adds, as Chrysostom says, a mention of "abundance of myrrh" which would have the effect of "*binding fast,*" like "the soldering of lead." At the same time, while substantially siding with Mark, John accepts the rare word of Matthew and Luke as expressing a fact, though not exactly the fact they describe. "There *was*"—John seems to say—"a '*wrapping,*' or rather a '*wrapping up,*' in connexion with the burial of the Lord. But it referred to *the burial garments alone*[2], not to the body itself."

[1866 (iv)] Some illustration of the facts above mentioned may be derived from the facts mentioned elsewhere (640—61) as regards what Mark (i. 10) calls the "*rending* (σχίζω)" of the heavens, whereas Matthew (iii. 16) and Luke (iii. 21) use the word "*open* (ἀνοίγω)." John omits this, but has later on (i. 51) "Ye shall see the heaven *set open* (ἀνοίγω)," agreeing verbally with Matthew and Luke but by no means in parallel context. Ἐντυλίσσω is far rarer than ἀνοίγω, and is used by the three Evangelists in contexts that are much more nearly parallel than those referring to ἀνοίγω. The demonstration, therefore, is far stronger here that John is writing allusively to the Synoptists, and he appears to be not only justifying Mark but also explaining what he may have thought a misunderstanding in Matthew and Luke.

---

[1] [1866 (ii) *a*] Aristoph. *Nub.* 983 ἐν ἱματίοις προδιδάσκεις ἐντετυλίχθαι, *Plut.* 692 Αὐτὴν ἐντυλίξασ' ἡσυχῇ. Steph. also quotes Athen. 3 p. 106 F, 107 A, where it describes the wrapping up of the liver etc. He refers to, but does not quote, Diocl. ap. Antiatt. Bekk. p. 97, 9. It does not occur in LXX (where ἐνειλεῖσθαι occurs once), and would seem to be a very rare word in Gk literature of all periods.

[2] [1866 (iii) *a*] Comp. Lk. [xxiv. 12] "*the linen cloths alone* (μόνα)," and Jn xx. 5—7 "*the linen cloths...the linen cloths...*the napkin...*not with the linen cloths, but apart,*" and see **1804** on "*the linen cloths alone,*" a phrase that may have been the subject of many interpretations.

CONCLUSION

§ 1. *Review of the evidence*

The Vocabularies given above have exhibited results that may be tabulated as follows:

[1867] (1) Synoptic Vocabulary, *i.e.* the Vocabulary of the Triple Tradition. This differs widely from the Johannine. Where the same words are used by all four Gospels, the Fourth often uses metaphorically what the Three use literally.

[1868] (2) Johannine Vocabulary. This would be found very small indeed as compared with the Vocabulary of Matthew by itself, or with that of Luke by itself, and even when compared above with the limited number of words used by Mark, Matthew, and Luke in common, it is small. It omits words of local or temporary interest and rings the changes on a small number of elementary words and their synonyms.

[1869] (3) John-Mark Agreements. The verbal agreements are few, Mark being the most concrete, and John being the most abstract, of the Evangelists. But the number of parallelisms is large, or—if regard be had to the small number of verbal agreements—very large indeed. They are also undeniable. For example, no one denies that the sayings about "buying for two hundred denarii" and "selling for three hundred denarii" are recorded by Mark and John in connexion, severally, with the same events.

[1870] (4) John-Matthew Agreements. The verbal agreements are more numerous than those in the John-Mark list.

CONCLUSION [1871]

But there are no parallelisms unless we suppose that John, when mentioning "*a* tribunal" in connexion with Pilate, wishes to distinguish it from "*the* tribunal" mentioned by Matthew. There are, however, the phrases "my brethren" and "light of the world," assigned both by Matthew and by John to our Lord but in different contexts—and the latter (1748) with the several prefixes, "Ye are," and "I am."

[1871] (5) John-Luke Agreements. The verbal agreements are very numerous indeed, exhibiting the two Evangelists as educated writers naturally using a similar vocabulary (except where Luke gave up, and John retained, special words of low-class Greek—perhaps endeared to some readers by old Evangelic associations). But parallelisms either are non-existent or are of a corrective character. For example, John twice uses Luke's word ἐκμάσσω to emphasize apparently the fact that the woman that "wiped" the Lord's feet was *not* a "sinner," but Mary the sister of Martha. Since also the evidence indicated that we ought to include in Luke's text the description of Peter's visit to Christ's sepulchre[1], there appeared to be another quasi-parallelism that must be described as corrective. And other corrective passages appeared to exist in John, in connexion with the phrase "stood in the midst," applied to our Lord after the Resurrection by him and Luke.

---

[1] [1871 *a*] The passage, like others in Luke's account of the Resurrection, might have been added by Luke himself in a second edition of his Gospel. I am informed by my friend Dr Israel Gollancz that there is evidence to shew that in the poems of Langland certainly, and perhaps in those of Chaucer, there are copies containing additions that proceeded from the author himself. In the days before printing, an author's second edition, if made shortly before his death, might appear at first in only a few copies, whereas the first edition might count its hundreds or thousands. This might discredit the additions in the second edition, so that even those scribes that copied it might think it necessary to correct the second by the first, omitting what appeared to some "the corrupt interpolations of the later copies."

[1872] (6) *John-Mark-Matthew Agreements.* Here, as in the John-Mark list, the number of verbal agreements is not large, but the parallelisms are proportionately very numerous; and the facts indicate that, in these, John is not following Matthew but Mark, whom Matthew has previously followed.

[1873] (7) *John-Mark-Luke Agreements.* The verbal agreements are not numerous—the vocabulary of Mark and that of Luke being seldom likely to be similar except where both are describing exorcisms, a subject never mentioned by John. There is only one parallelism, namely, in the description of the Baptist as not worthy to loose the "latchet" of Christ's shoe, where Matthew has "carry the shoes." One quasi-parallelism appears to be of a corrective nature, bearing on the "spices" used, or to be used, in embalming the body of Christ. Mark and Luke connect these with the women, Matthew omits "spices," and says that the women came to "behold" the tomb. John assigns the "spices" to Nicodemus and Joseph. The paucity of parallelisms contrasts with the abundance in the John-Mark-Matthew list.

[1874] (8) *John-Matthew-Luke Agreements.* The verbal agreements are very numerous indeed: but there is not a single parallelism. There is, however, an allusive use of Matthew-Luke's phrase "lay the head to rest," applied by John (**1839**) to the description of Christ's death. John sometimes alludes (**1450, 1784**) to Matthew's *or* Luke's version of the Double Tradition and (*e.g.* **1866** (i) foll.) to Matthew's *and* Luke's versions of the Triple Tradition; but in no case does John agree exactly with Matthew and Luke combined, or with either separately.

§ 2. *What remains to be done*

[1875] It may be objected against the preceding system of Vocabularies that it is incomplete, and—so far as concerns the attitude of the Fourth Gospel to the collective evidence of the Three—negative. "The first"—it may be said—"of the eight Vocabularies tells us what words are characteristic of Mark-Matthew-Luke and absent or rare in John: the second tells us what are characteristic of John and absent or rare in Mark-Matthew-Luke. But this is largely negative information. Where is the Vocabulary of *words common to the Four*, the *John-Mark-Matthew-Luke Vocabulary*? That would give us purely positive information, for want of which the preceding investigation must be pronounced defective."

[1876] Let us consider this objection in the light of facts as presented by page 1 A of Mr Rushbrooke's *Synopticon*, which prints in large red capitals all the words common to the Four Gospels in the description of John the Baptist and his baptism of Christ. They are as follows: "Voice of one crying in the wilderness, straight[en] the way of the Lord... Isaiah the prophet...I bapti[ze] in water...com[ing] of whom I am not...the shoe...Jordan...baptiz[ing]...Spirit descend[ing] as a dove from heaven...him...baptiz[ing] in the Holy Spirit... the Son (v.r. elect)." Now suppose we were to tabulate these words alphabetically, should we derive any information from them apart from a close examination of their context? For example, the last two words "the Son" (if genuine) occur in John the Baptist's testimony "I have borne witness that this is *the Son* of God." But the Synoptic mention of "Son" at the conclusion of the account of the Baptism refers it to a Voice from heaven, "This is (or, Thou art) my beloved *Son*." Again, Luke distinctly says that the Spirit "descended in bodily shape as a dove"; Mark and Matthew say "He saw" the descent, the former apparently, the latter certainly, referring "He" to Jesus (**596**). The Fourth Gospel makes the Baptist clear up this doubt by saying, "*I have beheld* the Spirit descending as a dove." These distinctions are most important. But what important gain would there be from simply reading, in a "John-Mark-Matthew-Luke Vocabulary," such an entry as "περιστερά Mk (2), Mt. (3), Lk. (2), Jn (3)"?

[1877] If mere tabulation would be useless as to the words specified above ("Son" and "dove") which belong to a narrative (the Baptism of Christ) where the Fourth Gospel intervenes in the Triple Tradition, much more would the charge of uselessness apply to such words as must necessarily form the common stock of all Gospels, *e.g.* "man," "woman," "live," "die," "soul," "spirit," "heaven," "earth," etc. We may therefore dismiss the project of a complete Fourfold Vocabulary as not likely to be what Bacon calls "luciferous." But we cannot dismiss so readily the thought—suggested by the last paragraph—that a close critical examination of the Johannine and the Synoptic narratives of the Baptism, and of other passages where John intervenes, would be of great value. Take, for example, the Feeding of the Five Thousand, where all the Evangelists except Luke mention "grass" in various ways. In a mere Fourfold Vocabulary this fact would not appear because Luke uses "grass" in other contexts. Even if a note were added, calling attention to Luke's omission, its significance would be lost among other notes necessarily attached to the word "grass" if it had to be annotated at all. It is only in a commentary on the four accounts of the miracle, that this and other points of Johannine agreement, or disagreement, with this or that Synoptist, could be satisfactorily discussed.

§ 3. *Johannine Grammar*

[1878] It might seem, then, that the next step should be to examine in order all the passages where the Fourth Gospel intervenes in the tradition of the Three. Equipped, as we now are from the preceding Vocabularies, with information as to the words that John favours and disfavours, his metaphorical method, and his apparent preference for Mark or Mark-Matthew (as compared with Luke) we could apply this knowledge to each narrative in turn, shewing how the Fourth

Gospel sometimes deviates from all three in virtue of his peculiar method or style, and sometimes approximates to one, or two, of the three in conformity with his rule of preference.

[1879] But we do not know quite enough about John as yet to do this effectually. It is not enough about any writer —least of all about a writer in Greek, a language abounding in facilities for expressing thought and emphasis by variety of order and construction—to know merely what verbs, nouns, and prepositions he likes and dislikes. We must also know something of his syntax. There are more ambiguities in the Fourth Gospel than in all the Three taken together, and it is easy to put one's finger on the cause of many of them. One, for example, is the attempt to express meaning by order of words or by reference to context. The very last words of Christ in freedom, uttered before He is led away in bonds to Annas, are what, proceeding from a classical Greek author, would have to be rendered, "The cup that my Father hath given me I will assuredly not drink it." There can be no doubt here that the words are to be read either interrogatively or as an exclamation implying surprise that Peter should try to prevent Him from drinking the cup: but there are many other passages where the meaning is far from clear until they have been illustrated by the comparison of a large number of similar instances.

[1880] Again, it is a peculiarity of John's style, and sometimes almost an obtrusive one, that he repeats some statements twice, others thrice, and that a sevenfold arrangement appears in parts of his narrative, and he occasionally prefers to make a literally inaccurate but practically accurate assertion, *e.g.* "Jesus baptized," and then, instead of cancelling it, to supplement it by an exact statement of the fact, that Jesus Himself did not baptize, but His disciples did. These peculiarities, and several others, fall under the head of Johannine Arrangement of Words, so that they have not been discussed in the preceding pages where words alone have been considered. Without some study of Johannine Grammar as well as Johannine Vocabulary, we should be at a disadvantage in approaching a discussion of the Fourfold Gospel. The next step, therefore, to be taken will be the publication of *Johannine Grammar*, as the Second Part of this work, with an Index to the two Parts.

APPENDIX

APPENDIX

PREPOSITIONS[1] IN THE FOUR GOSPELS

§ 1. *Introductory remarks*

[1881] No English alphabetical lists could well represent the differences between the Johannine and the Synoptic use of prepositions and particles. And even Greek statistics, without careful annotation, might be misleading. Prepositions that are used by the Synoptists frequently, but almost always literally, may be used by John almost as frequently but hardly ever literally. It is useless to be informed that two writers use "*in*" with the same frequency, if one mostly uses it in such phrases as "*in* that hour," "*in* those days," "*in* Capernaum," etc., and the other in such phrases as "abide *in* me."

[1882] The same thing holds good about "*to*" or "*into*." This, in the Synoptists, is mostly literal; but in John it is very frequently metaphorical—in the phrases "come *into* the world," "sent *into* the world." Frequently, too, John expresses "believe *in*" by "believe *into* (εἰς)." Luke uses ἀπό, "*from*," more than thrice as often as John, but John would be found

---

[1] The Johannine Prepositions will be discussed singly from the grammatical point of view in the Second Part of this work, the *Johannine Grammar*. Here they are treated collectively as illustrating the contrast between the Johannine and the Synoptic vocabulary. And the list will include one or two words (*e.g.* οὖν) of a specially illustrative character.

to exceed Luke in special phrases, *e.g.* "*from himself*," "*from myself*," "*from God*," etc., where the words have a moral or spiritual meaning. Hence ἐν, εἰς[1], ἐκ and πρός are not inserted in the following list; but "on" (ἐπί with gen.) is inserted for a special reason. It is not used by John in Christ's words more than once, and then only toward the end of his Gospel in the declaration of an accomplished mission, "I have glorified thee *on* the earth"; the reason is that this preposition does not lend itself to spiritual metaphor. So, too, παρά with accusative meaning "*by the side of*" occurs often in the Synoptic "*by* the sea" etc.; John uses it not with accusative but with genitive, to express the Son's coming "from the side of," or "from the house of," the Father. Lastly, the mediatorial preposition "*for*," ὑπέρ with the genitive, occurs far more frequently in the Fourth Gospel than in all the Three together.

[1883] In the *Johannine Grammar*, John's use of "*therefore*," οὖν, will be discussed under "Conjunctions," but some remarks on it may be useful here. In narrative, John is very fond of it, as carrying on the story from step to step in logical sequence. Οὖν in the Fourth Gospel is very much like the English "*so*" in a story for children: "He did this, *so* [as a natural consequence] she did that." John also frequently inserts it in describing the talk—often idle talk—of the multitudes, or of "the Jews," whom he represents as chattering with a false appearance of logical sequence. But he hardly ever inserts it in his record of Christ's words, perhaps because he does not like to represent Him as prone to arguing. Hence, though the particle occurs in the Fourth Gospel about 195 times, against 90 times in the Three, *it is not found more than* 8 *times in Christ's words* (**1885** *d*). In the Epistle it is never used at all.

---

[1] Except when εἰς is used for ἐν.

§ 2. A few statistics about Prepositions

	Mk	Mt.	Lk.	Jn
[1884] διά (accus. of pers.)[1]	4	4	0	9
εἰς (for ἐν)[2]	3	2	7	5
ἕνεκα, -εν, εἵνεκεν (1692 a)	4 or 5	7	5	0
ἐπί (accus.) (total)	34	c. 67	c. 100	19
„ (accus.) (Chri.)[3]	18	c. 41	c. 61	2
„ (dat.) (Chri.)	5	12	16	0
„ (gen.) (Chri.)[4]	9	22	17	1

[1] [1884 a] Διά τινα, in N.T., mostly means "for the sake of benefiting, satisfying, supporting, glorifying etc. a person" (not "*because of* what a person *has done* in the past"): nor can (Mk ii. 4, Lk. v. 19, viii. 19) "*because of* the crowd," with a negative, be regarded as exceptions, since "crowd" is there regarded impersonally. But "I come *for your sake* (διά σε)" might be used to mean "I come to see *you* [and not to see anyone else]," and so Jn xii. 9 οὐ διὰ τ. ʼΙ. μόνον means "not *to see* Jesus only." In Jn xii. 11 πολλοὶ δι' αὐτὸν ὑπῆγον... seems to mean " Many of the Pharisees were in the habit of going away [from their own party] *for the sake of seeing him* [Lazarus] and were becoming believers in Jesus." Jn vii. 43 "there was a division *for his sake*" may mean " for the sake of [supporting or attacking] him"; Jn xii. 42 "*for the sake of* the Pharisees they did not confess him" may be explained as Gal. ii. 4 "*for the sake of* the false brethren," which Lightfoot renders "*to satisfy, to disarm*, the false brethren."

[1884 b] All this bears on Jn vi. 57 where "living *for the sake of* the Father" and "living *for my sake*" must not be confused with living "*by means of*" (διά with gen.). It is true that "eating" is mentioned in the context. But the primary meaning probably is that the Son "lives *for the sake of* glorifying the Father." See 2294—2300.

[2] [1884 c] Εἰς for ἐν. These numbers are taken from Bruder—after rejecting Mk i. 39 (reading ἦλθεν not ἦν), ii. 1, Lk. xii. 21 (εἰς Θεὸν πλουτῶν), and inserting Jn xx. 19, 26 ἔστη εἰς τὸ μέσον. Jn's other instances are i. 18 ὁ ὢν εἰς τὸν κόλπον τοῦ πατρός, xvii. 23 ἵνα ὦσι τετελειωμένοι εἰς ἕν and xxi. 4 ἔστη ʼΙησοῦς εἰς (marg. ἐπί) τὸν αἰγιαλόν. Lk.'s instances are all local. Concerning Christ's manifestation after the Resurrection Lk. xxiv. 36 has αὐτὸς ἔστη ἐν μέσῳ αὐτῶν.

[3] [1884 d] ʼΕπί (accus.) (Chri.) in Jn, only i. 51 "the angels of God ascending and descending *upon* (ἐπί) the Son of man" (from Gen. xxviii. 12, LXX ἐπ' αὐτῆς, D ἐπ' αὐτῇ) and xiii. 18 "hath lifted up his heel *against* me" (from Ps. xli. 9).

[4] [1884 e] ʼΕπί (gen.) (Chri.) in Jn, only xvii. 4 "I [have] glorified thee *on* (ἐπί) the earth."

	Mk	Mt.	Lk.	Jn
ἕως (prep. w. noun)[1]	5	c. 19	8	[1]
κατά (accus.)	c. 14	21	37	7
,, (gen.)[2]	7	16	6	1
[1885] μηδείς[3]	8	5	9	0
μήποτε, or μή ποτε[4]	2	8	7	1
ὅστις (of persons)[5]	4	27	11	1
οὖν[6]	3 or 4	56	30	c. 195
παρά (accus.)	7	7	13	0
,, (gen.)[7]	6	5	9	25
περί (accus.)[8]	10	8	5	0
ὑπέρ (gen.)[9]	2	1	1+[2]	13

[1] Ἕως prep. w. noun, in Jn, is only in viii. 9 "from the first unto the last"—an interpolated passage.

[2] [1884 *f*] Κατά (gen.), in Jn, only xix. 11 Οὐκ εἶχες ἐξουσίαν κατ' ἐμοῦ οὐδεμίαν.

[3] [1885 *a*] Μηδείς. The Johannine non-use of any form of μηδείς indicates that Jn does not contain such prohibitions as "Tell *no man*," "Let *no man* know it," "Take *nothing* for the journey" etc. (Mk i. 44, Mt. viii. 4, ix. 30, Lk. v. 14 etc.).

[4] [1885 *b*] Μήποτε, in Synopt., alw. means "lest" exc. perh. Lk. iii. 15 "reasoning...(R.V.) *whether haply* he were the Christ." In Jn vii. 26 μήποτε...ἔγνωσαν, it means "*Can it be that...?*"

[5] [1885 *c*] Ὅστις, of pers., in Synopt., mostly means "every one that" or "that" used as a *defining* relative. But in Jn it seems to be a *supplementary* relative ("*who*"="*and he*") Jn viii. 53 "Art thou greater than our father Abraham *who* (ὅστις) is dead...?" See **2413**.

[6] [1885 *d*] Οὖν. Jn altogether differs from Mt.-Lk. in his use of οὖν. They mostly use it in Christ's words. Jn uses it freq. in the words of others (i. 21, 25, iv. 11 etc.) and in narrative i. 22, 39, ii. 18, 20 etc., but very rarely indeed in Christ's words (vi. 62, viii. 24, 36, 38, xii. 50, xiii. 14, xvi. 22, xviii. 8) about 8 times. In Mt.'s Sermon on the Mount alone, it occurs 13 times.

[7] [1885 *e*] Παρά (gen.). Jn's use is almost always in the phrase "*from* God (or, the Father)" *e.g.* i. 6, 14, v. 44, vi. 45, 46 etc.

[8] Περί (accus.), see n. on ὑπέρ.

[9] [1885 *f*] Ὑπέρ (gen.). Mk ix. 40 "He that is not against us is *for us*," and sim. Lk. ix. 50, but "against *you*...for *you*"; Mt. om., but has Mt. v. 44 "pray *for* them that persecute you," where Lk. vi. 28 has "pray *for*," expressed by περί. [Lk. xxii. 19, 20] is doubtful.

[1885 *g*] Jn's first instance is i. 30 "This is he *about* (ὑπέρ v. r. περί) whom I said...." John the Baptist is speaking of Christ, and ὑπέρ is all

	Mk	Mt.	Lk.	Jn
ὑπό (accus.)[1]	3 or 4	5	7	1
„ (gen.)[2]	8	23	23	1

the more remarkable because (1) he has, in Jn i. 15, Ἰωάνης μαρτυρεῖ περὶ αὐτοῦ, (2) everywhere else in Jn ὑπέρ means "*for the sake of.*" Perh. i. 30, having a shade of difference from i. 15, means "*in behalf of whom,*" i.e. as His representative.

[**1885** *h*] In Jn xiii. 37, 38 ὑπέρ is twice used about Peter's profession that he would "lay down his life *for*" Christ; in xvii. 19 "I sanctify myself *for* them" seems to refer to Christ's self-devotion on the cross; in almost all other passages the word is certainly used in connexion with Christ's dying *for* man, whether mentioned by Christ Himself, or (xi. 50—2, xviii. 14) by Caiaphas, or by the Evangelist referring to Caiaphas. *The prevalence of the word, therefore, in Jn is due to the prevalence of mediatorial doctrine.*

[1] [**1885** *i*] Ὑπό (accus.) in Jn, only i. 48 ὑπὸ τὴν συκῆν foll. by i. 50 ὑποκάτω τῆς συκῆς, on which see **2372—3**.

[2] [**1885** *j*] Ὑπό (gen.). The rarity of ὑπό w. gen. in Jn arises from his preference of active to passive, as in Jn x. 14 R.V. "mine own know me," but v. r. and A.V. "I am known of mine." The only genuine instance is Jn xiv. 21... ἐκεῖνός ἐστιν ὁ ἀγαπῶν με, ὁ δὲ ἀγαπῶν με ἀγαπηθήσεται ὑπὸ τοῦ πατρός μου, κἀγὼ ἀγαπήσω αὐτόν... where τὸν δὲ ἀγαπῶντα ἐμέ would be avoided by many writers as being in form, though not in fact, ambiguous.

ADDENDA

[1885 (i)] Vocabulary I (1672—96) gives a characteristic but not a complete list of words used in the Three Gospels and comparatively seldom or never in the Fourth. The textual list was intended for readers unacquainted with Greek. The annotations called attention to points some of which the author hopes to discuss in a treatise on "The Fourfold Gospel." The list omitted many words such as "camel," "candlestick" (A.V.), "herd," "mother-in-law," concerning which everybody knows that the Synoptists use them and John does not. Their inclusion appeared likely to make the Vocabulary inconveniently large without greatly increasing its utility for the general reader. But here, for the benefit of the student of the Greek Testament, the omitted words are set down in Greek alphabetical order. The list is not complete even now. It omits prepositions and particles discussed elsewhere, and also words used differently by the different Synoptists *e.g.* διαφέρω, καταρτίζω, κόπτω, and Λεγιών. But still, if the student combines the following list with the instances marked in Vocabulary I as Jn (0), he will have a tolerably complete view of *the words used by the Three Gospels and never used by the Fourth*. Ἀγέλη 2, 3, 2=ά. Mk (2), Mt. (3), Lk. (2), and so of the rest:—

[1885 (i) *a*] Ἀγέλη 2, 3, 2 : ἀδύνατος 1, 1, 1 : ἄζυμος 2, 1, 2 : ἄκρον 2, 2, 1 : ἀλάβαστρον 2, 1, 1 : ἁλιεύς 2, 2, 1 : Ἀλφαῖος 2, 1, 1 : ἀναγκάζω 1, 1, 1 : ἀνέχομαι 1, 1, 1 : ἀπαίρω 1, 1, 1 : ἀποδημέω 1, 3, 2 : ἀποδοκιμάζω 2, 1, 3 : ἀποκαθίστημι 3, 2, 1 : ἀποκεφαλίζω 2, 1, 1 : ἀποκυλίω 1, 1, 1 : ἄρσην 1, 1, 1 : ἀσκός 4, 4, 4 : ἀσπάζομαι 2, 2, 2 : ἀσπασμός 1, 1, 5 : ἀφαιρέω 1, 1, 4 (**1709** *d*). Βάθος 1, 1, 1 : βδέλυγμα 1, 1, 1 : βίβλος 1, 1, 2. Γαλήνη 1, 1, 1 : γαστήρ 1, 3, 2 : γένημα 1, 1, 1 : Γεννησαρέτ 1, 1, 1. Διαβλέπω 1, 1, 1 : διαθήκη 1, 1, 2 : διάνοια 1, 1, 2 : διαπεράω 2, 2, 1 : διαρήσσω 1, 1, 2 : δυσκόλως 1, 1, 1 : δῶμα 1, 2, 3. Εἰκών 1, 1, 1 : εἴωθα 1, 1, 1 : ἐκδίδωμι 1, 2, 1 : ἐνάτη ὥρα 2, 3, 1 : ἐντρέπομαι 1, 1, 3 : ἑξήκοντα 2, 2, 1 : ἐπίβλημα 1, 1, 2 : ἐπιγραφή 2, 1, 2 : ἐπισκιάζω 1, 1, 2 : ἐρήμωσις 1, 1, 1 : εὐθύς (adj.) 1, 1, 2 : εὐκοπώτερον 2, 2, 3. Ζημιόω 1, 1, 1. Θέρος 1, 1, 1 : θηλάζω 1, 2, 2 : θυσία 1, 2, 2. Κάμηλος 2, 3, 1 : καρποφορέω 2, 1, 1 : καταγελάω 1, 1, 1 : καταπέτασμα 1, 1, 1 : καταράομαι 1, 1, 1 : κατασκευάζω 1, 1, 2 : κατασκηνόω 1, 1, 1 : καταφιλέω 1, 1, 3 : κατέναντι 3, 2, 1 : κράσπεδον 1, 3, 1 : κρημνός 1, 1, 1 : Κυρηναῖος 1, 1, 1.

[1885 (i) *b*] Λάχανον 1, 1, 1 : λιμός 1, 1, 4 : λυχνία 1, 1, 2. Μετρέω 2, 2, 1 : μόδιος 1, 1, 1 : μυστήριον 1, 1, 1. Νεανίσκος 2, 2, 1 : νυμφών 1, 2, 1. Ξύλα (pl.) 2, 2, 1. Ὀδούς 1, 8, 1 : ὁρμάω 1, 1, 1 : ὀρχέομαι 1, 2, 1 : ὀσφύς 1, 1, 1. Παρέχω 1, 1, 4 : πενθερά 1, 2, 3 : περίλυπος 2, 1, 1 : περίσσευμα 1, 1, 1 : περισσότερος 3, 1, 4 (**1683** *c*) : πίναξ 2, 2, 1 : πόλεμος 2, 2, 2 : πονηρία 1, 1, 1 : πόρρω 1, 1, 2 : πρόθεσις 1,

ADDENDA [1885 (ii)b]

1, 1 : πρωτοκαθεδρία 1, 1, 2 : πρωτοκλισία 1, 1, 2 : πύργος 1, 1, 2. Ῥάβδος 1, 1, 1 : ῥήγνυμι 2, 2, 2. Σαλεύω 1, 2, 4 : σελήνη 1, 1, 1 : σίναπι 1, 2, 2 : σινδών 3, 1, 1 : σκηνή 1, 1, 2 : σκιά 1, 1, 1 : σκύλλω 1, 1, 2 : σπόριμος 1, 1, 1 : στάχυς 3, 1, 1 : στέγη 1, 1, 1 : σῦκον 1, 1, 1 : συνλαλέω 1, 1, 3 : συνπνίγω 2, 1, 2 : συντηρέω 1, 1, 1. Τελώνιον 1, 1, 1 : τίλλω 1, 1, 1 : τράχηλος 1, 1, 2. Ὑπακούω 2, 1, 2 : ὑπομένω 1, 2, 1. Φαίνομαι (mid. or pass.) 1+[1], 13, 2 : φιμόω 2, 2, 1 : φονεύω 1, 5, 1 : φόνος 2, 1, 2 : φραγμός 1, 1, 1. Ψευδοπροφήτης 1, 3, 1.

[1885 (ii)] Vocabulary II (1707—28) omitted a large number of words used by John alone, but used by him only once or twice, so that they could not be called characteristic, *e.g.* ἀλόη, ἄραφος, βαΐον, γενετή. These belong either to special narratives, or else to special details, not given by the Synoptists; and their inclusion seemed likely to make the Vocabulary inconveniently long without compensating advantage to the reader unacquainted with Greek. But there is much to be learned from some of these, *e.g.* from John's unique use of μιαίνω ("lest they (the chief priests) should *be defiled*") immediately before the priests accuse Christ of "*doing evil*," when compared with Matthew's statement "That which cometh out of the mouth *defileth* (κοινοῖ) the man." Some of them will be discussed in Part II of this work, *e.g.* ἅλλομαι (2314—6), others, it is hoped, in a future treatise. For the convenience of the student, instead of figures stating how often the word occurs in the Fourth Gospel, the list appends references to the several passages. No Synoptist uses the following words :

[1885 (ii) a] Ἀγγέλλω xx. 18, ἁγνίζω xi. 55, ἅλλομαι iv. 14, ἀλόη xix. 39, ἀμνός i. 29, 36, ἀνατρέπω ii. 15, ἀνέρχομαι vi. 3, ἀνθρωποκτόνος viii. 44, ἀπειθέω iii. 36, ἄραφος xix. 23, ἀρεστός viii. 29, ἀρνίον xxi. 15, ἀρχιτρίκλινος ii. 8—9. Βαΐον xii. 13 (2047), βασιλικός iv. 46, 49, βιβρώσκω vi. 13. Γενετή ix. 1, γέρων iii. 4, γηράσκω xxi. 18, γλωσσόκομον xii. 6, xiii. 29. Δακρύω xi. 35, διατρίβω iii. 22, διδακτός vi. 45, δωρεά iv. 10, s. also 1682 g. Ἑβδόμη ὥρα iv. 52, ἐκκεντέω xix. 37, ἐκνεύω v. 13, ἐλαττύω iii. 30, ἐλάττων ii. 10, ἕλιγμα xix. 39, ἐμπόριον ii. 16, ἐμφυσάω xx. 22, ἐνκαίνια x. 22, ἐπάρατος vii. 49, ἐπίγειος iii. 12, ἐπιλέγω v. 2, ἐπιχρίω ix. 11, ἐπουράνιος iii. 12, ἐραυνάω v. 39, vii. 52, εὐθύνω i. 23, ἐχθές iv. 52.

[1885 (ii) b] Ζῆλος ii. 17, ζήτησις iii. 25. Ἧλος xx. 25 (*bis*). Θεοσεβής ix. 31, θήκη xviii. 11, θρέμμα iv. 12. Καθαίρω xv. 2, κατηγορία xviii. 29, (τῶν) Κέδρων xviii. 1, κειρία xi. 44, κέρμα ii. 15, κερματιστής ii. 14, κηπουρός xx. 15, κλῆμα xv. 2—6 (4 times (1674)), Κλωπᾶς xix. 25, κοίμησις xi. 13, κομψότερον ἔχω iv. 52. Λατρεία xvi. 2, λέντιον xiii. 4, 5, λίθινος ii. 6, Λιθόστρωτος xix. 13, λίτρα xii. 3, xix. 39, λοιδορέω ix. 28. Μαίνομαι x. 28, Μάλχος xviii. 10, μάχομαι vi. 52, μεσόω vii. 14, μιαίνω xviii. 28. Νεύω xiii. 24, νιπτήρ xiii. 5. Ὁδοιπορία iv. 6, ὄζω xi. 39, οἶμαι xxi. 25, ὀνάριον xii. 14 (1736 e), ὅπλον xviii. 3, ὀσμή xii. 3, ὄψις vii. 24, xi. 44. Παιδάριον vi. 9 (1736 e), παραμυθέομαι xi. 19, 31, πενθερός

363

xviii. 13, περιδέω xi. 44, περιίστημι xi. 42, πορφύρεος xix. 2, 5, πόσις vi. 55, προβατική v. 2 (2216), προβάτιον xxi. 16, 17, προσαιτέω ix. 8 (s. also προσαίτης 1737 a), προσκυνητής iv. 23, προσφάγιον xxi. 5, πτέρνα xiii. 18, πτύσμα ix. 6 (s. also πτύω, 1737 b). [1885 (ii) c] 'Ρέω vii. 38. Σαμαρεῖτις iv. 9 (bis), σκέλος xix. 31, 32, 33, σκηνοπηγία vii. 2, σκηνόω i. 14, στοά v. 2, x. 23, συνεισέρχομαι vi. 22, xviii. 15, συνμαθητής xi. 16, σύρω xxi. 8, σχοινίον ii. 15. Τάχειον xiii. 27, xx. 4 (1918), τεκνίον xiii. 33 (1676 a), τεταρταῖος xi. 39, τετράμηνος iv. 35, τίτλος xix. 19, 20, τύπος xx. 25 (bis), τυφλόω xii. 40. 'Υδρία ii. 6, 7, iv. 28, ὑπόδειγμα xiii. 15, ὕσσωπος xix. 29, ὑφαντός xix. 23. Φαίνω (active) i. 5, v. 35, φανός xviii. 3, φαῦλος iii. 20, v. 29 (1772 b), φοῖνιξ xii. 13 (2047), φραγέλλιον ii. 15. Χαμαί ix. 6, xviii. 6, χείμαρρος xviii. 1, χολάω vii. 23. Ψεῦδος viii. 44, ψεύστης viii. 44, 55, ψῦχος xviii. 18.